Invisible Engines

Invisible Engines
How Software Platforms Drive Innovation and Transform Industries

David S. Evans, Andrei Hagiu, and Richard Schmalensee

The MIT Press
Cambridge, Massachusetts
London, England

MIT Press books may be purchased at special quantity discounts for business or sales promotional use. For information, please email special_sales@mitpress.mit. edu or write to Special Sales Department, The MIT Press, 55 Hayward Street, Cambridge, MA 02142.

This book was set in Sabon by SNP Best-set Typesetter Ltd., Hong Kong. Printed and bound in the United States of America.

An electronic version of this book is available under a Creative Commons license.

Library of Congress Cataloging-in-Publication Data

Evans, David S. (David Sparks)
  Invisible engines : how software platforms drive innovation and transform industries / David S. Evans, Andrei Hagiu, and Richard Schmalensee.
    p.   cm.
  Includes bibliographical references and index.
  ISBN 0-262-05085-4 (alk. paper)
  1. Application program interfaces (Computer software). 2. Industries—Data processing. I. Hagiu, Andrei. II. Schmalensee, Richard. III. Title.
QA76.76.A63 E93   2006
005.3—dc22

                                                              2006046629

10 9 8 7 6 5 4 3 2 1

Contents

Preface

If you have a RAZR mobile phone, a Windows personal computer (PC), a TiVo Digital Video recorder, a French credit card, an Xbox, or a Palm Pilot, you are using one. If you have bought anything on eBay or searched on Google you have used one too. All these products have at their core a software platform—a software program that makes services available to other software programs through Application Programming Interfaces (APIs). Those software platforms are at the heart of "economies" or "ecosystems" that consist of mutually dependent communities of businesses and consumers that have a symbiotic relationship with the platform. Software platforms are a general-purpose technology that first made its economic mark in the 1970s. These "invisible engines" have spawned many major industries—some directly, such as smart mobile telephones, and others indirectly, such as ringtones. They are in the process of transforming industries ranging from automobiles to home entertainment. They are likely to create more industries—one need only look at the applications that were quickly built with Google Maps soon after its release to see the potential. And, finally, they are challenging many long-established industries, some of which may not survive much longer. The PC rather quickly killed the typewriter industry, and the Internet may come close to finishing off the newspaper industry.

We speak loosely when we equate software platforms with the corresponding industries. It is easy to equate Windows and the PC industry, since Windows more or less defines that industry. It is harder to equate the Symbian operating system and the mobile telephone industry, however. The Symbian operating system is, in fact, only one element in a complex structure that links mobile phone operators, handset makers, application providers, and software platform makers. But the thesis of this book is that the underlying software platform technology shapes these industries, and the business strategies employed by firms in those industries, in fundamental and important ways. By focusing on the software platform we hope to offer the reader a perspective on the business dynamics and strategies of industries, old and new, that have been powered by these invisible engines.

Although two of us (Evans and Schmalensee) have worked on issues related to a major software platform, Windows, since the early 1990s as consultants for Microsoft in several prominent antitrust cases in the United States and Europe, our interest in the power of software platforms emanated from a totally different body of work. We have also been working on and thinking about the payment card industry since the early 1990s. An interesting aspect of that business is that successful payment card systems have to get people to use cards and merchants to accept them in order to even have a product. Two French economists, Jean-Charles Rochet and Jean Tirole, realized in studying the economics of the payment card industry that it shares this fundamental property with many other businesses. Think singles clubs—they need men and women and in the right proportions to even have a product. Similarly, advertising-supported media need both eyeballs and advertisers. Any type of exchange, such as Sotheby's, Deutsche Börse, or eBay, needs both buyers and sellers. These are all examples of two-sided platforms.

The two of us have been engaged in the study of two-sided industries ever since our colleagues Rochet and Tirole made this basic observation in 2001. We applied that framework in the second edition of an earlier book, *Paying with Plastic*, to study the business strategies and dynamics of the credit, debit, and charge card industry.

The third member of our team (Hagiu) decided to write his doctoral dissertation at Princeton University on the economics of two-sided markets during this same period. This document contains the first theoretical model designed specifically to study two-sided software platforms.

All of us quickly recognized that software platform businesses have at least two sides. Software platforms consist of services that are often made available to developers through APIs. They are also made available to computer users, but those computer users typically avail themselves of

API-based services by buying applications that in turn use APIs. It is only a slight exaggeration to say that *all* software platform makers *all* the time invest in getting *both* developers and users to use their platforms. The developers/users are like the men/women, cards/merchants, advertisers/eyeballs, and buyers/sellers that we mentioned above. In fact, software platforms sometimes appeal to more than two distinct groups—including hardware makers and content providers.

The economics of two-sided platforms provides a number of insights into pricing, design, organization, and governance of platform-based businesses. We were interested in understanding how this new economic learning could help shed light on the strategies followed by software platforms. On the flip side, we were interested in understanding how a diverse set of industries based on software platforms could be probed to provide insights for students of this new economics.

This book is the result. It blends economics, history, and business analysis. It is intended for anyone who wants to better understand the business strategies that have been followed in industries based on software platforms. We focus on pricing, product design, and integration into downstream or upstream suppliers. Entrepreneurs and managers should find insights that they can apply in their own businesses.

We hope that anyone who wants a concise business history of software platforms will find our discussion useful. We present detailed studies of the PC, video game console, personal digital assistant, smart phone, and digital media software platform industries. We present shorter discussions of auction-based and search engine–based software platforms.

This book does not cover government policies that affect software platforms. A serious treatment of that subject would require at least another book. Microsoft alone has been the subject of intense antitrust scrutiny since the late 1980s as a result of having more than a 90 percent share of PC operating system sales and engaging in various business practices that some antitrust authorities and courts around the world have questioned. There is also a vibrant policy debate over the extent to which governments, especially in emerging economies, should promote open-source software that is produced by cooperatives and made available for free at the expense of proprietary software that is made by for-profit firms and sold for profits. Google is increasingly at the center of a debate over the fair use of copyrighted material on the Internet. What can it, and similar services, copy and share with users? Does Google have to share any of its profits with the content owners? Our focus, however, is on what software platform businesses do and why they do it, and we stay away from debates about whether they should do it.

The book is not written in the technical language of economics journals, but we believe that our economist colleagues will nonetheless find that we have assembled factual material that both sheds light on the theory of two-sided markets and provides a useful reality check on that theory. We document several important regularities in software platforms. As in many two-sided industries, one side generally gets a really good deal. Developers get extremely valuable services for nominal cost from almost all software platform makers in almost all industries, but there is a notable exception. The size of software platforms expands exponentially because most makers in most industries add features over time. Less generally, the tendency is for software platforms to start as part of a vertically integrated business that becomes more decentralized over time as markets mature.

Software platforms, working closely with microprocessors in computing devices, have revolutionized many industries since they became commercially important in the 1970s. Looking forward, Web-centric software platforms that work on arrays of servers and that are connected to the Internet are, we believe, likely to produce changes that dwarf the revolution we have seen in the last quarter century. Our invisible engines aren't the whole story of the tectonic industrial shifts that are upon us. But they are a central part of the story, to which we now turn.

David S. Evans
Andrei Hagiu
Richard Schmalensee

Acknowledgments

This work could not have been completed without the help of many people and companies, to which we are profoundly thankful.

Melissa DiBella, Laura Gee, and Miroslav Skovajsa of LECG, LLC, along with Terry Xie of Market Platform Dynamics, helped enormously with the economic, business, and technical research that underlies this effort. Others who participated in this research effort at various times include Howard Chang, Anne Layne Farrar, Susan Hotelling, Albert Nichols, Brendan Reddy, Amy Stevenson, and Ori Stitelman. We also thank Karen Webster of Market Platform Dynamics for helping to make the book friendlier to business readers. Hagiu is also extremely grateful to the Research Institute of Economy Trade and Industry in Tokyo, where he was based during most of the writing and which provided invaluable research support and the kindest hospitality.

We benefited from talking to a number of people in the industries discussed in the book. We list them alphabetically and without company affiliations: J Allard, Raj Amin, Brian Arbogast, David Aronchick, Tim Attinger, Robbie Bach, Gerald Cavanagh, David Cole, Christa Davis, Michael Dearing, Suzanne DelBene, Alan Harper, James Healy, Carl Atsushi Hirano, Nanako Kato, Randy Komisar, Larry Kramer, Mitchell Kurtzman, Ed Lichty, Steve Lifflick, David Nagel, Takeshi Natsuno, Craig Neumark, Will Poole, Ray Ozzie, and Dwight Witherspoon. We are particularly grateful for these conversations because, even more than providing factual information, they helped shape and test our thinking about the issues discussed in this book. We wish we could have shared with the reader all of the insights we obtained from talking to these extraordinary individuals.

Much of the intellectual foundation for this book is based on work we have been conducting since around 2001 on two-sided platforms. We are grateful to Visa USA for funding our research efforts in that area and for numerous conversations with Jean-Charles Rochet and Jean Tirole on this area of economics. We are also grateful to Microsoft Corporation for funding much of the research that applies the theory of two-sided markets to software platforms, and for partially funding our writing in this area. We are especially grateful to Paul Allen, formerly general counsel of Visa USA, and David Heiner, deputy general counsel at Microsoft Corporation, for the value they have attached to stimulating academic research that sometimes seems quite distant from the issues of the moment.

Jean Tirole and several anonymous reviewers provided detailed and insightful comments on an earlier version of the manuscript that led to significant improvements. We are most grateful for their valuable help. Last, we thank our families for putting up with many late nights and weekends of writing and research.

We, of course, speak only for ourselves in the following pages. No one mentioned above necessarily agrees with us about anything. We retain all rights to any sins, errors, or omissions in what follows.

David S. Evans
Andrei Hagiu
Richard Schmalensee

1

Invisible Engines

But what . . . is it good for?

—*Anonymous engineer at the Advanced Computing Systems Division of IBM, 1968, commenting on the microchip.*[1]

INSIDE THIS CHAPTER

- The definition and history of software platforms
- The businesses powered by software platforms
- The basic economics of software platforms
- The plan of the book

Many modern products run on software platforms. Car engines and navigation systems have one, as do jumbo jets and the handheld devices we use for emailing and organizing ourselves. Video game consoles from Atari to Xbox are based on them. French debit cards have included them for years; these "smart cards" may eventually replace the magnetic stripe cards that are standard in the United States. Sophisticated mobile telephone services such as i-mode in Japan are based on software platforms. Personal music devices are as well. And, of course, all sorts of business and home computers also have them.

Software platforms are based on computer code. The code tells the microprocessors and other hardware components what to do. It is what

1. Caryn Yacowitz, Vittorio Zaccaria, Mariagiovanna Sami, Cristina Silvano, and Donatella Sciuto, *Power Estimation and Optimization Methodologies for Vliw-Based Embedded Systems* (Norwell, Mass.: Kluwer Academic Publishers, 2003).

makes your computer do calculations, or your personal music device play songs. And it provides services to applications, such as accessing the hardware or providing features that many applications would otherwise have to include themselves. It is what makes handwriting recognition possible on personal digital devices and enables your employer's human resources software to work on the company's computer system.

Yet these remarkable software engines are invisible to most of us. Their creators write them in a language that looks almost human. They then use other code to translate what they have written into machine language—combinations of 0s and 1s that microprocessors understand. Those digital data are then transferred to the physical memory or storage in the device itself.

Some software platforms are famous. Linux, the Mac OS, and Windows are household names. You cannot really see or touch these products, but at least you can buy a CD and a hefty manual. Others are known to many business users: z/OS, Solaris, and Unix, for instance. Many are known only to a few, such as Symbian for mobile phones or GeoWorks for handheld devices. Others, including the software platforms that are the real brains behind devices such as the Sony PlayStation or Tivo's digital video recorder, are truly anonymous.

Software platforms have generated great wealth. Windows has provided about 40 percent of Microsoft's revenues in the last decade.[2] It has helped make Bill Gates the richest man in the world. Linus Torvalds has become a modern icon as a result of writing the first version of the famous open-source platform, Linux. And software platforms have been partners in some of the most successful technological marriages of the last quarter century: the Macintosh, iPod, PalmPilot, Sony PlayStation, and Xbox are among the better known hardware-software platform couples.

The computer revolution has been changing our lives now for fifty years, at an accelerating rate, and much has been written about it. Many of the companies, products, and entrepreneurs behind this revolution have become household names. Stories of Steve Jobs and Steve Wozniak building the first Apple computer in their garage and Bill Gates getting

---

2. Microsoft 10-Ks, available from sec.gov.

the best of IBM are almost folklore at this point. Economists have written a fair amount about the computer industry, and business writers have scoured its history in search of the drivers of great success.

Yet little has been written about software platforms. This is not necessarily remarkable. They are not well-defined products like toothpaste. The software platform used in i-mode does not compete directly with the software platform used in Web servers. And they are not components, like the engines sold to automobile companies or even the chips sold to computer device manufacturers. There is no software platform industry defined in government statistics. Rather, software platforms are a technology—though one based on a written language—that can be deployed in a vast range of industries for a great multitude of purposes.

Many economic threads, however, tie diverse software platforms together. The most critical of these ties is their potential for supporting a multisided business—one in which value is created by bringing together on the same platform multiple distinct groups of customers who need each other in some way. Businesses that cater to the singles scene are one example of this sort of business. Heterosexual nightclubs must get men and women together in the same place. Shopping malls are also multisided: their developers create platforms that attract both merchants and consumers. Similarly, many software platforms provide services to application developers and platform users. Like shopping malls, they also provide a common meeting ground where one side can sell to the other side.

Once the multisided potential of software platforms is recognized, other similarities among businesses based on them become apparent, as do some intriguing differences.

Many charge one customer group little or nothing for using the platform. If you want to write applications for the Symbian operating system that runs on mobile phones, you can get all the necessary tools and information for very little money. The same is true for Apple, Microsoft, Palm, and most other software platform vendors. They make their money mainly from users. Manufacturers of video game consoles also have a skewed pricing model, but they make their money mainly from developers. Consumers can buy Sony PlayStations, Xboxes, and other consoles for prices that sometimes do not even cover manufacturing costs.

Manufacturers make their money mainly from game developers, who pay royalties to gain access to the information required to write games for these consoles.

Most successful software platforms have exploited positive feedbacks (or network effects) between applications and users: more applications attract more users, and more users attract more applications. Nurturing both sides of the market helped Microsoft garner thousands of applications and hundreds of millions of users for its Windows platform. The same strategy worked for Sony PlayStation in games and Palm in personal digital devices. But some software platform vendors have invested little in providing services to application developers. That was true for IBM's mainframe operating system for many years, and is still true for many manufacturers that make software platforms for dedicated devices such as ATM machines.

Software and hardware platforms have a symbiotic relationship. Neither could perform without the other. Businesses have adopted various ways of dealing with this relationship. Some have tightly integrated their hardware and software platforms; video game console companies are one example. Others have focused on the software platform and treat much of the hardware side as they do applications. Microsoft more so than most has operated a three-sided platform that tries to get users, application developers, and hardware manufacturers on board.

The multisided potential of software platforms is not their only common feature. They share all the characteristics of complex software. They are designed, written, and debugged almost entirely by humans. Much of this work is drudgery, but some of it requires solving difficult puzzles and writing sophisticated mathematical algorithms. Once created, a software program is cheaper to replicate and distribute than a book. After it sells enough copies to cover the costs of creating it, it becomes a money machine: each copy generates revenue at little extra cost. But, as with books, recorded songs, movies, and other information goods, this revenue is at risk from pirates, people who make copies for free. The intellectual effort that went into the creation of the program is also at risk. Most software businesses distribute their code only in almost indecipherable machine language and secure legal protections such as copyrights and patents to deter theft of their intellectual property.

Some people object to selling software platforms (and other software), and especially to keeping their code secret. They believe in what is known around the world as *software libre*. In some ways, they long for the earlier days of computing. Computer companies such as IBM used to include software with their machines; buyers did not consider it something they paid for separately. For many years after the birth of modern computing, software was shared among colleagues. The notion of selling software, and especially software platforms, did not arise until the 1970s, almost a quarter century after the sale of the first commercial computer. The software industry started booming in the 1980s and has generated over $500 billion in sales worldwide in the last three years (we leave all currency figures in their original amounts and do not adjust for inflation).[3] The free software movement has tried to return to the more collegial approach of the industry's youth. Its greatest success is Linux, which is developed through a collaborative process among programmers around the world working through the Internet and coordinated through various committees. Linux is known as open source because you can read the programming code in which it was written. It is available for free, subject to some important restrictions we discuss later.

Most software platforms share another feature: they grow over time. Version 9.0 of the Red Hat Linux OS, introduced in 2003, has 50 million lines of code, compared with 9 million for Version 5.0, which came out in 1997. The same is true for the Mac OS. It started with one-fifth of a megabyte in 1984 and takes up more than a thousand megabytes today.[4] Software platforms grow because they do more things—they provide more features for application writers, end users, or both. In some cases, they are just taking advantage of faster microprocessors and larger memory. In others they are absorbing features that were once performed by separate applications. As more people began wanting to connect to

3. Richard V. Heiman, Sally Hudson, Henry D. Morris, Albert Pang, and Anthony C. Picardi, "Worldwide Software Forecast Summary, 2003–2007" (IDC report no. 30099), September 2003; Richard V. Heiman and Anthony C. Picardi, "Worldwide Software 2004–2008 Research Summary" (IDC report no. 31785), August 2004.

4. http://applemuseum.bott.org/sections/os.html; http://www.apple.com/macosx/techspecs/.

the Internet, for example, software platforms started including communication protocols that made that easier to do.

The following pages document patterns and anomalies across businesses based in whole or in part on software platforms. These regularities and irregularities are the source of insights that we hope will be useful to entrepreneurs and investors as well as economists. The patterns result from the underlying economics of software platforms. The skewed pricing structures that appear for most software platforms are common in other multisided platform businesses. Not surprisingly, the anomalies are both more intriguing and harder to rationalize. Economics, however, can narrow down the possible explanations. The differences between software platforms for video game consoles and PCs could result from path dependence (they started from different points, which determined their futures) or fundamental differences in economics (the manufacturer needs to make a market for game consoles to induce application developers to write, or consumer tastes for applications differ from those for games).

The challenges faced by software platform businesses are encountered by many other businesses that are multisided, or could be. Deciding whether and when to rely on outsiders for crucial complementary products is critical. Microsoft has built a software platform empire through partnering with many other firms that produce complements for it. But Apple's iPod/iTunes music platform has found success by doing everything from making the music device, designing the software, and running the music store. Pricing is key as well: finding the right balance between the various sides is one of the hardest problems faced by platform businesses. 3DO's innovative game platform died a quick death when it priced its consoles too high and its royalties for game developers too low. An ill-chosen pricing strategy put Microsoft's Xbox on the brink of disaster but one that it averted in time. Other platform businesses could learn from how software platforms load features to get and keep both sides on board. Whether you use Windows, Linux, or the Mac OS, most of the code on your hard disk has no direct value to you. Much of it is there for developers of applications, most of which you will never use. Other portions are there to provide esoteric features that only a few of us use.

Making Computers Smaller

Products based on software platforms abound because of the micro-processor revolution that began in the 1970s.

The first general-purpose electronic computer, ENIAC, was created during World War II for calculations that helped aim artillery toward targets. Based on 18,000 vacuum tubes, it was 100 feet long, 8.5 feet high, and several feet wide. The development of the transistor, which began in the late 1940s, led to the second generation of computers. The transistor serves the same function as the vacuum tube but is much smaller, requires much less power, and is much more reliable. Second-generation computers were thus smaller and less expensive to run. Third-generation computers were made possible with the invention of the integrated circuit in 1959.

The integrated circuit, which combined several transistors and other circuit elements into a single component, not only further reduced the size and price of computers but also made them faster. Admiral Grace Hopper, a pioneering software programmer, was famous for carrying around a "nanosecond"—a footlong piece of telephone wire represent-ing the maximum distance electricity can travel in one nanosecond. She used it to illustrate that computers had to be small to be fast. And com-puters did get smaller. The popular IBM System/360 Model 30, intro-duced in 1964, took up about 106 cubic feet.[5] Minicomputers were even smaller. Digital Equipment Corporation's PDP-8, introduced in 1965, was only about 8 cubic feet. Minicomputers were small enough that manufacturers could, for the first time, integrate computing power into laboratory devices and other equipment.

The current generation of computers began with the development of a microprocessor at Intel. The microprocessor packs the whole central processing unit (CPU), which is often called the brains of the computer and which involves many transistors, onto a single semiconductor chip. This has made it possible to provide massive amounts of computing power in small devices. Produced in 1971, the Intel 4004 was the first microprocessor. It had 2,300 transistors on a silicon wafer the size of a

5. http://homepages.kcbbs.gen.nz/nbree/saga.html.

ladybug and could perform 60,000 instructions a second. Three years later Intel introduced the Intel 8080, which had 4,500 transistors on a silicon wafer of about the same size as the 4040 yet could perform more than 500,000 instructions per second. It is considered the first general-purpose microprocessor, and its release marked the birth of the microprocessor industry. It soon spawned the first microcomputer, the Altair 8800, and the first video game system, Midway's Gun Fight arcade game.

The computing power of microprocessors depends on the number of transistors on the chip. Manufacturers have approximately doubled that number about every 18 months since the 1970s (this regularity is known as Moore's Law).[6] A computer science textbook published in 2002 notes that "the highest-performance microprocessors of today outperform the supercomputer of less than 10 years ago."[7] That microprocessor is the size of a fingernail; the supercomputer filled a room.

The price of computing power has declined as well, in part because microprocessor production allows for extensive scale economies. This decline has been dramatic. For example, the number of integer operations per second per dollar grew more than 500-fold between 1990 and 2004.

Other hardware advances have helped miniaturize computing devices. The most notable is the decrease in the size and cost of disk storage. During this same time period, the amount of magnetic disk storage that could be purchased with a fixed dollar budget increased by about 500 times, and the disk density or the number of megabytes per square inch of disk surface increased by more than 1,200 times.

Advances in technology and computer design have provided ever smaller and cheaper computers. A comparison of specifications makes clear that a typical $1,000 computer bought around 2003 had greater computational performance, main memory, and disk storage than a $1,000,000 computer bought around 1980. Even more remarkable are consumer products that are based on computing devices.

6. Paul Freiberger and Michael Swaine, *Fire in the Valley*, 2nd ed. (New York: McGraw-Hill, 2000), p. 377.

7. John L. Hennessy and David A. Patterson, *Computer Architecture: A Quantitative Approach*, 3rd ed. (New York: Elsevier, 2002), chap. 1.

At less than 4 cubic inches, the 2004 iPod mini can easily fit in a shirt pocket. It has two 80-MHz microprocessors and can store more than 1,000 pop songs on its 6-gigabyte storage disk. At $249, it is several times more powerful than the multi-million-dollar IBM System/370 available in 1970.

The Growing Family of Computer-Based Products

The microcomputer industry grew rapidly as a result of these favorable technological and cost trends. In 1981, shortly after IBM added its microcomputer to the ones already introduced by Apple and others in the late 1970s, 344,000 microcomputers were sold in the United States. By 2004 there were an estimated 822 million computers in use worldwide. Almost every office worker in the United States now has one, and 56 percent of American households have at least one.[8]

The video game device was the first mass-produced good based on the microprocessor that was not a traditional computer. The early devices, introduced in the late 1970s, played a single game. Over time, video game consoles were developed that rivaled the most sophisticated personal computers. These were able to play numerous games that were compatible with their software and hardware. By 2002 the video game industry had reached $21 billion of annual revenue from the sale of consoles and games, surpassing the movie industry's $19 billion in annual box office revenues that same year.[9]

The increasing power and decreasing size of microprocessors and other hardware components made handheld computers feasible by the late 1980s. The Apple Newton was the first of these. The original Newton was about the size of a VHS cassette and functioned basically as an electronic notepad. It was technically interesting but a commercial failure. A few years later Palm introduced the PalmPilot, which had widespread appeal and helped create the handheld industry. At first these products were used mainly as sophisticated organizers; they competed with

8. Rex Crum, "*Computer Industry Almanac* Sees 1 Billion PCs by 2007," *CBS Market Watch*, March 9, 2005 (available from Lexis-Nexis); http://www.census.gov/population/socdemo/computer/ppl-175/tab01A.pdf.

9. "Gaming's New Frontier," *The Economist*, October 2, 2003.

Filofax. Over time they added Internet browsing and wireless email. In 2004, more than 31 million handheld devices ranging from BlackBerries to Treos were sold worldwide.[10]

Many, if not most, new mobile phones have calculators, games, and other computer-based features, and it is often possible to access more applications by downloading them directly from the Internet or downloading them to a PC and transferring them to a mobile phone. As wireless networks have gotten more sophisticated, wireless telephone companies have turned their phones into Web portals through which users can obtain various kinds of content and send email. Japan's DoCoMo was the pioneer here. Vodafone and other mobile networks have followed. There were more than 1.5 billion mobile phones in use worldwide in 2004.[11]

Digital music devices started becoming popular in the early 2000s. Their roots go back to the PC. Starting in the early 1990s, PCs could play CDs, and by the mid-1990s they could store and retrieve digital music tracks on disks. Various formats were developed for transmitting digital music over the Internet, including MP3, and several "media players" became popular for playing and manipulating music on PCs. Stand-alone MP3 players were introduced in the late 1990s. The industry is now synonymous with the iPod, introduced in 2001. More than 32 million handheld music devices were sold in 2003, and this industry is expected to expand dramatically with the increasing popularity of downloading music.[12]

Microprocessor-based computing devices were incorporated into many other products starting in the 1980s. ATMs are one example. Intel 8086 microprocessors powered cash dispensers in the late 1970s. Over time, ATMs have become PC-compatible devices that use stripped-down versions of common PC software platforms such as Windows or Linux. Cars are another example. Indeed, software gremlins are

10. David Linsalata, Kevin Burden, Ramon T. Llamas, and Randy Giusto, "Worldwide Smart Handheld Device 2005–2009 Forecast and Analysis: Passing the Torch" (IDC report no. 33415), May 2005, table 1.

11. http://www.itfacts.biz/index.php?id=P2193.

12. Susan Hevorhian, "Worldwide Compressed Audio Player 2004–2008 Forecast: MP3 Reaches Far and Wide" (IDC report no. 31811), August 2004, table 4.

behind a spate of complaints about windows going down on their own and temperature control systems turning up the heat on hot summer days.

The French payment card system started incorporating microprocessors into their debit cards in the late 1980s.[13] These were used mainly for verification. Cardholders entered their personal identification number on a reader that verified it against the number contained in the chip. These "smart cards" have gotten more capable and cheaper to produce. The major card systems have worked on developing software and hardware standards for these cards. Smart cards are being used at colleges to keep track of meals, for social welfare programs, and for secure purchasing over the Internet. Several card issuers in the United States have introduced "contactless" chip cards that are simply waved at a device at the point of sale. It is likely that within a decade, most of the cards used for payment around the world will be smart cards and thus based on small computers. (In 2003, there were already 220 million smart cards involved in banking-related uses alone worldwide.[14])

Software Platform Elements

A complete software platform does everything from telling the microprocessor to turn switches on or off to providing a host of full-fledged software features for application developers that save them the time of writing those features themselves. Many software platforms, though, are based on different software programs that provide different portions of these services. The boundaries between these programs are not always clear in practice and can change over time. To add to the confusion, these programs have names that are sometimes used interchangeably even though the programs do somewhat different things.

Moving from controlling the microprocessor to serving application developers, it is useful to distinguish four kinds of platform-related programs.

13. David Evans and Richard Schmalensee, *Paying with Plastic*, 2nd ed. (Cambridge, Mass.: MIT Press, 2005), p. 302.
14. http://www.epaynews.com/statistics/scardstats.html#7.

Software platforms are often, but not always, *operating systems*. The nucleus of a computer operating system is generally called the *kernel*. It manages the processors, memory, input and output, and certain support functions. It controls the hardware to calculate 2 + 2 and sends "4" to an output device. This is the first thing Linus Torvalds wrote to get Linux going.

The operating system generally also assists application programs in other ways. For example, it may help programs display complex graphics, such as a three-dimensional graphical depiction of 2 + 2 = 4, on a mobile phone screen or computer monitor. PC operating systems such as the Mac OS X are usually full-fledged software platforms; only the operating system stands between the hardware and the applications. In this case the terms *operating system* and *software platform* are synonymous.

Middleware typically refers to software that specializes in providing services to application developers. It does not have a kernel, and it relies on the operating system to control the hardware. Some middleware sits on top of an operating system kernel and does everything besides basic hardware support. For example, the operating system for the Sony PlayStation is little more than a kernel; game developers such as Electronic Arts write their own middleware, which provides support for various PlayStation games they create. Other middleware leaves tasks to an operating system that go beyond those generally performed by the kernel. And some middleware sits on top of a software platform: it may help applications run on many different software platforms, and it may compete with the software platform for the attention of application developers. That is the case with Sun's Java technologies.

Another critical aspect of a software platform's architecture is whether it is *open* or *closed*. With an open platform, anyone with the right technical knowledge can obtain access to the services provided by the platform or its underlying elements. Most PC platforms are open: one can write applications for the Mac OS or Windows without getting permission from the manufacturers. With a closed platform, only those with permission to use the platform can benefit from its services. Most game and mobile telephone platforms are walled off. Programmers have to get a "certificate" to get access to the operating system and hardware on these computing devices. Hacking is still possible, but much more difficult.

The Plan of the Book

This book is organized into four major parts. The next two chapters provide background. Chapter 2 describes software platforms from a technological standpoint. What do they do? How do they do it? How are they created? Chapter 3 considers their key economic aspects. It introduces the economics of two-sided markets, which is critical for understanding the nature of the demand for software platforms. It also explores characteristics that software platforms share with other software products and many information goods.

In the second part, Chapters 4 through 8 analyze important industries in which software platforms have played a prominent role, either as a standalone product or as an important component in a computer system consisting of hardware and software. The chapters in this section examine, in order, PCs, video games, handheld devices, mobile telephones, and digital music players and devices. These chapters are not intended to provide a complete history of these industries. After some initial background discussion, each chapter focuses on the strategies that companies pursued in these industries over time. In particular, we look closely at efforts to get multiple customer groups on board the platform, pricing, product design, and the organization of the supply chain and ecosystem. To help the reader understand the evolution of these industries, we present a timeline of the events we focus on for each chapter. (A historian of these industries would no doubt create a somewhat different timeline of key events.)

The third part, Chapters 9 through 11, examines the similarities and differences across these industries on several critical dimensions. Chapter 9 compares and contrasts business strategies for supplying software platforms. The focus is on business integration among the various levels of providing computer systems. Why have some companies chosen to provide both the hardware and the software platform, while others in the same segment have specialized in the software platform? How does the decision to disintegrate vertically vary over time, and why? Chapter

10 looks at pricing. We show that all these industries charge one customer side a "low" price. With the exception of video game consoles, all provide software developers with inexpensive access to valuable features in the platforms. What is the reason for the single exception? Chapter 11 examines the bundling of features. Like most information goods, software platforms combine features that attract very different groups of customers. What is extraordinary is the extent to which software platforms grow through the accumulation of features.

The fourth part, which consists of just Chapter 12, focuses on the role of software platforms in the process of creative destruction. Many software platforms have marched from the narrow market in which they were first introduced into other markets. PCs and video game consoles are both trying hard to get into your living room. Mobile phones are moving into digital cameras, personal music devices, personal digital assistants, and payment cards. The boundaries between software platforms and the industries they power are blurring. Many call this convergence. But it is also a life-and-death struggle for the businesses involved. As the iconic Pilot goes the way of the typewriter, the Palm OS may evolve into a successful mobile phone software platform, or it may just wither away. As some software platforms—and whole product categories—die, others are born.

Chapter 12 also looks at the role of two types of software platforms that were born shortly after the start of the commercial Internet in 1995. Both are Web-centric platforms. Both are designed to facilitate transactions between buyers and sellers in the economy. The code sits on servers that are connected to the Internet. One type is based on conducting auctions, the other on conducting searches. As of 2006, eBay and Google are the leaders in these respective categories.

Although these companies are not in the business mainly of providing software services to users or developers, they have opened their software code to developers and are providing services that facilitate developers writing applications. These Web-centric platforms will be sustaining a vast economy of developers, based on the experience of other software platforms we have examined. The symbiotic relationship between and among the platforms, developers, buyers, and sellers is expected to lead to profound changes in the retail economy.

INSIGHTS

• Software platforms are invisible engines based on written computer code. Software platforms power, to varying degrees, many modern industries, including digital music, mobile phones, on-line auctions, personal computers, video games, Web-based advertising, and online searches.

• Starting in 1970, the microprocessor revolution has stimulated the development of software platforms for diverse computing devices, enabled software platforms to migrate to smaller devices, and helped software platforms do more over time everywhere they are used.

• Software platforms usually provide valuable services to people who use computing devices, developers who write applications, and makers of computing hardware.

• Most businesses based on software platforms follow *multisided* strategies to get users, developers, and hardware makers on their platforms. These strategies are critical for harnessing positive feedbacks. For example, users value more applications, and applications developers value more users.

2

Speaking in Code

I have traveled the length and breadth of this country and talked with the best people, and I can assure you that data processing is a fad that won't last out the year.
—*The editor in charge of business books for Prentice Hall, 1957*[1]

INSIDE THIS CHAPTER

- The birth and evolution of modern computing
- The development of operating systems and software platforms
- The role of APIs in reducing duplication of programming efforts
- The production of commercial and open-source software

Software platforms come in several varieties, depending on what the code does and where among the various computing devices it resides.

Some have a single block of code that does everything from controlling the switches in the microprocessors to helping applications show three-dimensional objects. When you play Doom 3 on your Apple PC, the Mac OS X code is doing a lot of the work.

Others come in pieces. There is code on the device that controls the microprocessor. Then there is another piece that provides services to programmers who are writing applications for the device. The Nokia Series 60 Platform is what mobile phone applications use for many software services. The Nokia platform in turn relies on the Symbian OS to control the phone hardware.

1. Allan Afuah, *Innovation Management: Strategies, Implementation and Profits* (New York: Oxford University Press, 2003).

Still other software platforms are written so that they can work on multiple devices with different microprocessors and operating systems that control those microprocessors. The Java 2 Micro Edition provides technologies that enable developers to write programs that can run on consumer electronics devices with different chips and operating systems.

These alternatives for building and providing software platforms have key consequences for the structure of industries based on computer devices and the dynamics of competition within these industries.

The Historical Foundations of Computers and Programming

A program tells a computer what to do.

A loom designed by Joseph Jacquard in 1801 was the first programmable computing device. The Jacquard loom used punch cards made of stiff pasteboard to control the patterns of threading through the fabric. It revolutionized the textile industry—after a rebellion of weavers who feared it would eliminate their jobs was put down. Punch cards remained the dominant method for transmitting programs to computing devices until the late 1970s: "do not fold, spindle, or mutilate" was a famous programmer admonition.[2]

The origins of modern computing lie in efforts to make performing complex calculations easier. Charles Babbage developed the basic ideas behind mechanical computing and programming in the early nineteenth century out of frustration.[3] As Babbage wrote in his memoirs,

... I was sitting in the rooms of the Analytical Society, at Cambridge, my head leaning forward on the table in a kind of dreamy mood, with a table of logarithms lying open before me. Another member, coming into the room, and seeing me half asleep, called out, "Well, Babbage, what are you dreaming about?" to which I replied "I am thinking that all these tables" (pointing to the logarithms) "might be calculated by machinery."

He invented mechanical methods (using a machine called the Difference Engine) for calculating astronomical and mathematical tables, and

2. http://ccat.sas.upenn.edu/slubar/fsm.html.
3. Charles Babbage, *Passages from the Life of a Philosopher* (London, 1864), http://www-groups.dcs.st-and.ac.uk/~history/Mathematicians/Babbage.html.

reported them in an article published in 1822.[4] He went on to describe an "Analytical Engine" based on Jacquard's punch cards that contained many of the features of modern computers.

Though it was never actually built, Babbage's Analytical Engine led to a mathematical literature on how to write programs to solve problems with it. Ada King, the countess of Lovelace and Lord Byron's daughter, is often credited, along with Babbage, with whom she collaborated closely, with the first computer program—a set of instructions for calculating a sequence of numbers $(+1, -\frac{1}{2}, +\frac{1}{6}, \ldots)$ known as Bernoulli numbers. Although it is a matter of dispute whether she was an originator, interpreter, or popularizer, many of the ideas of contemporary programming were presented in her 1843 annotated translation of Menabrea's *Notions sur la machine analytique de Charles Babbage*.

The British government withdrew funding for an advanced version of Babbage's Difference Engine, and the Analytical Engine was beyond the technology available in the mid-nineteenth century. Further significant advances were not made until the demands of World War II, combined with technical progress, resulted in several breakthroughs, and until mathematicians Alan Turing, Claude Shannon, and John von Neumann laid the modern foundations of computer programming in the years before and after the war.

In the late 1930s, Turing, who is famous for writing programs that helped crack the Germans' Enigma code during World War II, published a paper that introduced what is now known as the Turing machine. It described the features of a mathematical computational device using a tape the machine can read and write on, and it defined a group of tasks that could be computed using this device.[5]

4. http://www-groups.dcs.st-and.ac.uk/~history/Mathematicians/Babbage.html. The Difference Engine was "programmed" to evaluate a polynomial such as $y = a \times x^2 + b \times x + c$ for successive values of x given the values of a, b, and c.

5. A Turing Machine is a "state machine": at any time it is in one of a finite number of states. It has a head that can read and write symbols—a 0 or 1, for example—onto an infinite tape. For every combination of a current state and the symbol under the head, a new state and action are defined. The action can be one of the following: change the symbol under the head, move the head one step right, or move the head one step left. The machine halts if there is no action defined for the current combination of a state and symbol under the head.

A program for this machine consists of a series of instructions:

X ← Read the symbol under the head;
If there is a transition rule for the combination of X and the current state
N
    Then write Y on the square under head or move the head one step left
or right
    Then change state to M
If not halt
Repeat

All current computers and higher programming languages are mathematically identical to a Turing machine, though much easier to use. The concepts of *if* and *then* are important parts of the programming idiom.

Claude Shannon recognized that 0s and 1s could be used to represent whether relay and switching circuits were on or off. In his 1938 MIT master's thesis, he demonstrated that these circuits could be used to perform complex calculations based on a series of 0s and 1s.[6] A decade later he coined the term bit—from *bi*nary digi*t*—in a paper on signal processing that founded modern information theory.

By the time of Shannon and Turing, hardware technology had progressed far enough that their ideas were soon put into action. Mechanical computing machines had been around for many years, ranging from the abacus for simple calculations to gear-shaft and cog systems that could solve differential equations. The demands of World War II saw the development of electronic computers in England, Germany, and the United States. The ENIAC, mentioned in the introduction, is considered the first fully operational electronic general-purpose computer. Unlike its special-purpose mechanical predecessors, it had "conditional jumps" (such as "if X go to instruction N") and could do many different kinds of calculations. Operators programmed it manually by setting switches and plugging cables. Data for programs were entered and stored on punch cards. This system was tedious.

6. Shannon relied on a branch of mathematics known as Boolean algebra.

John von Neumann helped devise what became the programming architecture of modern computers. His key insights were that instructions could be reduced to binary values and that both instructions and data could be stored efficiently in memory. This led to an architecture consisting of five components: an input unit, a control unit, memory, a calculating unit, and an output unit. The instructions are fetched and executed one at a time—sequentially—by the central processing unit (CPU). The CPU must have almost instantaneous access to memory for this to work. Practically, that resulted in a hierarchy of memory based on access speed, including what is now called random access memory (RAM). The stored program computer became the mainstay of the computer industry.

The Development of Programming Languages

A programming language has a vocabulary and grammatical rules that permit humans to communicate instructions to computers.

From the introduction of the ENIAC, machines have only understood a language consisting of 0s and 1s. That is called *machine language*. The invention of a stored program permitted computer operators to convey instructions through punch cards containing 0s and 1s rather than manipulating cables and toggles. That tedious process was made simpler by the invention of what is known as *assembly language* to convey these instructions. Something like the use of "LOL" for "laughing out loud," "li $t0 8" instructs the computer to load the value 8 into register t0 in the processor; this command replaces writing 001101 00000 01000 00000 00000 001000 in machine language.[7] Short Code, invented in the late 1940s, was the first programming language. The programmer used its symbols to write out a program. When complete, she then had to translate the symbols back into 0s and 1s. A few years later that tedious process was eliminated with the development of a *compiler* that did this translation automatically.

Higher-level languages were then developed that made "writing" complex programs substantially easier because the programming is done

7. 34080008 in hexadecimal notation.

at a level that is intuitive to humans. The programmer can simply instruct the computer to add two numbers, for instance, without keeping track of where in the CPU they and their sum are stored. FORTRAN, developed at IBM for scientific computing and introduced in 1957, was the first of these languages. Its vocabulary provides a sense of what it could do: IF, THEN, GOTO, DO, END, TRUE, FALSE. It was especially popular for scientific applications. Other languages were developed over time, such as COBOL, which was used mainly for writing business applications. FORTRAN and COBOL were used to develop applications for mainframe computers, large computers owned by enterprises. Today, most of the code running on mainframe computers is in COBOL.

Another popular language was BASIC. It was introduced as a teaching tool at Dartmouth College in 1963. It had a simple vocabulary and grammar and was easy for beginners to use. It became the leading language for the PCs introduced in the late 1970s in part because it required little memory. Microsoft's first product was a version of BASIC for the Altair, the first PC. Soon after dropping out of Harvard, Microsoft founder Bill Gates wrote a BASIC *interpreter*—which is similar to a compiler in the sense that it translates a higher-level language into something the machine can understand—that fits into 4 kilobytes (kb) of memory (about 10 percent of the memory on a smart credit card).[8]

The simple program in Figure 2.1 illustrates the role of a high-level language. We start with an algorithm for calculating 2 multiplied by itself n times (that is, 2 to the nth power), where the user can specify any n she would like. We then write a program in BASIC that communicates this algorithm to a computer. That program is then translated into 0s and 1s. We represent the 0s and 1s in hexadecimal notation (each pair of hexadecimal digits corresponds to a unique combination of eight 0s and 1s).

Even in the early days of computing, programs designed for business or technical applications might have had many thousands of lines of high-level code. In order to write such large programs in a timely fashion it was necessary to have many individuals working in parallel. Unfortunately, changes to any one part of a large program may affect how other

8. Smart cards have 24 kb of ROM and 16 kb of programmable ROM. http://electronics.howstuffworks.com/question332.htm.

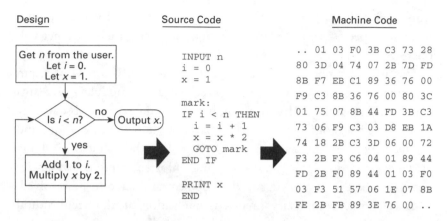

| Design | Source Code | Machine Code |

```
INPUT n
i = 0
x = 1

mark:
IF i < n THEN
    i = i + 1
    x = x * 2
    GOTO mark
END IF

PRINT x
END
```

```
.. 01 03 F0 3B C3 73 28
80 3D 04 74 07 2B 7D FD
8B F7 EB C1 89 36 76 00
F9 C3 8B 36 76 00 80 3C
01 75 07 8B 44 FD 3B C3
73 06 F9 C3 03 D8 EB 1A
74 18 2B C3 3D 06 00 72
F3 2B F3 C6 04 01 89 44
FD 2B F0 89 44 01 03 F0
03 F3 51 57 06 1E 07 8B
FE 2B FB 89 3E 76 00 ..
```

Figure 2.1
Simple program: from design to source code to machine code. The machine code is written in hexadecimal notation (where numbers go up to 16 and A–F represent 11–16).

parts operate, so the more individuals there are working in parallel on a single program, the more likely it is that they will create problems for one another and thus slow the effort down.[9]

The solution to this problem has been to exploit the power of *modularity* in software design.[10] The basic idea is to move from the specification of what a new program as a whole should do to the specification of an *architecture* that describes the overall program as a set of modules, specifies the functions that each module is to perform, and specifies the interfaces that link them. In a program to handle payroll, for instance, one module might be assigned the task of calculating each employee's Social Security contribution as a function of current law, this period's earnings, and past contributions—all supplied by other modules. If the program's architecture is sound, individuals or small

9. This is a general property of complex systems: changing the engine in a car, for instance, may require making changes in its brakes, fuel tank, frame, and many other components. The classic discussion in the context of software is Frederick P. Brooks, *The Mythical Man-Month: Essays in Software Engineering* (New York: Addison-Wesley, 1975).

10. This powerful idea is used in a wide variety of design contexts. See Carliss Y. Baldwin and Kim B. Clark, *Design Rules* (Cambridge, Mass.: MIT Press, 2000).

teams can work in parallel in the various modules, and if the modules meet their specifications, the program built by linking them together will operate as intended.

The modular approach has numerous advantages. If a new program (or other complex system) can be specified as *N* modules, *N* teams can work in parallel. Moreover, individual modules can subsequently be improved without touching other parts of the overall program, and they can be used in other programs. On the other hand, specifying an architecture in detail is complex, and unforeseen interdependencies between modules often occur in development and have to be resolved. Because of the complexity involved, innovation at the architectural (as opposed to modular) level is difficult. Finally, an architecture that facilitates program development (by having a large number of modules and simple interfaces, say) may fail to optimize performance (by, in effect, requiring excessive communication between modules, for instance). There are trade-offs between and among modularity, design costs, and efficiency.

Object-oriented programming is a recent innovation in high-level languages based on modularity. A program is written as a set of *objects*, each of which corresponds to particular functions and data. The other parts of the program can then use these objects to get access to the data and functions they include. These objects make it easier to reuse code for multiple purposes. The programmer can just take one of these components off the shelf, so to speak, and deploy it when needed. The programmer can also decide to make any object off-limits to certain other parts of the program in the interests of reliability.

Two high-level languages, C and Java, are widely used today for writing much of the software discussed in the following pages.

C, along with its variants (including C+, C++, and C#), is the most widely used programming language. It was developed at Bell Laboratories in the 1970s. Though difficult to learn, it is one of the most powerful and flexible languages for writing efficient programs. It is especially popular for writing system software such as the operating system. C++ added object-oriented programming to C.

Sun's Java programming language is part of a set of programming technologies that are designed so that applications can run on many different operating systems and hardware configurations: "write once, run everywhere" is its aspiration and mantra. It was originally developed for handheld devices and has become widely used for writing small Web-based applications. Similar to C++, Java is an object-oriented language. Java programs go through a series of translations that enable them to be run on different machines. The programs are first compiled into *byte code* files, which can then be translated into machine-level instructions by a *Java Virtual Machine* that is written specifically for an individual operating system or hardware platform.

Evolution of Operating Systems

Modern operating systems are software programs. If you think about the computer platform from the viewpoint of the microprocessor, the operating system is usually the only program from which the CPU receives instructions. All other programs sit on top of the operating system and interact with the CPU only through it. Today, most operating systems are written in a high-level language such as C++ and are then translated into machine language before being installed on the computer hardware.

There were no operating systems for the early computers. From the late 1940s to the mid-1950s, a person ran the machine from a console that had toggle switches and display lights. Programs in machine language were submitted to the machine through a punch card reader. Debugging programs required looking at lights for the processor registers and main memory to figure out the source of the errors. Moreover, it was hard to schedule time with the expensive computing hardware. Only one program could run at a time, and users had to schedule blocks of time. They might finish early and leave the computer idle for a time, or not get any results at all before their time ran out.

Batch operating systems were developed to maximize the utilization of these expensive machines. General Motors created the first in the mid-1950s for use on its IBM 701 computer.[11] Other customers followed

11. Frank Hayes, "The Story So Far: Bell Labs, GM and MIT Played Major Roles in the Development of Operating Systems," Computerworld, 30, March 17, 2003.

suit. By the early 1960s, many computer manufacturers had developed batch operating systems for their machines. These early systems had a *monitor*. Although now synonymous with the screens many of us look at for hours every day, the original monitor was a portion of the code that acted as a sentry. That sentry controlled the sequencing of instructions to the processor, prevented user programs from altering memory where the monitor program itself resided, reserved for itself certain privileged instructions such as input and output, and timed programs to prevent them from using system resources for too long. Users could communicate with the monitor using *job control language* (JCL). In these early days of computing, programmers put canned JCL instructions at the beginning and end of their programs—all on punch cards.

In those days, inputting instructions and outputting results accounted for most of the time it took to run a program. The CPU was mostly idle while this was going on. Multiprogramming (or multitasking) was developed to make better use of the CPU. It required hardware that enabled the processor to be interrupted when input and output operations were completed and there was computing to be done. And it required memory management that enabled several programs to be kept in the main memory and that juggled the execution of these programs around while input and output operations were being conducted. One of the first multiprogrammed, batch operating systems was the IBM OS/360 for the System/360 in 1964.[12]

"As more and more features have been added to operating systems, and as the underlying hardware has become more capable and versatile," William Stallings has observed, "the size and complexity of operating systems has grown."[13] UNIVAC's operating system for the 1107,

12. A related development during the late 1960s and 1970s was time-sharing. Programmers interacted directly with the computers during the very early years, and, although it was inconvenient, they could see and debug errors in real time. Batch processing cut the connection between the programmer and computer. The programmer had to submit a job and get the results back from the computer operator. Multiprogramming helped make it possible for multiple users to interact with a machine. Users submitted commands at a terminal and got responses back from the computer. Time-sharing systems traded increased processing use for decreased response time for the user.

13. William Stallings, *Operating Systems: Internals and Design Principles*, 4th ed. (Upper Saddle River, N.J.: Prentice Hall, 2001), p. 77.

announced in 1960, had 25,000 lines of code.[14] IBM's OS/360 had a million lines when introduced in 1964. The Multics operating system, developed by MIT and Bell Labs, had 20 million in 1975. Windows XP has about 40 million.[15] These are not apple-to-apple comparisons because they are for different programs written for different systems. Nonetheless, they highlight an important trend throughout the history of operating systems.

Operating system designers have added features that make improved use of the hardware or that control new hardware features. More important for the evolution of industries based on software platforms, operating system designers have also added many features that save programmers from having to write their own code. Just as object-oriented programming helps programmers avoid reinventing the proverbial wheel—such as code for displaying data in three dimensions—developing operating systems as rich sets of modules and making public the interfaces that link them saves programmers of diverse applications from having to write code for a wide variety of common tasks. Indeed, this modularity has transformed operating systems into software platforms. We explain how next.

Application Programming Interfaces

Operating systems provide services to applications through Application Programming Interfaces (APIs). These services range from rudimentary hardware services, such as moving a cursor on a monitor, to sophisticated software services, such as drawing and rotating three-dimensional objects. The APIs serve as interfaces between these services and applications. (As we discuss later, they may also serve as interfaces between modules of the operating system itself.)

Applications obtain services by passing specific information to the APIs and obtaining other information back. The API, which the programmer sees, calls on a black box (a system module), which the programmer does not see, to perform a specific task. The method is similar to the mathematical functions included in high-level programs. Suppose

14. http://www.cc.gatech.edu/gvu/people/randy.carpenter/folklore/v1n3.html.

15. http://en.wikipedia.org/wiki/Source_lines_of_code.

you wanted a computer to multiply two numbers, X and Y. You could write that program in machine language to get the microprocessor to do that. But since multiplication is a common problem that people face, high-level languages all have functions that do this for you. All you have to do is give the value of the two numbers to a function in the program and the function will return the result. In particular, you might write X = 6, Y = 7, and $Z = X * Y$; "*" is often the symbol that tells the high-level language that it should insert X and Y as arguments in its multiplication algorithm. You will get the answer 42, although you will never see the machine code that does the calculation.

The APIs for operating systems take "arguments" (like the 6 and 7 in the example above) from the application program and call on "system services" (like the machine code that calculates 6 times 7) to perform the work desired by the application program. The Linux kernel has an API, shown in Figure 2.2, that allocates memory for an object that the application intends to use. The application has to specify the size of the object in bytes and some parameter flags for the API. The Linux source code then allocates the memory necessary for this object and returns a pointer to enable the application to find the memory needed for the object. This API is simple. It just enters information into the function (_cache_alloc) that calls on the system services to do the work. There are at least 116 lines of source code in Linux that carry out the work required by this seven-line API.[16] As a result, the programmer can avoid writing more than 100 lines of code by inserting the necessary data into this seven-line API.

It is easy to see why application developers find the ability to access system services through APIs appealing. Rather than every application developer writing hundreds of lines of code to allocate memory to an object, to take the example above, the operating system developer writes 116 lines of code and makes the system services this code provides available to all application developers through the API.

Some operating systems provide fairly minimal services to applications. Others devote large amounts of code to features that applications

16. The 116 lines are part of methods one or two levels below the original API. Going deeper into the kernel would raise this number significantly.

```
void * __kmalloc (size_t size, int flags)
{

    struct cache_sizes *csizep = malloc_sizes;


    for (; csizep->cs_size; csizep++) {
        if (size > csizep->cs_size)
                continue;


        return__cache_alloc(flags & GFP_DMA ?
            csizep->cs_dmacachep : csizep->cs_cachep,
flags);
    }

    return NULL;
}
```

Figure 2.2
An example of a Linux API. (Source: Linux Kernel 2.6.10; File: slab.c.)

can use. The computer device itself influences this choice. Because a mobile phone has limited memory, for instance, an operating system for a mobile phone cannot do as much as an operating system for a PC. (Of course, today's mobile phone can do more than PCs could in the 1980s.) An operating system for a single-purpose device such as the temperature control system in a car need not cater to applications because at least for now, there is no demand for applications to run on such a device. The business model adopted by the operating system manufacturer also determines the services it provides to applications. Some manufacturers may decide to focus mainly on hardware and let others provide system services. Sony provides significantly fewer services to game developers on its PlayStation than Microsoft does on its Xbox, for instance.

Middleware also provides application services. These software programs leave most of the hardware interactions to the operating system that they work with. They specialize in providing more advanced software features on which application writers can rely.

Some middleware complements the operating system in the sense that there are few overlaps in services. That is true, for example, of the Symbian OS and the Nokia Series 60 and 80 Developer Platform.

Other middleware competes with the operating system by providing services that are also in the operating system. That is true of Java. It provides software services that programmers can use in place of the services available in the operating systems with which Java works—Linux, Mac OS, Windows, and a host of others. Then, on each hardware platform on which Java runs, Java leaves the job of controlling the hardware to the operating system running on that hardware.

Software Platforms

The software platform is the set of programs that stand between the hardware and an application. A particular computing device may have several possible software platforms for an application based on different combinations of operating systems and middleware programs.

Mobile telephones provide an interesting example. Consider a mobile telephone based on the Texas Instruments OMAP line of microprocessors; these are used in Nokia phones, for example. Possible software platforms are shown in Figure 2.3. In the first three stacks the operating system (Linux or Windows Mobile) provides APIs for mobile phone applications. In the fourth stack, Symbian, which is partly owned by Nokia, provides mainly hardware services and Nokia's middleware provides application services.

Consider also a PC based on an Intel chip. Figure 2.4 shows some of the possible software platform configurations. In this example there are two alternative operating systems, Linux and Windows. Each provides

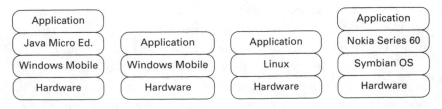

Figure 2.3
Alternative mobile telephone platforms.

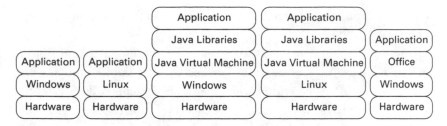

Figure 2.4
Alternative personal computer software platforms. Here, "Linux" includes both Linux kernel and utilities.

a rich set of application services through a series of APIs. However, either can work with Java middleware as long as there is a Java Virtual Machine running alongside the operating system. In addition, other applications may use specialized services made available in other software such as Office.

Three popular software platforms illustrate some of the diverse ways of building platforms.

Windows XP

Windows XP descends from Windows NT, which Microsoft released in 1993. Windows NT was written for processors that could handle instructions and numbers represented with 32 bits (that is, 32 sequential 0s or 1s), compared with 16 bits for earlier versions of Windows. Microsoft has upgraded (and renamed) Windows NT over time while retaining the same basic architecture. With Windows XP, Microsoft unified its lines of desktop operating systems for home (Windows 95, 98, and Me) and business (Windows NT and 2000). In addition, Windows XP added new technology for keeping track of items across computers on a network and other features that were appealing for inter-connected computing.

Written mainly in C++, versions of Windows XP have been available for client computers (the computers that sit on our desks or laps) and server computers (the networked computers that focus on such things as Web applications and corporate databases) using Intel-compatible microprocessors. The operating systems for clients and servers have much of their code and APIs in common, but the server operating systems include various services for servers on networks of computers.

Windows NT and its successors relied on the modular and object-oriented design concepts mentioned earlier. One can think of this as using the concept of APIs within the operating system code. A lower-level object provides services to higher-level objects. For example, in Microsoft Windows XP, Internet Explorer relies on a module called the Microsoft XML Core Services, which is used to interpret XML documents. The same Microsoft XML Core Services module is used by other parts of the operating system, such as the part that handles playing media.[17]

Windows XP also has an extensive set of application services that are known as the Win32 API Set. Bill Gates put the number of APIs in the initial version of Windows 2000 at more than 6,000.[18] The next version of the Windows operating system, Vista, will feature sophisticated support for digital rights management (see Chapter 8), a new user interface technology, and many new application services made available through the WinFX API Set. It will have a total of more than 1,000 APIs available to developers. (The number of APIs reported here is based on the ones that Microsoft documents and manages.)

Unix and Linux

Linux is an operating system that is widely used on server computers and is making headway in everything from embedded devices to mobile telephones to client computers. It has descended from Unix. Unix in turn is an operating system that was widely used for minicomputers and workstations during the 1970s and 1980s and remains popular for servers and other heavy-duty uses.

Computer scientists at Bell Labs developed the first versions of Unix. It was first used on a minicomputer made by Digital Equipment Corpo-

17. http://support.microsoft.com/?scid=kb;en-us;q272633;   http://download.microsoft.com/download/9/6/5/9657c01e-107f-409c-baac-7d249561629c/MSXML4SP_RelNote.htm; http://www.microsoft.com/downloads/details.aspx?FamilyID=3144b72b-b4f2-46da-b4b6-c5d7485f2b42&DisplayLang=en.

18. U.S. v. Microsoft, Civil Action No. 98–1233, Direct Testimony of Bill Gates, ¶56.

ration. Like most operating systems at the time, it was written in assembly language; at the time, this was considered the best approach for writing complex programs that were also efficient. In a major innovation a few years after its introduction, it was rewritten in C, thereby demonstrating the advantages of using a high-level language for writing most operating system code. Bell Labs licensed the Unix source code to universities and businesses. Several developers started modifying the code. Since they did not do this in concert, the Unix code "forked," leading over time to multiple versions of the operating system, and programs written for one version could not necessarily run on another version without modification. The most popular of these versions was BSD Unix, created at the University of California, Berkeley.

What is normally considered the Unix operating system is a collection of several components. These include the kernel, an interface that permitted applications to call on the services of the kernel and therefore the hardware, and a series of canned commands and libraries of programs that users can rely on for calling on system services directly or can use in applications written for Unix. Over time, the various versions of Unix have improved the kernel. For example, Sun's Solaris operating system is based on a version of Unix (System V Release 4) that AT&T and Sun Microsystems developed jointly. These partners completely rewrote the kernel that was the basis for the standard version of Unix at the time.

Linux is based on a variant of BSD Unix that can run on IBM-compatible personal computers. Linus Torvalds wrote the original Linux kernel in C and posted an early version on the Web in 1991. He used software tools that were developed by the Free Software Foundation. Working over the Internet, programmers from around the world suggested improvements and additions to the kernel as well as other utilities. Torvalds incorporated these periodically into releases of Linux. Over time, Torvalds secured the help of a number of individuals to help manage the process of building and releasing successive versions of Linux. (We discuss the Free Software Foundation and the production of open-source programs in more detail in the next chapter.)

The Linux kernel was organized as a collection of modules. Each module could be modified independently of the others, and new modules could be added to the system. This facilitated improvements in Linux and also made it possible for independent programmers to make contributions.

Working versions of Linux consist of the Linux kernel, various applications, and specialized configuration and installation tools that together form a Linux distribution such as Red Hat Linux. The Linux kernel is the core of the operating system, managing things like memory and task scheduling. The system is often modified to fit specialized tasks such as deployment in specialized devices (mobile phones, set-top boxes, robots) or in unique circumstances (security).

Java

Sun initially envisioned Java, first called Oak, as a programming language for digital devices for television and other media. The idea was to create a language that was useful for devices that lacked the processing power and memory of larger computers. It was also aimed for use on devices based on different microprocessors. Java's programming team first displayed Java's potential prowess by creating a digital entertainment device with an animated touch screen and Duke, Java's mascot, doing cartwheels on the screen.[19] Over time, this new language has evolved into a platform that can be used on many computing devices. As of 2006, however, Java is most commonly used for small Web applications, in enterprises as a component of applications on servers, in set-top boxes, and on portable devices.

The platform consists of three major components. First, Java is a programming language. Second, the Java Virtual Machine is the middleware layer that is at the core of Java's operating system independence. Unlike other programming languages, Java programs are not written for a particular operating system or device. Instead, they run on a Java Virtual Machine that serves as an intermediary between the program and the underlying operating system.

The Java Virtual Machine specific to a given operating system and hardware environment then converts the byte codes into machine code.

19. http://www.engin.umd.umich.edu/CIS/course.des/cis400/java/java.html; http://newsletter.paragon-systems.com/articles/58/1/ja/8427.

Thus the same program, without modification, runs on every system for which a Java Virtual Machine is available. However, the portability comes with a price: performance. The Java Virtual Machine is essentially another layer of instructions that sits between the application and the hardware. Consequently, Java applications run slower and require more memory than comparable applications written specifically for any given operating system. As a result, Java is rarely used for complex or demanding applications, and the applications are heavily optimized for specific operating systems and processors when it is used. Such optimization hurts portability.

Finally, Java also includes class libraries for each operating system. The class libraries are the services provided by the APIs and form the backbone of Java. They are also a limitation on Java's platform independence. Even if a particular system has a Java Virtual Machine, a Java program will run only if all the class libraries it relies on are available on that system. That is seldom an issue for PCs, but smaller, more limited devices such as mobile phones may not have room for the full class libraries. The Java Virtual Machine and the class libraries are sometimes referred to as the Java Runtime Environment.

The architecture of the Java technologies for an Audiovox SMT5600 mobile phone was shown in Figure 2.3.[20] This device has a microprocessor from Texas Instruments and uses the Windows Mobile 2003 operating system. The phone also supports the Java 2 platform. An application developer can write his program in Java and rely on the Java class libraries for the equivalent of APIs and underlying application services. He can then compile this program into Java byte codes.

Operating System and Software Platform Production

Modern operating systems have tens of millions of lines of code. Ten million lines of code have roughly the same information as the *Encyclopædia Britannica*. The many sections of this code—objects or modules—are highly interdependent, much like the parts of a modern jet aircraft. There is a further challenge. Users want their applications to

20. http://www.mobiletechreview.com/audiovox_SMT5600_smartphone.htm.

work with successive generations of the platform. Changes in the platform must maintain "backward compatibility" as much as possible.

Anyone who has programmed knows that it is rarely easy to make a complex program work properly with all possible inputs. One must typically write code, run it, watch it fail, find and remove the error or bug that caused the failure, try again, and keep debugging until the program does what it was intended to do. With long, complex programs written by many people, this process becomes distinctly harder: not only does each programmer have to make sure her module works correctly, but those in charge of the program need to make sure that all of the modules work properly when fit together. Debugging is easiest with single-purpose programs. Operating systems and software platforms are harder because they are designed to support many other programs that cause the many elements of the operating system to interact in an enormously large number of ways. They need to go through a testing process even after they seem to run well in normal use. This process often continues to what is known as alpha and beta testing by users.

There are important differences between the development process for operating systems that are manufactured by companies—what is known as proprietary software—and those that are produced through the open-source process.

Proprietary Operating Systems

Sophisticated operating systems are developed over many months by large teams of designers, programmers, and testers. New versions of an operating system can take several years from conception to release. It took Apple five years to develop the Mac OS X, and this involved a complete redesign and rewriting of its earlier operating system. Microsoft Windows NT, mentioned earlier, was developed over five years by a team that grew to more than 200 designers, programmers and testers working for Microsoft—in addition to the over 15,000 alpha and beta testers who volunteered to try early versions of the program.[21]

The process of developing a new operating system begins with its architecture that, like a building, will determine the constraints

21. Internal Microsoft information, obtained by interview.

on remodeling efforts for years to come. Programming teams then begin writing the code for each individual module of the operating system. In Microsoft's case, this involves working in parallel but linking the pieces daily and debugging the resulting system.[22] It also entails constant testing. Microsoft employs roughly one tester for every programmer.

This description makes it seem as if writing software was like writing a newspaper—and in some ways it is. There are many people working in loosely formed teams whose output is combined every day into a single document. But the outputs of the software teams must work together. And while journalism has its own complexities, software developers have many hard mathematical problems to conquer in the process of writing an operating system. For instance, software manufacturers face complex mathematical problems in designing and implementing systems for maintaining and updating directories in networks. Between 1995 and 2004, IBM, Microsoft, Novell, Sun Microsystems, and other companies were granted more than 290 patents for their programming methods. There is also a premium on writing code that is efficient—that maximizes the performance of the computer's hardware.

Open-Source Software

Open-source communities face similar problems in dealing with large, complex software programs, but solve them quite differently.

A program begins when one or more individuals conceive its architecture. Often these individuals will write a first draft of the program, or a significant segment, and then post the code and key elements of the overall architecture on the Internet. They will form a self-perpetuating committee that will guide further development by accepting changes contributed by others to current versions. Debugging and testing takes place mainly through people—usually the information technology savvy, but in later stages also interested members of the general public—identifying problems and reporting them to a site that is dedicated to the program. The

22. Michael A. Cusumano and Richard W. Selby, *Microsoft Secrets* (London: HarperCollins, 1995), pp. 269–270.

open-source community prides itself on having "a thousand eyeballs" look at and use program code and thereby steadily improve its quality.

Linux was developed more or less in this way. Torvalds and his lieutenants have been coordinating its development ever since he released the first kernel. For example, since mid-2001, approximately 4,000 programmers have made contributions to Linux.[23] The code for the kernel has expanded from about 2.5 million lines to more than 4 million lines in the same period, and many utilities, libraries, and other software platform-related modules have been written for it.

The Linux development process is much more organized than it might seem. Many of the contributors are employed and paid by large corporations, such as IBM and Hewlett-Packard (HP). Patches and new ideas for individual modules are conceived and started by individual developers or contributing enterprises. After that, the project begins a life of its own, depending on the idea's popularity within the Linux community. These projects are posted on the Internet and are usually run under some direction. The one below, taken from the Linux home page in February 2005, shows a project for creating a new sound API. The home page for the project advertises for programmers to work on further development.

Name: Advanced Linux Sound Architecture (ALSA) Project
Website: http://www.alsa-project.org/
Contact: perex@suse.cz
Description: Primary goals are create modern sound driver for Linux with new sound API which solves all OSS/Lite trouble and create good libraries for sound applications.

The Website says: We need users to use, test and provide feedback, programmers to work on low level drivers, writers to extend and improve our documentation, and application developers who choose to use ALSA as the basis for their programs. If you are interested, please subscribe to a mailing list. We welcome all constructive ideas, opinions and feedback!

---

23. Josh Lerner, Parag Pathak, and Jean Tirole, "The Dynamics of Open Source Contributions," *American Economic Review Papers and Proceedings* 96 (May 2006): forthcoming.

The contact for the project was located at SuSE, a company that distributes open-source software, in the Czech Republic (SuSE is a German company that is owned by Novell). We return to the open-source movement and its origins in the next chapter.

Operating System, Software Platforms, and Computing Devices

Several computing devices are the focus of discussion in the remaining chapters. Table 2.1 shows the main operating systems and software platforms that are used for these devices. It also shows the different manufacturers that provide the hardware, the operating system, and the middleware. There is great variety. The remainder of this book documents this heterogeneity and explores the business, economic, and historical reasons behind it.

Two features of software platforms have wide ramifications. The provision of services through APIs makes them inherently two-sided platforms that serve users and developers simultaneously. The fact that software platforms are no more than written symbols means that, like books, movies, patents, and other intellectual property, these platforms often cost much to create and little to reproduce. The next chapter examines the economic implications of these and other characteristics of software platforms.

INSIGHTS

• Software platforms were made possible by the development and improvement of programming languages that enable humans to tell computers what to do.

• The design of software platforms and the business models they serve have important consequences for the structure of industries based on computing devices.

• Most software platforms are composed of modules that provide software services to other software programs. APIs provide application programmers access to these services. In effect, the programmer submits

Table 2.1
Summary of Platforms

Platform, Examples	Microprocessor	Operating System	Middleware
PC			
Microsoft Windows	Intel, AMD	Windows	Windows, Java, more
Apple Macintosh	POWERPC, Intel	Mac OS	Mac OS, Java, more
Linux	Intel, AMD, POWERPC, more	Linux kernel	Linux Utilities, Java, more
Game Consoles			
Sony PlayStation 2	300 MHz Emotion Engine	Sony proprietary	Sony PS2 SDK (limited), sound and graphics APIs
Microsoft Xbox	733 MHz Intel Pentium 3*	Windows 2000*	XDK, sound and graphics APIs
PDA			
Palm OS	Intel, TI, ARM, Motorola, more	Palm OS	Palm OS, Java
Microsoft Windows Mobile	Intel, TI, ARM, Motorola, more	Windows Mobile	Windows Mobile, Java 2 Micro Edition, Mophun
BlackBerry	Intel, Motorola, more	RIM proprietary	Java
Smart Phones			
Symbian	Intel, TI, ARM, Motorola, more	Symbian	Nokia Series 60/80, Java 2 Micro Edition, Mophun
Microsoft Windows Mobile	Intel, TI, ARM, Motorola, more	Windows Mobile	Windows Mobile, Java 2 Micro Edition, Mophun
Linux	Intel, TI, ARM, Motorola, more	Linux	Linux Utilities, Vendor SDKs, Java 2 Micro Edition
Digital Media			
Microsoft Windows Media	NA	NA	Windows Media Player
RealNetworks	NA	NA	RealPlayer
Apple QuickTime	NA	NA	QuickTime
Apple iPod	NA	iPod OS	

* Modified for the needs of the game console.

information to the API, and the software platform performs the service requested.

• The use of APIs enables software platform developers to write code that can be used by many applications vendors, thus reducing duplication of effort.

• Open-source software is built through a decentralized process whereby an initial version of a program is posted on the worldwide Web and anyone who is interested may propose additions or corrections.

3

Both Sides Now

I'm basically a very lazy person who likes to take credit for things other people actually do.
—*Linus Torvalds*[1]

INSIDE THIS CHAPTER

- Software platforms as information-goods and multisided platforms
- Economic and strategic characteristics of multisided platforms
- Economic aspects of open-source software

Two features of the technology we described in the last chapter shape the economics of software platforms.

Software platforms are a written product of the mind. They are in effect documents, usually written in a high-level computer language. The code involved is malleable. It can be moved, altered, added to, and subtracted from with great ease. It is created almost entirely by people— "almost" because, like composers and writers, most programmers use computers for help.

Software platforms are inherently multisided. They usually serve distinct groups of customers, who benefit from having each other on the same platform. Application Programming Interfaces (APIs) forge the crucial relationship between application developers and end users. The developer can benefit from using APIs when she can sell the resulting software to users who have those APIs on their computing devices.

1. Eric Raymond, *The Cathedral and the Bazaar* (Sebastapol, Calif.: O'Reily Press, 1999).

Although we examine both of these features in this chapter, the multi-sided nature of software platforms is a main focus of the remainder of the book and the economic aspect of these invisible engines from which we will glean many insights. We conclude this chapter with a discussion of another remarkable aspect of the software business: people working collaboratively over the Internet, often without pay, produce software, including software platforms, that compete with software produced by for-profit firms.

Information Goods

Software is one of many information goods in modern economies. Books, songs, screenplays, patents, and secret formulas are others. Of course, there are differences among these products. Most books are a final product read for enjoyment or knowledge. Musical scores instruct musicians on what to do with their instruments. And software is ultimately a series of instructions that directly or indirectly makes computer hardware work. But these differences pale next to the similarities.

Like all information goods, software has four major economic characteristics. It is a creation of the human brain; it is made of pliable symbols; the consumption of these symbols by one person does not exclude consumption by another; and it is almost costless to reproduce an exact replica of these symbols. A musical score has all these features. A composer can use musical notes to make scores of infinite variety and length. When an orchestra plays a particular score, it does not reduce the value of the score to anyone else. And it is cheap to reproduce the score, as well as any orchestra's rendition of it.

These software features have consequences shared by other information goods. Without intellectual property protection there is no obvious way to make money. (The free software movement discussed at the end of this chapter has found some unusual ways to motivate its participants.) There are extreme scale economies: fixed costs are high, marginal costs quite low. The addition of features is relatively easy and an important source of dynamic competition, incremental innovation, and product differentiation.

Software Characteristics

Produced by an Educated Workforce   Software is designed and written by a diverse set of individuals, but typically they are college graduates who often have some training, and perhaps even a degree, in computer science. Software programmers and related professionals who worked in the U.S. software industry had an average of 15.3 years of education as of 2000. That compares with 13.8 years for the workforce on average and 14.7 years for professional service industries (including law, medicine, accounting, and architecture).[2]

There were 1,194 degree programs in computer science in American colleges and universities in 2006.[3] These programs usually offer courses in the design of operating systems. All of the top ten programs as ranked by *U.S. News and World Report* did.[4] There are a number of textbooks on the design of computer operating systems and related topics.

Microsoft is notable for screening people for intelligence and problem-solving skills. A 1995 study reported that Microsoft recruited from the top fifty colleges and universities and hired less than 3 percent of the people it initially interviewed. Microsoft is famous for asking job candidates to solve problems on the spot, such as estimating the number of gas stations in the United States. As of 2004, over 95 percent of the architects, designers, and programmers working on Windows had a college degree and 40 percent had computer science degrees. Ten years later Google has developed a reputation as a company where only brainiacs need apply.[5] It advertises mainly in technical magazines and puts people through numerous interviews that test intellectual skills before hiring one out of the 200 candidates who send in a résumé.

2. http://www.bls.gov/oco/ocos110.htm.

3. http://www.usnews.com/usnews/edu/college/tools/brief/cosearch_advanced_brief.php

4. "America's Best Graduate Schools 2005 Edition," *U.S. News and World Report*, December 31, 2004.

5. Michael A. Cusumano and Richard W. Selby, *Microsoft Secrets* (London: HarperCollins, 1996), pp. 92–93; Internal Microsoft information; John Battelle, *The Search: How Google and Its Rivals Rewrote the Rules of Business and Transformed Our Culture* (New York: Portfolio Press 2005); http://www.cbsnews.com/stories/2004/12/30/60minutes/main664063.shtml.

Made of Malleable Code   We have already seen that software programs, including platforms, are a series of instructions usually written in a language such as C++. Managing the creation of millions of lines of code that work together as planned is no mean feat. But one reason these programs have grown so large is that they have been designed to make it easy to add to them. In some respects, doing so is like adding a paragraph to a chapter of a book or another riff when playing jazz. The key difference is that since the ultimate product is digital, users do not experience the addition in the way that adding a chapter makes a book thicker.

Like the contents of a newspaper, the contours of a software program can be changed readily. Just as newspapers have suburban or regional editions that add coverage specific to a particular geographic area, modern software programs may have versions targeted to particular groups, such as Java for small devices. And just as newspapers can add sections to bring in more readers, so software programs can add features or functionality.

Many operating systems added features in the mid-1990s that helped users communicate over networks such as the Internet. Apple's Macintosh included AppleTalk proprietary networking protocols in 1985 and added protocols for communicating over the Internet in 1995.[6]

Easy to Reproduce   All information goods are easy to copy. But software programs, including platforms, are especially so because they are necessarily digital. The easiest way to see this is with the open-source operating system Linux. You can download this 5.7 million-line operating system over the Internet from numerous Web sites.[7] With a cable modem connection it takes a couple of minutes. Not surprisingly, piracy is a major problem for software firms that sell their products.

Software platforms are often installed on computer hardware before it is sold. The manufacturer does this itself when it makes both the soft-

6. Jim Carlton, *Apple: The Inside Story of Intrigue, Egomania, and Business Blunders* (New York: HarperCollins, 1997), p. 59; "Apple goes to the core; Apple introduces Power Macintosh 9500 that uses TCP/IP and PCI bus architecture; Product Announcement; Brief Article," *LAN Magazine*, October 1, 1995.

7. http://zdnet.com.com/2100-1104-864256.html.

ware and the hardware. Apple zaps its software right onto its iPods and Apple computers. Or the software manufacturer may license the software to other manufacturers that install it, often from a single master CD. Distribution costs are higher when the software platform is sold directly to users. Thus, Microsoft incurs some costs in reproducing its Windows software on CDs and distributing it through retail channels. The same is true for Linux distributors such as Red Hat. But even in these cases the per-unit costs are relatively low, as with other information goods such as music CDs.

Inexhaustible Once created, there is an inexhaustible supply of software such as platforms. Unlike most goods and services, but like all information goods, consumption by one user does not reduce the amount available for others. Indeed, software platforms are better than inexhaustible because consumption by one user is likely to increase the value of the software to others.

Complementarities and Network Effects System components are generally complements: adding another component to a system or improving an existing component generally increases the value of the other components. Moreover, in many cases, systems have what economists call *indirect network effects* linked to the presence of components.[8] That is, an increase in the number of users of one component often makes that component more valuable as a complement to the other components. As Sony's Internet–based game center for the PlayStation 2 draws more users, for instance, more PlayStation 2 owners will want to buy games supported by the Internet service. As its games become more popular, more consumers will prefer PlayStation 2 consoles to competitors' models. Likewise, an increase in the variety of components (printers for PCs, for example) often increases the value of other components to end users. In recent years

8. Michael Katz and Carl Shapiro, "Systems Competition and Network Effects," *Journal of Economic Perspectives* 8 (Spring 1994): 99. For a general discussion of network effects and their business implications, see Carl Shapiro and Hal Varian, *Information Rules* (Boston, Mass.: Harvard Business School Press, 1998).

economists have tended to apply the multisided platform framework to these situations, as we discuss in the next section.

There also may be direct network effects. These arise when an increase in the number of users of an application or platform directly makes that application or platform more valuable to each user. Its value increases because users can share information and work together more efficiently. When WordStar was the leading PC word-processing program, many people bought it at least in part because they could share documents with friends and co-workers.

Economic Consequences

These technological features shape the economics of software platforms just as they shape the economics of most software products.

Intellectual Property Protection   If people could get the source code for any software product, they could reproduce it for next to nothing. The price would fall to almost zero, and the original writer would derive no financial benefit.

Software companies rely on all three major forms of intellectual property protection to guard their investments against this fate.[9] First, they keep the source code secret as much as possible. Before they distribute the software they turn it into the 1s and 0s of machine code. In principle, an able, dedicated, and patient programmer could translate machine code back into a high-level language. But this sort of decompiling is forbidden by almost all commercial software licenses and all but impossible in practice for multi-million-line software platforms. In addition, "trade secret" law protects software developers from the unscrupulous employee or agent who might try to release the source code without authorization.

Software companies also copyright their code. As with a book, you cannot reproduce copies of software programs without violating copyright law. Of course, as with other information goods, piracy is nonetheless rampant, especially in countries with weak intellectual property laws. In India, an estimated 80 to 85 percent of the copies of Macro-

9. Suzanne Scotchmer, *Innovation and Incentives* (Cambridge, Mass.: MIT Press, 2004), chap. 3.

media Flash and Dreamweaver in use are not legal. Even in the United States, almost 30 percent of Macromedia software is pirated.[10]

Finally, software companies get patents on algorithms and other features. The United States had granted about 127,000 software patents through 2004. (It takes about 3.5 years on average for the grant of a patent application.[11]) Apple's iTunes software, for example, allows users to import an unlimited number of audio tracks and encode them into the popular MP3 format, as well as listen to MP3s, audio CDs, or hundreds of Internet radio stations. A patented system for accessing digital media across networks was important for the success of iTunes.

Economies and Diseconomies of Scale Although no one has ever quantified it, it is generally understood that there are diminishing returns to scale in writing software platforms. That is, doubling the size of a platform by adding more features more than doubles the cost (holding the quality of the code constant—one can always write inefficient code). Increases in size create more interdependencies (with N objects, there are N^2 possible pairwise interactions, for instance), thus raising the likelihood of bugs, and thereby raising development, debugging, and test costs more than proportionately.[12] (Object-oriented programming and the use of modules are designed to temper these diseconomies.) But once created, cheap reproduction means that additional copies cost little. The production technology is therefore as shown in Figure 3.1.

These economic features suggest some caution in characterizing the marginal cost of producing software. It is true that once the costs of creating software have been sunk, the marginal costs of reproducing and distributing it are very low. That is an ex post perspective on cost. But it is also true that the likely adoption of a software program is not independent of the costs that are incurred in creating it or revising it.

10. Venkatesh Ganesh, "The continuing story of software piracy," *The Financial Express* (August 8, 2005), http://www.macromedia.com/devnet/logged_in/swozniak_piracy.html.

11. It is difficult to define "software patents," but in 2004, 127,098 patents were granted under the G06F classification, which covers electronic data processing. Data set available from www.uspto.gov.

12. "Linux: Fewer Bugs Than Rivals," *Wired News*, December 14, 2004.

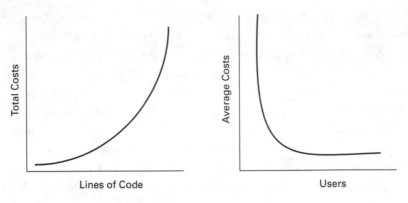

Figure 3.1
Diseconomies of scale.

Software designers add features in part to bring in more consumers; in the case of software platforms, those consumers include both users and developers of applications that run on top of the platforms. Ex ante, the marginal cost of acquiring additional customers by improving the platform, is likely to be much higher than the marginal cost of reproducing and distributing the software.

This distinction is also relevant for other information goods. Movies are a good example. The cost of making a completed movie available to an additional viewer is close to zero. However, the number of viewers a movie garners is partly dependent on the investment in the actors, special effects, and other features that make a movie popular. Movies made with low budgets are often aimed for a narrow audience, while movies with blockbuster potential typically have extravagant budgets. The marginal cost of garnering a viewer, viewed ex ante, is positive.

Pricing and the Recovery of Investments   As with all information goods, software poses some challenges related to recovering investments and earning profits. Pricing at ex post marginal cost or anything close to it would lead to bankruptcy. Software pricing thus depends primarily on demand (particularly the responsiveness of demand to changes in prices) rather than on cost and has as its main goal at least recovering fixed and sunk development costs. The pricing of software platforms is considerably more complex because of their multisided nature, as we discuss later.

Why have software prices not declined at the same pace as hardware prices? Basically because software development costs have not declined as rapidly as hardware costs, for two related reasons. The first is that educated labor, which is not becoming cheaper, accounts for most of the cost of producing software. In 2001, U.S. software firms paid about 33 percent of revenues to their employees, while semiconductor companies paid less than half that percentage.[13] The second reason is that software products are becoming more complex: with advances in hardware, software programs typically grow over time through the accretion of features. A typical PC game program in 1994 was 20 megabytes; a typical PC game program in 2004 was 2,200 megabytes.[14]

Bundling Features   Most goods are bundles of features, many of which could be provided separately but are not. Cars come with spark plugs and tires even though you could buy your own. Moreover, many goods are improved over time through the addition of features. Few cars come these days without air conditioners and rear window defrosters.[15] Many cereals add fruit and flavors over time, leading to many variations.

The same is true for computer systems. Microprocessors, memory, and other components are typically combined to create a hardware platform such as a Nokia mobile phone handset or an Xbox game console. With time, many peripherals come to be integrated into the hardware platform. Consider the case of the math coprocessor, which facilitates number crunching. Before the release of Intel's 486 chip, Intel's microprocessors did not include a math coprocessor. Customers who wanted one purchased it separately from one of several vendors at substantial cost. Today, one cannot buy an Intel x86 processor without a built-in math coprocessor.

13. 2002 Economic Census, Industry Series Reports, available at http://www. census.gov.

14. "Doom II Game Has 500,000 Pre-Orders," *Newsbytes News Network*, October 13, 1994; http://www.amazon.com/exec/obidos/tg/stores/detail/videogames/ B00006C2HA/tech-data/103-8949918-3544622.

15. David Evans and Michael Salinger, "Why do Firms Bundle and Tie? Evidence from Competitive Markets and Implications for Tying Law," *Yale Journal on Regulation* (January 2005): 37–89.

Creating products through feature addition is particularly easy with information goods. That is the beauty of the pliability of music and language. Pop music was mainly distributed as singles on seven-inch records until the early 1960s. The success of the Beatles' *Sergeant Pepper's Lonely Hearts Club Band* album made clear the value of compiling songs and helped make the market for long-playing albums. Bundling multiple songs into albums became standard practice, and the distribution of songs as singles became less common. (We return to this issue in Chapter 11, where we will see that music downloading is helping to promote unbundling.) Newspapers have added various features such as style and living sections over time.

Similar forces apply to software in general and platforms in particular. Where exactly the tasks performed by software are accomplished is a matter of business and design decisions. Many tasks that used to be performed by stand-alone applications have become integrated into other applications (such as spell checkers, which originally were sold separately from word processing programs) or into the software platform itself. Early operating systems, for example, did not include communications functionality.

The malleability of code reinforces several economic forces that encourage the inclusion and accretion of features in products.

Bundling and integration. Combining features in a single product reduces transaction costs for consumers. Rather than having to buy two products, they can buy just one. Moreover, the manufacturer can create additional value by creating connections between the features. An example is making the features of a spreadsheet program available to a word-processing program.

Economies of scope. When there are fixed costs in offering separate products, firms may find it profitable to bundle those products if demand for the separate components is not particularly strong. Several major automobile makers, for example, have decreased the number of different cars people can purchase.[16] They have done this by developing bundles of options that "most people" want, even though some people

16. Ibid.

would not value some of those options separately. For software there are cost savings from combining several features into a single package, as well as savings in distribution and product support. (There may be diseconomies, of course, if making the program larger and thus more complex results in disproportionately large increases in the costs of writing, debugging, testing, and supporting the package.)

Demand aggregation. When there are fixed costs of producing and distributing products but low marginal costs of adding components, it may be possible to lower average costs and reduce variation in what people are willing to pay by combining components that appeal to different groups of customers.[17] Hardware and software typically include many features that most consumers never use. However, by including these features vendors expand the number of consumers who find the product valuable at the offered price. This is why many word processors include equation editors, newspapers have horoscopes, and cable companies include channels that most of us never watch.

Multisided Platforms

That shopping malls and software platforms have much in common is one of the important insights of the economics of multisided markets. The mall is available to stores and shoppers. Once there, the merchants and consumers interact directly on the platform. The merchant rents space. The shoppers often get amenities such as free parking, in addition to getting into the mall for free.

Likewise, the software platform is available to developers and users. The developer licenses its software to the user, who then runs the application on the platform. Both user and developer rely on the services provided by the platform. For many software platforms the user pays to license the platform, while the developers get to use the platform services for free and may even get some subsidized software tools to help them do so.

17. Yannis Bakos and Eric Brynjolfsson, "Bundling and Competition on the Internet," *Marketing Science*, 1 (Winter 2000): 63–82.

Both platforms help reduce duplication and thereby lower the cost of providing services. Shopping malls provide parking, restrooms, and many other common facilities. Stores benefit because they do not have to provide these facilities on their own. Shoppers benefit because retailers have lower costs. Software platforms make services available through APIs. Developers benefit from these because they avoid having to write some of their own code. Users benefit from a greater variety of and lower prices for applications.

The economics of multisided platforms provides a set of tools for understanding the past, present, and future of software platforms.

The Economics of Multisided Platforms

Multisided platforms cater to two or more distinct groups of customers. Members of at least one customer group need members of the other group for a variety of reasons. Platforms help these customers get together in a variety of ways and thereby create value that the customers could not readily obtain otherwise. The village market is one of the oldest examples of a two-sided platform. It is a place where buyers and sellers can get together and trade. So is eBay. Another old example is the village matchmaker, who helped men and women find marriage partners. Match.com provides a similar service using Internet technology; speed dating is another important innovation. The publisher of this book operates a platform, too. It is in the business of finding authors in search of an audience and audiences in search of content.

Governments run some two-sided platforms. Cash is an example. The government institutions behind the euro help ensure that sellers will take it for payment and buyers will use it for payment. Standards sometimes give rise to two-sided platforms. Fax machines facilitate communication between senders and receivers. Cooperatives of firms also operate two-sided platforms—Visa is the most significant example. For-profit businesses operate two-sided platforms in a wide variety of industries and in many economically significant ones. Highly visible examples include American Express (travelers checks and charge cards), Google (search engine–based portal), and News Corporation (advertising-supported media).

William Baxter presented one of the first formal analyses of a two-sided business in 1983.[18] He was a law professor who was self-taught in economics. He observed that payment cards provided a service only if both cardholders and merchants jointly agreed to use a card for a transaction. He derived some of the fundamental economic consequences of this joint demand. (Baxter went on to become a highly innovative antitrust chief in the United States.)

The notion, however, that diverse industries are based on two-sided platforms and are governed by the same basic economic principles is due to a pathbreaking paper by Jean Tirole and Jean-Charles Rochet that began circulating in 2001.[19] They showed that businesses such as computer operating systems, dating clubs, exchanges, shopping malls, and video game consoles were two-sided.

Economists now recognize that many industries, including the manufacture of software platforms, are guided by economic principles that differ in important ways from those that govern traditional industries. Many of these two-sided or multisided industries are subject to network effects, which were studied extensively by economists during the 1980s and 1990s.[20] Network effects are also central to the economics of multisided platforms, and more recent analysis provides additional insight into their business implications.

Internalizing Externalities   Multisided platform businesses tend to arise in markets that have three characteristics:

1. There are two or more distinct groups of customers.
2. There is some benefit from connecting or coordinating members of the distinct groups.

18. William Baxter, "Bank Interchange of Transactional Paper: Legal and Economic Perspectives," *The Journal of Law and Economics* 26 (October 1983): 541–588.

19. Jean Tirole and Jean-Charles Rochet, "Platform Competition in Two-Sided Markets," *Journal of the European Economic Association* 1, no. 4 (2003): 990–1029.

20. Shapiro and Varian, *Information Rules*. See the articles in Symposium on Network Externalities, *Journal of Economic Perspectives*, 8 (Spring 1994): 93–150.

3. An intermediary can make each group better off through coordinating their demands. For example, dating clubs provide a service to men and women, who benefit from meeting each other, and provide an efficient way for men and women to connect.

As a practical matter, multisided platforms tend to arise when a stronger version of condition 2 applies: most platform businesses exhibit indirect network externalities. Consumers, for example, get more value from their credit cards when more merchants take them, and merchants get more value from accepting credit cards when more consumers use them. This has not been lost on the card systems. The current advertising slogans highlight merchant acceptance: "Visa. Everywhere you want to be." "MasterCard: No card is more accepted." American Express, MasterCard, and Visa persuade merchants to pay for taking their cards by emphasizing the millions of consumers that have these cards and want to use them to pay. The sales pitch for the merchants is similar: then the card systems tout the number of cardholders they have who could transact at the merchant if it accepted the card for payment.

Customer groups can sometimes get together without a platform. Men and women have found each other without matchmakers. Buyers and sellers figured out ways to transact before there was money. Merchants can advertise their wares without the media. Successful multisided platforms, however, generally reduce the transactions costs that members of different customer groups would incur in trying to reap the benefits of getting together.

The fact that a platform could exist does not mean that it necessarily will or that it will provide the only method for providing benefits to customers. As we discuss in Chapter 8, Apple has thus far operated its iPod/iTunes platform as a single-sided business. It buys music by paying publishers royalties and distributes this music to customers who want it. Similarly, many consumers have "store cards"—payment cards issued by stores such as Bloomingdale's. In fact, the payment card industry was based entirely on this single-sided model until Diners Club introduced a card in 1950 that put multiple merchants and consumers on the same platform. We explore the decision to become a platform—along with platforms' related decisions regarding which system components to produce and which to rely on the market to supply—in more detail in Chapter 9.

Similarly, many businesses deal with multiple diverse groups without being platforms. There is a sense in which auto companies bring tire manufacturers and consumers together, but they do not do so in a way that makes Toyota, for example, a multisided platform business. In this case there is no direct interaction between the two sides. Toyota substitutes itself for consumers when dealing with tire producers, just as Apple does before sending music to consumers through iTunes. By contrast, two-sided platform businesses provide support for direct interaction between the two sides. Thus, game developers sell directly to PlayStation users, for instance, not through Sony.

Multisided businesses can generate profits for themselves and benefits for their customers if they can figure out ways to increase and then capture indirect network externalities. There are three major ways in which they do this.

First, they serve as matchmakers. Financial exchanges such as NASDAQ and on-line auction sites such as eBay match buyers and sellers. The Yahoo! Personals and 8MinuteDating match men and women.

Second, they build audiences. Advertising-supported media do mainly that: they use content to attract eyeballs and then sell access to those eyeballs to advertisers. Many platforms engage in less overt audience building. Auction houses such as Sotheby's try to build an audience of buyers for the art they sell on consignment. Nightclubs sometimes try to build an audience of women for men, and vice versa. We saw that payment card systems try to build an audience of cardholders for merchants and an audience of merchants for cardholders.

Third, they reduce costs by providing shared facilities for the customers on each side. That's the shopping mall case with which we began. But other platforms also do this to some degree. Buyers and sellers have shared auction institutions and auction sites from the Roman forum to eBay. Readers and advertisers share the pages of *Vogue*. Payment card systems provide a shared network for conducting transactions between merchants and consumers.

Software platforms provide value through matchmaking and building audiences, as well as through reducing duplication. Apple, for example, helped bring commercial artists and developers of design software together. It did this by including services in the Mac OS that developers could use to develop programs such as Adobe Photoshop for commercial artists. Sony PlayStation has developed an audience of console users that it can make available to game developers. The main economic value of software platforms, however, is in economizing on the amount of code that developers must write to serve the needs of consumers.

The Pricing Balancing Act   In single-sided markets, price usually tracks costs and demand for the product pretty closely. Firms figure out what their marginal cost will be and then mark it up—a little if customers are price-sensitive because there is a lot of competition, more if there is little competition. Particularly in stable markets, this is not rocket science. That is why how-to books on starting your own small business can offer reliable advice, such as "charge X times cost in sector Y." For example, one guide advises that the markup is generally 40 percent of the retail price in hardware stores and that for jewelry it ranges between 400 and 800 percent.[21]

In multisided markets, pricing is more complicated because of indirect network effects between the distinct customer groups. If you charge women the same price as men to enter your singles club, you may not get enough women. If this happens, men will not come, and suddenly you will have an empty club. Many Internet publications discovered that viewers deserted in droves when they attempted to charge them, although some did make the successful transition to paid subscriptions plus advertising.[22]

Multisided platform economics shows that it may make sense for firms to charge very low prices to one or more groups or even to pay them to

21. Stephen C. Harper, *The McGraw-Hill Guide to Starting Your Own Business*, 2nd ed. (New York: McGraw-Hill, 2003), pp. 100–101; Jan Kingaard, *Start Your Own Successful Retail Business* (Irvine, Calif.: Entrepreneur, 2003), pp. 152–153.

22. Michael Liedtke, "Online Subscriptions Herald the End of Web Freedom," Associated Press newswires, March 18, 2002; Thomas E. Weber, "Web Users May Balk at New Fee Services That Deliver Little Value," *Wall Street Journal*, April 8, 2002; Timothy J. Mullaney, "Sites Worth Paying For? The Paid Web Is a Work in Progress, But Some Are Already Getting It Right," *Business Week*, May 14, 2001.

take the product. And that is what multisided businesses do. Magazines, newspapers, and television broadcasters typically earn the preponderance of their revenues from advertisers.[23] Charge card companies such as American Express earn the bulk of their revenue from merchants.

Businesses in multisided markets often subsidize one side of the market to get the other side on board—sometimes explicitly by charging low or negative prices. At other times subsidies are less apparent, such as when the platform makes significant investments in one side and does not charge for it. Table 3.1 shows some examples. We will see that all software platforms make services available to at least one side for free. Most make free services available to developers through the APIs.

Table 3.1
Revenue in Selected Multisided Platforms

Industry	Multisided Platform	Sides	Side That Is "Charged Less"
Real estate	Residential property brokerage	• Buyer • Seller	Buyer
Real estate	Apartment brokerage	• Renter • Owner/landlord	Typically renter
Media	Newspapers and magazines	• Reader • Advertiser	Reader
Media	Network television	• Viewer • Advertiser	Viewer
Media	Portals and Web publications	• Web "surfer" • Advertiser	Web "surfer"
Finance	Proprietary terminals	• Trader/analyst • Content provider	Content provider
Shopping malls	Mall	• Merchant • Shopper	Shopper
Payment system	Travelers' checks	• Check holders • Merchant	Merchant
Payment system	Charge/debit card	• Cardholder • Merchant	Cardholder

23. Lisa George and Joel Waldfogel, "Who Benefits Whom in Daily Newspaper Markets?" NBER Working Paper no. 7944 (October 2000), p. 9.

The economics of pricing for multisided platform businesses has another key implication. In single-sided businesses, the principle that the one who causes the cost should pay the cost is good advice, for businesses as well as for policymakers. For example, a car buyer "causes" the cost of manufacturing the car, and thus pays the full cost. That principle usually does not make any sense in multisided markets, however. Often a product cannot exist unless several different customers participate simultaneously. They all "cause" costs and "cause" benefits. That is true even if it is possible to identify costs that increase as a result of an additional user on one side—for example, the cost of printing another copy of the Yellow Pages. Economists have shown that the best prices—either from the standpoint of the business maximizing profits or from the standpoint of policymakers maximizing social welfare—involve complex relationships between the price sensitivity of each side, interdependencies between these demands, and marginal costs.

Is There Anything New Here?   Multisided platforms have a number of features that economists have examined before. Yet traditional learning does not deal with the role of intermediaries in internalizing network externalities. Most businesses have distinct consumer types: workers or retirees, households or corporate entities, men or women. But multisided platforms differ in that they must serve two or more distinct types of consumers to generate demand from any of them. Hair salons may cater to men, women, or both. Heterosexual dating clubs *must* cater to men *and* women. For hair salons the ratio of men to women does not matter much; for heterosexual dating enterprises it is absolutely critical.

Most businesses in single-sided and multisided markets engage in price discrimination (charging different prices that aren't proportional to the corresponding marginal costs) because it is possible to increase revenue by doing so and because, in the case of businesses with extensive scale economies, it may be the only way to cover fixed costs. A dating club may charge men a higher price just because they have more inelastic demand and because it is easy to identify that group of consumers. But businesses in multisided markets have an additional reason to price discriminate: by charging one group a lower price the business can charge another group a higher price; and unless prices are low enough to attract sufficient numbers of the former group, the business cannot obtain any sales at all.

Like firms in multisided markets, many firms in single-sided markets sell multiple products, and there is extensive economic literature explaining why they do so. The standard explanations for why firms produce multiple products probably apply to many of the platforms discussed here. But firms that make multiple products for several one-sided markets (for example, General Electric makes light bulbs and turbine engines) or several complementary products for the same set of consumers (for example, IBM sells computer hardware and computer services) do not secure profit opportunities from internalizing indirect network effects.

Finally, it is important to ask how the business implications of the recent work on multisided markets differ from those of the older economic literature on network effects. This is not as simple as it might seem, since popular discussions of network effects often missed important subtleties in the academic literature.

Take the case of single-sided markets with direct network effects. Because of those effects it follows that there is an advantage to size, all else equal. But it does not follow that this advantage, if present, is large, and it certainly does not follow that the firm with the biggest market share always wins in the end, let alone that the first entrant always wins. Nonetheless, in the frenetic days of the Internet bubble, lots of businesses were founded on the assumption that network effects were present and important in their markets and that the key to success was to get in fast, price low, and build share at any cost. Proponents of this simplistic view emphasized tipping—you build up critical mass, and then the whole market flocks to you. And they emphasized an extreme sort of lock-in— once you get most of the customers, nobody can enter against you, even with a better product.

As Brian Arthur, an author of several influential papers in network economics, put it, "You want to build up market share, you want to build up user base. If you do you can lock in that market."[24] This is a nice, simple theory—much simpler than the economic literature from which it claimed to be derived. But it is hard to find many businesses that succeeded by following it. Unfortunately, many dot-com entrepreneurs and investors thought that "build share fast" was the path to great riches. Only a few made it very far down that path before reality closed it off and supposedly locked-in buyers left en masse. It turns out that only rarely are direct network effects strong enough to prevent buyers from switching to a better product, as the massive defections of buyers from once dominant word-processing programs illustrates.

Those who believed that riches could be made quickly and easily by harnessing network effects tended not to distinguish sharply between direct and indirect network effects. In both cases the managerial prescription was to build share rapidly; indirect network effects, like direct network effects, would kick in automatically and both fuel and protect further growth. Work on two-sided markets makes it clear that this is dangerously simplistic in two important respects.

First, even though at least two distinct groups must be involved or there to be indirect network effects, the network enthusiasts assumed both that it is obvious that one should pay and the other should not, and that it is obvious which group should pay.

Second, they generally assumed that the group that did not pay could be ignored in setting business strategy because it would automatically fall into line and generate valuable network effects. In contrast, economic analyses of multisided platforms, along with the industry case studies discussed in the following chapters, show that successful multisided platform businesses must pay careful attention to all relevant groups, and typically must worry more about balance among them than about building share with one of them. The multi-sided approach is consistent with asymmetric treatment of customer groups, but getting it right requires great luck or careful analysis.

The popular network economics literature also suggested that markets with direct or indirect network effects would tend to tip toward a single

24. Joel Kurtzman, "An Interview with W. Brian Arthur," *Strategy+Business* 11 (1998): 100.

provider.[25] That does not happen much in practice, though. Sometimes congestion costs outweigh network effects—that is the case with night-clubs, trading pits, and shopping malls. Platforms also differentiate themselves, and thereby counter the network effects of their rivals, by trying to appeal to different consumer preferences. That is one of the reasons for the proliferation of magazines.

Consider some markets that seem to display important indirect network externalities: PC operating systems, real estate agencies, payment cards, auction houses, local and national newspapers, broadcast networks, parcel delivery services, banks, dating services, standards for encoding DVDs, financial information services, music publishers, and recorded music manufacturers. Of these many markets, the only ones in which a single large player accounts for the preponderance of sales are PC operating systems (i.e., Windows) and some local newspaper markets (such as the *Los Angeles Times*).

Most software platform categories are competitive as a result of providers differentiating themselves to appeal to different types of customers on either side of the market.

Business Models in Multisided Platform Markets   Making a platform a success is a delicate process. Businesses have to get the pricing structure right; they must balance the demands of the various customer groups and nurture the several sides of the market. Getting the balance right seems to be more important than building shares. Platform markets do not tip quickly because as a practical matter, it takes time to get things right. And the first entrant often does not win in the end: many other firms may come in and successfully tweak the pricing structure, product design, or business model. eBay is a successful business-to-business (B2B)

25. Some of the network effects models allowed for differentiated tastes and the coexistence of multiple networks. See Jeffrey Church and Neil Gandal, "Network Effects, Software Provision and Standardization," *Journal of Industrial Economics* 40, no. 1 (March 1992): 85–104. S.J. Liebowitz and S.E. Margolis, "Network Externality: An Uncommon Tragedy" *Journal of Economic Perspectives* 8 (1994): 133–150. However, this literature was often taken to suggest overall that network effects naturally lead to a single firm dominating a category. See Brian Arthur, "Increasing Returns and the New World of Business," *Harvard Business Review* 74 (July–August 1996): 100–109.

exchange now, for example, but many earlier B2Bs failed.[26] Most B2Bs tried a big-bang strategy: make substantial investments in a platform and hope both sides show up when the platform opens for trading. The first and third entrants into the payment card industry, Diners Club and Carte Blanche, barely exist today. The second entrant, American Express, had a 14 percent share of credit and debit card purchase volume in 2003.[27]

Getting All Sides on Board   An important characteristic of multisided markets is that the demand on each side vanishes if there is no demand on the others, regardless of what the price is. Merchants will not accept a payment card if no customer carries it because no transactions will materialize. Computer users will not use an operating system for which the applications they need to run have not been written (except those rare users who plan to write their own applications). The businesses that participate in such industries have to figure out ways to get both sides on board.

One way to do this is to obtain a critical mass of users on one side of the market by giving them the service for free or even paying them to take it. Especially at the entry phase of firms in multisided markets, it is not uncommon to see precisely this strategy. Diners Club gave away its charge card to cardholders at first—there was no annual fee, and users got the benefit of the float.[28] Netscape gave away its browser to many users, particularly students, to get a critical mass on the end-user side of

26. eBay was not begun as a B2B Web site, but as more and more businesses began to do business on it, it became one. In 2003, eBay officially launched a separate B2B site. "Prior to the B2B site, eBay listed more than 500,000 business items for sale every week on its consumer site, with business buyers representing more than $1 billion in annualized gross merchandise sales, officials said." Renee Boucher Ferguson, "eBay Launches B2B Site," *eWeek*, January 28, 2003 (http://www.eweek.com/print_article/0,3048,a=36363,00.asp); eBay Press Release, "eBay Launches eBay Business to Serve Its Growing Community of Business Buyers," January 28, 2002 (http://investor.ebay.com/news/20030128-100772.cfm); Mark Berniker, "SAP, eBay Setup Industrial B2B Marketplace," *internet News.com*, June 16, 2003 (http://www.internetnews.com/xSP/article.php/2222371).

27. Nilson Report 805 (February 2004).

28. "Credit Cards for Diners," *New York Times*, March 30, 1950, p. 37; Diners Club display advertisement, *New York Times*, March 30, 1950, p. 42.

its business.[29] (Initially the other side was providers of Web sites, to whom Netscape sold its server software.)

Another way to solve the problem of getting the two sides on board simultaneously is to invest to lower the costs of consumers on one side of the market. As we saw earlier, for instance, Microsoft invests in the creation of software tools that make it easier for application developers to write application software for Microsoft operating systems and provides other assistance that makes developers' jobs easier. In some cases, firms may initially take over one side of the business in order to get the market going. Palm would never have succeeded in creating the vibrant Palm economy, with thousands of software applications and hardware add-on developers and millions of users, had it not provided the first applications itself (especially Graffiti, the handwriting recognition system).[30]

Providing low prices or transfers to one side of the market may help the platform solve the simultaneity problem by encouraging the benefited group's participation—which in turn, owing to network effects, encourages the nonbenefited group's participation. In addition, providing benefits to one side can discourage its use of competing multisided platforms. For example, when Palm provides free tools and support to PDA applications software developers, it encourages those developers to write programs that work on the Palm OS platform and automatically induces those developers to spend less time writing programs for other operating systems.[31]

Pricing Strategies and Balancing Interests   Firms in mature multisided markets—those that have already gone through the entry phase, in which the focus is on getting the various sides on board—still have to devise

29. David Plotnikoff, "Internet Born with Netscape," *Mercury News*, February 28, 2003 (http://www.tc.umn.edu/~jbshank/7_NetscapeIPO.html).

30. Annabelle Gawer and Michael Cusumano, *Platform Leadership: How Intel, Microsoft and Cisco Drive Industry Innovation* (Boston: Harvard Business School Press, 2003).

31. Jean-Charles Rochet and Jean Tirole, "Platform Competition in Two-Sided Markets," working paper, December 13, 2002; http://www.palmsource.com/developers/why_develop.html.

and maintain an effective pricing structure. In most observed multisided markets, companies seem to settle on pricing structures that are heavily skewed toward one side of the market, as Table 3.1 shows. Google earns the preponderance of its revenue from advertisers, for instance, and real estate brokers usually earn most or all of their revenues from sellers.

Sometimes all competing platforms converge on the same pricing strategy. In principle, Microsoft, Apple, IBM, Palm, and other operating system companies could probably have charged higher fees to applications developers and lower fees to hardware makers or end users. Most discovered that it made sense to charge developers relatively modest fees for developer kits and, especially in the case of Microsoft, to give away a lot for free.

Getting the pricing balance right, however, requires considerable care. For example, in 2000, Yahoo!'s Internet auction site was second only to eBay in terms of the number of listings. Sellers found the site appealing because unlike eBay, Yahoo! did not charge sellers a fee for listing their products. In 2001, Yahoo! changed its pricing strategy and began charging a fee. Yahoo!'s listings dropped by 90 percent as sellers presumably moved to the larger venue, eBay.[32] The price change affected Yahoo!'s buyer-side market as well, since buyers were now left with little to bid on.

Two important factors influence multisided pricing structures. There may be certain customers on one side of the market—Rochet and Tirole refer to them as "marquee buyers"[33]—who are extremely valuable to customers on the other side of the market. The existence of marquee customers who create strong network effects tends to reduce the price to all customers on the same side of the market and increase it to customers on the other side. A similar phenomenon occurs when certain customers are extremely loyal (or captive) to the multisided platform firm, perhaps because of long-term contracts or sunk cost investments. The effect is then opposite: the presence of captive customers leads to an increase in the price charged to those on the same side and a decrease in the price charged to the other side.

32. Saul Hansell, "Red Face for the Internet's Blue Chip," *New York Times*, March 11, 2001, section 3, p. 1.
33. Rochet and Tirole, "Platform Competition in Two-Sided Markets," pp. 23–24.

For example, American Express has been able to charge a relatively high merchant discount as compared to other card brands, especially for its corporate card, because merchants have viewed the American Express business clientele as extremely attractive.[34] Corporate executives on expense accounts were "marquee" customers, who allowed American Express to raise its prices to the other side of the market, merchants. Similarly, marquee customers—in the guise of popular stores, often called anchor tenants—are important for shopping malls as well: by attracting customers they make a mall more attractive to other stores. The decline of a marquee store can sound the death knell for an entire mall.

In the software world, marquee customers are usually businesses on the user side and "killer applications"—an application so innovative and popular that people and businesses buy the computer system mainly because they want the app—on the developer side. VisiCalc was the killer app for the Apple II computer. It was one of the most important reasons behind the initial popularity of this platform. Likewise, Mario Bros. was largely responsible for Nintendo's millions of sales of its NES video game console in the United States, and Sonic the Hedgehog was the main reason for its displacement by Sega's Genesis as the dominant console several years later.

Multihoming   As Table 3.2 illustrates, customers on at least one side of a multisided market often belong to several different networks. This is known as multihoming. Take payment cards. Most merchants accept charge, credit, and debit cards associated with several systems; consider how many card symbols there are at the next gasoline pump you use. On the other side of the market, the average consumer has 3.6 payment cards.[35] Advertisers typically place advertisements in several different magazines, and consumers read various magazines.

In general, multihoming by one side of the market relaxes platform competition for that side and intensifies it on the other. For instance, if game developers suddenly become more prone to porting their games to

---

34. Jon Friedman and John Meehan, *House of Cards: Inside the Troubled Empire of American Express* (New York: Kensington Publishing, 1992), pp. 13, 56.

35. http://www.cardweb.com/cardtrak/pastissues/april2004.html.

Table 3.2
The Presence of Multihoming in Selected Multisided Platforms

Multisided Platform	Sides	Presence of Multihoming
U.S. residential property brokerage	• Buyer • Seller	*Uncommon*: Multihoming may be unnecessary, since a multiple listing service allows the listed property to be seen by all member agencies' customers and agents.
Securities brokerage	• Buyer • Seller	*Common*: The average securities brokerage client has accounts at three firms. Note that clients can be either buyers or sellers, or both.
Newspapers and magazines	• Reader • Advertiser	*Common*: In 1996, the average number of magazine issues read per person per month was 12.3. Also common for advertisers: for example, on August 26, 2003, AT&T Wireless advertised in the *New York Times*, (the) *Wall Street Journal*, and the *Chicago Tribune*, among many other newspapers.
Network television	• Viewer • Advertiser	*Common*: For example, viewers in Boston, Chicago, Los Angeles, and Houston, among other major metropolitan areas, have access to at least four main network television channels: ABC, CBS, FOX, and NBC. Also common for advertisers: for example, Sprint places television advertisements on ABC, CBS, FOX, and NBC.
Operating system	• End user • Application developer	*Uncommon for users*: Individuals typically use only one operating system. *Common for developers*: As noted earlier, the number of developers that develop for various operating systems indicates that developers engage in significant multihoming.
Video game console	• Game player • Game developer	*Varies for players*: The average household (that owns at least one console) owns 1.4 consoles.

Table 3.2
(continued)

Multisided Platform	Sides	Presence of Multihoming
		Common for developers: For example, in 2003, Electronic Arts, a game developer, developed for the Nintendo, Microsoft, and Sony platforms.
Payment card	• Cardholder • Merchant	*Common*: Most American Express cardholders also carry at least one Visa or MasterCard. In addition, American Express cardholders can use Visa and MasterCard at almost all places that take American Express.

both Sony PlayStation 3 and Microsoft Xbox 360, there would be less reason for Sony and Microsoft to hold royalties down to attract developers. Moreover, in this case the two consoles would become closer substitutes from the users' perspective, since they would have more games in common, so one might expect the battle for the end users (many of whom buy only one console) to become fiercer, resulting in lower console prices.

Sometimes unrelated platforms evolve into intersecting ones, which target one or more groups of customers in common; we will see this for digital media platforms. Platform competition can be fierce when either group of customers is price-sensitive because they have other alternatives. The *Houston Chronicle* may have 89 percent of the newspaper readers in Houston, but that does not mean that it can exercise a great deal of pricing power.[36] Advertisers have many other ways of getting messages to readers, so they are sensitive to prices. And while readers may not have many newspaper alternatives, they do have other ways of getting the news, and having a lot of readers is what makes advertisers pay.

36. This number is the total daily circulation of the *Houston Chronicle* divided by the total daily circulation of all daily newspapers in the Houston area. *Circulation* 2003, SRDS (2002), p. 67.

Scaling   Many successful multisided firms seem to have adopted a fairly gradual entry strategy in which they scale up their platform over time.[37] Many payment card systems, for example, started in one city or region before expanding nationally. It is often difficult to predict just what the right technology and operations infrastructure will be. Therefore, the multisided firm may find it advantageous to establish efficient buyer-seller transactions and balanced pricing first, and make large investments only after the platform has been tested. Platforms such as eBay, Palm, and Yahoo! have expanded gradually and methodically, building up customers on both sides of their markets.

Strategy   Markets hardly ever cooperate with professors by following simple textbook rules exactly. But in traditional markets there are classic truisms that can at least serve as a benchmark, a starting point for more nuanced analysis. By contrast, multisided platforms, especially those in new markets, all too often require clean-sheet planning. With multiple yet interdependent business constituencies to serve, costs provide little guidance for pricing strategies. By the same token, early entry may yield first-mover advantages or provide an instructive failure that simplifies the search for successful strategies by businesses that follow. And, in light of the interdependence between different stakeholders, changes in the business environment may have multisided effects that are very difficult to anticipate.

Open-Source Software

The fortune made by the founders of Google is built in part on the efforts of thousands of volunteers around the world who helped develop the operating system that powers the massive array of server computers that helps us conduct searches and in return peppers us with customized

37. An example of a failed strategy is the case of Chemdex, a business-to-business marketplace, and its parent company, Ventro, which made initial technological and operational investments in the hundreds of millions of dollars (http://www.zdnet.com.au/newstech/enterprise/story/0,2000025001,20107754,0 0.htm).

advertising messages. Google uses Linux. Like anyone else, it can download this software platform for free from the Internet and customize the source code to meet its own needs. As of 2004, around 19 percent of server computers ran Linux worldwide.[38]

This is almost unthinkable in any other industry. It could not happen in manufacturing, because someone would have to pay for the raw materials to assemble an automobile, for example. Yet even in intellectual property-based businesses such as movies one seldom sees products made by volunteers beating those built by for-profit firms. Linux is the result of the remarkable open-source production model. We turn now to the underlying economics of that model.

Open source is based on a decentralized method for producing software that relies heavily on the Internet. Programmers working on their own or through their companies contribute code to open-source projects. The source code of the resulting programs is made available for free; hence the term open source. Users must sign a license that requires that if they redistribute the program, even in modified form, they must make the source code available. As a result, it is hard to make money directly from open-source programs or anything derived from open-source programs. Open source began as an ideology—"free software is a matter of liberty," according to Richard Stallman—but has evolved into a multi-billion-dollar business based on selling hardware, software, and services that are complementary to open-source programs.[39]

The Production of Open-Source Software

In its early days, individuals who donated their time to work on projects that interested them were the main contributors to open-source software. Typically, a person or a small group of people gets an idea for a project that is interesting, useful, or both. The original developers begin work on the project and eventually solicit support from other interested pro-

38. Al Gillen and Dan Kusnetzky, "Worldwide Client and Server Operating Environments 2004–2008 Forecast: Microsoft Consolidates Its Grip" (ID C report no. 32452), December 2004, table 2.

39. http://www.fsf.org/philosophy/free-sw.html.

grammers. Over the course of the project, programmers, including the original developers, may come and go as they complete work and as their interest waxes or wanes.

The programmers communicate with each other over the Internet. A core group, often consisting of one or more of the original developers, has responsibility for incorporating changes and suggesting things that need to be done. Modified versions of the source code are posted on the Internet and available for free to anyone who wants to use them or modify them further. Over time, users regularly identify bugs that had originally escaped detection, and worthwhile features to add. These users can provide feedback to the developers (or become developers themselves). Through this ongoing process the software becomes tested, debugged, and developed.

The Apache Web server is one of the most successful and famous open-source projects. An early version was written at the National Center for Supercomputing Applications (NCSA) and became the most popular Web server by 1995. Development stalled when Rob McCool, the core developer, left NCSA. Following his departure, some Webmasters began coordinating their fixes via email. Eventually, the Apache group, consisting of eight core contributors, was formed. In April 1995 the first version of the Apache server (version 0.6.2) was released, and became a huge success. The server was completely revamped during the second half of 1995, and Apache 1.0 was released in December 1995. Less than a year after its release, Apache 1.0 became the most popular Web server in the world.[40] The Apache group was incorporated in June 1999 as the Apache Software Foundation. Apache 2.0 was released in 2002, and minor fixes and updates have been periodically released since then. Apache remains the most popular Web server in use, with more than a 50 percent share of its segment.[41]

This production method differs from the commercial approach.

First, there is typically little analysis of consumer needs other than introspection: "What would I like my software to do?" This may be augmented by user feedback, but these users are self-selected; except in

40. http://httpd.apache.org/ABOUT_APACHE.html.
41. http://en.wikipedia.org/wiki/Apache_web_server.

unusual circumstances, they are not drawn randomly from the universe of potential users of the software.

Second, there is little formal testing of the type that commercial firms often must engage in: internal testing using hundreds, perhaps thousands of hardware and software configurations in a controlled manner. Testing is instead performed by the users who try versions of the software in uncontrolled environments, much like beta tests for commercial software developers (although perhaps with more sophisticated users providing feedback to the developers).

Third, the development of open-source software is less structured than the development of proprietary software. Although the core developers may provide direction, changes in the software result much more from individual action.

As open source has evolved, commercial businesses have become more intimately involved in steering open-source projects. They do this by having their employees spend time contributing open-source code and working on the various committees that oversee open-source projects. In a 2003 survey of open-source contributors, nearly 15 percent reported that their employer paid them to develop open-source code, 13 percent noted they were paid to "support" open source, and 13 percent stated they were paid to "administer" open-source projects.[42]

IBM is arguably the best example of a traditional for-profit company with strong ties to open-source software. The bond was officially created in 2000, when IBM announced a $1 billion investment (including marketing expenditures) in a variety of open-source initiatives, including adapting Linux and Apache to IBM's various computer hardware platforms.[43] IBM's hardware business was unusual in that it marketed several fundamentally different types of servers with mutually incompatible operating systems. Adopting Linux permitted IBM to unify its server product line, so that proprietary IBM software (and other software) could be used on all the different servers. By making Linux available on all of its servers, from the smallest to the largest, IBM added consistency to its product line

42. http://www.idei.fr/doc/conf/sic/papers_2005/pdavid_slides.pdf.

43. Joe Wilcox, "IBM to Spend $1 Billion on Linux in 2001," *CNETNews.com*, December 12, 2000 (http://news.com.com/2100-1001-249750.html).

that was missing before. IBM therefore had an incentive to do open-source development that would make Linux run (or run better) on its servers because the investment would provide benefits to IBM.[44]

The open-source investment strategy appears to have paid off handsomely for IBM. For example, China's postal service hired IBM to build Linux-based networks for over 1,200 of its branch offices.[45] A year after its initial $1 billion investment, the company announced that it had already recouped that amount and more.

Intellectual Property Rights

The proponents of open-source software faced a problem. On the one hand they wanted to make open-source software widely available. That meant that they did not want to use copyrights, patents, or trade secrets to limit the distribution of open-source programs. On the other hand, they wanted to make sure that commercial enterprises could not free-ride on the efforts of the open-source community by making minor changes or additions to open-source programs but then enforcing their own intellectual property rights on the entire modified programs.

The General Public License (GPL) was an ingenious solution to this dilemma. The GPL is based on "copyleft":

You must cause any work that you distribute or publish, that in whole or in part contains or is derived from the Program or any part thereof, to be licensed as a whole at no charge to all third parties under the terms of this License.[46]

(Despite the copyleft name, the GPL is enforced by copyright law. Copyright is the source of the property protection that enables those who release software under a GPL to impose conditions on others who obtain that code.) The copyleft provision means that if people choose to distribute software that is based in part on other software covered by the GPL, they must distribute their new software under the GPL. GPL soft-

---

44. James Evans, "IBM to Invest Almost $1 Billion on Linux Development," *InfoWorld*, December 12, 2000 (http://www.infoworld.com/articles/hn/xml/00/12/12/001212hnibmlin.html).

45. http://www.infoworld.com/articles/hn/xml/03/01/23/030123hnibmlinux.html?0124fram.

46. http://www.fsf.org/licensing/licenses/gpl.html.

ware thereby propagates itself. Copyleft makes it difficult for anyone to earn significant profits from selling software code subject to the GPL. As Richard Stallman observed,

We encourage two-way cooperation by rejecting parasites: whoever wishes to copy parts of our software into his program must let us use parts of that program in our programs. Nobody is forced to join our club, but those who wish to participate must offer us the same cooperation they receive from us.[47]

Proprietary programs can use or communicate with GPL programs in some limited ways without themselves becoming subject to the viral license condition, but the FSF recognizes that the dividing line can be murky. The terms of the GPL apply only to the distribution of software licensed under the GPL, although what "distribution" means in this context is not entirely clear either. It may be possible for an enterprise to modify a GPL program and use it internally without being legally bound to make the source code for its modified version available to others. On the other hand, if the same enterprise distributed its modified GPL program to a subsidiary, the terms of the GPL might well require it to make the source code available to all comers.

Most open-source projects are subject to the GPL. However, several commercial ventures have chosen to use modified licenses. The two most prominent examples are the Common Development and Distribution License (CDDL) that covered Sun's Solaris as it went open source and the Mozilla Public License (MPL) that governs the Firefox browser, among other products. Both contain provisions that GPL does not, and thus code cannot be freely moved between GPL and projects covered under these other licenses. Opponents of this balkanization of open-source licenses contend that it leads to islands of legally incompatible code. For example, owing to different licenses, no cross-pollination between Linux (GPL) and Solaris (CDDL) is possible. Proponents argue that companies have varying needs and catering to these differences is necessary for open-source software to flourish. In addition to relying on more restrictive licenses some open-source software companies are using intellectual property rights to help protect their investments and guard

47. http://www.rons.net.cn/RMS/ms_oss.html.

their profits. Red Hat, for example, has used trademark law to help protect its compilation of Linux from others.

Incentives

The incentives for writing open-source software are different from those for writing commercial software. Many people write open-source code without being paid directly for it. These are volunteers who write code in their spare time because it interests them. Others write code because their companies have asked them to. This may sound traditional but is not, since their employers cannot sell the resulting code or obtain intellectual property rights over it.

Why Individuals Work on Open-Source Software   Why programmers donate time to open-source software projects is a subject that has generated considerable discussion.[48] Open-source advocates have suggested several motives, four of which involve nonfinancial rewards:

• It is a good way to learn how to program and develop skills.
• It is fun. Since a programmer is free to pick and choose among open-source projects, he need only work on matters of interest.
• It is prestigious. Success at open-source development rates highly among those whose opinions most programmers most value—other programmers.
• It "scratches an itch." Programmers attack problems that they personally face or because they are intrigued by the intellectual challenge.
• It meets an ideological urge—the desire for free software and the "liberty" it entails.

The "scratches an itch" motive has been considered by some analysts as leading to something like a cooperative of users. A number of developers all consider a particular type of software potentially useful, so they pool their talents to develop the software. With this type of motivation, the GPL has sometimes been considered beneficial as an enforcement mechanism: it ensures that no one can take the collective intellectual

---

48. For a more detailed discussion of open-source software development, see Joshua Lerner and Jean Tirole, "Some Simple Economics of Open Source," *Journal of Industrial Economics*, 2002; Joshua Lerner and Jean Tirole, "The Open Source Movement: Key Research Questions," *European Economic Review* 45, nos. 4–6 (2001): 819–826.

property, add some private intellectual property, and treat the whole as a private good.

Business Models Based on the Open-Source Concept Businesses have incentives to "donate" employees to the development of open-source projects that stimulate the demand for other products or services sold by the firm. This has become an increasingly large source of labor for open-source projects.[49] IBM and Red Hat illustrate the motivations. As discussed earlier, IBM's model is built on driving the sales of its key products: supporting Linux software increases IBM's sales of hardware, proprietary software, and services. Linux offered a way for IBM to integrate its entire line of servers without having to develop a software platform of its own, and without having to shoulder the continued support and development of that system on its own.

Red Hat is a somewhat different story. That company began as a pure open-source vendor offering a distribution of Linux. Over time, it has gradually moved toward more traditional software licensing, presumably because it is difficult to support a for-profit company with a pure open-source business model. Red Hat is focused on solving a problem inherent in the Linux development model. For major proprietary operating systems such as Windows, the components of the software are integrated by the distributor and sold as a single program. Since no one developer exists for Linux, bits and pieces of the operating system tend to float around—some in forms unusable by nonprofessionals. Specific Linux distributions consolidate these bits and pieces into a convenient package.

Red Hat is arguably the premiere Linux distribution, with more than 46 percent of Linux server distribution shipments in 2004.[50] The company was founded in 1995 and subsequently enjoyed significant

49. "OpenOffice Team Wants IBM Contribution," *VNUNet*, April 25, 2005; Timothy Prickett Morgan, "Novell Creates Hula Open Source Collaboration Server," *ComputerWire*, February 16, 2005 (http://www.computerwire.com/industries/research/?pid=23554158-E49D-4ED2-9482-72B4B5D4119F&type=CW%20News).

50. Al Gillen, Milla Kantcheva, and Dan Kusnetzky, "Worldwide Linux Operating Environments 2005–2009 Forecast and Analysis: Product Transitions Continue" (IDC report no. 34390), table 2.

growth, topped off with an IPO in 1999 that generated the eighth biggest first-day percentage gain in Wall Street history.[51] Like many other high-tech companies, Red Hat lost quite a bit of value in the dot-com crash, but it has since rebounded successfully.

Red Hat really does three things. First, it integrates components of Linux into a cohesive distribution, including commonly used open-source products along with the core operating system. Second, it adds its own software to provide a better user experience and to make installation and updating easier. Third, it sells support packages and certifies that external administrators are qualified to work on Red Hat products. The company includes only open-source software, and the code it writes is licensed mainly under the GPL.

Red Hat changed its business model drastically in 2003 by splitting its distribution into two products—the Fedora Project, a more traditional open-source project, and Red Hat Enterprise Linux (RHEL), the flagship product. Fedora is the place for experiments to run and outside developers to submit code, while RHEL is a stable version of Linux for paying customers. Along with the split came a new licensing agreement. RHEL source code is available for free from Red Hat, but the code computers need to run the operating system is available only with the purchase of a support subscription.[52] And support subscriptions must be purchased for *each* computer, just like traditional proprietary software licenses.

One fundamental problem with generating revenue from GPL software is that anyone can take the source code, "compile" it for computers to read, and resell it without incurring the original creator's development costs. Red Hat has tried to sidestep this problem. Another company could rebuild RHEL from freely available source code, but it would have to strip out all references to Red Hat to comply with trademark law. Purchasers could not be certain that the distribution really contained all of the pieces in Red Hat's, or that the installation would

51. W. G. Rohm, "Inside The Red Hat IPO," *Linux Magazine*, November 15, 1999 (http://www.linux-mag.com/1999-11/redhatipo_01.html).

52. Advanced users could compile the source code themselves. As discussed later in the chapter, this has many disadvantages for corporate customers.

work as seamlessly. Thus, Red Hat has used its reputation in combination with trademark law to limit the potential for another company to undercut its profits.

Open source seems so New Age. Yet when one looks over the history of the computer industry, it turns out that the business of selling software—including software platforms—really didn't take hold until the late 1970s. Microprocessors created a mass market for software that attracted entrepreneurs. Many of these pioneers wrote applications that would run on the new microprocessor-based personal computers. A few focused on refining software platforms whose shared code could be used by many developers and customers at the same time. The next two chapters examine the almost contemporaneous birth of software platforms on PCs and video game consoles.

INSIGHTS

• Like other information goods, software platforms are produced by educated workers, are malleable and easily changed, and are reproducible at virtually no cost.

• Bundling features into the software platform is often efficient for the platform producer and for end users, as it is for most information goods, because it lowers distribution costs and expands demand.

• Software platforms create value by reducing the costs for their multiple customer groups to come together and thereby enhance the value that each customer group delivers to the other. They do this mainly through providing shared services—made available through APIs—that reduce costs for developers and users.

• Multisided platforms must consider marginal costs and price sensitivity in pricing, like single-sided businesses, but they must also consider which side values the other side more. Software platforms generally charge low prices on one side in order to attract customers who can then be made available to the other side. Getting the balance right among all sides is more important than building market share.

• Commercial and open-source production methods have both proved viable models for producing software platforms. Commercial methods seem better suited for managing the multisided aspects of platforms, while open-source methods have produced reliable platforms and applications.

4

Dropouts and Evangelists

So we went to Atari and said, "Hey, we've got this amazing thing, even built with some of your parts, and what do you think about funding us? Or we'll give it to you. We just want to do it. Pay our salary, we'll come work for you." And they said, "No." So then we went to Hewlett-Packard, and they said, "Hey, we don't need you. You haven't got through college yet."

—*Steve Jobs, founder of Apple Computer Inc., on attempts to get Atari and H-P interested in his personal computer.*[1]

INSIDE THIS CHAPTER

· The history of PC software platforms
· The role of multisided strategies in promoting growth and profits
· Hardware integration and its effect on the growth of the Apple and Microsoft platforms

In the first years of the computer industry, every computer was on its own island. In the early 1950s, a few large corporations, government agencies, and universities bought mainframe computers from a few large companies such as Sperry Rand. They didn't get much beyond the hardware. They got a few manuals and the basic software they needed to run programs written in assembly language. They didn't even get an operating system. Each computer's owner needed a team of in-house programmers who, perhaps with some technical help from Sperry, would write applications customized for that organization and that computer. Buying a new computer, even from the same

1. Blech, Benjamin, *Taking Stock: A Spiritual Guide to Rising Above Life's Financial Ups and Downs* (New York: AMACOM, 2003).

Chapter 4: Personal Computer Timeline

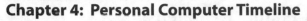

1950s First mainframe computers are purchased by government agencies, universities, and large corporations. Vendors begin bundling rudimentary operating systems with hardware and develop high-level programming languages such as FORTRAN and COBOL. By the end of the 1950s, more than 4,000 computers are in use worldwide.

1970 Minicomputers debut and time-sharing takes off.
AT & T develops Unix.

1974 Intel 8080 microprocessor debuts.

1960s ADR, commissioned by RCA, develops Autoflow, the first third-party software application, and sells 300 copies. Informatics' Mark IV file management software sells thousands of copies.

Altair introduces the first PC. **1975**

Steve Jobs and Steve Wozniak found Apple Computer. **1976**

The Apple II is launched, based on Apple DOS. **1977**

Late 70s: Gary Kildall and his company Digital Research develop CP/M.

Apple II begins using Apple DOS. **1978**

1979

1980

IBM chooses Microsoft over Digital Research to write the operating system and programming languages for PCs running Intel's 8088 microprocessor. Digital Research licenses CP/M to 200 PC makers.

1981 IBM launches the Intel 8088-based PC running PCDOS by Microsoft.

Atari introduces its line of home computers. VisiCalc becomes the killer app for Apple II.

1982 Compaq produces the first IBM clone.

1983 Nearly 1 million IBM clones are produced. The average price of a PC falls to $1,300. Lotus 1-2-3 becomes the killer app for the IBM PC. Morrow Design, Osbourne, and Franklin stop producing computers. DEC unsuccessfully enters the PC market.

Microsoft forms **1984** Developer Relations Group. Apple releases the Mac.

1985

Bill Gates sends letter to Apple CEO John Sculley and Apple Products' president Jean-Louis Gassée advising them to license the Mac OS to manufacturers.

Atari unveils IBM PC-compatible computers.
1987 IBM introduces OS/2 1.0.

IBM's share of the PC market drops to 14%. Microsoft releases Windows 3.0.
1990 AMD produces the Am386, challenging Intel's dominance in the chip-making business.

1991

Early version of Linux appears. Microsoft and IBM part company. MS, Apple integrate True Type software into OS. MS adds peer-to-peer networking. Sun creates Java.

1992 IBM introduces OS/2 2.0.

1994 Linux 1.0 becomes a full-fledged operating system.

1996 IBM scales back support for OS/2

1998

More than 450,000 developers take part in MS training programs, and MS spends $630 million on developer programs.

2000 Over 10,000 US businesses are writing PC applications. Over 1 million people in the U.S are working in programming-type jobs.

Global software industry revenues reach $189 billion. Intel provides Linux drivers for Centrino chips.
2004 Apples sales are reinvigorated by the success of iPod.

More than 90% of PCs have an operating system licensed by Microsoft. Linux has 3% of all desktop operating systems.
2005

manufacturer, often meant laboriously rewriting those applications almost from scratch.

The isolation of computer centers began changing at the end of the 1950s, when there were around 4,000 computers in use worldwide. Computer vendors began bundling rudimentary operating systems with their hardware. And the development of high-level programming languages such as FORTRAN and COBOL made programming simpler and made it easier, though hardly simple, to move programs from one machine to another. Computer owners could also start calling out for help. Two computer analysts who worked in the aerospace industry, for example, started one of the first programmers-for-hire companies— Computer Sciences Corporation—in 1959. Others followed suit. At first these software companies focused on helping companies write specialized software, from compilers to applications, for their expensive mainframe computers.

It didn't take much longer, though, for computer entrepreneurs to realize that there could be a market for general-purpose software that many companies would find useful. In the early 1960s, RCA, a computer manufacturer, commissioned Applied Data Research (ADR) to develop software that would automate the flow-charting of programs so as to facilitate debugging new applications and updating old ones. RCA had planned to give away the ADR product to help sell its computers, but it ultimately decided not to do this. Other computer manufacturers showed no interest in bundling ADR's software with their machines either. So ADR decided to try something new: it marketed its product, christened Autoflow, directly to computer users. It was hardly a mass market success by today's standards. But by 1968 ADR had sold about 300 copies of AutoFlow for operating systems from RCA, IBM, and Honeywell.

Others followed in ADR's footsteps. Informatics was one of the most influential. Its Mark IV file management software was, for computers, selling like hotcakes in the late 1960s. It sold thousands of copies of Mark IV, which ran on IBM's System/360 computer, for $30,000 each. That amounted to over $100 million in sales from late 1967 to the early 1980s. The "packaged" software industry was born. IBM gave this new arrival a significant boost in 1970 when the largest producer of mainframes began charging for all its software products (except its operating systems) rather than including them at no charge with its computers.[2]

Fast-forward to today's personal computer industry. The changes in industry structure are dramatic. Millions of people buy computers from dozens of manufacturers. Most computer users have never written a program of any sort. More than 90 percent of today's PCs have an operating system licensed from Microsoft, which plays a major role in the industry, even though it doesn't make computers.[3] Microsoft and many other firms sell a wide range of applications that can be run on most new computers.

Indeed, the software industry has become enormous: in 2003, the global software industry had revenues of $178 billion for packaged software. More than 10,000 businesses specialized in writing applications—Independent Software Vendors (ISVs), to use the industry jargon—in the United States alone.[4] More than one million people worked in programming-type occupations in the United States at the turn of the twenty-first century.[5] And, increasingly, large quantities of programming work are outsourced to software factories in India.

In addition, a large number of other firms produce monitors, printers, mice, and other peripheral equipment that can be used with virtually any PC. Those few isolated individuals struggling to make computers useful in the early 1950s might have been able to imagine much more powerful machines than those available then. But they would almost

2. Martin Campbell-Kelly, *From Airline Reservations to Sonic the Hedgehog: A History of the Software Industry* (Cambridge, Mass.: MIT Press, 2003), pp. 36, 101, 103–118.

3. Al Gillen and Dan Kusnetzky, "Worldwide Client and Server Operating Environments 2004–2008 Forecast: Microsoft Consolidates Its Grip" (IDC report no. 32452), December 2004.

4. Richard W. Heiman and Anthony C. Picardi, "Worldwide Software 2004–2008 Forecast Summary" (IDC report no. 31785), August 2004.

5. In the 2000 Census, there were 521,105 full-time year-round workers in the Computer Programmers title and 595,965 Computer Software Engineers, for a total of 1,117,070 people doing programming-related jobs. In addition, there were 554,720 Computer Scientists and System Analysts, which if included would bring the total to 1,671,790. http://www.census.gov/hhes/income/earnings/call2usboth.html.

certainly have been unable even to dream of today's rich and lively PC ecosystem, and they would never have been able to imagine the key role that software in general and operating systems in particular play in that ecosystem. The chronicle of this great structural transformation is mainly about the emergence of popular PC software platforms that sit between the hardware and applications. It is a tale, at the human level, driven by entrepreneurs who dropped out of college to pursue dreams that came true, and, more important for our purposes, of evangelists who worked at popularizing software platforms and thereby helped stoke the indirect network effects that propelled the PC revolution.

The Apple and Microsoft Software Platforms

Innovation was already shaking the stodgy mainframe computer industry by the mid-1970s. Computer power was coming to the masses—sort of. Companies such as Digital Equipment Corporation (DEC) were making minicomputers that were far less expensive than IBM's mainframes and that more businesses could use for more applications. And schools, too: Bill Gates learned how to program on his high school's DEC PDP computer. The time-sharing business was taking off: companies rented access to powerful computers to businesses with remote terminals. And companies such as Wang had developed specialized computers for office work. Innovations were occurring in operating systems as well, as we saw in Chapter 2. AT&T had developed Unix, which, in its several somewhat incompatible variants, became a powerful operating system for many of the new minicomputers and workstations.[6]

Minicomputer makers, however, still largely followed the highly integrated model pioneered by mainframe makers. They provided hardware, operating systems, and some applications—though they often charged separately for the apps. The biggest challenges to the industry's traditional structure and way of doing business were under way but almost invisible. Few noticed as the foundations were being laid for the PC revolution. The ensuing story has been told often, so we will just sketch some of the highlights.

6. Campbell-Kelly, *From Airline Reservations to Sonic the Hedgehog*, pp. 143–144, 159.

The Intel 8080 microprocessor, which debuted in 1974, made it possible to produce cheap electronic devices for a variety of purposes. The first PC was the Altair 8800, which became available in 1975. It came as a kit that hobbyists could use to build their own computers with 8080 chips. Like the earliest mainframes, the Altair came without an operating system. Bill Gates famously dropped out of Harvard to work with his childhood friend Paul Allen on a program that would allow users to compile and run BASIC programs on the Altair.[7]

Two years later Steve Jobs and Steve Wozniak (dropouts from Reed and Berkeley, respectively) took the next step. They sold the Apple II as a product bundled with a keyboard, a monitor, and a 6502 microprocessor from MOS Technology. It also came with a tape drive and Apple's version of BASIC. Apple later shipped a floppy disk drive for the Apple II that included a disk operating system called DOS or Apple DOS. Before that, BASIC was used to run programs.

Commodore Business Machines' Commodore PET and Radio Shack's TRS-80 were two of the more popular contemporaries of the Apple II. Like the Apple II, these machines came with a BASIC interpreter that functioned as the software platform. The TRS-80 also came with TRSDOS, a disk operating system, and a floppy disk drive.

None of these machines came with any applications to speak of. Many applications soon became available, though, especially for the Apple II. Most were programs that people shared freely.

By the early 1980s, hundreds of new computer companies were selling machines based on 8-bit processors. Then IBM appeared with its Intel 8088-based PC in 1981. It came with a version of Microsoft BASIC, and most purchasers also bought a new operating system produced by Microsoft called MS-DOS (more on this later).[8]

Early Software Platforms

After Bill Gates and Paul Allen developed their BASIC compiler for the Altair 8800, they went on to develop BASIC programming languages and tools for other early PCs. BASIC, which had been developed in 1963 at

7. Ibid., pp. 202–204.
8. http://inventors.about.com/library/weekly/aa033099.htm.

Dartmouth College as a teaching tool, became a software platform for these machines. Many PC owners, particularly hobbyists, used BASIC to write their own programs. Often users could copy BASIC source code from magazines and books such as *BASIC Computer Games*. BASIC applications could use the commands in BASIC (such as those controlling printing) to perform various tasks so programmers didn't have to write assembly language code themselves to perform those tasks. These commands thus played something like the role of the APIs we discussed in the last chapter.

BASIC and other programming languages were Microsoft's core business through the late 1970s. They accounted for about 30 percent of its revenue in 1984, shortly before the firm went public in 1986.[9] While BASIC was important during these early days, most prospective users weren't programmers, and BASIC never became for any manufacturer what Apple quickly acquired—a killer app.

Microsoft's pricing of BASIC departed from industry practice. Other software companies had translated various programming languages for specific operating systems used for mainframes and workstations. They had generally licensed the code to computer vendors for a substantial flat fee. Microsoft, though, charged PC makers a royalty for each copy they distributed—$30 a copy in the case of the MITS Altair 8800.

This approach worked well for both buyer and seller. Especially for cash-poor computer startups, it reduced their upfront costs. It also reduced their risks: if they didn't do well, they didn't have to pay much. They could also easily pass on the per-copy royalty cost to their customers. Per-copy charges also helped Microsoft capitalize on its investment in programming languages in the face of great uncertainty as to which computer makers would succeed. A flat fee would have earned less from the top sellers and would have discouraged other makers from even trying. Microsoft retained this basic pricing model when it went into the operating system business.

Another software platform seemed very promising during the late 1970s. Gary Kindall developed an operating system for the Intel 8080

9. Andrew Pollack, "Lotus Is the Spoiler at Microsoft's Party," *New York Times*, September 9, 1985.

chip called CP/M. He initially sold copies to hobbyists by mail for $75 each. He also gave one of the new computer makers, IMSAI, a blanket license for $25,000 in 1977. Kindall's company, Digital Research, wrote versions of CP/M for other new startups.

CP/M was important in the early days for two reasons. First, it relieved PC startups of the cost of designing their own operating systems, thereby reducing barriers to entry into the PC market. By 1980, Digital Research had licensed versions of CP/M to some 200 PC makers.[10] Second, CP/M to some extent provided a cross-platform environment for third-party application developers. Even though CP/M applications were not perfectly portable between computers from different manufacturers, the widespread use of CP/M significantly reduced the burden of writing applications for multiple otherwise incompatible computers.

From the beginning, Jobs and Wozniak decided that Apple should develop its own proprietary operating system. They followed the same model as mainframe and minicomputer companies. At first this seemed to be an enormous competitive advantage. A killer application for the Apple II, the VisiCalc electronic spreadsheet, appeared in 1979 and helped turn the Apple II into a highly successful computer platform shortly after its introduction.

VisiCalc didn't run at first on the competing CP/M software platforms. And while the CP/M machines were popular, there was no killer application for them in this period. Moreover, had one appeared, it is unlikely that it would have lighted a fire under any one of the manufacturers of CP/M computers—the flip side of low barriers to entry is generally low ability to sustain the profits needed to recoup investments. But a CP/M killer app might have given at least a short-term boost to the fortunes of Digital Research.

Many other companies followed Apple's highly integrated model, including Tandy, Commodore, Texas Instruments, Coleco, Atari, Timex, and Sinclair. Like the CP/M-based computers, they now appear mainly in trivia quizzes for computer buffs.

10. Campbell-Kelly, *From Airline Reservations to Sonic the Hedgehog*, pp. 205–206.

Atari became a household name thanks to its popular VCS game console and, to a lesser extent, its arcade games. However, the company was making home computers as early as 1979. After producing several 8-bit machines, Atari released the ST line of computers in the mid-1980s with the slogan "Power without the Price." These computers compared favorably with IBM PCs, Apple Macintoshes, and Commodore Amigas in terms of performance per dollar. They also included a MIDI port that made them popular with musicians.

Microsoft, IBM, and the Birth of a New Platform

In 1980, mighty IBM was in the uncomfortable position of playing catch-up in the PC market; Apple, Commodore, and Atari, among others, were already well established. Contrary to its usual practice of doing almost everything itself, IBM decided to speed development by securing partners to make much of the necessary hardware and systems software. The company offered Microsoft a contract to produce programming languages, its specialty at the time, for its new PC. Microsoft didn't have the time or interest to write an operating system and thought CP/M was their and IBM's best bet to meet their deadlines. According to Bob O'Rear, who led the IBM technical efforts at Microsoft, "[O]ur first shot at IBM was to get them to pick up CP/M from DRI and Bill helped set up a meeting."[11] When DR failed to come to terms quickly with Big Blue, IBM came back to Microsoft; Microsoft realized its programming language deal required an operating system and agreed to do it.[12] According to O'Rear,

The [operating system] we thought fit the best for a personal computer was CP/M. It was small, it was targeted at the right audience, it was something we could build on. We had a lot of faith in DR. [But] that didn't work, so we folded MS-DOS into the technical proposal and submitted that and IBM went for it. And then they also went for a huge list of modifications that had to be done to 86-DOS.

IBM was in a hurry for its new operating system. Microsoft bought a rudimentary operating system for the Intel 8086 from neighboring Seattle Computer Products to get a quick start. Seattle Computer Products had been waiting for a version of CP/M for a computer they had

---

11. O'Rear interview notes from MS-DOS encyclopedia project. Ray Duncan, ed., *The MS-DOS Encyclopedia* (Redmond, Wash.: Microsoft Press, 1988).

12. Campbell-Kelly, *From Airline Reservations to Sonic the Hedgehog*, pp. 206–207.

built. Frustrated by delays, they had one of their employees, Tim Patterson, write a "quick and dirty operating system" (dubbed Q-DOS) for it. Seattle Computer Products didn't want to be in the software business. Patterson joined Microsoft to help lead the effort to turn his Q-DOS into something that would meet IBM's specifications.

Microsoft's programmers then wrestled with a multitude of bugs and complexities to produce a finished operating system that was more efficient and included numerous enhancements. Among other things, it offered increased hardware independence, improved disk space allocation and management, and greater ease of use for users with less technical know-how. Microsoft turned over the completed version of PC-DOS modified for the 8088 chip nine months after sealing its deal with IBM. The basic system consisted of roughly 4,000 lines of assembly language code that took up 12 kilobytes of memory. IBM was able to ship its PC with PC-DOS a year after its aggressive decision to take on Apple and the other startups.[13] (Under Microsoft's agreement it could also license DOS to others, and it did so under the name MS-DOS.)

The computer giant thought it had kept control of the platform it was developing. It had a royalty-free license for PC-DOS. It was IBM that shipped PC-DOS, not Microsoft. And IBM planned to make it possible for its hardware platform to work with several operating systems. It reached an agreement with Softech for the UCSD p-System. The USCD p-System was available when the new IBM PC was launched, but it ran very slowly. IBM also belatedly reached a deal with Digital Research to produce a version of CP/M for its new machine. CP/M-86 for the IBM PC appeared several months after the launch, but Digital Research decided to price it at $240, four times the $60 cost of PC-DOS.[14]

13. Duncan, *The MS-DOS Encyclopedia*, pp. 15–24; Daniel Ichbiah and Susan L. Knepper, *The Making of Microsoft: How Bill Gates and His Team Created the World's Most Successful Software Company* (New York: Prima Publishing, 1991), p. 85; Campbell-Kelly, *From Airline Reservations to Sonic the Hedgehog*, p. 207.

14. Michael A. Cusumano and Richard W. Selby, *Microsoft Secrets* (London: HarperCollins, 1995), p. 159; Campbell-Kelly, *From Airline Reservations to Sonic the Hedgehog*, pp. 239–240.

In retrospect, having multiple operating systems run on a hardware platform is a poor strategy. The idea, of course, was to ensure that the hardware, not the operating system, became the standard that defined the platform and determined its evolution. Indeed, IBM followed an important economic principle for traditional industries: all firms would like everyone else in the supply chain to be competitive. IBM didn't seem to recognize that this was far from a traditional industry.

If IBM's strategy *had* worked, and if several operating systems had been installed on substantial numbers of IBM PCs, what would have happened? Most likely, having multiple operating systems would have made the hardware platform less popular than having a single operating system. Applications are generally written for software platforms, not the underlying hardware. The more fragmented the installed base of operating systems, the less attractive it is to write an application for any one of them. Thus, operating system fragmentation would have reduced the number of compatible applications for each of them, reducing their attractiveness to end users and thus reducing the value of the underlying hardware platform.

As we noted in Chapter 2, that is in fact what happened with the UNIX operating system for minicomputers. Several versions were created, and applications weren't compatible across them. That fragmentation (often called "forking") stunted the growth of UNIX. As of 2006, Linux, a stepchild of UNIX, has managed to overtake UNIX in part because Linus Torvalds and the rest of the committee that manages Linux have worked very hard to prevent fragmentation (more on this later).

But, as we now know, IBM's multiple-OS strategy did not work.

In order to get to market quickly and hold down system cost, IBM decided to create an open hardware platform—one quite unlike the walled garden it had tended for years in mainframes. And, of course, it had outsourced operating systems to Microsoft and other firms over which it had limited control. It appears to have believed nonetheless—one can only conjecture at this point—that it could reap the lion's share of profits from this innovative computer platform through its brand name, its marketing muscle, and its intellectual property in the basic input-output system (BIOS) that starts the computer when it is turned on. After all, it was selling the computers and should be able to charge a premium for them, as it had always done.

Things didn't work out that way. Microsoft had retained the rights to license MS-DOS—an exact replica of PC-DOS—to other computer manufacturers. It was keen to do so. At the same time, dozens of manufacturers started trying to clone the IBM PC. Their main stumbling block was the BIOS. Copyright law wouldn't allow them just to copy it. But nothing prevented them from reverse-engineering it. Like recreating a gourmet meal without the chef's secret recipe, this involved writing code for the BIOS by observing what the code did rather than what the code was.

Compaq produced the first truly legal IBM PC clone after reportedly spending $1 million to figure out the secrets of the BIOS. By 1983, IBM competitors had produced almost one million IBM PC clones. All ran MS-DOS, which was already the most popular operating system for PCs. And the price was right—an estimated $10 per computer at a time when the average PC went for about $1,300.[15] IBM tried to develop other proprietary technology to recapture control, but it had to give up the fight by the end of the 1980s. IBM's share of IBM-compatible PC sales tumbled to 14 percent by 1990.[16] It stopped making PCs altogether with the sale of its PC division to Lenovo in 2004.

The IBM/DOS-compatible PCs quickly killed off the many CP/M-compatible manufacturers. Between 1981 and 1986, Morrow Design, Osborne, and Franklin went out of business, and the rest failed not much later.[17] Companies like DEC tried to enter with CP/M-compatible machines during this period but had little success.

15. Campbell-Kelly, *From Airline Reservations to Sonic the Hedgehog*, pp. 207, 240–242; Dataquest, "Personal Computer Industry Service Worldwide Shipments and Forecast," tables 1.3.5 and 1.3.13.

16. Bruce Stephen and Mark Levitt, "Worldwide PC Market Review and Forecast 1990–1995" (IDC report no. 6077), December 1991, table 3.

17. Helen Grant, "Zenith High But Maker Goes Broke," *Australian Financial Review*, March 13, 1986; http://www.absoluteastronomy.com/encyclopedia/O/Os/Osborne_Computer_Corporation.htm; http://www.ti99ers.org/timeline/time1984.htm.

By the mid-1980s it seemed clear that the battle would be between two PC platforms, Apple computers and "IBM-compatible" computers. By the early 1990s, when IBM and Microsoft had competing operating systems for PC's based on Intel microprocessors, the phrase "IBM-compatible" was no longer in use. In the mid-1990s, IBM decisively lost the competition between these two operating systems. Since then, platform competition has been between Apple's Macintosh platform and the "Wintel" platform: Microsoft's Windows operating system running on computers based on Intel's microprocessors.

IBM's OS/2 versus Microsoft's Windows

In 1985, IBM and Microsoft agreed to develop a new operating system for the PC. IBM led the project and provided most of the resources.[18] The first version, OS/2 1.0, was released in 1987 but was intended mainly as a preview for developers. Among other things, it lacked a graphical user interface (GUI) and a comprehensive hardware support.

The relationship between Microsoft and IBM was always difficult, in part because of the very different styles of the two companies. For example, IBM measured programmers' contributions by the number of lines of code they wrote, which Microsoft thought encouraged the production of sloppy, inefficient code. The fact that Microsoft was developing Windows in parallel to OS/2 did not help the relationship. Moreover, IBM and Microsoft had different visions for OS/2. From the beginning, Microsoft urged IBM to base the OS/2 GUI on Windows APIs. However, IBM had different plans. It sought to create a single graphical interface across all of its platforms, from mainframes to PCs. Consequently it rejected Windows and included features in OS/2 that added little for PC users. OS/2 would also run only on the then most powerful PCs. In a joint statement in the late 1980s, IBM and Microsoft positioned OS/2 as the operating system of choice for powerful PCs, with Windows the alternative for lower-end machines, which constituted about 75 percent of the shipments at the time.[19]

18. At times, IBM devoted as many as 10,000 developers to the project, compared with Microsoft's 100. In 1986 IBM had roughly 150 times Microsoft's sales and 120 times its market capitalization. Microsoft Corporation 1986 Annual Report and Form 10-K; Fact Set Research Systems, CompuStat Database, 2001.

19. Maurice F Estabrooks, *Electronic Technology, Corporate Strategy, and World Transformation* (Westport, Conn.: Greenwood Publishing, 1995), p. 64.

(continued)

In 1990, Microsoft released Windows 3.0. Not only was Windows 3.0 very successful, it was also a viable option for the upper end of the market. Later that year, Microsoft and IBM parted company in one of the most famous corporate divorces. IBM got the project that would produce the next version of OS/2, while Microsoft got the research in progress on what would eventually become Windows NT.

IBM released OS/2 2.0 in 1992 with the slogan, "a better DOS than DOS, and a better Windows than Windows."[20] It was the first PC operating system to run on 32-bit microprocessors, which could support more ambitious applications, yet it was also able to run programs written for DOS and contemporary versions of Windows. OS/2 was backed by the IBM brand name and IBM's research capacity and marketing muscle. Moreover, the company seemed committed to making the platform work, advertising heavily (if sporadically) and regularly updating OS/2 through 1996. But version 2.0 and its successors never effectively challenged Windows. Why not?

Some argue that IBM didn't invest enough in developer support and evangelization. "The company stupidly reckoned that if you give developers a good operating system, coders will code for it," wrote the computer columnist John C. Dvorak.[21] IBM also charged substantial prices for developer tools. The incompatibility of Windows and OS/2 APIs also made it harder for developers to write simultaneously for OS/2 and Windows. Forced to choose, most chose Windows.

IBM also sent confusing signals to developers. OS/2 was only one of at least four operating systems for microcomputers under development at IBM.[22] IBM was also unable to explain its overall strategy to developers, prompting an editor to exclaim that "IBM's strategy is about as comprehensive [sic] as Balkan politics."[23] In 1996, IBM scaled back its OS/2 efforts, and in July 2005, IBM finally withdrew support for OS/2.

20. http://en.wikipedia.org/wiki/OS/2.

21. John C. Dvorak, "Obituary: O/S," *PC Magazine*, December 16, 2002 (http://www.pcmag.com/article2/0,4149,767456,00.asp).

22. Instead of OS/2, IBM used AIX, its version of Unix, for its workstations running its PowerPC processors. In 1991, Apple and IBM reportedly were jointly developing a new version of Unix, PowerOpen. In 1992, they formed a joint venture, Taligent, which started out with the goal of developing yet another new operating system, code-named Pink. Roy A. Allan, *A History of the Personal Computer: The People and the Technology* (Allan Publishing, 2001), p. 19.

23. Doug Barney, "Big Blue Pitches a Play-to-Play of Its OS Plan," *InfoWorld*, July 11, 1994, pp. 21–22.

Apple versus Microsoft

During the 1980s, Apple operated a two-sided platform. The company made its own hardware, which it sold with its own operating systems. It also branded its own peripheral equipment. Until 1998 it also refused to include industry-standard ports to facilitate connections to peripherals made by others.[24] Even today, Apple computers are designed in ways that discourage the use of third-party peripherals. Some of its models, for example, integrate a proprietary monitor, disk drives, and speakers in a single computer unit. Apple also wrote applications software for its operating systems. But early on, its managers understood the importance of building and sustaining a two-sided platform, attracting software applications from independent developers (including Microsoft) to add to the appeal of the Mac.

Microsoft went four-sided. Like Apple, it encouraged third-party development of applications for MS-DOS and subsequent operating systems while also writing applications software for its own operating systems. But it did not sell computers, only dabbled in peripheral equipment, and stayed out of the markets for big-ticket items such as monitors and printers. Instead, it encouraged computer and peripheral makers to make best use of its software platform.

The Microsoft platform was therefore more complex than the Apple platform: Microsoft had to harness the indirect network externalities between computer manufacturers, peripheral equipment makers, software developers, and, of course, computer users. That meant getting them all on the same platform—Microsoft's operating system for Intel-compatible computers—and generating positive indirect network effects between them. The multisided strategies we discussed in Chapter 3 were critical to its success.

24. "Hands On–Mac–Universal Solution," *Personal Computer World*, February 1, 1999; "Mac Ports, Past and Present," http://charm.cs.uiuc.edu/users/olawlor/ref/mac_ports/.

Apple's Blunder?

It is now commonplace to view Apple's choice of an integrated two-sided platform as an unpardonable strategic error, one that consigned erstwhile market leader Apple to a marginally viable niche in PCs. Indeed, to this day, some argue that sticking with an integrated hardware-software platform undermines the profitability of workstation and server computer makers ranging from IBM to Sun.

Bill Gates wrote to Apple's CEO John Sculley and Apple Products' President Jean-Louis Gassée in 1985, a year after Apple reported a $40 million loss as lower-cost IBM clones grabbed an ever-greater chunk of the PC market. He advised them to license the highly regarded Macintosh operating system to clone-makers, concluding as follows:

As the independent investment in a 'standard' architecture grows, so does the momentum for that architecture. The industry has reached the point where it is now impossible for Apple to create a standard out of their innovative technology without support from, and the resulting credibility of other personal computer manufacturers. Thus, Apple must open the Macintosh architecture to have the independent support required to gain momentum and establish a standard. (From a memo dated June 25, 1985, Quoted by permission from Microsoft.)

This wasn't just friendly advice. At the time, Microsoft earned about half of its revenue from applications for the Macintosh (including its hot Word word-processing package, which hadn't yet made a dent in the IBM-PC segment, as well as its Excel spreadsheet program, which accounted for 90 percent of Macintosh spreadsheet sales by September 1985) and only about 20 percent from MS-DOS.[25] It wasn't at all clear at the time that Microsoft would get a second home run after DOS. So Gates was covering his bets. Microsoft might have done extremely well as a leading application developer for a dominant Mac OS.

But hindsight has a way of making uncertain outcomes seem inevitable. A closer look suggests that integrating the hardware and software platforms tightly had significant advantages over letting a thousand hardware makers bloom. Apple was able to tailor its operating system software to its hardware during a period in which operating systems were rapidly growing more complex and hardware performance was rapidly improving. And since it controlled both the hardware and the operating system, it was possible to test the operating system with every possible hardware

25. Campbell-Kelly, *From Airline Reservations to Sonic the Hedgehog*, p. 253; Jonathan Chevreau, "Apple Hopes Macintosh Will Take Bite of Market," *The Globe and Mail*, January 23, 1984; "Lotus Is the Spoiler at Microsoft's Party," *San Francisco Chronicle*, September 1985; Owen Linzmeyer, *Apple Confidential* (San Francisco: No Starch Press, 1999), p. 134.

(continued)

> combination before Apple computers were put on the market, something Microsoft could not possibly do. Apple had a powerful graphical user interface before Microsoft, and its systems have long been viewed as more stable.
>
> What we know in hindsight is that Apple's share of the PC business plummeted, so that today it has only a 4 percent share of sales.[26] But unlike the many CP/M clone-makers it once faced, Apple is still around and quite well known. Apple either knows its own strengths or is stunningly stubborn—it has chosen the same vertically integrated hardware/software strategy for its latest hit product, the iPod, which we discuss further in Chapter 8.

Managing the Software Side

Both Apple and Microsoft have focused considerable efforts on persuading third-party producers to write applications for their software platforms. These efforts paid off and were critical to the success of these operating systems.

Killer Apps   In the first decade or so of the PC industry, several computer platforms took off after the emergence of a killer app for them. VisiCalc, the first spreadsheet application for PCs, was a killer app for Apple. Dan Bricklin, its inventor, and his team wrote it in assembly language—the tedious process required in those days to get good performance—for the microprocessor used in the Apple II.

After a number of limited-distribution versions—we would call them demos, alpha, and beta versions today—the first "real" release came out in October 1979. An analyst report captured its significance: "VisiCalc could some day become the software tail that wags (and sells) the personal computer dog."[27] Although VisiCalc was quickly ported to other platforms, Apple had the early lead. And, most important, businesses realized that these tiny new computers were not toys; they really could provide important productivity tools for their workers.

26. "Worldwide Client and Server Operating Environments 2005–2009 Forecast: Modest Growth Ahead" (IDC report no. 34599), December 2005.

27. http://www.bricklin.com/history/saiproduct1.htm; http://www.bricklin.com/history/rosenletter.htm.

Spreadsheets continued to provide the spark needed for platforms to get off the ground over the next decade or so. Lotus 1-2-3 appeared in 1983, not long after the IBM PC had started building momentum, and it only ran on PC/MS-DOS. It was a major advance over VisiCalc because it combined a spreadsheet, a rudimentary database, and the ability to create graphs into one product. Microsoft's Excel turned out to be one of the hot apps—killer is perhaps too strong a term at this point—that finally got Windows off the ground in its third release.

Killer apps have also played important roles for the other software platforms we consider in later chapters. These applications helped set up the positive network effects that make platforms grow. More people got a computer system with a particular software platform. That encouraged more application developers to write more applications for that platform.[28]

Apple, though, had no role in the development of VisiCalc. Dan Bricklin's Web site on the history of the development of his product makes no mention of interactions with anyone from that company. Likewise, neither Microsoft nor IBM helped Lotus create a killer application for their software-hardware platform. IBM even declined the exclusive marketing rights to the Lotus 1-2-3 spreadsheet.[29] VisiCalc had already been ported to DOS, after all; what more did they need?

Nevertheless, it didn't take long for Apple, Microsoft, and others to recognize that applications were so important to the success of their platforms that they needed to nurture their development and not just sit back and hope they became available.

Evangelization   The realization that independent software vendors were vital to their success led both Apple and Microsoft to mount aggressive, ongoing efforts to recruit independent software developers to their platforms. In part, these efforts took the form of old-fashioned "you must believe" marketing long practiced by tent revivalists and self-help gurus, and perfected by Apple's Guy Kawasaki. The author of books with titles such as *The Art of the Start, Rules for Revolutionaries, Selling the*

---

28. Campbell-Kelly, *From Airline Reservations to Sonic the Hedgehog*, p. 216.
29. Paul Carroll, *Big Blues: The Unmaking of IBM* (New York: Crown, 1993), pp. 77–78.

Dream, and *The Macintosh Way*, Kawasaki led the charge to give the Apple Macintosh cult status among both early computer users and software developers.[30] To hear Kawasaki tell it, the interdependence between the user and developer sides of the platform was not behind the original effort: "I was never told, 'OK, you go get XYZ to write software, and they in turn will get more customers to buy your software and to buy Macs.' That's what happened, but that was not the plan."[31]

Kawasaki's marketing innovations ranged from developer conferences, which were part technical presentations and part pep rallies, to EvangeList, an email newsletter sent to Apple devotees in the mid-1990s that was designed to counter worries that Apple would disappear as its market share dwindled. To this day, his success has set the tone for marketing to software developers. It was an important contribution to the development of the positive indirect network effects needed to grow these multisided platforms. We will see that "evangelism of the platform" has been critical to all of the successful software platforms we consider. Indeed, Google appointed Vinton Cerf, one of the intellectual founders of the Internet, to be its first chief evangelist in September 2005.

As a practical matter, though, Microsoft's formation of its Developer Relations Group (DRG) in 1984 probably had more impact on the way computer platforms evolved than Kawasaki's barnstorming. This team was charged with attracting independent developers to the then-unborn Windows platform: "Drive the success of Microsoft's strategic platforms by creating a critical mass of third-party applications" was its mission.[32] DRG has pursued this goal with a determination reflected in both the degree of long-term planning and the significant resources invested. Long before Microsoft introduces a new operating system, it solicits advice on the tools that developers will need to create applications to run on it. For example, it sent tentative specifications for Windows NT to developers in November 1990, asking for feedback three years before the operating system was released.

30. http://www.guykawasaki.com/about/index.shtml.

31. Ben McConnel and Jackie Huba, *Creating Customer Evangelists* (Chicago: Dearborn Trade Publishing, 2003), p. 13.

32. "Microsoft Developer Relations: Microsoft's Commitment to Third-Party Developer Success," Microsoft Corporation white paper (Redmond, Wash.: Microsoft Corp., 1998).

Many developers belong to the Microsoft Developer Network (MSDN). They are regularly sent information on how to create applications to run on Microsoft platforms: between 1993 and 1998, Microsoft shipped 100 million CDs with this sort of information. The company sponsors several series of conferences to keep the programming community both informed and involved. In 1998 alone, some 450,000 developers took part in various Microsoft training programs. All told, the company spent $630 million on its evangelism effort that year.[33]

Application Program Interfaces Evangelization is unlikely to succeed with application developers without a good product—in particular, software services made available through APIs. On the one hand, it is important to convince developers that the platform will attract many end users interested in their products: hence direct, visible advertising to end users and the pep rally aspects of evangelization. On the other hand, it is important to convince developers that they can write attractive programs to run on the platform relatively easily: hence efforts to reduce the costs of writing applications for the Apple and Windows platforms.

The platform owners make heavy investments in technical assistance to developers as part of this effort. All platform managers maintain the so-called developer networks. MSDN, with over 3 million members, is one of the biggest, while the Apple Developer Connection has about 500,000 members.[34] These networks are subscription-based, with annual charges ranging from a few hundred dollars to over $10,000, depending on the services provided. They offer access to news, technical documentation, developer forums, and online support. Members may receive discounts on select developer tools or conference fees. Although the open-source Linux platform has no formal platform manager, Linux developer forums are regarded as some of the best because all the members of the ecosystem participate, including IT managers, application developers, and platform developers.

33. *United States v. Microsoft*, Civil Action No. 90–1232, Testimony of Paul Maritz, January 20, 1999, § 140, § 136–152.

34. http://www.edn.com/blog/400000040/post/740000874.html; "Microsoft Announces Unprecedented Momentum for MSDN at 3 Million Members," *M2 Presswire*, March 7, 2000.

Platforms make another key investment in reducing developer costs: they constantly add and improve the software services provided through the APIs discussed in Chapter 2. For example, the Apple Mac OS X, introduced in 1999, has about 8,000 APIs that expose underlying software services. Some (called Cocoa) were designed to support new software applications and others (called Carbon) were designed to ease the transition from the Mac OS 9.[35]

These numbers by themselves don't say much, of course; it is the range of services these APIs offer to developers that is impressive. The original MS-DOS offered developers APIs for keyboard input, file operations, and time control, to name a few. In the late 1980s, Windows came with many more, including APIs that enabled developers to use memory in a much more sophisticated way, to take advantage of the GUI, and to use a mouse for input. Media functionality was added in the early 1990s, CD support in the mid-1990s and DVD APIs at the turn of the twenty-first century. Throughout the 1990s, operating systems added support for new networking technologies such as infrared, Bluetooth, and WiFi.

The end user does not see any of this. Instead, she sees the applications that are built on top of these APIs. The many media players on PCs these days, for instance, rely on the underlying operating system for the core media functionality, in addition to using the APIs that display the media player on the screen and let the user control it with a mouse. Instant messengers, Palm synchronization, and other applications use networking APIs, while games use the operating systems' 3D graphics support.

Managing the Hardware Side

Apple treats hardware from other suppliers in much the same way that a vertically integrated automobile company like Toyota treats parts and optional equipment made by others: it buys many components from independent suppliers. Over the years, for example, Apple's microprocessors have come largely from Motorola and IBM.[36] But as a major customer,

35. William Peterson, Jean Bozman, and Dan Kusnetzky, "Apple Announces New Operating System Strategy for the Mac" (IDCFlash no. 16257), May 1999; http://en.wikipedia.org/wiki/Mac_OS_X_history.

36. Stephen Shankland, "Apple to Ditch IBM, Switch to Intel Chips," *CNET News.com*, June 3, 2003 (http://news.com.com/2100-1006_3-5731398.html).

Apple has a strong say in their design and specifications. Apple's first commercial computer, the Apple II, was an open system and owes a large part of its success to the availability of many third-party hardware add-ons. However, Steve Jobs felt that a true PC should be an appliance like a TV that requires no interaction with the circuitry, no technical knowledge, and no assembly. He realized this vision in the original Macintosh, released in 1984. This machine had no expansion slots, no hard disk drive, and no standard ports. Its keyboard also lacked arrow keys, to force the user to use the mouse. After Jobs' departure, the Macintosh design was relaxed and expansion slots, standard ports, hard drives, and arrow keys all appeared on the models released in 1986.[37]

One of Apple's most successful branded products was the LaserWriter line of printers. Launched in 1985, they helped create what is now known as desktop publishing. As of 2005, Apple's high-end thin-screen displays are one its most popular branded peripherals. They, like other Apple products, including the iPod discussed in Chapter 8, are sold in Apple's chain of retail stores, among other places.

Microsoft, by contrast, has specialized in software from the outset— a "stick to your knitting" strategy. It has made only a few forays into hardware, such as the Microsoft mouse and its wireless keyboards. Microsoft makes hardware, however, mainly to help sell more software. Microsoft's SoftCard, introduced in 1980, for example, enabled Apple II computers to run CP/M applications, including Microsoft BASIC. Similarly, Microsoft introduced its mouse in 1983 to help spur sales of Microsoft Windows, which was in development at the time.[38]

These exceptions aside, Microsoft mainly relies on third parties to make the complementary hardware that helps sell PCs and thereby its operating systems. This may seem like a difference without a distinction. After all, Apple purchases many of the parts for its machines, and it has to make sure these suppliers provide technology that will help Apple sell its computers. But Microsoft, like other multisided platform firms, has structured a complex series of relationships with third parties to promote

37. http://lowendmac.com/history/1984dk.shtml; http://www.lowendmac.com/history/1986dk.shtml.

38. Paul Freiberger and Michael Swaine, *Fire in the Valley: The Making of the Personal Computer*, 2nd ed. (New York: McGraw-Hill, 2000), p. 329; Stephen Manes and Paul Andrews, *Gates* (New York: Simon & Schuster, 1994), p. 221.

the licensing of its operating system software. These relationships are managed partly through financial incentives and partly through developing the software platform in close cooperation with these third parties to promote their sales as well as Microsoft's sales.

That difference is best seen in the incorporation of CD-ROM drives into computers. Apple could just decide to do this, buy CD-ROM drives from third parties, and build them into its computers. Microsoft had to encourage the computer manufacturers in its ecosystem to install them. Those manufacturers didn't have much incentive to do this, however, when there wasn't much software that relied on CD-ROMs. Microsoft provided financial incentives to install CD-ROM drives and promised that its software platform would ensure the development of applications that used CD-ROMs. We return to this later.

The Microsoft-Intel partnership has been central to the hardware-software platform that is the basis for the PCs that most of us use. Intel had virtually no competition until 1990, when AMD, Intel's former second source supplier, released the Am386 chip. As of 2004, Intel had an 82 percent share of the global PC microprocessor business.[39] Intel and Microsoft have had to work closely to ensure that Microsoft operating systems get the computing power they need from Intel processors and that Intel's processors get the support they need from the software platform. Not surprisingly, the relationship between these two elephants has not been free of conflict. Each has sought more control over the Wintel platform, and with it, presumably, a larger share of the profits associated with the platform's spectacular success.

Both have sought to hedge their bets with other partners. Microsoft has long dealt with Intel's microprocessor rival, AMD. Intel, for its part, is reportedly underwriting efforts to develop applications for the Linux platform in China, India, and Brazil.

Microsoft's relationship with makers of branded PCs is simpler. Virtually all PCs are now sold with an operating system installed. Microsoft provides information to PC makers on how changes in the operating

39. AMD had already been making Intel compatible chips. It had a cross-license agreement with Intel until 1986, when Intel ended the contract. A lengthy legal battle between the two companies ensued. AMD, http://www.amd.com/us-en/Weblets/0,,7832_12670_12686,00.html; Shane Ran "Worldwide PC Processor 2004 Vendor Shares" (IDC report no. 33398), May 2005.

system will affect the optimal design of the hardware, and it solicits feedback during the development process. Manufacturers pay license fees to Microsoft, which they pass on, as they would any costs, to end users as part of the price of the box.

Microsoft offers some discounts on its licensing fees in return for computer makers doing certain things that improve the overall quality of the entire platform. For example, Microsoft provided a small discount to computer makers in 1996 to give them incentives to install USB ports on their computers. Microsoft benefited from these incentives: USB ports promoted the addition of various peripherals that Windows would support, and that made Windows a more valuable platform. Of course, the computer makers and peripheral manufacturers in aggregate benefited from additional sales. But none of them individually had the incentive to promote the inclusion of USB ports. Microsoft as the maestro of the multisided platform had both the incentive to subsidize the inclusion of USB ports and the ability to do so.

These sorts of financial incentives are only one aspect of the platform strategy to get customers on board. As we noted earlier, in the mid-1980s Microsoft pressed hard to accelerate the development of CD-ROM technology as a cornerstone of multimedia computers. It held annual developers conferences for interested parties, worked with major manufacturers to create an industry-standard format, and evangelized computer makers to package built-in CD-ROM drives with new machines. Beginning with Windows 95, Microsoft has included code to create a relatively seamless "plug-and-play" experience with thousands of peripheral devices.[40] As we will see throughout this book, this sort of platform management is hardly unique to Microsoft. Most software platforms engage in similar activities, if not always with Microsoft's drive and skill.

Platform Pricing and Hardware Integration

Pricing is key for getting customers on board a platform and harnessing network effects to increase its size, as we saw in Chapter 3. The PC

---

40. Randall E. Stross, *The Microsoft Way* (Reading, Mass.: Addison-Wesley, 1996), p. 65; http://searchwin2000.techtarget.com/sDefinition/ 0,,sid1_gci212799,00.html.

industry quickly settled on a particular *pricing structure*. Virtually all revenue and profit have come from end users, not from the businesses that have relied on the services provided by APIs to write applications. No commercial maker of PC software platforms—whether integrated into hardware, as was the case with Apple and Atari, or sold separately, as was the case with Microsoft, Digital Research, and IBM—has tried to make money from application developers. So the "end user pays/the developer gets a free ride" pricing structure has held firm for more than a quarter of a century over several significant shifts in the industry.

It took longer to settle on *pricing methods*. Several of the early operating system companies licensed their code to manufacturers for a flat fee and allowed the manufacturers to modify the source code for their machines. Microsoft took a different approach. It licensed the binary code on a per-machine basis. Neither computer makers nor end users could modify the software platform easily. Apple took yet another approach. It didn't license its operating system at all (with the exception of a short period in the late 1990s). Nor did it make the source code available for modification.

The different makers of operating systems also took very different approaches to the *price levels* they were charging. We already saw the stark contrast between Microsoft and CP/M for the early IBM PCs. Later, IBM initially priced OS/2 at $325, compared with Microsoft Windows 3.0 at $149. A more interesting although difficult comparison is between Microsoft and Apple, since Apple's operating system generally comes bundled with its hardware, with no separate price. However, there is a clue: the 1990 upgrade to Windows 3.0 was $50, about half the price ($99) of a 1991 upgrade to Apple's System 7.0. Another useful clue comes from a comparison between computers with similar hardware: in this same period the average price of an Apple PC was over $200 more than the average price of a similarly equipped and powerful Compaq PC sold with Microsoft operating systems.[41]

41. Campbell-Kelly, *From Airline Reservations to Sonic the Hedgehog*, p. 250; "Microsoft Corp.: Windows 3.0 Is Here," *Business Wire*, May 22, 1990; Ron Wolf, "Apple Begins Shipping Long-Awaited System 7.0 Operating System," *Austin American-Statesman*, May 13, 1991; Dataquest, "Personal Computers U.S. Vendor Segmentation: 1998," April 19, 1999.

Thus, it appears that Microsoft chose a low-price strategy relative both to other stand-alone operating system vendors and to sellers of integrated software-hardware platforms. This encouraged computer makers to sell more machines with Microsoft's operating systems installed. Competition among them forced hardware prices down further. That extended the pricing advantage of the DOS/Intel and later Windows/Intel computer platform.

We examine the determinants of these pricing choices—and why they differed dramatically from the choices made in the video game industry—in Chapter 10. In the next chapter we learn that the video game console platform took a "developer pays/console user gets a cheap ride" pricing strategy.

Bundling

Early PC operating systems did relatively little, just managing basic functions like the input and output of data and the loading and execution of applications. Operating systems were only as capable as the computers on which they ran and accordingly provided only a fraction of functionality of their modern counterparts. But as computer technology advanced, operating systems expanded their reach—often into areas previously served by applications software made by others. For example, all modern PC operating systems include code for applications as basic as arithmetic calculators and as advanced as automating connection to networks.

Competition in PC operating systems has served to accelerate this trend. For example, in 1991, both the Mac OS and Windows integrated TrueType software for manipulating font sizes. Likewise, Apple offered QuickTime, a collection of multimedia functionalities, as a free add-on for the Mac OS in 1991; Microsoft followed with Video for Windows in 1994. Both Apple and Microsoft added peer-to-peer networking features in 1991 and 1992, respectively. IBM scored a first by adding an Internet browser to OS/2 Warp in 1994. Microsoft, playing catch-up with IBM as well as the independent release of Netscape Navigator, offered a Windows browser in 1995, based largely on code licensed from Spyglass. Microsoft included Outlook Express email software with Windows 2000, and Apple followed with its Mail email client in the first release of the Mac OS X, early in 2001. Both Windows XP (2001) and the "Jaguar" version of the Mac OS X (2002) included instant messaging applications.[42]

The Linux platform for desktop PCs does not have a single manager with competitive incentives to bundle applications. However, all the companies that package and support Linux include most of the features now bundled with Windows and the Mac OS X. Indeed, because many Linux applications are free, Linux distributors often include more. Novell's Desktop 9 distribution, for instance, includes an Office-like productivity suite as well as instant messaging software that is compatible with AOL, MSN, and Yahoo IM applications. Red Hat does the same.

The Platforms in Perspective

Microsoft came to dominate PC platforms in the 1990s by pricing low and by capitalizing on what we now see as the strategic errors of others in the 1980s. Network effects associated with DOS's head start may well have given the company a competitive advantage. But Microsoft was able to translate that advantage into success only by understanding what it took to nurture its multisided platform and acting decisively on that knowledge to bring application developers on board and keep them there.

After some very rough patches, Apple has managed to stabilize revenues from its tightly integrated hardware-software platform and may

42. http://en.wikipedia.org/wiki/System_7_(Macintosh); "Windows 3.1: What's New Is for the Users on Networks," *LAN Times*, April 6, 1992; http://www.macos.utah.edu/Documentation/MacOSXClasses/macosxone/macintosh.html; http://www.microsoft.com/windows/windowsmedia/press/dmtimeline. aspx; http://support.microsoft.com/default.aspx?scid=kb;EN-US;q126746; http://www.macos.utah.edu/Documentation/MacOSXClasses/macosxone/ macintosh.html; http://channel9.msdn.com/ShowPost.aspx?PostID=10049; http://en.wikipedia.org/wiki/Spyglass; http://en.wikipedia.org/wiki/Spyglass; "Outlook Express," *Internet Magazine*, May 1, 2000; http://en.wikipedia.org/ wiki/Mac_OS_X_v10.0; Joe Wilcox, "Apple to Unleash Jaguar OS Upgrade," *CNET News.com*, August 29, 2002 (http://news.com.com/ Apple+to+unleash+Jaguar+OS+upgrade/2100-1001_3-955063.html); http://en. wikipedia.org/wiki/Windows_xp#Windows_XP_Starter_Edition.

yet be able to profit from its inherent strengths. By controlling both the hardware and the operating system, it has been able to produce an exceptionally benign computing environment that attracts nonbusiness users who are prepared to pay more for handsome design and superior stability. And it may find ways to leverage its great success in portable digital devices—specifically, the iPod—to the benefit of the Mac OS platform. Indeed, surveys of iPod users indicate that the "halo effect" from the iPod has given a very substantial boost to sales of computers based on the Mac OS X platform.[43]

Still, it would be folly to make predictions about the evolution of the PC platform competition in coming years with any confidence. For one thing, technological change—for example, greater penetration of broadband that made server-based platforms practical—could undermine today's PC platforms. Google looms large as of this writing. This advertising-supported search engine offers an extremely popular platform that seems to reside on what we call the Web but of course really resides on Google's vast array of Linux-based servers. Many take it for granted that this new firm, so different from Apple and Microsoft, could push these old warriors aside. We return to this in Chapter 12.

For another, regulation—or corporate response to the threat of greater regulation—could slow innovation in Windows the way it impaired innovation at IBM in the 1970s and 1980s. Microsoft is subject to regulation stemming from adverse antitrust decisions in both the United States and the European Union—economies that together account for 59 percent of the world's gross domestic product and at least 70 percent of Microsoft's sales.[44] The U.S. regulation expires in 2007, while the EU regulation is perpetual, although it is the subject of an ongoing legal appeal. Then again, Microsoft's rival of the moment, Google, is coming

43. Daniel Drew Turner, "Apple Could See Near Doubling of Market Share," *eWeek.com*, March 22, 2005 (http://www.eweek.com/article2/0,1759, 1778538,00.asp).

44. http://en.wikipedia.org/wiki/List_of_countries_by_GDP_%28nominal%29; http://www.sec.gov/Archives/edgar/data/789019/000119312505174825/d10k. htm.

under scrutiny from many quarters, and that could slow any challenge it might make to Microsoft.

Yet another wild card, to which we now turn, is the Linux open-source platform, which has made great inroads in server software but is only now beginning to make a dent in platforms geared for client computers in business uses.

The New Challenger with No Owner: Linux

Windows' tens of millions of lines of code are a well-guarded trade secret. Until recently, only carefully screened outsiders—major software and hardware developers, along with government experts seeking to uncover security flaws in the code—ever got to see the proprietary code, and then only under strict conditions of secrecy. Apple used some publicly available code as a key building block for the Macintosh OS X platform, and the company made portions of Mac OS X available to the programming community, both as a gesture of goodwill and as an enticement to develop applications for the platform. But vital features of the operating system remain secret, including Apple's GUI and the code that makes the operating system compatible with earlier generations of Apple applications. Windows and the Mac OS, moreover, are both owned and carefully managed by companies that seek a return on their investments in these systems.

There is an alternative model, though. Open-source software, designed and maintained by volunteer programmers, has been successful in several areas[45]—something of a surprise in light of the worldwide success of market-driven incentives and the general failure of communal production. For example, the Apache Web Server is widely used on standard server computer platforms, as well as being distributed with major proprietary operating systems such as Sun's Solaris. And

45. Surprisingly at least to economists, who have long assumed that profit incentives were critical to the design of modern software. David Evans, "Is Free Software the Wave of the Future?" *Milken Institute Review* (4th Quarter, 2001); Josh Lerner and Jean Tirole, "The Scope of Open Source Licensing," NBER working paper, 2002.

many have argued in recent years that the most potent competitive threat faced by Windows comes not from Apple but from a PC operating system that is built entirely from open, publicly available source code and that, accordingly, nobody owns or manages for a profit: Linux. Linux has already secured a strong presence as an operating system for server computers—it had a 12 percent share of paid shipments (from firms like Red Hat) in 2004, along with a large but unknown number of free downloads, and is clearly a significant competitor for Microsoft, Sun, Novell, and other companies in that business.[46] The big open question is whether this un-owned, open-source alternative will evolve into a major multisided platform for desktop PCs that competes successfully with Windows and the Macintosh operating systems.

An early version of Linux, a rudimentary kernel, appeared in 1991 for use with Intel 386-compatible hardware. By 1994, with the release of Linux 1.0, it had evolved into a full-fledged operating system. Unlike the other multisided OS platforms, however, Linux had—and has— no corporate parent to guide its development or to evangelize about either the development of applications software or the development of device drivers to make it compatible with peripheral equipment. Instead, hundreds of open-source enthusiasts, loosely organized and uncompensated, have both directed and executed the work of enhancing the Linux platform. One can debate its merits, but one can't dispute that many sophisticated users choose it for a significant number of important tasks.

Over the years, Linux has made an important transition from an operating system created mainly by volunteers with little money to gain from its success to one that is supported by many employees of companies that do have money to gain. As Linux's popularity has grown, technology companies have started contributing code and evangelizing the operating system. As of 2006, large companies, including IBM, Computer Associates, and HP, contribute code to Linux development. IBM has modified Linux for use with its zSeries mainframes. Similarly, Intel is working to

46. "Worldwide Client and Server Operating Environments 2005–2009, Forecast: Modest Growth Ahead" (IDC report no. 34599), December 2005, table 2.

make its chips and Linux fully compatible, presumably in order to sell chips for "Lintel" equipment and to reduce its dependence on the Windows software platforms.

Customers who choose Linux today are different from those who choose proprietary operating systems for servers such as Sun's Solaris or Windows. Numerous information technology specialists in charge of corporate and government networks have embraced Linux. They can customize Linux to their own needs, since they can see and alter its source code. IT specialists are able to fix bugs in Linux without help or permission from the licensor. Desktop users, on the other hand, rarely benefit from access to the operating system's source code. Also, volunteer programmers don't have as much incentive as salaried employees to do the more mundane work necessary to make a desktop operating system easier to use—for example, writing the device drivers necessary for the thousands of peripherals available for PCs to be compatible with the operating system or making the user interface easy for novices to master. With the increasing popularity of Linux, however, some vendors of peripheral equipment are starting to fill the device driver void themselves, a process that is arguably made easier by easy access to the source code. But until enough desktop users demand such drivers for Linux, most of the burden of producing them will continue to fall on volunteers, making it more difficult to balance the sides of the Linux platform. The challenge of producing an easy-to-use graphical interface seems to have proven even more difficult.

To date, Linux has yet to dent the market for desktop operating systems, with only a 2 percent share of such systems delivered in 2004. Still, that's doing about as well as Apple, which has been around much longer.[47] If the un-owned Linux desktop platform does continue to make headway against the competition, it seems most likely that the advance will be led by large businesses that have long experience with Linux servers and that can provide internal support for free applications. Or it may come in rapidly emerging economies such as South Korea, where the government subsidizes Linux applications development, or China,

47. Ibid.

where mandatory use of Chinese-produced software by government agencies has motivated adoption of Linux by many local and national organizations.[48]

In any case, the success that Linux has attained has interesting implications for those contemplating developing software platforms. On the one hand, it provides an alternative production model that has obviously achieved some successes. Many companies are learning from the Linux experience. On the other hand, it is a bit scary to proprietary software firms and their backers. One wouldn't have thought that an un-owned platform that is free to all sides of the market could have taken almost 20 percent of the server business in competition with Microsoft, Novell, and Sun in about a decade.

Yet open source hasn't had any significant impact yet on video games, personal digital assistants, mobile telephones, or digital devices. We therefore won't see it mentioned much in what follows. We turn next to a hardware-software platform that looks almost identical to PCs but has evolved very differently—video game consoles.

INSIGHTS

• The PC software platform has changed the way computer power is delivered to businesses and consumers. Today it coordinates a nonintegrated and decentralized process in which separate firms deliver hardware, peripherals, applications, and software platforms.

• Killer applications were important for the early success of PC software platforms; many people bought systems because they could run a particular killer application, such as VisiCalc. That in turn stimulated more applications developers to write for the underlying software platform.

• Platform "evangelists" were also crucial to the success of PC platforms. They helped persuade independent developers to write applications

48. http://news.com.com/China+Local+software+for+local+people/
2100-7344_3-5951629.html; http://linux.slashdot.org/linux/05/03/29/0322248.
shtml?tid=163&tid=190&tid=106.

for the platform. Evangelism went hand-in-hand with the development of software services for developers that were made available through APIs.

• All commercial PC software platform vendors have adopted the "charge users/let developers free-ride" pricing structure in order to encourage software developers to write applications for their platform.

• Four key strategies helped Microsoft obtain the leading position in personal computers: (1) offering lower prices to users than its competitors; (2) intensely promoting API-based software services to developers; (3) promoting the development of peripherals, sometimes through direct subsidies, in order to increase the value of the Windows platform to developers and users; and (4) continually developing software services that provide value to developers directly and to end users indirectly.

5

PONG

Video games are bad for you? That's what they said about rock and roll.

—*Shigeru Miyamoto, the most famous game developer in history (Mario Bros and Donkey Kong, among others)*[1]

INSIDE THIS CHAPTER

· What ignited the market for video games

· Why video game business models are different from other software platforms

· How the video game industry operates today

In 1991, Trip Hawkins seemed to be trying to do for video games what Bill Gates had done for PCs. He started 3DO as a new kind of game console company. Instead of making its own consoles, it licensed its technology to manufacturers in return for royalties. Matsushita, Sanyo, AT&T, and other major players agreed to make 3DO's Multiplayer, a 32-bit CD-based console released in 1993. Further departing from industry practice, 3DO charged game developers royalties that were about a fifth of what its competitors were asking.

It was an interesting idea, but it didn't work. Even though analysts had said the Multiplayer was based on some of the finest technology in the market, the public didn't rush to buy it. It isn't hard to see why. The hardware manufacturers sold the Multiplayer for $700, compared to prices ranging from $150 to $200 for competing consoles from Sony and Sega. There weren't many games for 3DO's product either, despite the

---

1. http://www.answers.com/topic/shigeru-miyamoto.

Chapter 5: Video Game Console Timeline

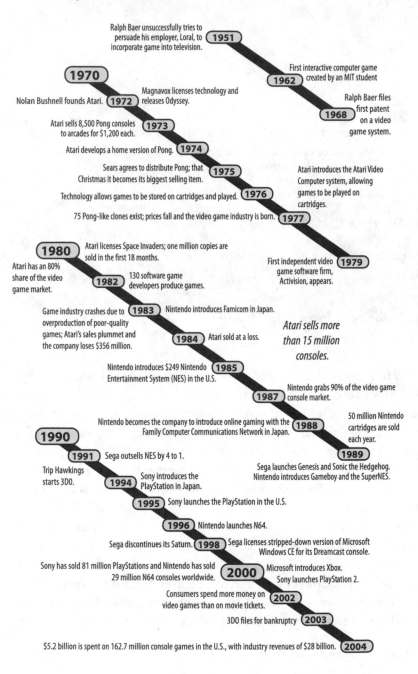

Ralph Baer unsuccessfully tries to persuade his employer, Loral, to incorporate game into television. **1951**

First interactive computer game created by an MIT student **1962**

1970

Magnavox licenses technology and releases Odyssey.

Nolan Bushnell founds Atari. **1972**

Ralph Baer files first patent **1968** on a video game system.

Atari sells 8,500 Pong consoles to arcades for $1,200 each. **1973**

Atari develops a home version of Pong. **1974**

Sears agrees to distribute Pong; that Christmas it becomes its biggest selling item. **1975**

Atari introduces the Atari Video Computer system, allowing games to be played on cartridges.

Technology allows games to be stored on cartridges and played. **1976**

75 Pong-like clones exist; prices fall and the video game industry is born. **1977**

1980
Atari licenses Space Invaders; one million copies are sold in the first 18 months.

Atari has an 80% share of the video game market.

First independent video game software firm, Activision, appears. **1979**

1982
130 software game developers produce games.

Game industry crashes due to overproduction of poor-quality games; Atari's sales plummet and the company loses $356 million. **1983** Nintendo introduces Famicom in Japan.

Atari sells more than 15 million consoles.

1984 Atari sold at a loss.

Nintendo introduces $249 Nintendo Entertainment System (NES) in the U.S. **1985**

Nintendo grabs 90% of the video game **1987** console market.

Nintendo becomes the company to introduce online gaming with the Family Computer Communications Network in Japan. **1988**

50 million Nintendo cartridges are sold each year.

1990

1991 Sega outsells NES by 4 to 1.

1989

Trip Hawkings starts 3DO.

1994 Sony introduces the PlayStation in Japan.

Sega launches Genesis and Sonic the Hedgehog. Nintendo introduces Gameboy and the SuperNES.

1995 Sony launches the PlayStation in the U.S.

1996 Nintendo launches N64.

Sega discontinues its Saturn. **1998** Sega licenses stripped-down version of Microsoft Windows CE for its Dreamcast console.

Sony has sold 81 million PlayStations and Nintendo has sold 29 million N64 consoles worldwide. **2000** Microsoft introduces Xbox. Sony launches PlayStation 2.

Consumers spend more money on video games than on movie tickets. **2002**

3DO files for bankruptcy **2003**

$5.2 billion is spent on 162.7 million console games in the U.S., with industry revenues of $28 billion. **2004**

low royalty rate developers paid. Game developers likely figured out that at more than three times the price of the competition, Multiplayers weren't going to fly off the shelves. There wouldn't be enough demand to justify the cost of writing games. In 1996, 3DO stopped selling console technology, and in 2003 it filed for bankruptcy.[2]

3DO tried a product pricing and integration strategy that was much closer to the long-standing PC model than the long-standing video game console model. As it went under, it became the exception that proved the rule.

Almost from the beginning, makers of game consoles have followed an approach that stands the PC model on its head. They integrate the hardware and the core software. Consumers can't get one without the other. They sell this integrated console to end users at a price that often doesn't even cover the manufacturing cost. The console producers make their profits from games they develop for their own consoles and, more important, from licensing their console's proprietary coding information to third-party game developers.

The difference between the PC strategy and the video game strategy presents an intriguing puzzle. Video game consoles and PCs are technically similar. Developers write games for both platforms and consumers use both platforms for playing games. The console platform rules, though. U.S. consumers spent five times more on video games than on PC games in the first half of 2005. Indeed, video games have become a major entertainment industry. By 2002, consumers around the world were spending more money annually on video games than on movie tickets. That year, the top-selling game, Halo 2, sold 2.4 million copies and earned about $125 million in its first *24 hours* on store shelves. That was more than three times as much the highest-grossing Hollywood movie that year, *Spider-Man 2*, which earned a mere $40.5 million in its first day.[3]

This chapter examines the puzzle of the video game pricing model in the course of describing an industry that has revolutionized how people

2. Harvard Business School, "Power Play (C): 3DO in 32-bit Video Games," July 12, 1995; http://en.wikipedia.org/wiki/The_3DO_Company.

3. http://www.npd.com/dynamic/releases/press_050728.html; video game sales were $21 billion in 2002, whereas box office sales were $19 billion. "Gaming's New Frontier," *The Economist*, October 2, 2003; http://www.usatoday.com/life/movies/news/2004-07-01-spider-man-2-opening_x.htm; http://money.cnn.com/2004/11/11/technology/halosales/.

play games, a millennia-old pastime, and how people, especially those who grew up after the twin birth of the PC and the video game console in the late 1970s, entertain themselves at home.

The Birth of the Video Game Industry

In 1951, Ralph Baer was designing a television for aerospace electronics manufacturer Loral. He wanted to make the television interactive and incorporate a game, but his employer didn't like the idea. Fifteen years later, working for another defense contractor, Baer got permission to try television-based games. His team developed a chase game, tennis, Ping-Pong, and a "gun" that could sense light on the television screen. He filed what is considered the first patent on a video game system in 1968.[4]

Magnavox, a television manufacturer, licensed the technology and released the Odyssey game system in early 1972. For $100 it came with twelve games, each on a printed circuit board. For another $25 buyers could get a rifle to use with the system. Magnavox limited retail outlets for the Odyssey to its own dealers. Its advertising—plus its exclusive use of Magnavox dealers—suggested, incorrectly, that people needed a Magnavox television to use the system. Magnavox might have stimulated its television sales with this strategy had Odyssey been more appealing. Instead, it limited sales to the 10 percent of households that had a Magnavox television. It sold more than 100,000 game systems by year end, but sales quickly trailed off, and Odyssey was pulled from the market.[5]

Meanwhile, significant innovations in games were taking place elsewhere. Nolan Bushnell had played the Spacewar game on a minicomputer while in graduate school. Created in 1962 by an MIT student, it used the machine's toggle switches as controls for dueling rocket ships.[6]

4. Rusel Demaria and Johnny L. Wilson, *High Score!: The Illustrated History of Electronic Games* (Berkeley, Calif.: McGraw-Hill/Osborne, 2002), p. 14; http://www.emuunlim.com/doteaters/play1sta1.htm.

5. http://www.pong-story.com/odyssey.htm;   http://www.gbrc.jp/GBRC.files/journal/abas/pdf/ABAS4-1-1.pdf. David Sheff, *Game Over: Press Start to Continue* (Wilton, Conn.: Game Press, 1999), p. 141.

6. Demaria and Wilson, *High Score!*, p. 12; Steven L. Kent, *The Ultimate History of Video Games* (Roseville, Calif.: Prima Publishing, 2001), p. 18.

A decade later, Bushnell came up with the idea of using the new microprocessor technology to develop a coin-operated arcade version of Spacewar called Computer Space. The console he conceived and licensed to a manufacturer had a circuit board with only Computer Space hardwired into it, a black-and-white monitor, and a mechanism for handling coins put in through a coin drop. Computer Space didn't do well—it was too complex for inebriated bar patrons. The manufacturer liked the console design, however, and asked Bushnell for another game. They couldn't come to terms, however, and Bushnell started Atari instead.[7]

Atari's first game hit was a version of Ping-Pong called Pong. Atari sold 8,500 Pong consoles in its first year, a high volume for an arcade-type game, for about $1,200 each. The buyers got to keep all the quarters that people paid to play the game. Atari, like Apple in PCs, did everything—it designed the hardware and software for the arcade game consoles and manufactured them itself.

The arcade game business boomed in the 1970s. Numerous variants on Pong were introduced as multiple players searched for the next killer app for arcade machines. Over time, arcade games have declined as home video games have become more popular. We focus exclusively on the latter in what follows.

Magnavox Collects

Ralph Baer patented the idea of projecting electronic games onto a television screen and the design of a Ping-Pong game. Magnavox sued Atari for patent infringement and claimed that Bushnell had gotten the idea for Pong from seeing the Odyssey demo in a trade show. Bushnell managed to negotiate an out-of-court settlement with Magnavox that allowed Atari to become Magnavox's sole licensee in exchange for a one-time fixed fee of $700,000. As more Pong-based games came into the market, Magnavox successfully prosecuted a number of patent claims during the 1970s. Most game system makers paid Magnavox royalties for use of its video game patents. Magnavox reportedly received more than $80 million in royalty payments or settlement checks.

7. Sheff, *Game Over*, p. 135. http://lavender.fortunecity.com/fullmonty/22/atari.htm.

Although a television maker for living rooms tried to start the home video game industry, it was an arcade game maker for bars that succeeded. Atari developed a home version of Pong in 1974. Having seen the Odyssey system fizzle, retailers weren't interested. But in 1975, Sears agreed to distribute it, and ordered 150,000 systems. At $100 each, they flew off the shelves. By Christmas, Pong had become the biggest-selling item at Sears, with lines of parents waiting outside the stores.[8]

Meanwhile General Instruments had developed a $5 chip with four tennis-like games and two shooting games programmed into it. That allowed any toy maker to produce Pong clones. Dozens of manufacturers introduced game systems based on these chips. By 1977 there were almost 75 Pong-style clones, each of which sold for a few dollars. The home video game industry had arrived.

These early manufacturers sold complete systems that included one or more games. Consumers had no way to install additional games. These were single-sided businesses. Moreover, the machines didn't make significant use of microprocessors or rely on software to develop the games.

The Emergence of the Video Game Platform

The foundations for the two-sided business model that dominates the video game industry today were laid in the late 1970s. Video games were separated from the console so that end users could add games over time. This separation made it possible for companies to specialize in developing games for these consoles. It also raised the basic pricing question: Should console makers raise prices for the console, given that third-party games make those consoles more valuable, or should console makers figure out some way to charge third-party game producers for games—or both?

8. http://en.wikipedia.org/wiki/Pong; Demaria and Wilson, *High Score!*, p. 26.

Adding Games

In 1976, Fairchild Camera introduced the Channel F console. It could play games stored on cartridges. Each cartridge had a memory chip that had one or more games programmed into it. Fairchild sold the cartridges for $19.95 each and eventually released twenty-one versions of them. The Channel F console itself went for about $170.

A year after Channel F came out, Atari introduced the Video Computer System (VCS). It had an 8-bit microprocessor and could play games that came in cartridges. The console sold for $199—a little more than manufacturing cost—and the "carts" containing the games sold for $30 each (it cost less than $10 to manufacture a cartridge).[9] The console came with what became an important peripheral, a joystick.

The Atari VCS didn't sell well at first. That changed in 1980 when it licensed the popular arcade game, Space Invaders. This killer app for the VCS sold one million copies in its first 18 months, and helped Atari sell more than 15 million VCS consoles between 1979 and 1982. Atari earned about $512 million in 1980 and had an 80 percent share of the gaming market. As an Atari history Web site notes, "designers had unknowingly created a console whose hidden potential was quickly discovered by programmers who created games far outperforming what the console was originally conceived to do."[10]

From then on, video game consoles have been based on microprocessors and games have been stored mainly on removable media rather than being hardwired into the console. The Atari VCS was an inflection point for the video game industry.

Sell the Blades

Now that it had separated the console and the games, Atari—and its copycat competitors—had more flexibility in how they priced their products. Earlier, single-game console makers had to recover their investments

9. Demaria and Wilson, *High Score!*, p. 29; Kent, *The Ultimate History of Video Games*, p. 107; http://en.wikipedia.org/wiki/Atari_2600.

10. http://en.wikipedia.org/wiki/Atari_2600; http://www.biggeworld.com/archive/atarishift.html; http://www.atarimuseum.com/videogames/consoles/atari_videogame_consoles.htm.

and earn a return from selling the integrated game consoles. They had to do it in a hurry before a rival came out with a more attractive game.

Atari decided to sell the VCS at or below manufacturing cost and make its profit from selling games over time to its installed base of console owners. This was a novel strategy in the 1970s: computer makers then were giving away software to sell more hardware, from which they earned their profits. Atari turned this strategy upside down. Like many critical innovations, it is obvious in hindsight. The economic theory of two-part pricing offers some hints as to Atari's thinking and also suggests why this approach worked for video game consoles but not other computer hardware.[11] (We return to these matters in Chapter 10.)

There's an old business strategy often described as giving away razors to sell blades. It isn't literally used much by razor manufacturers anymore. But the basic idea is still employed by many other makers of durable goods who sell the durable good at little or no markup over cost, or even at a loss, and make their profit from products that work with the durable good. The basic idea is that selling the razor at cost, or even at a loss, encourages people to buy the razor and increases the demand for blades. Technically, the razor and blades are complements: because lowering the price of the razor raises the demand for blades, which are sold at a profit, the optimal razor price is lower than it would be for a firm that didn't sell blades.

But there is more to the story. Not only can the razor-blade business make money from people who buy blades, it can make more money from people who shave a lot, either because they have fast-growing beards or because they care more about their appearance. By making money mainly or exclusively on the blades, the business sorts customers so that those who value the system (razor + blade) more end up paying more for it.

11. Thomas T. Nagle and Reed K. Holden, *The Strategy and Tactics of Pricing*, 3rd ed. (Englewood Cliffs, N.J.: Prentice-Hall, 2002); Richard Schmalensee, "Monopolistic Two-Part Pricing Arrangements," *Bell Journal of Economics* 11 (Autumn 1981): 445–466.

Technically, this is a two-part tariff, consisting of an access fee (the price of the razor) plus a usage fee (the price of the blade). Here the blade can be thought of as having two related roles. It meters the use of the durable good, and it sorts customers into those who are willing to pay more and those who are willing to pay less. These metering devices tend to increase profits and help companies better recover their fixed costs of investment. Because it is particularly attractive to make money on the blades, it is especially attractive to reduce the price of the razor, perhaps to below cost, or perhaps even to zero in extreme cases.

For video game console makers this razor-blade strategy made a lot of sense. Getting the console into the hands of many people increased the demand for the games it could play. Moreover, it made buying a console less risky for households, who had no good way of knowing how valuable the console would be until they saw the games produced for it. The game-console company, which was in the best position to forecast the quality of those games, took the risk: it lost money if consumers didn't buy many games, and it made money if they did. The people who ultimately bought a lot of games were those who valued the console the most, so making profits mainly or even entirely on games enabled the console makers to earn the most from those willing to pay the most for their system.

Even though royalties are paid to console makers by game developers, the above discussion implicitly assumes that they are passed along dollar-for-dollar to consumers. In this textbook case, the only reason to charge royalties to developers rather than directly to consumers is convenience. As we discuss in Chapter 10, however, because competition among game developers involves the production of highly differentiated products, even if convenience were not an issue, console makers would probably earn more charging game developers.

The video game pricing strategy wouldn't have made sense for computer makers. There's probably not much correlation between the number of applications that someone uses on a computer and the value that person places on that computer. An engineering firm might use more applications than an electrical utility, but most likely both are using the computer to its maximum capacity. Likewise, there's no apparent reason why an author who uses her PC only for word processing and email will value it any less than a retired person who runs dozens of different applications for fun.

The Emergence of the Two-Sided Platform

When games were separated from consoles, it became possible for console makers to adopt a two-sided model by encouraging other companies to develop games for them. But none took that step at first.

Several game programmers left Atari to start the first independent video game software firm, Activision, in 1979. Using their knowledge of the Atari VCS, they developed a number of very popular games. Other third-party game developers quickly appeared. Some of their games were great. Others weren't.

These game makers had all developed their games without obtaining permission from the console makers or paying anything to them. Since the console makers had invested to develop the underlying technology and were earning returns on those investments by selling games, this third-party entry posed a direct threat to their profits. Notice the contrast with PC software platforms: the major players didn't specialize in making applications for their platforms, had other sources of revenues, and quickly encouraged developers to free-ride on their platform code. The game console makers, on the other hand, saw independent game developers as a scourge. Atari sued Activision repeatedly.[12]

The bottom fell out of the video game industry in 1983. According to one source, of more than 130 significant video game software firms in 1982, only five or six survived the crash. Atari, the industry leader, was the biggest victim. Its sales fell from 5.1 million units in 1982 to 3 million units in 1983, when it lost $356 million, taking down the share price of the company to which Bushnell had sold it, Warner Communications, by 50 percent over 10 months. The next year, Warner sold

12. SN Kent, *The Ultimate History of Video Games*, p. 194.

Atari at a loss. The other publicly held companies such as Mattel and Coleco took similar hits. Many video game magazines also went out of business.[13] We leave the causes of the great video game depression to others. Some say it was the proliferation of bad games. Others at the time thought a fad had merely run its course.

A new entrant, however, soon appeared that embraced the two-sided platform model and reignited the industry. Nintendo introduced its Famicom system in Japan in 1983 and its Nintendo Entertainment System (NES) two years later in the United States. The console was sold for $249, at an operating loss.

Nintendo had actively pursued licensing agreements with third-party game publishers to get a critical mass of games for its new system. However, having witnessed the 1983 U.S. video game market crash, it concluded that in order to succeed, it had to control the quality of games sold for its platform. Accordingly, each NES cartridge contained an authentication chip that was necessary to provide access to the console circuits. Nintendo also kept tight control over the games supplied for its console through its Nintendo "Seal of Quality" policy and, in the interest of quality control, forbade any single developer to publish more than five games every year for the NES.[14]

The authentication chip also allowed Nintendo to charge royalties to third-party game developers, thus converting them from enemies to allies. Nintendo determined the selling price of all games and charged its third-party developers a 20 percent royalty on sales. Since Nintendo made the cartridges and required licensees to order them in advance and be subject to strict inventory management policies, it knew how many

13. Martin Campbell-Kelly, *From Airline Reservations to Sonic The Hedgehog: A History of the Software Industry* (Cambridge, Mass.: MIT Press, 2003), p. 280; http://www.dbbs.gr/hcg/cop36.htm; Warner Communications historical share prices; Kent, *Ultimate History of Video Games*, pp. 239, 252–255; Leonard Herman, *Phoenix: The Fall and Rise of Videogames* (Union City, N.J.: Rolenta Press, 1997), p. 128.

14. Later, several very successful developers such as Acclaim and Konami were granted licenses for an additional five games a year.

games each licensee was producing. Nintendo also adopted the novel policy of prohibiting game makers from publishing their games on a rival system for at least two years.[15]

A year after Nintendo entered, there were more than twenty-four games for the NES. By 1989 Nintendo games were selling at a rate of 50 million cartridges per year. Some of these are all-time classics, such as Donkey-Kong. Nintendo wrote many of its games itself, including Mario Brothers, which was the killer game for the NES. This reflected both its strong previous experience in arcade games and its inability to sign up more than four developers, all Japanese, by NES's launch. Despite countless visits and evangelization efforts, major American developers that had survived the 1983 crash preferred to remain focused on the emerging PC gaming market, which we discuss below.[16]

As Nintendo captured a larger share of the U.S. video game console market—reaching 90 percent in 1987—American third-party game developers began to come on board. At the same time, however, the Federal Trade Commission also started taking an interest in Nintendo. Under its scrutiny, Nintendo stopped setting retail prices for its games, dropped the exclusivity clause in its licensing agreements, and let developers make their own cartridges. Nintendo kept its security chips, though, and continued to charge royalties.[17]

15. Campbell-Kelly, *From Airline Reservations to Sonic The Hedgehog*, pp. 284–286.

16. "Robot Lets Firm Toy with Success: Electronic Playmate Opens Doors for Redmond Video-Game Maker," *The Seattle Times*, February 11, 1986; "Home Electronics: Video Wars," Associated Press, October 16, 1989; Kent, *The Ultimate History of Video Games*, p. 307.

17. http://www.nationmaster.com/encyclopedia/List-of-NES-games; http://www.cyberiapc.com/vgg/nintendo_nes.htm; "Will Justice Dept. Probe Nintendo? (Antitrust Investigation)," *HFD—The Weekly Home Furnishings Newspaper*, December 18, 1989; "Nintendo Agrees to Settle FTC Charges," *Los Angeles Times*, April 11, 1991; "FTC Action Takes No Bite Out of Nintendo (Federal Trade Commission, Nintendo Company Ltd) (Washington Report)," *Discount Store News*, August 5, 1991. Nintendo thought their antitrust problems were over, but not long after the price fixing settlement in 1991 the FTC began a new investigation into monopolization charges. The investigation was dropped in 1992. "FTC Halts Probe of Nintendo: Two-Year Investigation Looked Into Accusations of Antitrust Activity," *Seattle Post-Intelligencer*, December 3, 1992.

The Game Boy

In 1989, Nintendo introduced another gaming platform, the handheld
Game Boy. Like the NES, the Game Boy was initially driven by one killer
app, Tetris. Tetris had been created by a Russian mathematician, Aleksey
Pajitnov. In 1986, Robert Stein, the president of a London-based software
company, encountered a pirated copy of Tetris and negotiated with
Pajitnov for the right to license it. Stein apparently did not realize that
he needed to obtain the rights from the Russian authorities, not Pajitnov.
Stein went on to negotiate deals for the European and American computer
rights to the game before the Russians had actually given him the authority to do so. Atari also obtained the rights to the game and in turn sold
the Japanese coin-operated rights to Sega. Multiple firms obtained the same
rights to Tetris from Stein, who did not have the authority to
issue any of these contracts. At this point Nintendo realized no one truly
owned the rights to Tetris, negotiated with the Russians, and obtained the
worldwide video game rights to Tetris. Nintendo then introduced the
Game Boy handheld console with the Tetris game bundled. The Game
Boy sold over 1 million units and over 2.4 million games in its first year
on the market. By 1992, worldwide shipments were 10 million units per
year.[18]

The licensing contracts for third-party Game Boy developers were
identical to those for the NES. When the Game Boy was first released,
there were only four games in addition to Tetris available, but twenty-
three of the licensees for the NES had signed on to develop more titles.
By May 1990 there were seventy titles available for the Game Boy, and
at the June Expo Center show of the same year there were 200 titles available for trial.[19]

Nintendo's lead didn't last. In 1989, Sega launched its 16-bit console,
Genesis, several months before Nintendo came up with its own 16-bit
Super NES. With its killer game, Sonic the Hedgehog, Genesis had
outsold Super NES four to one by 1991. Sega relied on the same
platform strategy as Nintendo: it used a security system to lock out

18. Kent, *The Ultimate History of Video Games*, pp. 377–381. "Nintendo
Doesn't Intend to Sell 16-Bit Game," *Los Angeles Daily News*, March 23, 1990;
"Grown-up Game Boy Still Has Youthful Charm," *Plain Dealer Cleveland*,
December 22, 1997.

19. "Nintendo Nirvana: Thousands of Devotees of Electronic Games Plan
to Converge on Portland for Expo Center show," *Portland Oregonian*, June
27, 1990; "A Video Shootout in Hand-held Games," *The Dallas Morning*

unlicensed game developers, and it relied on first-party game sales and royalties charged to licensees (virtually identical to those charged by Nintendo) for the bulk of its profits. All subsequent significant game console makers have followed the same basic strategy. While it is possible that the strategy could be improved upon, 3DO's failure suggests that low-priced games can't make up for a high-priced console and that "charge developers/subsidize consoles" is the more profitable model.

The Other Video Game Platform: PC

Personal computers arose as a gaming platform when the first cheap PCs appeared in the wake of the 1983 video game crash. Introduced in 1982 at a price of $600, the Commodore 64 (C64) claimed to rival the Apple II, priced at more than $1,000, in power. The C64 helped shift the market's attention from dedicated video game consoles to PCs.

Trip Hawkins created Electronic Arts in 1983 to develop games for the C64. Within 6 months of introducing its first products, Electronic Arts was supporting the Apple II and the Atari 800, in addition to the C64. When Nintendo introduced the NES in the United States, Electronic Arts refused to support it. Like many others in the industry, Hawkins thought the PC platform had definitively supplanted the console platform as a gaming medium.

Three years and 28 million NES video game consoles later, it became clear that he was wrong. (Note that while Hawkins has gotten two major things wrong so far in this chapter, Electronic Arts is the world's largest game developer, with annual revenues of over $3 billion.) In the 1990s, console game software outsold PC game software by two to one in unit terms and four to one in revenue terms, even though there were nearly ten times more computer game titles than console titles on the market. In 2004, U.S. consumers spent $5.2 billion on 162.7 million console games, compared to $1.1 billion on 45 million PC

News, May 30, 1990; "Atari's Handheld Video Game Bows With Color LCD Monitor," *HFD—The Weekly Home Furnishings Newspaper*, June 12, 1989.

games and $1.0 billion on games for Game Boy and other portable devices.[20]

Clearly, neither of the two overlapping platforms has driven the other out of the market. They are still competing today for both game developers and users, as we discuss later. Remarkably, they are overlapping multisided platforms (see Chapter 3) with opposite two-sided pricing strategies. Their coexistence is a testament to the power of product differentiation in multisided platform industries.

The Sony PlayStation

Sony solidified the two-sided platform model. And it introduced the first commercially successful machine with an operating system and with applications that came on a CD rather than a chip.[21]

Sony's first contact with the video game market occurred when Nintendo approached it in 1988 with a proposal to manufacture a CD-ROM drive for the Super-NES. That deal never materialized, and Sony opted to design its own console. The PlayStation hit the market in 1994 in Japan, and at its 1995 U.S. launch the console sold for $299 and the games for about $40–$50 each.[22] It was competing against Sega's Saturn, Nintendo's Super NES, and later against Nintendo's N64, which was launched in 1996.

Unlike Nintendo and Sega, Sony didn't have much experience in developing games and decided to rely mainly on third parties. By 1999, about 77 percent of the games developed for PlayStation came from third parties, whereas they supplied only 43 percent of N64's games. To ensure

20. "The Power of Nintendo (Direct Marketing Success of Nintendo America Inc.)," *Direct Marketing*, September 1, 1989; Electronic Arts, Income Statement, 2004; Peter Coughlan, "*Competitive Dynamics in Home Video Games* (K): Playstation vs. Nintendo64," Harvard Business Online, June 13, 2001; http://www.writenews.com/2005/021105_gamesales_04.htm.

21. Among a slew of ill-fated video game consoles introduced at the beginning of the 1990s, 3DO's Multiplayer and NEC's Turbografx were the first machines to play games on CDs.

22. http://www.scee.com/about/sonyHistory.jhtml http://en.wikipedia.org/wiki/Sony_Playstation; "Console Yourself—It's Only Money," *The Independent–London*, January 8, 1996.

the availability of some quality titles, the company purchased a leading game developer before launching the PlayStation.[23] Sony also pursued alliances with other developers to secure the exclusive support of their games for its console.

Users preferred the Sony PlayStation because it was sleeker and had more games than Sega's Saturn. Also, though the Saturn came bundled with the highly desirable Virtual Fighter game, it cost $100 more than the PlayStation.[24]

The software platform for the PlayStation was a proprietary Sony operating system developed in-house. It was designed exclusively for the PlayStation and optimized to make the most of the console's hardware capabilities, including a very capable microprocessor. It was also designed to read game software from CD-ROMs, just as PCs did. CD-ROMs were much cheaper to manufacture than cartridges, had more storage capacity, making possible a significant improvement in game complexity, and could be easily obtained if game makers needed to increase production. The only drawback was that the data access speed was somewhat slower. Sega's Saturn also relied on CD-ROMs, but Nintendo decided to continue using cartridges, both for the Super NES and for the N64.

By the time the PlayStation launched, Sony had signed up nearly a hundred game companies, and with its licensees had more than 300 individual game projects under way. An important factor in Sony's success was its provision of an unprecedented array of development tools and software libraries that made it easier to write games to the PlayStation than to the competing systems from Nintendo and Sega. The latter were believed to discriminate in favor of their own game developers when it came to supplying tools. (This is a tension that runs through businesses that produce applications as well as software platforms. Many software platform makers, however, also do applications for their platforms. Providing developers assurance that there is a level playing field is a business necessity.)

Over time Sony has nurtured the PlayStation platform by continuing to encourage third-party game developers. Its library of titles grew

23. Coughlan, "Competitive Dynamics in Home Video Games," p. 1; Kent, *The Ultimate History of Video Games*, p. 505.

24. Kent, *The Ultimate History of Video Games*, p. 517.

from 19 in 1995 to 300 in 1997 and 2,600 in 2000. It managed to sell almost 10 million consoles within its first two years on the market, and 26 million consoles by the end of 1997 (three years after release). Even the launch of Nintendo's N64 in 1996 was not enough to stop it. By 2000, there were more than 81 million PlayStations worldwide, compared to 29 million N64s. Sega's Saturn fared very poorly, with only 17 million units sold by 1998, when it was discontinued. Between 1996 and 2000, PlayStation's market share never dropped below 33 percent.[25]

PlayStation 2

Launched in 2000, PlayStation 2 continued Sony's dominance into the current generation of 128-bit consoles, where it faced Sega's Dreamcast, Nintendo's GameCube, and the new kid on the block, Microsoft's Xbox.

Like the original PlayStation, PlayStation 2 was initially priced at $299 when it was released in the United States. It followed the established industry pattern of selling hardware below cost (at least initially)—according to some estimates, its manufacturing cost was over $400—and recouping through sales of first-party game software and royalties charged to third-party game publishers. Component costs fell over time and manufacturing efficiency increased over time, so that in 2004 a Sony executive could assert that there was a "positive gross margin" on PlayStation 2 sales. But the largest share of PlayStation's profits (between 60 and 70 percent, according to interviews with Sony executives) still comes from sales of Sony-produced games and royalties ($3 to $9 per disk) paid by third-party game publishers.[26]

25. "Sony Sets Up New Games Companies," *Music & Copyright*, February 1, 1995, "PlayStation Game Console Sells More Than One Million Units in November," *Business Wire*, December 8, 1997; "Video Game War Heats Up Sony Re-enters Fray with Playstation 2," *The New Orleans Times-Picayune*, February 19, 2000; "Worldwide Videogame Forecast and Analysis, 2001–2006" (IDC report no. 26906), 2002, table 4; Installed Base "Video Game Consoles: Sony, Nintendo and Sega Brace for Microsoft Challenge," *In-Stat*, December 2000, table 2.

26. Dean Takahashi, *Opening the Xbox* (Prima Lifestyles, 2003); Takao Yuhara, Sony Corporation earnings conference call, January 28, 2004; Adam Brandenburger, "Power Play (C): 3DO in 32-bit Video Games," *Harvard Business Online*, April 10, 1995; Coughlan, "Competitive Dynamics in Home Video Games (K)."

Built around a new processor, the "Emotion Engine," PlayStation 2 was a powerful machine, able to process graphics fifty times faster than the PlayStation 1, according to a standard measure of speed. PlayStation 2 games were loaded on DVDs, with twenty-five times the capacity of a conventional CD. The new console could also play movies stored on DVDs.

The PlayStation 2 suffered, though, from a lack of investment in development tools. Developers complained that the system was very difficult to work with. Shinji Mikami, the designer behind several such hit games, complained that unlike the original PlayStation, the PlayStation 2 had "no library." Developers needed "to create [their] own library, which poses its own set of problems in that there are so many choices to achieve the same effects." And Gozo Kitao, the general manager of Konami, stated, "If you focus on making full use of all the specs, it will be very expensive and time-consuming to produce a game."[27]

In addition to being sparse, the developer tools for PlayStation 2 were also released quite late, only nine months before its Japanese launch. By contrast, game developers for Xbox had received their tools from Microsoft 18 months before that console launched. It is therefore not surprising that at Sony's PlayStation Festival 2000 trade show, which took place about a month before the Japanese launch, only nineteen games were in development for the PlayStation 2.

PlayStation 2 managed to win the support of third-party game developers in part because it was compatible with PlayStation 1. Manufacturers had previously reasoned that incompatibility would help drive sales of game software developed for new machines. It turned out, however, that backward compatibility was especially attractive to PlayStation 1 users, who valued the ability to play their library of games on the new console. These users upgraded even though there were relatively few new games initially available for PlayStation 2. By 2004, PlayStation 2 had more than 1,000 titles, compared to roughly 700 for Xbox and 600 for GameCube.[28]

27. Kent, *The Ultimate History of Video Games*, pp. 568–569.

28. Anthony N. Gihas and Stephanie S. Wissink, "The Video Game Industry" (Piper Jaffray & Co.), April 2005, p. 18.

PlayStation 2 emerged as the clear winner of this round of console competition. In 2004, it sold 15.2 million consoles worldwide and had a 58 percent market share.[29] Sony has announced that it hopes to transform its game console into a rich home entertainment device. But so does Microsoft. The bundling of new features this broader role involves has become a major focus of the competition between consoles.

The Xbox

Microsoft made its first foray into the video game market when Sega decided to use a stripped-down version of Microsoft's Windows CE software platform as a development environment for its 1998 Dreamcast console. Sega had invested heavily in Dreamcast development tools. It standardized the interface between its development environment and the Windows CE development environment. As a result, developers could easily port games to and from PCs. Good theory, bad execution. The performance of game software using the Microsoft APIs was much slower than that of software using Sega's original Ninja library of APIs. In the end, only one of the forty games available within six months of Dreamcast's launch used the joint development tools.[30] Although the reasons for the failure may be different, Microsoft, like 3DO, found that licensing software platforms to hardware makers was not the road to riches in the video game industry.

Microsoft got the execution right the next time. Rather than build a new gaming platform for its Xbox, Microsoft relied on a version of the Windows NT/2000 operating system, stripped down and modified in order to focus it on gaming. It built the Xbox software platform around DirectX, a collection of Windows software services that were specially designed to help PC game developers deal with the diversity of user hardware, particularly the sound and graphics cards that were so important to games. In the words of J Allard, one of the key executives on the

29. "Worldwide Videogame Hardware and Software 2004–2008 Forecast and Analysis: Predicting the Future" (IDC report no. 31260), May 2004.

30. Stegan Thomke and Andrew Robertson, "Project Dreamcast: Serious Play at Sega Enterprises Ltd.," Harvard Business Online, September 9, 1999, p. 11.

Xbox team: "We started taking things out of Windows NT, or rather putting things in DirectX, to put the software together. It was more or less a DirectX operating system."[31]

The Xbox operating system resides on the DVD disk with each game rather than, as in a PC, on the console's hard disk. This enables developers to customize the operating system to some extent and thereby to enhance memory usage. If a game does not make use of online capabilities, for example, the corresponding networking code can be left off the DVD.

The original Xbox hardware had two important innovations: an 8-gigabyte hard drive and a high-speed Ethernet adapter. Earlier consoles had not included hard drives because of the cost involved. Indeed, Microsoft spent almost $50 per machine for the hard drive. However, the company reasoned that a hard drive would give more flexibility to game developers and would help improve the online gaming experience by providing a storage medium for game data.

PlayStation 2 and GameCube did not come with built-in network connections but could be connected through either a 56K modem or an Ethernet adapter. By contrast, Microsoft chose to integrate a broadband-only connector to simplify the life of online game developers, who did not program for slower forms of Internet access. Of course, this was a gamble on the growing penetration of broadband connectivity, but it was one that paid off. Microsoft's subscription-based online gaming service, Xbox Live, has grown from 750,000 users in 2004 to about 2 million in 2005. The PlayStation 2 boasts the same number of online gamers, but that is a much lower proportion of the console's installed base, 6 percent of the PlayStation 2 installed base compared to 16 percent for Xbox.[32]

To ensure the availability of attractive first-party titles, Microsoft recruited game developers and acquired game companies. These

31. Takahashi, *Opening the Xbox*, pp. 150–153.

32. "Microsoft Quarterly Revenue Tops $10 Billion Launch of Office 2003 and Strength in PC Market Fuels Demand for Desktop Software," *PR Newswire*, January 22, 2004; "Xbox Dedication: With 3-Day Jump, Greenfield Teen Finds Lot to Love in New Machine," *The Milwaukee Journal Sentinel*, November 22, 2005; "Nintendo Gives Gamers a Reason to Chat," *The Boston Globe*, May 23, 2005.

supplemented its in-house team, which had done only PC games. The most significant acquisition was the highly acclaimed game development firm Bungie, whose Halo has been by far the strongest selling Xbox game and has largely driven purchases of Xbox.[33] Overall, there were three first-party and twelve third-party titles available for Xbox when it was released. That number doubled to more than thirty games available during the 2001 holiday season.[34]

Even though Microsoft chose to follow video game industry practice, rather than its policy regarding PC games, and to act as a careful gatekeeper for third-party games with the Xbox, it courted developers to an extent unprecedented in the video game industry. Before the Xbox launch, it set up an Independent Developer Program. It also established the Incubator Program to encourage smaller developers by providing free software tools, and it waived the normal prepublishing requirements.[35] The presence of DirectX and its evangelization were particularly successful. The tools used for creating Xbox games were quite similar to PC game tools, which made life particularly easy for developers with PC experience.

Like most consoles since the Atari VCS, the Xbox console is a loss leader: its launch price was $260, which was $100 less than its estimated manufacturing cost. Microsoft has continued to lose at least $100 on each console sold, as price cuts have tracked reductions in manufacturing costs. From its 2001 launch through December 2003, the company had gross revenues of $961 million from Xbox software sales—direct sales of its own games plus $7 per unit royalties levied on third-party games—and $313 million gross revenues from sales of peripherals such

33. Analysts estimated that over 80% of Xboxes sold at launch were sold with Halo. Takahashi, *Opening the Xbox*, p. 319.

34. "Microsoft Playing Out of the Box," *The Hartford Courant*, November 4, 2001; "Game on! Sony, Nintendo and Microsoft Get Ready to Rumble in the Battle for North America's $8-Billion Video-Game Market," *Winnipeg Free Press*, November 10, 2001; "Game Wars," *The Tampa Tribune*, November 19, 2001.

35. Microsoft PressPass, "Microsoft Embraces the Worldwide Independent Video Game Developer Community," November 7, 2000 (http://www.microsoft. com/presspass/press/2000/Nov00/XPKPR.asp [downloaded 21 June 2004]); http://news.com.com/2100-1040-248875.html?legacy = cnet.

as game controllers, memory cards and other plug-ins, and remote controls. (First-party games accounted for roughly 70 percent of total game software revenues over this period.) Because of negative hardware margins, however, through the end of 2003 Xbox had incurred a total loss of roughly $590 million.[36]

The foregoing may suggest that Microsoft simply accepted the core elements of the standard video game business model. In fact, in the process of creating Xbox it challenged almost every element of that model, from the vertical integration between software and hardware in the platform and the below-cost pricing of the console to the royalty-based model with quality control for third-party games. For example, it considered making money on the console but learned from developers that they wouldn't write games unless they were confident that many consumers would buy the console. The fact that Microsoft ended up adopting the standard business model despite its initial skepticism suggests that model makes good economic sense for this industry, at least at this time.

Microsoft (Almost) Channels 3DO

Xbox started as Project Midway in 1999 inside Microsoft—a bow to the critical World War II battle in the Pacific and an expression of the company's intention to produce something midway between a PC gaming platform and a console. Indeed, the original idea was to come up with a low-cost personal computer specialized for playing games, in order to counter the threat posed by Sony's ambitious PlayStation 2.[37] Remarkably, the Windows Entertainment Platform, as the machine was to be called in the beginning, was initially supposed to run a future version of the Windows 98 operating system, function as an open platform like the PC (in the sense that game developers could program anything they wanted without constraints or having to pay royalties), and be made according to Microsoft's specifications by licensed third-party OEMs. Microsoft knew about 3DO's failure six years earlier, but it concluded that overpriced hardware had been the main flaw and decided it had what it took to make the

36. This estimate and the next are based on J.P. Morgan North American Equity Research, "Microsoft Corporation: Patience Is a Virtue," January 6, 2004, table 12.

37. Takahashi, *Opening the Xbox*.

(continued)

same strategy succeed. After all, if anyone could successfully bring the PC platform model into the gaming industry, it would surely be Microsoft.

Not surprisingly, the initial hardware strategy did not work. Dell, Panasonic (Matsushita), Sharp, Toshiba, Mitsubishi, and Samsung all declined to produce hardware under license, arguing (quite reasonably) that there was no way for them to make money. Everyone was aware of the negative hardware margins characteristic of the video game industry, and a third-party hardware maker had no way to recoup its losses because it did not sell any game software. In the end, Microsoft had to rely on a contract manufacturer for Xbox, just like all other console vendors.

Similarly, the Xbox was in the end designed as a closed system, and Microsoft charged royalties to third-party developers, just like all the other console vendors. One reason for this shift was that Microsoft came to the conclusion that it was important to control the quality of titles supplied for the console. (In particular, it understood that it had to exclude the mediocre games that flooded the PC platform, especially if it planned to charge royalties to developers; a security system was accordingly developed to prevent quick-and-dirty porting of PC games.) A second reason for this shift was financial: after long brainstorming sessions with senior executives, it became clear that the company needed the royalty revenues from third-party game developers to help offset the losses incurred on console sales. The case for royalties was even stronger when Microsoft realized it had to supply the hardware itself. In the end, it settled on the $7 per game royalty charged by everyone else.

Today's Video Game Industry

When Pong came out thirty years ago, mainly young boys played video games. The industry has grown up along with those boys: the average age of video game players had crept up to 28 by 2004. More games are written for young adults: they are rated, like movies, and many have explicit sexual content. Online gaming is also beginning to take off, to the point that the "currency" used in these games is now bought and sold on eBay so that game players can purchase some of the virtual weapons of war needed in their favorite online games.[38]

38. "Reel fakes; Phony Web sites are the movie studios' latest advertising tactic. But have they gone too far?," *St. Paul Pioneer Press*, May 30, 2004. In the United

The video game industry had global revenues of $28 billion in 2004 from the sale of video game consoles and games. It is still only one-fifth the overall size of the movie industry, which had global revenues of $129 billion in 2004 from all sources, although, as mentioned earlier, video game sales exceed movie ticket sales. But the video game industry has grown at an average rate of 17 percent per year in the last four years, compared with 4 percent for movies, and if these trends continue, video games will overtake movies in a decade.[39] Whether they do or do not, what is striking is how these software platforms coupled to specialized computers have revolutionized home entertainment.

Console Makers

At the software platform level, the video game industry is far less concentrated than the PC industry. In 2004, Sony's PlayStation (1 and 2) accounted for about 65 percent of both console and game sales worldwide. Xbox was second in console sales, with a 17.6 percent share, and had a 15.5 percent share of software sales. And Nintendo's GameCube also had a 16.9 percent share of console sales, which well exceeds Apple's 4 percent share in PCs.[40]

Though there has generally been a clear leader among each crop of new consoles, none has attained shares like those enjoyed by Microsoft in PCs. Why not? After all, video games have the same sorts of network effects: users like platforms with more games, and developers like

---

States, for example, rating is done by the Entertainment Software Rating Board. There are similar organizations in many other countries, including Japan, Australia, and Germany. http://en.wikipedia.org/wiki/Entertainment_Software_Rating_Board "Patti Waldmeir: Cyber World is Heading for Regulation," March 30, 2005.

39. "Global—Movies & Entertainment—Market Value," Datamonitor Market Research Profiles, May 1, 2004; "Worldwide Videogame Forecast and Analysis, 2001–2006" (IDC report no. 26906), 2002, table 20 (derived 2000 revenues from growth percentage and 2001 numbers).

40. "Worldwide Videogame Hardware and Software 2004–2008 Forecast and Analysis: Predicting the Future (IDC report no. 31260)," May 2004; "Worldwide Client and Server Operating Environments 2004–2008 Forecast: Modest Growth Ahead" (IDC report no. 34599), December 2005. Apple's share is 3.7%.

platforms with more users. There are scale economies in software platforms and scale and learning economies in console production.

We can see at least three reasons.

First, there has been less demand by customers for standardization of video game consoles. People don't use these devices for the sort of collaborative work that requires file sharing on PCs and that places a premium on compatibility. If Billy has a PlayStation, he might actually prefer that his buddy Johnny buy an Xbox; that way Billy will get to play a new set of games. In addition, games aren't like word-processing packages that people keep upgrading. Game players like diversity, just as moviegoers and television watchers do. Indeed, until the PlayStation, console vendors explicitly rejected backward compatibility to differentiate new products from old ones; that stands in sharp contract to the considerable investments Apple and Microsoft regularly make to ensure that new versions of their operating systems are able to run old applications. As the stock of games increased, console makers realized that some game players didn't want to lose their entire investment in games or to have to maintain two consoles. Nevertheless, as the leap-frog competition in this industry shows, consumers care far more about "new features" than backward compatibility of their games or having the same console as their friends do. The demand for product differentiation counters direct network effects and makes it hard for a single platform to emerge triumphant and secure.

A second reason why console leaders' shares have stayed well short of 100 percent is related to their basic business model. By pricing consoles low (at or below manufacturing cost) and relying on games (their own and third parties') for profit, they have been able to weaken consumers' resistance to buying new consoles before the full set of compatible games is known.[41] Because consoles are both differentiated and relatively cheap, there is significant multihoming on the consumer side in this market: 60

41. It is worth noting just how much cheaper these consoles are than similarly equipped PCs. The Xbox 360, for instance, comes with a Power PC processor, 500 megabytes of memory, and an operating system that allows users to play movies and connect to the Internet. At $399, it is around a tenth of what a similarly powerful Apple PC costs. See the prices for Apple Power Mac G5 at http://store.apple.com/, checked August 22, 2005.

Table 5.1
Technical Specifications for Selected Consoles

Console	CPU Width	CPU Speed	Memory	Media	Release Date
Atari VCS 2600	8-bit	1.19 MHz	128 bytes	4 kb	1977
NES	8-bit	1.79 MHz	2 kb	0.5 Mb	1983
Genesis	16-bit	7.61 MHz	64 kb	4 Mb	1989
SNES	16-bit	3.58 MHz	128 kb	6 Mb	1991
PlayStation	32-bit	33 MHz	2 Mb	CD (650 Mb)	1994
Saturn	32-bit	2 × 28.6 MHz	2 Mb	CD (650 Mb)	1994
N64	64-bit	93.75 MHz	4 Mb	64 Mb	1996
Dreamcast	128/64-bit	200 MHz	16 Mb	1 Gb	1998
PlayStation II	128-bit	300 MHz	32 Mb	DVD (4 Gb)	2000
Xbox	128-bit	733 MHz	64 Mb	DVD (8 Gb)	2001
Game Cube	128-bit	485 MHz	40 Mb	1.5 Gb	2001

percent of American households who play video games own more than one console.[42]

Last, technology has moved fast enough (Table 5.1) that using technological advances to make significantly better consoles and games has helped console makers displace or least seriously challenge the leading platform maker several times in the short history of the industry. From 1989 to 1994, Sega's Genesis machine was clearly the leading console, but it was displaced by the Nintendo Super NES shortly after its 1995 launch. After a very brief reign, the Super NES was outsold by the PlayStation in 1996. The PlayStation led the market until 2001, when it was replaced by the PlayStation 2, which, as this is

42. "Tales of the Gamer: IDC's 2004 Videogamer Survey" (IDC report no. 31760), September 2004, fig. 7.

written (just after the Xbox 360 launch), remains the market leader.[43] Network effects don't always favor incumbents: a hot new console can attract consumers because it plays a few great games, or it can attract game developers because they can obtain its software platform and development tools to write great games at reasonable cost, or both. Once both sides race to climb on board a hot new platform, there is little a market leader with an inferior platform can do to lure them back.

The software platform has become an important part of this competition. As we have seen above, Xbox placed unprecedented emphasis on the software platform. Although many see Sony's strategy as quite different because it emphasizes hardware capabilities, a closer look makes it clear that PlayStation's appeal to developers also rests on the extensive software development tools that Sony and licensees provide.[44]

Game Developers and Publishers

Since Activision began writing third-party games in 1979, this niche in the ecosystem has grown rapidly (Table 5.2). By 2005, the bulk of games were developed by third-party publishers. Nintendo, for example, developed only 10 percent of the games currently available for its GameCube and Sony only 9 percent for its PlayStation 2.[45]

Electronic Arts

Electronic Arts (EA) was founded by entrepreneur Trip Hawkins after he left Apple Computer in 1982. EA started as a game developer for the PC platform and, having observed the 1983 video game crash, ignored Nintendo's NES console initially. Later Hawkins admitted his mistake, and EA entered the console gaming market in 1990 as a licensee of Sega's Genesis.

Today EA is the world's largest video game publisher, with 2005 fiscal year sales of $3 billion and market capitalization in 2005 of over $16

43. IDC reports nos. 31260, 29404, 28282, and 26906; "Video Game Consoles: Sony, Nintendo and Sega Brace for Microsoft Challenge," *In-Stat*, December 2000, table 2.

44. See, for example, "Video Games: A Serious Contest," *The Economist*, May 8, 2004.

45. http://www.us.playstation.com/gamefinder.aspx; http://www.nintendo.com/gamelist.

(continued)

billion.[46] It supports all major gaming platforms: PC, Xbox, PlayStation, and GameCube. It also runs its own Internet gaming Web site, Pogo.com, that provides small Internet games for brief entertainment.

Hawkins's key innovation was the so-called Hollywood model of game production. At a time when game developers were not well rewarded by their employers, he decided to treat them as artists. He attracted top development talent by offering attractive bonuses and introducing the practice of printing the authors' names clearly and visibly on game packages, to some extent imitating album covers in the music industry. In general, EA paid more attention to the packaging and marketing of games than its rivals. By careful management of the creative process, coupled with creative marketing, EA transformed game development into the complex process we see today. Games are no longer created only by programmers: video layout artists, sound and music directors, and script editors are also employed, as well as marketing specialists.

EA's other major innovation was the introduction of sports tie-ins. It began by paying the modest sum (by today's sports industry standards) of $25,000 to legendary NBA star Julius Erving for using his image in a basketball game. Today EA owns the rights to several extremely profitable sports game franchises (NBA Live, Madden NFL, FIFA soccer, and others), some of which are exclusive, others of which are shared with competitors. For example, in December 2004, EA obtained from the NFL the exclusive rights to publish games using the league's image and that of its players for five years, in exchange for an amount speculated to be in the neighborhood of $300 million. In contrast, the NBA has licensed the rights to produce basketball games to EA, Take Two Interactive, Sony, and Atari. EA is rumored to have paid up to $20 million each for the rights to both the *Harry Potter* and the *Lord of the Rings* franchises.[47]

EA operates nine in-house development studios around the world. In addition, it frequently publishes games from independent studios that lack the capital and marketing savvy necessary to go it alone. Sometimes EA buys out promising studios altogether and creates episodic franchises based on their successful games. For example, it bought Origin Systems Inc. in 1992, and after the success of Ultima Online, released in 1997, it decided to focus Origin on building the Ultima franchise, the latest incarnation of which is Ultima IX: Ascension.

46. http://en.wikipedia.org/wiki/Electronic_Arts; Yahoo! Finance Electronic Arts, August 22, 2005.

47. Kent, *The Ultimate History of Video Games*, pp. 260–266; http://money.cnn.com/2004/01/20/commentary/game_over/column_gaming/?cnn = yes.

Table 5.2
United States Third-Party Game Developers

Publisher/ Developer	2004 Revenues[48] (millions)	Platforms Supported (no. of titles)[49]	Hit Titles
Electronic Arts	$444	GameCube (74); PS 2 (121); Xbox (80); PC (15)	NBA Live (2003: GC, PS2, Xbox), 007: Agent Under Fire (2003: GC, PS2, Xbox)
Nintendo of America	$231	GameCube (53); PS 2 (0); Xbox (0)	Super Mario Sunshine (2002: GC); Donkey Kong Jungle (2005: GC)
THQ	$133	GameCube (40); PS 2 (55); Xbox (30); PC (23)	SpongeBob SquarePants: Battle for Bikini Bottom (2003: GC, PS2); Evil Dead (2002: PS2, Xbox)
Activision	$125	GameCube (35); PS 2 (43); Xbox (40); PC (43)	Spiderman (2002: GC, Xbox); Tony Hawk's Underground (2003: GC, PS2, Xbox)
Sony[50]	$116	GameCube (0); PS 2 (98); Xbox (0)	EverQuest Online Adventures (2003: PS2)
Konami	$77	GameCube (21); PS 2 (69); Xbox (20); PC (22)	Yu-Gi-Oh! (2003: GC, PS2, Xbox); Dance Dance Revolution Extreme (2004: PS2, Xbox)
Sega	$69	GameCube (29); PS 2(42); Xbox (34); PC (7)	ESPN College Hoops (2003: PS2, Xbox); SEGA Sports NHL 2K3 (2002: GC)

48. Piper Jaffray, "The Video Game Iindustry."

49. http://www.nintendo.com/gamelist; http://www.us.playstation.com/ gamefinder.aspx; http://www.xbox.com/en-US/games/catalog.htm; http://www. sega.com/home.php?hsid=235711; http://www.ea.com/home/ pccd.jsp?src=11001hometab5linknone; http://www.activision.com/en_US/ game_list/game_list.jsp; http://www.konami.com/gs/, http://www.konami.com/ gs/; http://www.namco.com/platform/pc/; http://www.microsoft.com/games/pc/ default.aspx.

50. Includes games published by SCEA and Sony Online Entertainment.

Table 5.2
(continued)

Publisher/ Developer	2004 Revenues[48] (millions)	Platforms Supported (no. of titles)[49]	Hit Titles
Midway	$59	GameCube (4); PS 2 (40);Xbox (31); PC (4)	Mortal Kombat (2002: GC, PS2, Xbox); MLB Slugfest (2002: GC, PS2, Xbox)
Microsoft	$58	GameCube (0); PS 2 (0); Xbox (53); PC (42)	Project Gotham Racing (2003: Xbox); Amped: Freestyle Snowboarding (2001: Xbox)
Namco	$57	GameCube (16); PS 2 (44); Xbox (11); PC (5)	SoulCalibur II (2003: Xbox); Moto GP (2000: PS2, Xbox)

Most video game developers write games for several competing platforms (that is, they multihome), as shown in Table 5.2. Often they will write a game for one platform and, if it is successful, port it to other platforms. This happens much more in video games than it does in software applications because there are comparably large markets on multiple consoles.

Technical progress in hardware has made it possible to write and play increasingly sophisticated games. As a consequence, the game development process has become longer and more complex. During the early days of Atari (1977–1982), individual developers sometimes produced games in as little as 3 months. A quarter-century later, video games are developed by large teams of software engineers, 3D graphic designers, and sound artists. These teams may devote 18 months or more to a single game. For example, reportedly more than 100 developers are currently working on Halo 3 for Xbox 360. Developing a video game is becoming more like producing a movie with extensive special effects than like writing a typical software application.

The tools used in the development process have also become more sophisticated. In the early days, game developers wrote in assembly language and worked directly with the console. As the hardware platforms, software platforms, and the games themselves have become more complex, the modeling, graphics and design work, and actual coding have moved to workstations or PCs. Developers use higher-level programming languages, development tools, and software libraries provided by the console's manufacturer or third-party firms. Development tools include development environments emulating the upcoming console's capabilities (usually a modified console plus a PC), APIs, documentation, demos that can be used as prototypes, and more.[51]

Console manufacturers generally price the assistance they provide developers just to cover costs. In addition, in exchange for a modest fixed licensing fee (approximately $12,000 for PlayStation 2) covering administrative costs, developers and publishers can get technical information about the console and the right to sell their products to licensed game developers.[52] The provision of good development aids at attractive prices is one of the major ways of getting and keeping developers on board the platform. Particularly intense efforts go into providing game developers and publishers with development tools in a timely manner so as to allow the latter to maximize the number of attractive games ready at console launch.

Console makers use multiple channels and venues for reaching their development communities. At the industry's two most prominent events, the annual Electronic Entertainment Expo and the semi-annual Consumer Electronics Show, they expend large sums of money on lavish parties and fancy booths, which are used to showcase cool technologies, as a public relations vehicle and as a way to advertise their clout to game developers and (via the media in attendance) end users. Console makers also hold regular briefing sessions for licensees, with announcements and technical presentations regarding upcoming consoles, features, and business schemes, as well as some hands-on opportunities for developers in attendance.

51. For example, Sony offers both a professional developer toolkit (T10K) and a Linux kit for PlayStation 2. See http://playstation2-linux.com/faq.php#Availability__When_Where_and_how_much.

52. http://www.tmstation.scei.co.jp/ps2/public/license.html.

Other creative initiatives abound. For instance, Sony launched a developer kit for hobbyists that it sent to college programmers eager to take a stab at game development for PlayStation 2. And Microsoft sent two key members of its Xbox team on a three-week worldwide evangelization tour to visit some forty game publishers, introduce and demonstrate the Xbox, and convince them to work with it.[53]

As with many economic activities, the growth, maturation, and increasing complexity of the game development process has led to a division of labor among specialist firms. Development studios do most of the actual game programming. Game publishers provide seed money, take responsibility for most of the financial risks associated with the marketing and distribution of games, and negotiate the licensing agreements with the console manufacturers. Some firms are integrated across this boundary, others cross it by contract. The contracts between a publisher and an independent development studio generally involve payments made by the publisher in the form of a cash advance and, in case a game is successful (if sales exceed a certain threshold), royalties ranging from 10 to 40 percent of the game's retail price, depending on the studio's reputation and self-financing ability.

A third category of firms has recently emerged, specializing in providing development tools and middleware to game developers. These products can significantly lower development time and costs and reduce the expertise required by developers in order to be able to program for a specific console. There are currently over fifty third-party providers of tools and middleware for the PlayStation 2 and over thirty for Xbox.[54] Their products range from 3D graphics APIs and console-specific compilers to speech recognition software and music playback systems.

Thus, as with PCs, a complex ecosystem of interdependent companies has developed around multisided platforms (Figure 5.1). The key difference is that several significant software platforms coexist.

53. http://www.xboxusersgroup.com/forums/showthread.php?t = 167.
54. http://www.tmstation.scei.co.jp/ps2/public/TM_liste.html http://www.xbox.com/en-US/dev/tools.html.

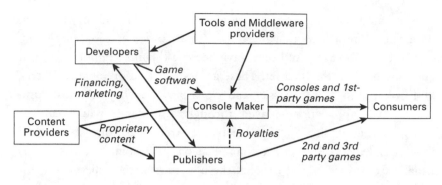

Figure 5.1
Platform ecosystem for consoles.

PC Games

As noted earlier, console gaming has led PC gaming in terms of revenues since the late 1980s. Nevertheless, PC gaming hasn't disappeared. It remains strong in some segments, particularly online gaming, which first appeared on the PC platform. In 2005, there were about 62 million online PC gamers in the United States.[55]

There are three main categories of PC games. Classic CD-based games usually focus on single-player experiences, although multiplayer support has become more common. Like sellers of any other software application, the publishers of these games receive revenue only from CD sales. Not surprisingly, they suffer from extensive piracy.

Games in the second category, known as massive multi-player online role-playing games (or MMPORPGs), are played online simultaneously by thousands of users 24 hours a day, 7 days a week. They are the most expensive PC games to develop, with budgets ranging from $5 million to $30 million. They are hosted on the publishers' servers. Users pay a fixed fee to buy the game CD, usually around $50, after which they are charged monthly subscription rates, typically between $6 and $15.

55. http://blogs.zdnet.com/ITFacts/?p=920156. Another option chosen by Real, for example, is to allow users to play the full version for free but for a limited time only.

Web-based games, the third category, are short, fun, and easy to learn, designed to appeal to casual gamers (think office employees playing during coffee breaks). And they have become the most popular form of entertainment on the Internet. These games range from Solitaire, Tetris, and Collapse to arcade classics and word puzzles. They are most commonly Java applications played through a browser, which can be accessed through sites such as Electronic Arts' pogo.com, Real's Real One Arcade, and Shockwave.com. The basic version of the game is usually free and designed to whet the appetite for the full version, for which the publisher charges a one-time fixed fee for unlimited play thereafter. Upgrade rates from free downloaders to paying customers are low (between 1 and 5 percent), and game sites have turned to advertising as a source of revenue.

As with console games, there are development studios, game publishers, and middleware providers involved in developing PC games. Most firms in each of these three segments are active on both platforms, consoles and PCs. All this makes for a rather rich ecosystem around the PC gaming platform, similar to the console ecosystems but with several new actors. We illustrate it in Figure 5.2.

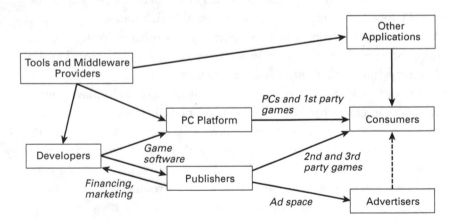

Figure 5.2
Platform ecosystem for PC games.

PC versus Consoles: Platform Competition

At first glance it is quite surprising that the PC and console gaming platforms have coexisted for a long time by the standards of computer-based industries, even though they employ radically different business models. A closer look suggests a straightforward economic explanation.

As two-sided platforms, PCs and consoles compete for both game developers and game users. The most obvious difference is on the developer side: PCs are open platforms, while developing games for a console requires access to proprietary information supplied by its vendor, as well as the payment of royalties. On the other hand, thanks to the gatekeeper role played by console vendors, console games compete against fewer titles (there are approximately ten times more PC game titles) and are not "diluted" into the mass of low- to mediocre-quality games that flood the PC market. On the PC side, games are only one category of application among many. Nonetheless, games are an important category of PC applications, and PC software platform vendors have accordingly been interested in attracting them. Perhaps the best illustration is Microsoft's development of the DirectX collection of APIs specifically geared for PC game development, discussed earlier.

There is much multihoming by both developers and users. Most publishers of console games are also very active in the PC game business. For example, in June 2006 the Electronic Arts Web site listed fifty-two games on CD for PCs, fifty-four games for Xbox, and fifty-four games for PlayStation 2, with at least fifteen titles available on all three platforms. Similarly, 91 percent of console gamers who own a PC also use their PC for playing games.[56] These facts suggest that consumers and therefore developers value the different features offered by these alternative platforms. They like variety.

From the point of view of users, the game technologies are quite different. PC games use a keyboard and a mouse, whereas consoles use a controller and/or a joystick. The latter are more suitable for "fast twitch"

56. Coughlan, "Competitive Dynamics in Home Video Games."

games, and it is thus not surprising that console game developers generally focus on racing and shooting games. Strategy games such as Civilization, by contrast, are available exclusively on PCs. Another interesting source of differentiation on the consumer side is that consoles are naturally geared for a more social gaming experience: most people play console games in the living room, often with friends or family competing against each other. By contrast, PC games are more solitary experiences: users sit alone in front of a computer and play either against the machine or against other players in remote locations.

Thus the PC and console gaming platforms offer rather different experiences to end users, with many enjoying both, and game developers seem to find it easy to participate in both ecosystems. As long as both sides of the market continue to benefit from both platforms, both platforms will survive. This is consistent with a more general pattern that we will see in later chapters: when consumers value product differentiation and platforms can offer innovative and unique features, multiple platforms can coexist despite indirect network effects that make bigger better.

Online Games

Lured by the prospect of profits that a subscription-based online service could create for a video game console, Nintendo was the first to get into online games, back in 1988, with the Famicom, the Japanese version of the NES. Nintendo sold a $100 modem, which allowed the Famicom to hook up to a telephone line. With this connection, Famicom users could play games with each other and also get stock prices, make purchases, read news, or do the many things one does on the Internet nowadays. Despite the potential to become a nascent online community in Japan, the Famicom network failed. Only 130,000 households purchased the modem, and only a fraction of those ended up using the services. Sega also sold a modem peripheral for the Genesis that allowed players to compete against each other via the phone lines, but it wasn't a great success either.[57]

57. Ibid.

Microsoft and Sony have started online gaming platforms more recently. They have gotten multiple sides on board and are growing rapidly. They have adopted different strategies in doing so.

Microsoft built an integrated, centralized, closed platform, Xbox Live, that provides a variety of services to both users and game developers. Developers must comply with Microsoft's technical specifications and cannot rely on their own online infrastructure. At the same time, they can benefit from a host of features built into Xbox Live: matchmaking, authentication, friends service, statistics storage, content delivery, and, most notably, support for voice communication. Meanwhile, users, who pay about $50 a year for a subscription, benefit from a centralized service with a consistent interface across games.

Sony, by contrast, has chosen an open approach for its online gaming platform. It simply supplies the network and the security system, as well as the option to host third-party games on its servers. However, it leaves the task of providing additional features such as matchmaking to individual developers. This approach works for big publishers such as Electronic Arts that can use their existing infrastructures, but not for many smaller publishers. Because each developer can add its own features, this approach results in fragmentation of the platform, and each publisher offers a few games for its "flavor" of the platform.

Platform Expansion

The guts of any game console are basically the same as those of a PC. Video game platform vendors have long realized that their consoles are capable of much more than just playing games. Since the start of the industry, some vendors have looked to expand the functionality of their machines and to invade formerly separated markets. As we discussed above, for instance, in 1988 Nintendo launched the Family Computer Communications Network System in Japan. A modem and a special cartridge allowed the Famicom console to interact with other networked Famicoms and with computers. This ultimately unsuccessful system offered users services such as online stock trading, banking, travel reservations, and game-related information.

The most radical expansions occurred in the early 2000s. Industry experts dubbed the Sony PlayStation a Trojan horse for taking control of the living room. The PlayStation and Sega's Dreamcast could play music CDs, while Xbox and PlayStation 2 are capable of playing movies as well as music, both on DVD and on traditional CD-ROM formats. In 2003, Sony launched PlayStation X, a souped-up version of PlayStation 2, including a hard-disk–based video recorder, satellite and analog TV tuners, and photo album and music playback features. Pushing the limits even further, the Xbox 360, which went on the market in late 2005, can check email, surf the Internet, and record television programs, as well as connect with the version of Windows that Microsoft has developed for home entertainment use.[58] Not to be outdone, PlayStation 3, due in November 2006, will be an even more powerful home computer, making all PlayStation 2's features available in high definition and adding the ability to connect to various consumer electronics devices.

This is all part of the continuing quest for the living room, to which we return in Chapter 12.

INSIGHTS

• The console video gaming industry operates a radically different business model from other software platform industries. Game manufacturers tightly integrate hardware and software systems; they offer consoles to consumers at less than manufacturing cost, and they earn profits by developing games and charging third-party game developers for access to their platforms.

• In 1977, Atari's VCS 2600 established this "razor/blade" strategy, by pricing that encouraged people to buy the console (the razor) so that Atari could earn profits from the sale of games (blades) to them.

58. "Microsoft Gambles With Xbox 360," *Wall Street Journal*, May 13, 2005; "Power-Packed Chatty Xbox," *The Australian*, May 17, 2005.

• In the early 1980s, Nintendo was the first to embrace the now-standard two-sided business model; it recruited independent third-party game developers by offering them a 20 percent royalty on game sales while imposing procedures to control game quality.

• The PC and console video game platforms have maintained opposite business models, even though many game developers and others participate in both ecosystems. This has been possible because the two platforms offer products that users consider significantly different.

• Video game consoles have greatly expanded beyond games and have become platforms for all kinds of home entertainment with the addition of such features as DVD playing and recording capabilities, photo management, Internet access, and on-line shopping.

6

The Palm Economy

I rigged my cellular to send a message to my PDA, which is online with my PC, to get it to activate the voicemail, which sends the message to the inbox of my email, which routes it to the PDA, which beams it back to the cellular. Then I realized my gadgets have a better social life than I do!

—*Tom Ostad, comic artist*[1]

INSIDE THIS CHAPTER

· How PDAs were born and came of age

· Multisided strategies and the "Palm economy"

· Changing patterns of integration over time

During the late 1990s, many a young executive carried a PalmPilot and pecked her appointments into the device's screen using its special handwriting recognition software. PalmPilots were mainly organizers—computerized versions of the once hot FiloFax—that could do a few other things, including email. By 2001 Palm had sold over 21 million of its personal digital assistants (PDAs). Palm's shipments had grown at an average rate of 115 percent in the previous five years. Then growth suddenly stopped and turned into decline. Between 2001 and 2004, Palm sales decreased at an average annual rate of 13 percent. Annual unit sales were more than a million lower in 2004 than in 2003.[2]

1. http://www.uhv.edu/it/IT_staff/quotes.asp.

2. Diana Hwang, "Technology Road Map of Smart Handheld Devices" (IDC report no. 16225), June 1998; Jill House and Diana Hwang, "Pocketful of Palms: The Smart Handheld Devices Market Forecast Update and Outlook, 1999–2003" (IDC report no. 21177), December 1999; Jill House, "Market

Chapter 6: PDA Timeline

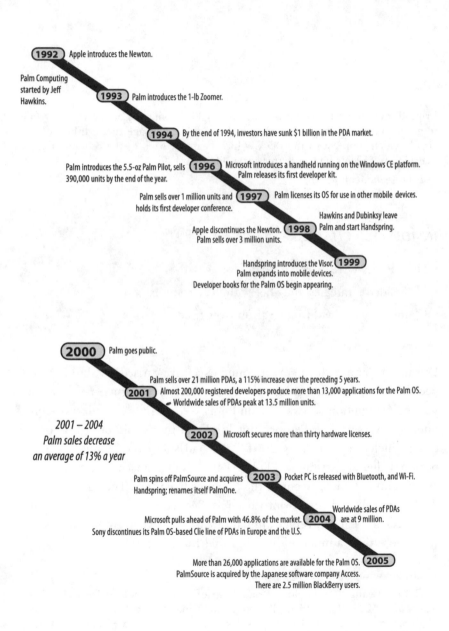

1992 Apple introduces the Newton.

Palm Computing started by Jeff Hawkins.

1993 Palm introduces the 1-lb Zoomer.

1994 By the end of 1994, investors have sunk $1 billion in the PDA market.

Palm introduces the 5.5-oz Palm Pilot, sells 390,000 units by the end of the year. **1996** Microsoft introduces a handheld running on the Windows CE platform. Palm releases its first developer kit.

Palm sells over 1 million units and **1997** Palm licenses its OS for use in other mobile devices. holds its first developer conference.

Apple discontinues the Newton. **1998** Hawkins and Dubinksy leave Palm and start Handspring. Palm sells over 3 million units.

Handspring introduces the Visor. **1999** Palm expands into mobile devices. Developer books for the Palm OS begin appearing.

2000 Palm goes public.

Palm sells over 21 million PDAs, a 115% increase over the preceding 5 years. **2001** Almost 200,000 registered developers produce more than 13,000 applications for the Palm OS. Worldwide sales of PDAs peak at 13.5 million units.

2001 – 2004 Palm sales decrease an average of 13% a year

2002 Microsoft secures more than thirty hardware licenses.

Palm spins off PalmSource and acquires **2003** Pocket PC is released with Bluetooth, and Wi-Fi. Handspring; renames itself PalmOne.

Worldwide sales of PDAs
Microsoft pulls ahead of Palm with 46.8% of the market. **2004** are at 9 million.
Sony discontinues its Palm OS-based Clie line of PDAs in Europe and the U.S.

More than 26,000 applications are available for the Palm OS. **2005** PalmSource is acquired by the Japanese software company Access. There are 2.5 million BlackBerry users.

This chapter is about the spectacular and surprising rise, and slow but (at least as this is written) uncertain decline of Palm.

It is an interesting story at several levels.

For one, Palm executed a multisided platform strategy with aplomb. It grew quickly as users and developers made it an increasingly valuable platform for each other. It succeeded where many others, including Apple, had failed miserably.

For another, Palm is mainly a software story. Palm got into hardware mainly because it needed to make sure it got the overall initial system right. But its focus was on handwriting software and the underlying operating system. The Palm Economy, as it was called, was built on the Palm OS.

At yet another level Palm illustrates the choices platform providers make in integrating into different elements of the platform. It started out as a pure software company, integrated into hardware, and then divided itself into independent software and hardware companies.

Finally, Palm shows how the flexibility of software and hardware platforms enables them to seize categories quickly but also leaves them open to quick destruction by other categories. PalmPilots were great organizers that did some other things, such as email, well enough. Palm's growth has slowed for a number of reasons, but chief among these is that many consumers prefer great email devices or mobile phones that do organizing well enough.

Mayhem: The Smart Handheld Devices Market Forecast and Analysis, 1999–2004" (IDC report no. 22430), June 2000; Kevin Burden and Alex Slawsby, "Hand Check: The Smart Handheld Devices Market Forecast and Analysis, 2000–2005" (IDC report no. 24859), July 2001; Kevin Burden, Weili Su, Alex Slawsby, and Jennifer Gallo, "Sync or Swim: Worldwide Smart Handheld Devices Forecast and Analysis, 2002–2006" (IDC report no. 26865), April 2002; Alex Slawsby, Randy Giusto, Kevin Burden, Ross Sealfon, and David Linsalata, "Worldwide Smart Handheld Devices Forecast and Analysis, 2003–2007" (IDC report no. 29586), June 2003; Kevin Burden, David Linsalata, Alex Slawsby, and Randy Giusto, "Worldwide Smart Handheld Device 2004–2008 Forecast Update: First Quarter Triggers Downward Revision" (IDC report no. 31554), August 2004; David Linsalata, Kevin Burden, Ramon T. Llamas, and Randy Giusto, "Worldwide Smart Handheld Device 2005–2009 Forecast and Analysis: Passing the Torch" (IDC report no. 33415), May 2005.

Palm could rise again, though. The Palm OS is now competing against other operating systems for smart mobile phones. We leave this transition from PDAs to phones to the next chapter.

The Birth of PDAs

Palm started as a software company. The PalmPilot grew out of its inventor's early interest in handwriting recognition software. Jeff Hawkins (no relation to Trip Hawkins of video game fame) had developed software for recognizing hand-printed characters while at the University of California, Berkeley. He joined GriD, a computer company that was making a device for pen computing, and licensed his PalmPrint software to his new employer. Aimed at the corporate market, the $2,500 4.5-pound GriDPad did not catch on. Nor did other pen-operated computing devices, despite Microsoft's hyped entry into the category.

Hawkins began looking for a market that could be served by his software. He started Palm Computing in January 1992 with the idea of taking his software to consumers. The Zoomer (derived from "consumer") appeared late the next year.[3]

Palm collaborated with three other partners to produce this new small computing device. Casio manufactured it. GeoWorks designed an operating system for it based on its GEOS operating system. Tandy distributed it. And Palm made the application software. AOL and Intuit became partners as well, providing applications.[4]

The $700 one-pound Zoomer came loaded with an organizer that had scheduling and address features; a dictionary, spell-checker, and thesaurus; a calculator; and other applications. Intuit provided PocketQuicken for the Zoomer, and AOL provided an email program. Zoomer also came with PalmPrint, which provided the way for users to enter information into the organizer. Unfortunately, this handwriting

---

3. Andrea Butter and David Pogue, *Piloting Palm* (New York: John Wiley & Sons, 2002), pp. 7, 10.

4. Walter S. Mossberg, "Personal Technology," *The Wall Street Journal*, October 28, 1993; "Tandy, Casio Unveil 'Zoomer' Plans," *Computer Reseller News*, January 18, 1993.

recognition software didn't work well.[5] And the device was loaded with so many features that it was slow. As Jeff Hawkins reflected some years later, "It was the slowest computer ever made by man. It was too big and too expensive. We executed badly."[6]

It was also second to market. Apple had introduced the Apple Newton to great publicity a few months before Palm launched the Zoomer. The $1,000 Apple Newton had the same problems as the Zoomer. Its handwriting recognition software was lampooned in a series of Doonesbury cartoons and an episode of the Simpsons. Apple continued to improve the Newton, but its sales remained dismal—only 85,000 in its first year—and it was discontinued by 1998.[7]

The Newton was a hit, though, compared to the Zoomer. Estimates of sales vary widely, but all reports agree that fewer than 60,000 Zoomers were ever sold. Palm's partners lost interest.[8]

They were not alone. According to an interview with Hawkins's number two, by the end of 1994, venture capitalists and consumer elec-

5. Tom Thompson, Tom R. Halfhill, et al., "Hands-on Evaluations of the Apple Newton MessagePad, Tandy/Casio Zoomer, and the Eo 440 Personal Communicator," *BYTE*, October 1, 1993.

6. http://www.palmloyal.com/modules.php?name=News&file=article&sid=26.

7. John Markoff, "Apple's Newton Reborn: Will It Still the Critics?" *The New York Times*, March 4, 1994; http://www.pdasupport.com/PDAencyclopediaAppleNewton.htm.

8. *PC Week* estimated that 20,000 Zoomers had been sold by November 1993, whereas *PC World* estimated 60,000 units by February 1994, yet *Electronic*

tronics companies had invested $1 billion in the PDA market. No one had anything to show for it.[9] Go, one of the PDA contenders, liquidated itself in 1994. The trade press suggested that PDAs had gone the way of pen-based computers.

The Apple Newton

Like the PalmPilot, the Apple Newton had its roots in software. It became known as the Newton because it was powered by the Newton OS. Apple had been developing the Newton OS as part of a revolutionary new programming environment and operating system based on a "rich object-oriented graphics kernel."[10] The Newton was originally conceived as a sophisticated PC that would be especially useful for architecture and other graphic design uses. Apple reportedly feared the Newton computer would cannibalize Macintosh sales, and diverted the effort toward PDAs.

For developers, Apple offered an object-oriented programming system called NewtonScript. According to one source, programmers complained that "the programming environment was overpriced—on top of purchasing a Newton for nearly $1,000 US [the list price], the Toolbox programming environment cost an additional $1,000 US."[11] Apple developed other toolkits to help application developers and eventually provided the programming environment for free. A number of applications were developed for the Newton; many are still available. Some of these helped transform the Apple Newton into a specialized device for certain businesses or professions. In the medical industry, doctors ran programs like Pocket Doc and Hippocrates to assist with medical records and billing, for instance, and Apple was awarded a $1 million contract to investigate the Newton's use in the medical operations of the Department of Defense.[12]

Engineering Times said no more than 40,000 of the model had been sold by November of that same year. Mike McGuire, "PDA Shipments Are Meeting Goals of Manufacturers and Analysts," *PC Week*, November 8, 1993; James Daly, "Newton PDA Faces Uphill Struggle: Interest in Entire Genre Wanes," *Computer-World*, February 7, 1994; Rick Boyd-Merritt, "PDAs Fall into Disfavor; Concentration on Cellphones, Pagers," *Electronic Engineering Times*, 28 November 1994.

9. Pat Dillon, "The Next Small Thing," *Fast Company*, June 1998 (http://www.fastcompany.com/online/15/smallthing.html).

10. http://en.wikipedia.org/wiki/Apple_Newton.

11. http://www.pdasupport.com/PDAencyclopediaAppleNewton.htm.

12. Mark H. Ebell, "Pocket Doc 1.1," *Journal of Family Practice* 41 (October 1, 1995); Mary Heng, "Apple's Newton Offers Firm A Slice of Software Business," *The Omaha World-Herald*, October 18, 1993, "Apple Computer Gets Defense Contract To Study 'Newton' Use," Dow Jones News Service, December 6, 1993.

(continued)

> Apple discontinued the Newton PDA in 1998 as a result of its poor sales in the face of the PalmPilot's success. Apple had initially planned to continue the development of the Newton OS, which was designed to work in small mobile devices. However, after Steve Jobs returned to lead the company, it decided to focus its operating system development on the Mac OS and to develop a version of this for small devices. As it turned out, Apple has not become a competitor in this arena. It bought an operating system from another vendor for its iPod device, as we discuss in Chapter 8.

Palm, on the other hand, regrouped. It surveyed Zoomer buyers to find out what they liked and didn't like, what they used and didn't use:

What these people said opened the company's eyes. More than 90% of Zoomer owners also owned a PC. More than half of them bought Zoomer because of software (offered as an add-on) that transferred data to and from a PC. These were business users, not retail consumers. And they didn't want to replace their PCs—they wanted to complement them. People weren't asking for a PDA that was smart enough to compete with a computer. They wanted a PDA that was simple enough to compete with paper.[13]

Making the Market

Palm couldn't find partners interested in pursuing its new vision of the PDA. Making a virtue out of necessity, Palm decided to go it alone and became a vertically integrated PDA maker.

Development of the PalmPilot

Reflecting on the failure of the Zoomer, Palm decided that to be successful a device had to adhere to several principles. The software had to be simple so the device could run quickly enough. The device had to be small enough to fit into a shirt pocket. And it had to be cheap.

Handwriting recognition software had to recognize a wide variety of writing styles. That necesssarily required complex code. And at the time

13. Dillon, "The Next Small Thing."

even the best handwriting software—the software in the Newton was state-of-the-art—was not very good. Palm decided to reverse the logic. Rather than having software learn how to recognize people's handwriting, have people learn how to write for the device. Hawkins argued that it was easier to teach people to learn a single new writing style than to write software that could recognize their many individual writing styles.

This insight led to the development of Graffiti. Each letter is based on a single stroke, so that an A is written as an inverted V and an F as an inverted L. The simple style made the software efficient and accurate, although of course it required users to go to the trouble of learning this odd script.

The original PDAs were like bricks. The Zoomer weighed a pound and the Newton 0.9 pounds. The Newton was 7.25 inches × 4.5 inches × 0.75 inches. Neither could fit into a shirt pocket. Hawkins reportedly paced the Palm halls, measuring employee pockets against balsa wood prototypes. Palm's new device weighed about 5.5 ounces and measured 4.6 inches × 3.1 inches × 0.6 inches.[14] Its volume was just over a third of the original Newton's.

Hawkins complained that his business partners for the Zoomer had kept insisting on adding more and more features to the product. That's one reason it was large, cumbersome, and slow. Simplicity was key in Palm's second act. The basic applications were a calendar, an address book, a to-do list, and a memo writer, along with easy connectivity to and synchronization with PCs.

The target price for the product was $299.

Starting as a Single Silo

Palm's lead investor advised Hawkins to become a "self-sufficient company that designed, built, and marketed" the new PDA.[15] Rather than taking on partners, as it had done with the Zoomer, Palm outsourced the hardware design and manufacturing to other companies while it focused on the operating system and applications. Palm still

14. http://www.pdasupport.com/Newton.htm; Rich Schwerin, "Portable Pocket Assistant," *PC/Computing*, March 1, 1996.
15. Dillon, "The Next Small Thing."

needed help with marketing. It approached US Robotics, then a leading PC modem manufacturer, about becoming a partner. US Robotics offered instead to buy Palm for $44 million in stock. Palm accepted and became a division of US Robotics.

Several commentators have suggested that Hawkins and his colleagues were not interested in pursuing a platform strategy. Yoffie and Kwak quote Hawkins as saying in the context of competition with Microsoft: "We are not about the operating systems. . . . we are about a highly integrated product that delivers an end user results. . . . In all honesty, if Microsoft walked in today with a great environment that we could build great products on, we'd absolutely consider it."[16] That comment seems dubious in light of Palm's past as a software company through 1995 and its aggressive software platform strategy after 1996. And we doubt that Palm would have wanted to become another Windows CE device manufacturer any more than Apple would have wanted to become yet another manufacturer of Wintel PCs. Instead, it appears that Palm integrated into hardware in part because it wanted to maintain its revolutionary design vision and in part because it had little choice.

The 5.5-ounce PalmPilot debuted in April 1996. Consumers and reviewers agreed that Palm had gotten it just right. Palm sold 390,000 units by year end and could barely keep pace with demand.[17] According to one review, "If you're searching for the ultimate palm-size organizer, look no further."[18] Graffiti was also a hit. Some called it the killer application for the Palm, although it was part of the software platform rather than an application. It was a user interface that had value only because it made it easy for consumers to use the applications on the device.

The PalmPilot quickly dominated the PDA category. It garnered almost one-third of PDA shipments in 1996, and became the market leader only a year after being introduced. It had sold over 1 million units by the end

16. Annabelle Gawer and Michael A. Cusumano, *Platform Leadership*, 2002, p. 195.
17. Diana Hwang, "Technology Road Map of Smart Handheld Devices."
18. Schwerin, "Portable Pocket Assistant."

of 1997 and over 3 million by the end of 1998. Its market share climbed to just over 65 percent by 2000 before it started falling as a result of increased competition (mainly from Windows CE-based devices) in PDAs. Table 6.1 shows how the different PDA software platforms fared in market share terms from 1996 to 2004.

The fact that Palm had produced a breakthrough device was important to its success. But so too was its low-price strategy. At $299 it was one of the least expensive PDAs available. Apple was still asking about $1,000 for its Newton. Donna Dubinsky, Hawkins's right-hand person at Palm, later emphasized that the low price was important to get penetration and secure network effects, a point we return to later. Like the iPod and BlackBerry devices, Palm's PDA became a cultural icon. In 2000, the supermodel Claudia Schiffer released a Palm Vx Claudia Schiffer Edition through her Web site.[19]

Palm made the market for PDAs. Most of the early makers with their own operating systems, such as Apple, exited the business. Palm soon faced competition from Microsoft, which had developed Windows CE for handheld devices. Microsoft followed its traditional strategy of focusing on the software platform and encouraging computer manufacturers to make devices based on it. Moreover, Palm had to endure the management problems that resulted from 3Com's disastrous acquisition of US Robotics in 1997 and the difficulty that Palm's key employees had in working within large established organizations. Hawkins and Dubinsky left Palm in mid-1998, and many of the key engineers and managers left within the next year. Within 3Com, Palm had four presidents over the next year. Nonetheless, Palm managed to maintain its lead in traditional PDAs until 2004, as Table 6.1 shows. But it was a lead in a shrinking category.

Disintegration

Palm started moving away from its single silo approach in late 1997, when it decided to license the Palm OS for other mobile

19. Ian Fried, "Palm Shows New OS with Wireless Voice, Data Feature," CNET News.com, December 12, 2000.

Table 6.1
Market Share by Operating System

	1996	1997	1998	1999	2000	2001	2002	2003	2004
Palm	25.7%	34.2%	46.3%	60.6%	66.5%	55.1%	57.5%	51.0%	46.0%
Microsoft Powered	4.5%	17.5%	25.8%	19.3%	16.6%	16.6%	23.3%	38.0%	46.8%
EPOC	19.0%	12.2%	8.3%	8.5%	—	—	—	—	—
Synergy (Zaurus)	32.5%	15.2%	—	—	—	—	—	—	—
Newton	4.4%	—	—	—	0.3%	0.1%	1.1%	1.6%	1.1%
Linux	—	—	—	—	—	—	—	—	—
DOS	10.1%	1.2%	0.5%	0.3%	—	—	—	—	—
Other	3.9%	19.9%	19.1%	11.4%	16.7%	28.1%	18.0%	9.5%	6.2%
Total	100.0%	100.0%	100.0%	100.0%	100.0%	100.0%	100.0%	100.0%	100.0%

Source: IDC reports.

devices, such as bar code scanners, smart cards, and mobile phones.[20] Palm soon signed up Symbol, Nokia, Sony, and Motorola.

Even more aggressive licensing followed, partly precipitated by disagreements between Palm's founders, Hawkins and Dubinsky, and 3Com's management. The pair tried to persuade 3Com to spin off the Palm division. When it refused, they decided to leave. They persuaded 3Com to grant them a license to the Palm OS. (Ironically, 3Com's leaders had earlier advocated licensing the Palm OS widely, but Hawkins and Dubinsky had opposed this.) They started a new company called Handspring in October 1998 and introduced the Visor PDA the next year;[21] they focused on innovative hardware design.

Meanwhile, 3Com decided to spin Palm off as a separate company that would license the Palm OS to other PDA manufacturers. In the next five years these would include Handspring, Sony, Kyocera, Nokia, Symbol, and Qualcomm. Hardware makers like Handspring produced popular models running the Palm OS. The Handspring Visor Deluxe, released in 2001, came with a springboard expansion slot that was not a part of Palm's PDAs. This expansion slot allowed owners of the Handspring Visor Deluxe to attach other hardware modules to make their PDA a pager, mobile phone, or voice recorder. The Handspring Visor Deluxe was also available in five colors. By 2001, the Palm OS was on 55 percent of PDAs sold that year; and 40 percent of those were not made by Palm.[22]

Palm went public in 2000. A year later Palm divided itself into two companies—one making and licensing the operating system and the other making the hardware—although both were still under common ownership. The rationale for the separation was that hardware manufacturers would be more comfortable licensing the Palm OS

20. "In the Palm of its Hand: Why Windows CE Has Been Unable to Unseat the Palm Operating System," Red Herring, December 1, 1998.

21. Stephanie Miles, "PalmPilot Creators Form New Firm," CNET News.com, November 6, 1998; Dawn Kawamoto, "New Handheld Device Firm Formed," CNET News.com, October 9, 1998 (http://news.com.com/New+handheld+device+firm+formed/2100-1001_3-216527.html?tag=st.rn).

22. Alex Slawsby, Randy Giusto, Kevin Burden, Ross Sealfon, and Dave Linsalata, "Worldwide Smart Handheld Devices Forecast and Analysis, 2003–2007."

from a company that didn't compete with them.[23] It completed this process of disintegration in 2003 when it spun off the operating system as PalmSource. Palm, the remaining hardware company, acquired Handspring and renamed itself PalmOne. PalmOne received a license to the Palm OS (which it renewed in May 2005 through 2009) and agreed that if it used a different operating system it would not brand its PDA as Palm.

This last and radical step was supposed to enable the Palm OS to be licensed widely, giving it the scale necessary to face growing competition from the charging legions of Windows CE–based devices. However, when we asked David Nagel, until recently CEO of PalmSource, his view was that the separation of Palm was too slow (it took about two years) and was completed too late. With Palm's purchase of Handspring and Sony's decision to discontinue sales of its Palm OS–based PDAs in Europe and the United States in 2004 (and Japan in 2005), the fortunes of the Palm OS software platform remained essentially tied to a single hardware maker, PalmOne.

Meanwhile, by 2004 the market was rife with rumors that PalmOne was about to release devices based on Windows CE, which would end its exclusive allegiance to the Palm OS software platform. That year, the Palm OS's share of sales for PDA devices fell behind Windows CE for the first time.

Although the formal announcement that PalmOne would build devices running on Windows CE did not come until September 2005 (and no such device has been sold as of this writing), this lingering rumor weakened PalmSource considerably in the eyes of investors and consumers. This led to the purchase of PalmSource by the Japanese software company Access in September 2005 for about $324 million.[24] On the one hand, this acquisition reflected investors' lack of confidence that the Palm OS could survive as a stand-alone software platform. On the other hand, Access's prominence in software for mobile devices

---

23. Authors' interviews with David Nagel, CEO of PalmSource, December 2001 to May 2005 passim; Piu-Wing Tam, "Palm Plans Split Into Two Firms: Holders Will Be Asked to Approve Separation of Gadget Division from Company's Software Unit," *Wall Street Journal Europe*, October 28, 2003.

24. http://www.palmsource.com/press/2005/111405_access.html.

may breathe new life into the Palm OS and help it break into other domains of mobile computing beyond PDAs. Indeed, Access produces the highly regarded NetFront Web browser for use on a variety of electronic devices (from digital television to car navigation systems), the most prominent of which are NTT DoCoMo's third-generation i-mode mobile phones, which we will encounter in the next chapter.[25]

Palm's Platform Strategy

Palm adopted a sophisticated multisided platform strategy to secure its position in handhelds. According to Dubinsky, "We are a platform business. The idea in the beginning of a platform business is to get as much market share and installed base as possible, to draw as many developers as possible."[26]

The tactics were similar to those we have seen already for PCs and video games: adding features that helped software companies develop valuable applications, providing them with tools and other assistance for writing programs, and evangelizing the platform.

Palm supported developers from the beginning of its introduction of the PalmPilot. In early 1996, it released its first software development kit (SDK) for developers. This free software included the source code for the applications it had bundled with the Palm, including the calendar, to-do list, address book, and memo pad. Developers could use these applications as reference models for building their own application. As Dubinsky explained,

This [application] source code was in the SDK, so [it] was under a license, but a royalty-free license. We found many developers that took advantage of this. Some would just use the source code for specific elements, such as picking up the code for a scroll bar. Others looked at it as sample code, and others took a whole application and created an enhanced version.[27]

25. It is noteworthy that as of November 30, 2005, NTT DoCoMo has increased its investment share in Access from 7.12 percent to 11.66 percent (http://www.nttdocomo.com/presscenter/pressreleases/press/pressrelease.html?param%5Bno%5D=597).

26. Gawer and Cusumano, *Platform Leadership*, p. 198.

27. Gawer and Cusumano, *Platform Leadership*, p. 199.

The Palm OS included software services made available to developers through APIs. Like the PalmPilot itself, the API-based services were simple but highly functional. Although there were few frills, the APIs gave developers access to a rich set of tools to use to build programs. Palm also provided documentation, white papers, frequently asked questions, tech notes, a tutorial, and an emulator environment through its Web site. By 2000, Palm was also making its Conduit Development Kit available for free; it had cost $99 just a year previously.[28] (Each application designed for a Pilot has two parts: the part that runs on the handheld, and the "conduit," which allows the handheld application to sync with a computer. Palm included a default conduit in the operating system, so that if a developer did not design a specific conduit portion of his or her application the Palm would still synchronize the relevant data.)

Within 18 months of its introduction in 1996 Palm had gotten developers on board its platform. According to an article in *Wired*, "On its way to becoming the bestselling handheld computer of all time, the 3Com PalmPilot has spawned an intense, emotional, and fanatical developer following not seen since the glory days of the Mac."[29] By then there were hundreds of third-party applications for the PalmPilot.[30] Books geared for developers who wanted to write programs for the Palm OS started appearing. *Palm OS Programming: The Developers Guide*, for example, was published in January 1999.

After Palm had established itself as the leading PDA, it started to spend more effort on evangelizing its operating system. It held its first developer conference in late 1997. Palm also offered business development

28. Neil Rhodes and Julie McKeehan, *Palm Programming: The Developers Guide* (Sebastopol, Calif.: O'Reilly & Associates, 1999), pp. 19, 27–29; Robert Mykland, *Palm OS Programming from the Ground Up* (Berkeley, Calif.: Osborne/McGraw-Hill, 2000), pp. 389–390.

29. "How PalmPilot Became a Hacker Cult," *Wired*, February 20, 1998.

30. In March 1997, only 11 months after its introduction, there were 180 applications for the PalmPilot ("Personal Organizer: U.S. Robotics Adds Support to Palm OS Enabling Development of Internet- and Network-Based Software Applications; More than 2,000 Developers Creating Software for PalmPilot Connected Organizers," EDGE: Work-Group Computing Report, March 17, 1997), later articles just generalize to hundreds. "3Com Corporation Releases Spanish Language Version of the Best-Selling PalmPilot Professional Edition Connected Organizer," *Business Wire*, November 3, 1997.

resources to developers, including joint development, marketing, and bundling. By 1998 it had 3,595 registered developers. In 2000, Palm launched PluggedIn@Palm, a program providing resources and advice to its developers. During the same year, Palm also set up a $50 million venture capital unit called Palm Ventures to support businesses focusing on Palm OS applications. It offered Palm OS development classes regularly and encouraged other activities among its community of users through developer portals.[31]

The growth in developers is shown in Figure 6.1. In 2001 there were almost 200,000 registered developers of software applications, who had

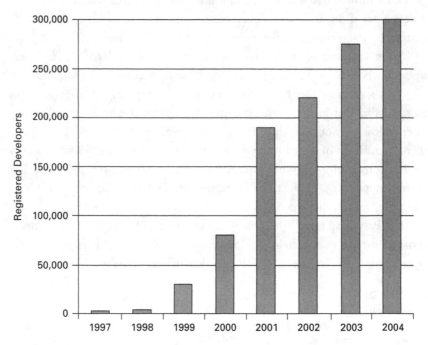

Figure 6.1
Growth of Palm registered developers. (Source: Palm press releases and SEC filings.)

31. http://www.palmone.com/us/company/pr/1998/devpr.html; http://www. palmone.com/us/company/corporate/timeline.html; Richard Shim, "Microsoft Crashes Palm Developer Party," CNET News.com, December 7, 2000; Gawer and Cusumano, *Platform Leadership*, pp. 203–206.

Table 6.2
Selected Top-Selling Palm OS Applications

2004	2005
SplashID (information security)	AOL (account access)
Splash Wallet Suite (productivity apps)	Agendus Professional Edition (PIM enhancement)
Agendus Standard Edition (PIM enhancement)	Ringo Pro (ringtone manager)
Agendus Professional Edition (PIM enhancement)	Agendus for Windows Outlook (contact manager)
Diet & Exercise Asst. (fitness and diet manager)	PocketMirror Std. (Outlook synchronization)

Source: Handango.com.

produced more than 13,000 commercial applications for the Palm OS. The existence of a large variety of applications was integral to fueling further sales of Palm OS PDAs. Applications like those listed in Table 6.2 encouraged consumers to purchase PDAs running the Palm OS. As of February 2005, people could choose from over 26,000 applications for the Palm OS.

PalmSource has continued to pursue an aggressive two-sided platform strategy since Palm spun off this operating system company. It had 400,000 registered developers as of April 2005. It courts these developers in several ways. First, it provides them a range of development tools. The Palm OS Developer Suite, for example, "provides a convenient and streamlined path to create compelling, robust, and professional applications for Palm OS smart phones and traditional Palm OS devices."[32] These tools are all available at no charge. However, PalmSource offers additional priority access to certain developers' tools through its Inside Track program for a $149 annual fee. Second, it maintains regular contact with developers through conferences and other ways. Its recent developer conference in May 2005 attracted over 1,000 developers. Third, it hosts a software store on its Web site that helps promote the sale of third-party applications.[33]

32. http://www.palmos.com/dev/tools/dev_suite.html.

33. The Palm OS Developer Suite is free to members of the Palm OS Developer's Program, which is free to register for at the lowest level (http://www.palmos.com/dev/programs/pdp/). http://www.palmos.com/dev/programs/insidetrack/learn.

As a result, developers continue to write applications for the Palm OS. More than 650 new applications appeared in the first quarter of 2005. Recent arrivals in 2005 include the Galaga game, for $14.99, and a free guide to the FIFA World Cup football (soccer, for American readers) championship.[34]

From a two-sided platform pricing perspective, Palm has therefore followed the model of PC operating system vendors such as Microsoft. Palm (and later PalmSource) charges software and hardware developers little or nothing for the various forms of support it provides.[35] And, just as Microsoft charges computer manufacturers a licensing fee for installing Windows on computers, PalmSource charges a license fee of approximately $11 per PDA for its Palm OS. In both cases, we would expect manufacturers to pass most of these fees on to end users. From 2002 to 2004, PalmSource made an average of 93 percent of its revenues and 96 percent of its gross margins from licensing and royalties on its Palm OS and therefore, in effect, from end users. Palm received the remaining 7 percent of its revenues and 4 percent of its gross margin from developer and manufacturer support.[36] As with all the software platforms we

---

html; "Palmsource Affirms Linux Commitment," Linuxdevices.com, May 24, 2005; http://palmsource.palmgear.com/.

34. PalmSource 10-Q, January 2005, p. 9; PalmSource 10-Q, April 2005, p. 41; PalmSource 10-Q January 12, 2005. http://www.handango.com/Software Catalog.jsp?siteId=1&jid=46AF5AX2F73CACD44A29426F29CDF764& platformId=1&N=96804&Ntk=All&Ntt=Galaga; http://www.freewarepalm.com/database/fifaconfederationscup2005.shtml

35. One could, however, argue that venture capital support to (selected) developers possesses a variable fee dimension, since it provides Palm with an equity position in these firms. This would generally enable it to capitalize on at least some successful complements, much as video game console makers capitalize on successful games through royalties. We were unable to find any detailed data regarding the funding deals made by Palm Ventures; this suggests that net revenues from venture capital deals are small compared to revenues from licensing the Palm OS.

36. We can approximate the royalty fee by taking the revenue from royalties (e.g., $15,952,000 for three months ending May 2005) and dividing by number of devices shipped in that same time period (e.g., 1.4 million), for an average royalty of $11.40 per device (PalmSource 8-K, March 2005; PalmSource 10-K 2004). Gross margin here is computed by dividing total revenue minus cost of revenue by total revenue from each business section.

encounter in this book, the business model is based on highly skewed pricing.

Windows CE

Following launches by Apple, Palm and other PDA manufacturers, Microsoft made its own entry into the handheld device market in November 1996 with Windows CE, a new operating system for small, handheld computers.[37] And, like Palm, Microsoft didn't get it right from the beginning. Microsoft spent five years and three iterations building a software platform that could compete with the Palm OS for PDAs.

Initially, Microsoft's lack of integration and reliance on third-party hardware manufacturers seemed to be a relative disadvantage. Following its customary PC-like approach, Microsoft developed the software platform and teamed up with computer makers that produced devices based on its hardware specifications. However, until the release of Windows CE 3.0 and Pocket PC 2000, Microsoft and the computer makers had concentrated their efforts on the "wrong" handheld platform. They were building handheld PCs, a rather bulky and expensive species, closer to PCs than to true pocket-size PDAs like the PalmPilot. Microsoft even avoided using the term "PDA" and preferred talking about "PC companions" and later about "Palm-tops." The Windows CE software platform itself was viewed as too complex for the needs of PDA users, especially when compared to the simplicity of the Palm OS.

Despite Microsoft's having six big-name computer manufacturers—Casio, Compaq, HP, LG, NEC, and Phillips—on board, fewer than 500,000 Windows CE-based handheld PCs were sold in 1997.[38] Palm,

37. Contrary to what is commonly believed, Windows CE was built from the ground up and was not a trimmed-down version of Windows 98 (http://www. hpcfactor.com/support/windowsce/). Stephanie Miles, "Microsoft Unveils Anticipated Pocket PC for Handhelds," CNET News.com, April 19, 2000.

38. Windows CE was started as the project Pegasus within Microsoft. OEMs were selected based on the work carried out up to the fourth beta (i.e., preliminary) release of the new operating system. http://www.hpcfactor.com/support/windowsce/; Jill House and Diana Hwang, "Pocketful of Palms: The Smart Handheld Devices Market Forecast Update and Outlook, 1999–2003" (IDC report no. 21177), December 1999.

by contrast, sold almost one million units that year. Over the next three years, Palm's PDA sales rose spectacularly, while sales of Windows CE devices were sluggish. From 1997 to 2000, shipments of Palm-powered PDAs exceeded those of Windows CE–based devices by an average of one million units per year.

Failure to attract end users meant that Windows CE also had a hard time getting developers on board. Ed Colligan, vice president for marketing at Palm, put it very plainly: "They'd offer funding for the initial development. They [Microsoft] held all the development kitchens. They always put on a big dog-and-pony show, and we our little nothing thing. [. . .] In the end, all the schmoozing and all the tools and all those things really don't matter if the products aren't selling."[39]

Faced with a stagnating platform, Microsoft shifted gears. In the Pocket PC operating system and corresponding hardware specifications that it released in April 2000, it abandoned the familiar desktop Windows look in favor of a simpler GUI better adapted for PDAs.[40] The devices were no longer to be called Palm-tops but Pocket PCs. Microsoft's hardware partners took advantage of the new software platform to release smaller PDAs, such as HP's Jordana and Compaq's iPAQ.

The sleeker Pocket PC platform has permitted Microsoft to compete with the Palm OS and its entourage. Microsoft offered comprehensive development tools such as Platform Builder 3.0 and eMbedded Visual Tools 3.0, which allowed developers and hardware manufacturers to build "rich embedded devices that demand dynamic applications and Internet services."[41] For example, Pocket PC sported an upgraded version of Windows Media Player, a new Internet browser, and improved email software.

39. Gawer and Cusumano, *Platform Leadership*, pp. 199–200.

40. Pocket PC was the direct successor of Windows CE 2.0 (September 1998) and 3.0 (April 2000). These latter incarnations of the Windows CE software platform were modular, enabling hardware makers to pick the parts they needed and use them to power a variety of devices, including ATMs, cars, video game consoles such as Sega's Dreamcast, and even kitchen utensils. Miles, "Microsoft Unveils Anticipated Pocket PC for Handhelds."

41. http://members.fortunecity.com/pcmuseum/windows.htm.

Still, Palm's lead remained more than comfortable. In 2001, end-user market shares were 55 percent for Palm versus 16 percent for Pocket PC.[42] At the time, Palm OS had about 190,000 developers providing 13,000 commercial applications, whereas Pocket PC had only 1,600 developers. And Palm devices remained significantly cheaper, starting as low as $99, while Pocket PCs did not go below $200.[43]

Microsoft intensified its efforts on all fronts. It started courting PDA software developers more actively, in particular those that had been supporting the Palm OS platform exclusively and had been a major source of the latter's strong competitive advantage over Windows CE. For example, Vindingo, the vendor of the popular electronic city guides on Palm, decided to start offering them on Pocket PC devices as well in 2001.

Microsoft expanded the number of its hardware licensees from six in 2000 to more than thirty in 2002, and it added major hardware makers such as Toshiba, Dell, Gateway Computers, Samsung, and JVC. Some of these computer manufacturers started making inroads into the low-cost PDA category, long Palm's exclusive territory.[44]

Most important, over time Microsoft integrated a number of new features into its software platform that made it particularly attractive for corporate mobile workers. The 2001 and 2003 subsequent releases of Pocket PC added virtual private networking, instant messaging, remote control of office PCs, and the wireless technologies Wi-Fi and Bluetooth. Microsoft also made the hardware specifications for Pocket

42. Although some sources claim that Palm had a 71% market share in 2001 and Pocket PC had only a 15% share, these figures are based on a more narrow definition of the handheld market. http://palmtops.about.com/cs/pdafacts/a/Palm_Pocket_PC_p.htm; Alex Slawsby, Randy Giusto, Kevin Burden, Ross Sealfon, and Dave Linsalata, "Worldwide Smart Handheld Devices Forecast and Analysis, 2003–2007."

43. Arthur Gasch, "Receiving Stations to PDAs, New Products Set the Pace at ACEP (Personal Digital Assistants) (American College of Emergency Physicians)," *The BBI Newsletter*, January 1, 2003; http://www.palmsource.com/press/2002/012102.html; http://palmtops.about.com/cs/pdafacts/a/Palm_Pocket_PC_p.htm.

44. Richard Shim, "Microsoft Extends Hand on Low-Cost PDAs," CNET News.com, November 11, 2002; Mitch Irsfeld, "New Foodservice Tools Could Flow from Microsoft's Expanded PDA Initiative," *Nation's Restaurant News*, May 29, 2000.

PCs more stringent, requiring its licensees to use more powerful microprocessors.[45]

These additions and improvements were a key factor in raising Pocket PC's fortunes against Palm OS. Windows pulled ahead, with a full-year market share of 46.8 percent, compared to Palm's share of 46.0 percent in 2004.[46]

Palm emphasized simplicity and ease of use when it started. That was a wise re-entry strategy, given the failure of the bulky Newton and Zoomer. Microsoft focused on providing lots of features. That didn't help at first. But as happened with Windows, the hardware platform eventually caught up to the software platform. The learning and development of the richer platform eventually paid off, enabling Microsoft's Pocket PC to close the gap with the Palm OS.

The BlackBerry

The other significant competitor to Palm, attacking from a different angle, is the BlackBerry handheld device, the product of the Canadian firm Research in Motion. BlackBerry—also known as CrackBerry, an allusion to its addictive nature—is a PDA, the star feature of which is mobile email: users send and receive their email through the device's always-on wireless connection. The mere access to email, however, did not make BlackBerrry unique or drive its popularity. Its killer feature has been that email is "pushed" onto the device as soon as it arrives at the server, while users of other PDAs have had to contact their server to see whether they had email. While well-known, especially to likely readers of this book, the BlackBerry remains a niche product. There were 5 million BlackBerry users in May 2006.[47] RIM produces the devices, then sells them either directly, in bunches, to companies, which can also buy RIM's email software to integrate with their corporate email servers, as well as to mobile network operators, which then resell them to their customers, just as they do with mobile phones.

45. http://news.com.com/Pocket+PC+2002+debuts/2100-1040_3-273912.html; http://news.com.com/Microsoft+preps+new+handheld+OS/2100-1041_3-1015726.html.

46. David Linsalata, Kevin Burden, Ramon T. Llamas, and Randy Giusto, "Worldwide Smart Handheld Device 2005–2009 Forecast and Analysis: Passing the Torch."

47. http://www.blackberry.com/news/press/2006/pr_30_05_2006_01.shtml.

(continued)

Like Palm, RIM started by selling Blackberries as fully integrated systems: hardware plus software. The company manufactures the hardware and has developed a proprietary operating system that takes advantage of the device's unique input system, particularly its thumbwheel. In addition, RIM licenses the BlackBerry Enterprise Server (BES) software, which allows organizations to integrate their employees' BlackBerry devices with their email system. In other words, if your company does BlackBerry, then you have a small box on your corporate email server that handles email transit to and from BlackBerries and also ensures that emails sent from a user's BlackBerry will also appear in his PC mailbox. There are versions of BES for most major email servers: Microsoft Exchange, Lotus Domino, and Novell Groupwise.

Initially, RIM provided all BlackBerry applications bundled with the device. Recently, however, the rising popularity of the device has attracted many third-party applications software providers, which have turned the BlackBerry into a true two-sided platform, very similar to the way in which Palm became two-sided. RIM seems to be following in Palm's footsteps with respect to its hardware strategy as well. In an effort to expand the market for its technology, the firm recently started licensing the BlackBerry software (the operating system and BES) to prominent mobile phone manufacturers such as Nokia, Motorola, and Samsung.[48] The devices built by the latter are therefore competing against the BlackBerry, just as PDAs running Palm OS and built by Sony and Handspring were competing against Palm's own Pilot. RIM's hope seems to be to move into the mass market and focus more on the software platform and related services, as the hardware becomes commoditized.

Like Palm and all other software platforms we have encountered except for video games, RIM derives the largest share of its revenues from end users, either directly (through sales of BlackBerry devices, licensing of the BES software and subscription revenues) or indirectly (through licensing of the BlackBerry operating system to third-party handheld manufacturers). For example, in 2004, handhelds accounted for 57.7 percent of BlackBerry's revenues; the remainder came from service (28.8 percent) and software (13.5 percent).[49] The service revenues came from individual subscribers to the BlackBerry Wireless Solution: either they are collected directly from the customer or the customer pays a third-party carrier that in turn pays BlackBerry. The software revenue comes from the licensing of BES, maintenance, and upgrades.

48. "Attack of the BlackBerry Killers," *The Economist*, March 17, 2005.

49. http://www.rim.net/investors/pdf/2004rim_ar.pdf.

(continued)

> This is not surprising given that RIM charges very low (if any) prices to independent software developers. The SDK and the emulator are downloadable free of charge from BlackBerry's Web site. The only restriction imposed by RIM is that certain controlled APIs must be "signed" in order to become functional on a BlackBerry handheld. To obtain and use these controlled APIs, developers must register and pay a $100 registration fee.[50]

Bundling

Much of the competitive dynamics between Palm and its rivals and much of the innovation that has taken place in PDAs has involved bundling new features. The holy grail of PDA makers has been a collection of features that consumers wanted in a handheld device that could deliver them well. The Apple Newton and Zoomer failed because they misjudged the applications that people ultimately cared about and because they bundled more into their products than the hardware could deliver well. The same goes for Microsoft and its Windows CE hardware licensees before Pocket PC came on the market.

The PalmPilot was the first PDA to strike the right balance between the key applications that consumers wanted and the device speed that made these applications attractive. One of the key features that Palm included—and that was copied by all that followed—was PC connectivity. Consumers wanted to be able to move data between their PCs and PDAs and, most important, to synchronize their address books and calendars. That required bundling software and hardware features to make this possible. The PalmPilot came with a cradle in which the user put the device to sync it with the user's PC.

Table 6.3 shows the history of key product features for users in PDAs from 1993 to 2004. (A similar set of features offered to developers was included in the operating system.)

50. http://www.blackberry.com/developers/downloads/jde/api.shtml.

Table 6.3
Timeline of major features added to PDAs

	Operating System	Capabilities
1993	Apple Newton, Palm Zoomer	Handwriting recognition, Infrared beaming, Organizer, Address book, Dictionary, Thesaurus, Spellcheck, Calculator
1996	Palm OS 1, Windows CE 1.0	Graffitti handwriting recognition, computer synchronization, Basic email, Spreadsheet, Word processor, Expansion cards, Networking
1997	Palm OS 2, Windows CE 2.0	32-bit color, on-screen keyboard, True Type fonts, TCP/IP and Ethernet support
1998	Palm OS 3, Windows CE 2.1	USB support, Network printing, Better audio support, Encryption, Device-device synchronization
1999	Windows CE 2.12	Wireless networking, Text messaging
2000	Palm OS 3.5, Windows CE 3.0: Pocket PC 2000 Edition	Media Player, HTTP Server, Language localization, XML support, E-Book support
2001	Palm OS 4, Windows CE: Pocket PC 2002 Edition	Bluetooth support, Third party 128-bit encryption, 160 × 160 resolution, MP3 playback
2002	Palm OS 5, Windows CE 4.0	Voice recording, 320 × 320 resolution, Camera
2003	Palm OS 6, Windows CE 4.2	Basic voiceover IP, Java virtual machine
2004	Palm OS 6.1: Cobalt, Windows CE 5.0	USB on-the-go support, Asian language, QVGA, HVGA resolution

Convergence of Categories

The worldwide sales of PDAs peaked in 2001 at 13.5 million units. It fell to 9 million units as of 2004.[51] It is generally expected to continue to fall.

This decline illustrates some important principles about computer-based platforms in general and software platforms in particular. These platforms are bundles of features that appeal to different users for

51. David Linsalata, Kevin Burden, Ramon T. Llamas, and Randy Giusto, "Worldwide Smart Handheld Device 2005–2009 Forecast and Analysis.

different reasons. It is easy to add or subtract features. The PDA was originally conceived of as a bundle of hardware and software features that would compete with PCs. The idea was that some people didn't need all the power that came with a PC and would be happy with something smaller that did less. That assumption was wrong. People didn't like the feature bundles they got from the Newton or Zoomer. After Zoomer, Palm tried a different bundle of features that turned out to give consumers what they wanted: a complement to their PCs rather than a substitute.

It turns out, however, that the PDA was a much less stable category than video games or PCs. People liked handheld devices, but over time they found other bundles of characteristics more appealing than those that came with a PDA. The RIM BlackBerry has been a major turn-of-the-century hit. These handheld devices mainly send and receive email, but they can organize contacts and maintain calendars as well. They have their own operating system, and RIM is pursuing its own platform strategy, as we saw above. A more important hit has been mobile phones—or, more precisely, smart mobile phones, which have operating systems and can run applications. As a result of this competition, PDAs and BlackBerries have started bundling mobile telephone features. The PalmOne Treo 650 smart phone has all the capabilities of a PDA: organizer, messenger, Web access, and Bluetooth technology.

As the Treo shows, Palm OS isn't limited to running PDAs. Palm diversified into other mobile devices in late 1999, as we noted earlier. As the smart mobile telephone business has taken off, Palm has increased its efforts to persuade phone manufacturers and wireless carriers to rely on its operating system. There are advantages (the large base of Palm applications and end users familiar with them) and disadvantages (there are other operating systems that were designed specifically for mobile phones) to doing so. Palm secured a 6 percent share of mobile telephone operating systems in 2004.[52] But it faces tough competition, to which we now turn.

52. Ibid.

INSIGHTS

• Palm made the market for PDAs in the mid-1990s after the first generation of personal organizers flopped in the early 1990s. Handwriting recognition was the device's "killer app"; it made a variety of applications easy to use.

• Palm, which started as an application software company, created its hit Pilot as an integrated hardware/application/software platform and then disintegrated by encouraging others to develop applications and make hardware.

• Palm followed multisided strategies of promoting its platform to developers and encouraging the creation of third-party applications. It also innovated by adding features to its hardware and software platforms.

• Palm's PDA success has proven short-lived, both because Microsoft's competing software platform has gained traction and because smart phones and other handheld devices have reduced the demand for PDAs.

• RIM's popular BlackBerry has attracted a developer following that has turned it into a two-sided platform. BlackBerry's decision to license its operating system to mobile phone manufacturers has turned these customers into competitors, just as Palm created competitors when it licensed its OS to Nokia, Motorola, and Sony.

• Bundling decisions are at the core of competition in the PDA segment. Early PDAs failed because they came with more features than the hardware could support. When PDAs included only features that people really wanted on devices fast enough to make those features attractive to users, sales took off.

7

Ba-BA-Ba-BAAAAH

This "telephone" has too many shortcomings to be seriously considered as a means of communication. The device is inherently of no value to us.
—*Western Union internal memo, 1876*[1]

INSIDE THIS CHAPTER

• The complex structure of the mobile phone industry

• Software platforms for smart mobile phones

• Multisided strategies and the development of DoCoMo's i-mode phone platform

---

Many years ago, most telephones alerted people that they had a call with a single jarring ring. The same unchangeable ringtone was bundled into every phone. As we all know from the cacophony of mobile phones ringing in public places, people now hear many sounds that tell them they have incoming calls. Mobile manufacturers have different standard tones, and many makers allow people to choose among several possible rings.

Moreover, people are no longer restricted to the ringtones that come with their phone. They can buy ringtones from various Web sites and download them into their phones. If you want to hear Simon and Garfunkel singing "Bridge Over Troubled Water" to announce a call, you can get it for $2.49 from www.cingular.com, among other places. These downloadable ringtones are small software applications. They

---

1. Morgan, Michael, *Making Innovation Happen: A Simple and Effective Guide to Turning Ideas Into Reality* (Warriewood, Australia: Australian Print Group, 2000).

Chapter 7: Mobile Phone Timeline

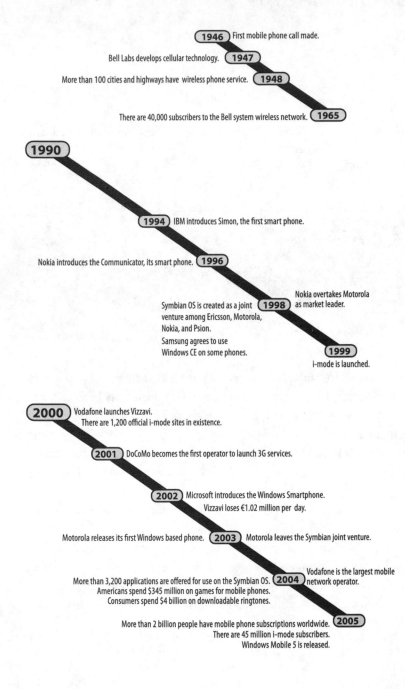

1946 First mobile phone call made.

Bell Labs develops cellular technology. **1947**

More than 100 cities and highways have wireless phone service. **1948**

There are 40,000 subscribers to the Bell system wireless network. **1965**

1990

1994 IBM introduces Simon, the first smart phone.

Nokia introduces the Communicator, its smart phone. **1996**

Nokia overtakes Motorola
as market leader.

Symbian OS is created as a joint **1998**
venture among Ericsson, Motorola,
Nokia, and Psion.
Samsung agrees to use
Windows CE on some phones.

1999
i-mode is launched.

2000 Vodafone launches Vizzavi.
There are 1,200 official i-mode sites in existence.

2001 DoCoMo becomes the first operator to launch 3G services.

2002 Microsoft introduces the Windows Smartphone.
Vizzavi loses €1.02 million per day.

Motorola releases its first Windows based phone. **2003** Motorola leaves the Symbian joint venture.

Vodafone is the largest mobile
More than 3,200 applications are offered for use on the Symbian OS. **2004** network operator.
Americans spend $345 million on games for mobile phones.
Consumers spend $4 billion on downloadable ringtones.

More than 2 billion people have mobile phone subscriptions worldwide. **2005**
There are 45 million i-mode subscribers.
Windows Mobile 5 is released.

include 15 seconds of digital sound and code that works with the software platform that's on the phone to make the digital sound audible.

With the spread of increasingly sophisticated mobile telephones, ringtones have become a big business. Consumers around the world spent an estimated $4 billion in 2004 on downloadable ringtones.[2] Most mobile operators sell these on their Web sites, and many Web portals specialize in providing them. The segment has attracted hundreds of software developers in the last few years.

That something as frivolous as ringtones has become such a moneymaker for mobile operators, music owners and publishers, and software developers is early evidence of the power of the software platforms that power these small computing devices.

Most of the mobile phones used by subscribers in the world aren't smart enough for ringtones or other software or Web-based applications. They don't have the microprocessor and operating system required for an intelligent phone. (Many data sources restrict "smart phones" to those that are closer to the PDAs of the last chapter—ones onto which it is easy to download sophisticated applications. These data sources would not include many of the sophisticated phones we discuss here.) That is changing rapidly in many countries. Mobile network operators have seen Web-based services as a driver of revenues and profits. They have developed capacious networks for delivering data and have started encouraging their subscribers to take ever-smarter phones that can rely on these services.

Japan is far ahead of the pack. Most phones there are smart, with 79 percent connected to the Internet in 2004. A June 2005 article in the *Business Telegraph* describes what anyone who has lived recently in Japan knows:

There are some things that a teenage girl in Tokyo cannot leave the house without. Her gladiator sandals, her Mac strobe cream moisturiser, and her i-mode mobile phone. With i-mode she can be constantly connected to a virtual playground of web-based treats: ringtones, chat, email, games, horoscopes and whacky cartoon characters.[3]

2. Reinhardt Krause, "Cellular Carriers Search for Piece of Music Biz," *Investor's Business Daily*, May 13, 2005.

3. *Business Telegraph*, June 24, 2005.

If the Japanese experience is any indication of the future elsewhere, these small computing devices promise to revolutionize many industries. People with certain i-mode phones in Japan can wave them at a device at the store counter to automatically pay for things. The transaction generally goes through the i-mode mobile phone network (and its associated billing system) rather than through a payment system network like that operated by MasterCard.

This chapter is about how mobile phone software platforms are driving innovation and transforming industries. It is a story once again of the power of these invisible engines and the role of multisided strategies in getting diverse customer groups on board. Pricing, bundling, and evangelizing remain the key tactics.

The Mobile Phone Business

The company that operates the wireless network has a critical influence on mobile telephone platforms. These "mobile operators" ultimately control what mobile telephones their subscribers use, what software platform runs those phones, and what applications can be downloaded onto them. We begin with these networks and then consider the other key players in the ecosystem: the phone manufacturers, software platform providers, application developers, and content providers. A simplified sketch of the relationships among the players is shown in Figure 7.1. (Americans refer to cell phones. We use the term mobile phones or

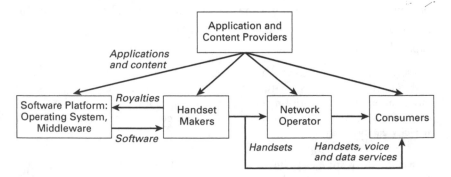

Figure 7.1
Platform ecosystem for mobile phones.

mobiles, which seems to be the more common term outside the United States.)

Mobile Operators

The first mobile phone call—made with a handset in a car—took place on June 17, 1946. More than 100 cities and highways had wireless phone service by 1948. There were 5,000 subscribers using clunky handsets. The wireless network, then controlled by the nationwide Bell telephone system, grew slowly. There were only 40,000 subscribers in 1965. The 2,000 New York City subscribers had to wait 30 minutes to place a call on one of the limited number of channels available. At this point, the wireless network was based on a single transmitter serving each wide geographic area.

Cellular telephone technology originated at Bell Laboratories. In 1947, the well-named D. H. Ring came up with the idea of having low-power transmitters spread across a grid and handing off calls from one cell to another of this grid as a person moved around it. Further development of computers was necessary to make this idea workable. A Motorola employee walking the streets of New York finally made the first cellular telephone call on April 3, 1973. AT&T started field-testing cellular telephone service in the late 1970s. The first commercial cellular network in the United States was started in Illinois in 1983. Japan, however, had started one four years earlier. Cellular technology soon displaced single-transmitter systems.[4]

Before the mid-1980s, telephone systems in most countries were monopolies, either public utilities or state-run enterprises. The United States started introducing competition in telephone service in the 1970s. As a result of the settlement of a government antitrust case, on January 1, 1984, AT&T divided itself into a separate long-distance company, operating in competition with other long-distance providers, and seven regional operating companies. Although few other countries went this far, the idea of promoting more competition in telephone service had widespread appeal. When the promise of cellular technology became apparent, many countries decided to create competition in this area by making licenses for the necessary radio spectrum available to several

4. http://www.ideafinder.com/history/inventions/mobilephone.htm.

competing companies. As of 2005 there were four major mobile operators in the United States, five in the United Kingdom, three in France, four
in Germany, and three in Japan.

Mobile networks are multisided platforms. They link people who
make calls and people who receive calls (we discuss more sides below).
The subscribers to a mobile telephone network make calls to, and receive
calls from, other subscribers on the same mobile network, subscribers of
other mobile networks, and individuals with traditional fixed-line telephones. Mobile operators around the world have followed a similar
pricing strategy. They generally subsidize the purchase of mobile telephone handsets by prospective subscribers. They then recover the costs
of these handsets through various subscription plans for making calls
and other fees that callers pay, as well as from the many new mobile telephone services discussed below. For example, Vodafone offers several
mobile telephones for free in the United Kingdom as part of an initial
subscription package that also includes reduced calling charges. A three-
month subscription that costs £12.50 per month includes a Motorola V3
telephone that is sold separately on amazon.uk for £199.99.[5]

Mobile telephone companies compete for subscribers. After investing
in subsidized phones and sales efforts to sign them up, they try to make
these subscribers as "sticky" as possible to their networks. In many countries, for instance, people who switch carriers lose their telephone
numbers. They also usually have to switch telephones, and that often
means losing all of the telephone numbers and other information they
have programmed into their handsets.[6]

The mobile operators also try to get their subscribers to use the
network as much as possible. Until recently that meant encouraging

5. Vodafone: http://shop.vodafone.co.uk/index.cfm?fuseaction=home.
viewPressOffers&WT_ref=HOM-15-07-2005-H005 (downloaded October 10,
2005); Amazon.co.uk, Motorola V3: http://www.amazon.co.uk/exec/obidos/
ASIN/B000980PVM/qid=1128958244/sr=8-2/ref=sr_8_xs_ap_i2_xgl/
026-6708820-8480445 (downloaded October 10, 2005).

6. Local number portability has been available in the United States and the
United Kingdom for years, and Japan began to offer local number portability
in 2006. http://www.fcc.gov/cgb/consumerfacts/wirelessportability.html;
http://www.ofcom.org.uk/consult/condocs/uk_numb_port/uk_numb_port_cons/
#content; "KDDI to Turn Its Handsets into Wallets," *Financial Times*, July 12,
2005.

people to make and take phone calls. With Internet connectivity, these companies are trying to get their customers to use the networks for other services, such as messaging, buying things online, and downloading content. One of the most successful of these is DoCoMo, whose i-mode service we discuss in this chapter.

The mobile operators serve as gatekeepers to their subscribers, a role that doesn't exist in other computer-based industries. One cannot call a subscriber without going through the operator's switch. Although it is possible for manufacturers to sell handsets directly to subscribers, it is more convenient for the subscriber to get both the phone and the network subscription from the operator. Most mobile phones are sold through system operators.[7]

Mobile network operators have consolidated over time in most nations, and several global operators have appeared. The largest by revenue as of 2004 were Vodafone, followed by NTT DoCoMo and T-Mobile, as shown in Table 7.1.

The United States has lagged behind Europe and Japan in the use of mobile telephones. For many years just about everyone under the age of thirty has had a mobile telephone in Europe and Japan. Young people outside the United States have used these computing devices since the mid-1990s for tapping out short messages (SMS) to each other, often using a dialect that economizes on keystrokes, such as the common "ttyl" (talk to you later) or "cu" (see you). The United States is catching up. But SMS is less popular in the United States because of the relatively low cost of voice telephone calls and high Internet penetration.[8]

Mobile telephones are particularly attractive for emerging economies that haven't invested in their fixed-line systems. More than 330 million residents of China have a mobile phone. Estimates are that more than 545 million—about 41 percent of the Chinese population—will have one by 2009.[9] Eventually most of these phones will be smart enough for the

7. "The NPD Group," *Business Wire*, November 21, 2005.

8. Charles S. Golvin, "Sizing the US Mobile Messaging Market" (Cambridge, Mass.: Forrester Research, July 30, 2004).

9. "China: Telecoms and Technology Forecast," Economist Intelligence Unit—Executive Briefing, April 19, 2005.

Table 7.1
Largest Mobile Operators by Revenue, 2004

Carrier	Revenues (billions)	Subscribers (millions)	Countries
1 Vodafone	$58.7	$154.8	Australia, New Zealand, Germany, Greece, Hungary, Ireland, Italy, Portugal, Spain, Sweden, U.K.
2 NTT DoCoMo	$45.1	$117.0	Japan
3 T-Mobile	$29.9	$120.0	U.S., Australia, Germany, U.K., Slovakia
4 Verizon Wireless	$24.4	$45.5	U.S.
5 Orange (France Telecom)	$23.5	$50.0	Australia, Hong Kong, Thailand, France, Netherlands, Poland, U.K.
6 China Mobile	$23.2	$220.5	China
7 Cingular	$19.4	$50.0	U.S.
8 MoviStar	$14.4	$74.0	Argentina, Spain
9 China Unicom	$9.6	$112.0	China
10 Mobile TeleSystems	$3.9	$42.3	Russian Federation

Note: Vodafone also owns 49% of Verizon Wireless (not included in the Vodafone total).
Source: Operator Web sites, and the press.

kinds of services we describe in this chapter. Worldwide, some analysts predict that the smart phone share of mobile shipments will more than quadruple over the next few years to about 18 percent in 2009, so that more than 180 million will be shipped annually.[10] Many of these people probably won't have a PC and will be connected to the Internet mainly through their mobile phones.

Mobile Phone Manufacturers

As we noted earlier, Motorola made the first mobile telephone for use with a cellular network. For a while it owned the business, but aggressive competitors soon appeared.

10. Kevin Burden, Randy Giusto, David Linsalata, Ramon T. Llamas, and Allen M. Liebovitch, "Worldwide Mobile Phone 2005–2009 Forecast Update and 1H05 Vendor Analysis" (IDC report no. 34408), November 2005.

One of them, Nokia, overtook Motorola as market leader in 1998.[11] It had moved more quickly than Motorola to respond to the emergence of digital networks in the early 1990s. It also recognized that people who carried mobile phones around all the time cared about how they looked. Nokia excelled at creating fashionable phones that initially appealed to the burgeoning European market, and eventually to Americans as well. Motorola fought back by continuing to improve its popular StarTac phone, which it originally introduced in 1996.[12]

An important dimension of competition among manufacturers has become how smart the phone is[13]: the sophistication of the hardware and software platform and therefore its functionality. Motorola introduced the first mobile that could receive wireless email, for instance, while Alcatel had the first phone that could both send and receive wireless email, and Samsung offered the first mobile that could play streaming video.[14] Competition has also included adding features that weren't

11. http://nds2.ir.nokia.com/aboutnokia/downloads/archive/pdf/eng/nok98eng. pdf.

12. http://www.motorola.com/content/0,,123-288,00.html.

13. The wireless transmission standards are the other noteworthy technological dimension: they are embodied in the phone chips and determine how data (voice and other) are transmitted on the network. For second-generation (2G) networks there are three main standards: GSM, accounting for 75% of worldwide users, especially in Europe; CDMA, with 17% of users, prevalent in South Korea, China, and North America; and TDMA, an old U.S. standard, which is fading away. Patents for the GSM standards are owned by a consortium of major handset manufacturers, including Nokia, Motorola, and Ericsson. By contrast, virtually all patents for CDMA are owned by U.S. firm Qualcomm, which in 2003 was virtually the sole provider of chips for CDMA phones and the overall world's number 2 cell phone chip provider, after Texas Instruments. For advanced, third-generation (3G) networks capable of supporting higher bandwidth and faster data transmission, the two main standards are WCDMA (Wideband CDMA, known in Europe as UMTS), the upgrade for GSM used by carriers such as NTT DoCoMo, Vodafone, T-Mobile, and Cingular; and CDMA2000, the upgrade for CDMA used by Verizon Wireless, SK Telecom, and Sprint, among others. Qualcomm owns all patents on CDMA2000 but only 20% of those for WCDMA, at least 60% of which is owned by Nokia, Ericsson, NTT DoCoMo, and Siemens together.

14. "Samsung Electronics Launch Streaming Video Cell Phone," *Israel Business Today*, October 1, 2000; "Motorola Debuts Internet Service At Wireless '96,"

originally associated with mobile phones. The now famous example is bundling a digital camera with a phone. Some phones now do almost everything one could do with a PDA—they include calendars, contact managers, and other features of an electronic organizer.

Because network operators serve as gatekeepers, competition among mobile telephone makers has a dimension that we haven't seen in other industries based on software platforms. Manufacturers sell their phones mainly through the operators, giving those operators considerable influence over the features that get included on the phones. After all, these phones are ultimately designed to benefit subscribers and thereby to help each operator sell calling and other services to its subscribers. Thus, when DoCoMo decided that it wanted its phones to include a smart card so that its subscribers could pay for things, it asked Fujitsu, NEC, Panasonic, Sharp, and other manufacturers that supply its phones to include this feature.[15]

Ultimately, of course, the consumer determines the popularity of different mobile phones. There is a choice among operators in many countries. The operators therefore have strong incentives to make sure that consumers are getting the phones they value most highly. In addition, most operators give prospective subscribers the ability to choose among different phones. For example, Verizon offers various mobile phone models from Kyocera, Audiovox, Samsung, Motorola, and LG at its wireless stores. The pricing of mobile telephones to the consumer is, however, less transparent than hardware-software platform pricing in other industries. Mobile operators enter into deals with manufacturers to supply phones. These are then bundled by the operators into packages that are designed to appeal to different customer groups.

Operating Systems, Middleware, and Software Platforms

For mobile telephones to become smarter, they needed increasingly sophisticated operating systems to exploit advances in microprocessors and other elements of the mobile hardware platform.

Mobile Phone News, March 25, 1996; Saunthra Thambyrajah, "New Alcatel Phones with Net Capabilities," *The New Straits Times*, June 18, 1998.

15. Ben Charney, "Carrier Turns Cell Phones into Wallets: NTT DoCoMo Launches a Service That Lets People Make Credit Card Transactions and Bank Withdrawals via a Handset," *Cnet*, August 9, 2004.

IBM made the first smart phone. Dubbed Simon, it was distributed for use with Bell South's mobile network in 1994.[16] It was an early PDA—it included an address book, appointment calendar, notepad, sketchpad, calculator and to-do programs, plus utilities for setting system preferences and managing data files. In addition to making telephone calls, subscribers could also send and receive emails and faxes. The operating system was primitive—a version of DOS. The Simon died a quick death, just as other early PDAs introduced around this time did.

Nokia introduced its Communicator phone two years later. The Communicator could send and receive faxes, emails, and SMS messages, as well as access corporate or public databases and the Internet. It also included a calendar, calculator, address book, and notepad. It was more of a success than the Simon. Nokia sold 100,000 Communicators in the six months after the release.[17] The Communicator used an operating system from Geoworks, the company that made the operating system for Palm's failed Zoomer.

These and other early smart phones had only those applications that had been embedded in the phone by the manufacturer or mobile operator. There was no significant community of third-party application developers.

With the development of the World Wide Web, the increasing sophistication of mobile networks, and greater interest on the part of consumers for email services, the demand for smart telephones increased, and the need to develop sophisticated platform software grew.

Three major operating systems have emerged for smart mobile phones: the Symbian OS, Windows CE-based Microsoft systems, and the Palm OS. Table 7.2 shows their shares over time. Together they have about 75 percent of all operating systems for mobile phones, with the remainder divided between Linux, voice-enabled BlackBerries that have the BlackBerry OS, and other smaller operating systems.

Creating a sophisticated operating system for a mobile telephone is a significant undertaking. As the need for such systems became apparent,

16. Chris O'Malley, "Simonizing the PDA," *Byte*, December 1994.

17. "Nokia 9000 Communicator Named Best New Product of '97," *Business-World*, January 30, 1998; Mark Moore, "Smart Phones Get Smarter," *PC Week*, February 10, 1997.

Table 7.2
Operating Systems Market Shares (%)

	2002	2003	2004
Microsoft powered	11.9	9.7	12.7
Palm OS	17.6	8.0	6.3
Symbian	45.6	66.0	55.9
Other	24.9	16.2	25.2
Total	100.0	100.0	100.0

Source: IDC reports nos. 29586, 31554, and 33415.

so did the reluctance of individual hardware manufacturers to go it alone. On the other hand, the large makers didn't want to leave this to Microsoft. They feared that mobile telephone manufacturing would become like computer manufacturing—a highly competitive industry in which each firm struggles to differentiate itself from its rivals. The mobile manufacturers also didn't want to leave this to competition. They feared they might repeat the fragmentation of the early days of personal computing, with many incompatible operating systems and applications.

So in 1998, the hardware manufacturers formed a joint venture to create an operating system they could all use. Symbian, as the joint venture was called, initially consisted of the three largest handset makers at the time—Ericsson, Motorola, and Nokia—together with Psion, a British maker of a PDA with its own operating system. This cooperative venture developed the Symbian OS and released it in 1999. (It was based on Psion's EPOC 321 OS for its PDAs.) Nokia was the first to release a phone based on the Symbian OS, the Nokia 9210 Communicator.

Symbian licenses its operating system both to the manufacturers who own the joint venture and to other manufacturers of telephones and other small computing devices. It has become the leading operating system for smart phones. Of the 22 million smart phones sold worldwide in 2004, 12 million used the Symbian OS.[18]

18. David Linsalata, Kevin Burden, Ramon T. Llamas, and Randy Giusto, "Worldwide Smart Handheld Device 2005–2009: Forecast and Analysis: Passing the Torch" (IDC report no. 33451), May 2005, Table 27.

As of April 2005, Symbian's shareholders consisted of Nokia, Ericsson, Panasonic, Samsung, Siemens, and Sony. Nokia had the largest stake, at 48 percent, followed by Ericsson, at about 15 percent.[19] All the shareholders license Symbian. Motorola dropped out of the joint venture in 2003 as a result of Nokia's growing influence. But it continues to license Symbian. So do a number of other mobile makers that don't belong to the venture.

Microsoft has had less success in this business than Symbian. It has had trouble getting the largest manufacturers to take its software platforms for mobile phones—Windows Smartphone, released in October 2002, and Windows Mobile 5, released in May 2005. As a result, its approach as of 2005 has been to form partnerships with low–cost, original design manufacturers (ODMs) to produce mobile phones. It tailors its mobile software platform to the needs of individual network operators.[20]

Microsoft thereby effectively bypassed the brand-name handset makers by dealing directly with the network operators. For example, it got Taiwanese ODMs to build phones that use Windows Mobile, and Orange, a French network operator, to sell these phones to its subscribers. Orange benefited from the greater flexibility it had to customize the phones it sells and from being able to market them under its own brand.[21]

Motorola and Samsung have decided to use Windows-powered operating systems on some lines. Samsung did this quite early, beginning in 1998. Motorola did so as part of its strategy to reduce its participation in and reliance on Nokia-controlled Symbian. It released its first Windows-based phone in September 2003. Both companies are multi-homers: they both use Symbian as well as Windows Mobile; Motorola also uses an operating system it developed based on Linux. Most other mobile manufacturers have standardized on a single operating system.[22]

19. http://www.symbian.com/about/ownership.html (accessed April 28, 2005).

20. "The Third Way," *The Economist*, September 18, 2003.

21. For instance, operators seem to think that one-touch access to their portals through a button common to all their handsets (such as the "i" button on i-mode handsets) can work wonders in increasing revenues from customers. Sue Marek, "Customisation? Suits You, Sir!" *Mobile*, April 14, 2005.

22. "News in Brief," *Digital Cellular Report*, April 23, 1998; "Mobile Phones: Battling for the Palm of your Hand," *The Economist*, April 29, 2004; Ben King,

Palm was well positioned to take the lead in smart mobile phones. Its Palm OS was a well-regarded operating system for small computing devices. It had a significant share of mobile operating systems in the first few years of the twenty-first century. But it has declined precipitously since. Symbian was a major obstacle for it, as for everyone, since the large mobile phone makers had a stake in and control over Symbian and feared losing control of the platform to anyone else. The rising fortunes of Windows CE in both the PDA (as we saw in the previous chapter) and the smart phone spaces have also hurt Palm OS. In particular, in late 2005 PalmOne itself (the hardware company resulting from the 2003 split of Palm) added a model to its popular line of Treo smart phones that used the Windows Mobile 5 software platform.[23] But Palm OS may yet find a way to rise from the ashes through its new owner, Access Co.,[24] the main provider of Internet browsers for NTT DoCoMo's i-mode phones.

This doesn't quite complete the story of software platforms. Windows CE and the Palm OS are sophisticated software platforms with rich sets of software services for developers. Symbian is a more bare-bones operating system. Early on, Symbian decided to separate the software platform into a rudimentary operating system and middleware that would run on top of it. Meanwhile, some of the handset manufacturers have chosen to develop their own proprietary middleware. Nokia is perhaps the most advanced in this regard, as we discuss later in the chapter.

Applications

Writing applications for mobile telephones isn't like writing them for Wintel or Apple computers. Different mobile phones have different operating systems and middleware. Developers have to customize their

---

"Challenger Is Open Source of Debate: LINUX," *Financial Times*, February 18, 2004.

23. http://www.microsoft.com/presspass/press/2005/sep05/09-26MobilityPR.mspx.

24. As mentioned at the end of Chapter 6, Access bought PalmSource for $324 million in September 2005.

applications for each of the packages on which they want their applications to run. Developers sometimes need to customize their applications to run on different phones running the same operating system and middleware (such as a Samsung phone running Series 60 and a Nokia phone also running Series 60). The varying screen sizes and other hardware components may also require nontrivial adjustments.

Given these difficulties, it is perhaps not surprising that the leading consumer application is something as simple as a ringtone. This is not a killer application in the sense we have used that term. People bought Apple IIs just because they wanted to use VisiCalc. People—at least people we know—don't buy mobile phones just because they want to hear "Toxic" from Britney Spears every time they get a call.

Ringtones may be trite, but they are hardly trivial applications. They are supposed to make the mobile phone play a replica of up to 15 seconds of a song you choose. How close they come to the original depends on the cleverness of the programmers in using the mobile platform to replicate the tones of the song. It also, of course, depends on the mobile phone. The smart phones available in 2005 aren't known for the quality of their speakers.

As in the Palm economy, most ringtone developers are small shops and startups. Faith, Inc. was one of the largest in 2005. It developed the specific polyphonic ringtone MIDI format first used in Japan and now worldwide. It has a market capitalization of less than $500 million—quite small for a publicly traded company.[25]

Three other types of businesses besides the developers earn profits from ringtones and are therefore relevant for understanding this niche of the mobile software platform ecosystem. The most popular ringtones are based on popular songs that are protected by copyright. The music publishers that own these copyrights (and the songwriters who get royalties from the publishers) benefit whenever a ringtone is sold. The producer of a $2 ringtone usually pays $0.40, or 20 percent, to the music publisher. (Publishers usually charge more for higher-fidelity ring tones—

25. "Faith—Mobile Solution," http://www.faith.co.jp/hp_engl/e_mobile.htm. "Faith, Inc." http://quote.tse.or.jp/tse/quote.cgi?F=listing/EDetail1&MKTN=T&QCODE=4295 (downloaded October 10, 2005).

between 35 and 55 percent of the ringtone price.[26]) Many mobile phone operators sell ringtones from their Web sites and take a piece of the action; they also profit when their subscribers download ringtones from other sites. And finally, there are a number of Internet businesses such as RingTonesGalore that aggregate ringtones and sell them to consumers.

Ringtones are by far the most popular application for mobile phones as of early 2006. Games are another popular application. American consumers spent almost $345 million dollars on games for mobile phones in 2004, and estimates indicate this will rise to $1.4 billion by 2008.[27] Other applications for personalizing mobile phones, such as wallpapers and screen savers, and personal productivity applications, such as contact organizers, are also popular. Some mobile phones based on the Symbian OS support mobile versions of the Adobe Acrobat document reader, the Opera browser, and the RealPlayer media player.

Many applications are sold directly to consumers through the Internet or the mobile carriers. However, developers also license applications to the operating system makers or handset manufacturers directly, and they in turn bundle the applications with their own offering.

The development of applications for mobile phone software platforms has taken longer to take off than for personal computers, video game consoles, or PDAs. This side of the mobile platform is still in its infancy in 2006. The explanation for this difference is quite simple. Unlike these other industries, the mobile phone software platforms lack the ability to control the ecosystem and drive innovation in it. Much of the power that other software platforms have is dissipated in the mobile phone industry as a result of the fragmentation of control in this global industry among many network operators and device makers.

26. Lewis Ward, "U. S. Wireless Ring Tone 2004–2008 Forecast and Analysis" (IDC report no. 34713), August 2004.

27. David Linsalata, Schelley Olhava, and Lewis Ward, "U.S. Wireless Gaming 2004–2008 Forecast and Analysis: Gaming . . . Together" (IDC report no. 32644), December 2004.

The Role of the Software Platform

Symbian has the largest share of mobile telephone operating systems, but it leaves the provision of many platform features to others. Take the Nokia 6620. It has the Symbian OS 7.0. That operating system takes care of all low-level tasks of the phone, such as sending and receiving voice and other data, updating the date and time, and connecting to the wireless network. The Nokia phone also has Nokia's Series 60 platform, a middleware platform that runs on top of the Symbian OS. This middleware platform provides a graphical user interface, an organizer, a media player, and application support. Nokia licenses its middleware software to other mobile makers, including LG Electronics, Lenovo, Panasonic, Samsung, Sendo, and Siemens. These makers customize it for their phones. Other mobile makers, such as Sony Ericsson, Fujitsu, and Mitsubishi, use different middleware with the Symbian OS. All of the middleware makers provide third-party applications developers with software development kits for writing to their middleware. Symbian does the same for its operating system.

All of the software platforms for mobile phones, whether middleware or not, engage in the basic tactics that all software platforms pursue. They keep adding services exposed through APIs that help developers, they provide tools that facilitate writing applications, they do all this with minimum charges, and they evangelize. Symbian and Nokia provide examples of tactics pursued in some form by all of the mobile software platforms.

Symbian

Although the middleware provides additional features not present in the Symbian OS, Symbian has been very successful in encouraging the development of applications that work directly with the OS. The number of Symbian applications offered by third-party vendors rose from 1,700 in 2003 to more than 4,700 in 2006. Macromedia's Flash Player for the Symbian OS enables people to navigate through interactive content provided in sleek graphic formats, the Adobe Acrobat reader allows people to read Adobe documents, people can stream audio and video with RealNetworks' RealPlayer, and they can browse the Web with the Opera web browser.[28] Some of the more important applications such as RealPlayer resulted from joint development efforts.

Symbian has an active program for encouraging application developers. Its Web site enables independent developers to download software development kits, programming languages (Java, C++, OPL,[29] and Visual Basic) customized for various middleware packages, and other development tools and documentation. It also holds industry-wide events and organizes contests for the best applications.[30]

Although many development aids can be downloaded from Symbian's Web site at no cost, some tools for development and customization of the operating system are available only to those who enroll in Symbian's Platinum Partnering Program. Affiliation with the partnership program costs $5,000 per year for Platinum members and $1,000 per year for Affiliate members.[31] In exchange for these participation fees, Platinum members receive the Symbian OS development and customization kits,[32] technical, commercial, and marketing support from Symbian, and participation and showcase opportunities at industry events. Membership in the Platinum Program allows a company to purchase a development kit license for Symbian OS v7 for $15,000 (with optional updates at $3,000 per year), Symbian OS v8 for $18,000 (updates at $3,600), or for v9 and above for $25,000. But according to Symbian, these programs

28. "Total Cumulative Shipments Reach 70.5 m," Symbian press release, May 16, 2006; "RealNetworks Launches New Mobile Media Solutions for Content Providers," *Asia Pulse*, February 19, 2004; "Adobe Expands Reach of Adobe Reader and PDF on Consumer Electronics Devices," *Business Wire*, June 10, 2004; "Symbian Enhances Wireless Internet Offering with Opera," Symbian press release, May 29, 2001.

29. Open Programming Language.

30. "At the Heart of Smartphone Evolution," *Symbian News*, March 11, 2002; "Symbian Exposium03—Invitation to Press," Symbian press release, April 10, 2003; "Nokia Names Top Symbian Applications Globally," Symbian press release, April 15, 2002.

31. Emails to Laura Gee of LECG from Pamela Annund of Symbian, May 5, 2005.

32. They are available free to Symbian's licensees.

Table 7.3
Symbian Revenue Structure

	2004	2003	2002
Symbian OS Units	14.38 m	6.67 m	2.00 m
Average royalty/unit*	US$5.72	US$6.24	US$5.75
Royalty revenue* (£m)	45.2	25.5	7.7
Consulting services revenue (£m)	17.5	17.1	20.2
Revenues from partnering and other revenues† (£m)	3.8	2.8	1.6
Total (£m)	**66.5**	**45.4**	**29.5**

* Royalties comprise Symbian OS and UIQ.
† "Partnering and other revenues" include revenues from training, partner activities, and trade shows.

are "priced only to enable cost recovery."[33] (These programs accounted for only 5.7 percent of Symbian's total revenues in 2004.)

Symbian earns its keep from licensing its OS to mobile phone makers. From Symbian OS version 7.0 onward, the royalty has been set at $7.25 per unit for the first 2 million phones and $5 per unit thereafter. It also charges its licensees for the consulting services it provides during the installation and customization of the Symbian OS. The share of royalty revenues has dramatically increased over time, as shown in Table 7.3: it went from 26 percent of total revenues in 2002 to 68 percent in 2004.

Nokia

Nokia established an independent division called Nokia Mobile Software to write and evangelize its middleware. It set up a "Chinese wall" between this division and the rest of the firm in an attempt to assure competing manufacturers that licensed its middleware that Nokia would not seek a software advantage at its competitors' expense.

Nokia's Series 60 middleware has software services exposed through APIs for supporting a variety of applications such as games, navigation,

33. "Symbian OS Phone Shipments Reach 14.4 m in 2004," Symbian press release, February 14, 2005.

dictionaries, voice recognition, and multimedia. The current version comes bundled with a variety of features. These include a Web browser, streaming audio and video based on RealPlayer, a camcorder application, organizational software, a mobile wallet, and video telephony.[34]

I-Mode

A new breed of platform, portals for mobile Internet services, has emerged with the advent of smart phones and advanced-generation mobile networks with greater bandwidth. I-mode is the focus here.[35] It was created by DoCoMo, the Japanese mobile network operator that is owned by NTT, Japan's largest telephone company. It was the first 3G network and remains the most successful to date.

The Japanese mobile market differs from others in several ways that have proved important for the emergence of i-mode in Japan and the lack of emergence of similar services in the American and European markets. DoCoMo has a much higher share of the Japanese mobile market (56 percent in March 2005[36]) than most mobile operators have in their national markets. DoCoMo therefore has considerable bargaining power over handset manufacturers that hope to sell in Japan. There's another difference. Japanese households are far less likely to have a PC at home than American households and households in many European Union countries.[37] The mobile telephone became the major way for

34. "Series 60 Platform 3rd Edition Overview," Nokia Corporation, February 2005; available at http://www.series60.com.

35. Most of the analysis is informed by our conversations with Takeshi Natsuno, i-mode's architect and chief strategist.

36. "DoCoMo Will Sell Nokia Phones for 3G Network From October," *Bloomberg*, May 27, 2005.

37. "USA: Telecoms and Technology Forecast," Economist Intelligence Unit—Executive Briefing, June 9, 2005; "Japan: Telecoms and Technology Forecast," Economist Intelligence Unit—Executive Briefing, June 9, 2005; "Singapore: Telecoms and Technology Forecast," Economist Intelligence Unit—Executive Briefing, June 6, 2005; "France: Telecoms and Technology Forecast," Economist Intelligence Unit—Executive Briefing, February 10, 2005; "Germany: Telecoms and Technology Forecast," Economist Intelligence Unit—Executive Briefing, February 1, 2005.

Japanese consumers to surf the World Wide Web. Finally, a love of gadgets and games appears to be deeper for Japanese consumers than for American and European consumers. The conditions were ripe for i-mode.

The I-Mode Technology

The other software platforms we have examined up to this point all reside on the computing device. By contrast, the i-mode software platform consists of many pieces that reside in several places. Some are on the handset and others are on a variety of server computers that handle requests from the handsets and pass information to and from the Internet. The core of the i-mode platform is a set of rules for transmitting data between the mobile handsets, DoCoMo's wireless network, and DoCoMo's server computer farm. Much of the platform lives on the server computers. These pieces count packets sent and received by each i-mode user, manage user email and subscriber accounts for various content sites, handle billing information, and connect i-mode mobile phones to the content providers' application servers. A portion of the platform therefore sits on top of the operating systems used by the several handset makers (including Linux and Symbian).

Getting Two Sides on Board

I-mode is a two-sided platform that serves subscribers to DoCoMo's mobile phone network, on one side, and Internet content providers on the other. Before i-mode was launched in February 1999, the company signed up sixty-seven content providers, handpicked by Mr. Natsuno, its chief strategist. He sought a diverse portfolio from the beginning. Mobile banking, perceived as vital to the success of i-mode, had twenty-one sites. The remaining forty-six sites covered gaming, fortune telling, news, sports, airline information, train and other travel information, real estate listings, and weather forecasts.[38] This variety set the stage for a marketing campaign that emphasized the myriad of amazing things subscribers could do with their mobile phones other than making phone calls.

38. Takeshi Natsuno, *i-mode Strategy* (New York: John Wiley & Sons, 2002), p. 49.

I-mode gained one million subscribers in six months, 5.6 million in one year and 32.2 million in three years. Subscribers totaled 45 million in August 2005. That is a remarkable market penetration for a premium service in a nation with a population of 127 million. The content provider side today includes some 5,000 "official" i-mode sites and another 88,000 unofficial ones.[39] Official sites can be accessed directly from the i-mode menu on subscribers' handsets. To access unofficial sites, users must type in the Web address manually.

Three strategic decisions were key to i-mode's success.

Adopt standards. I-mode chose standard formats and protocols with which Internet content providers were already familiar. This dramatically lowered the cost to content providers of providing content for the new service. To begin with, i-mode supported the compact HyperText Markup Language (c-HTML) for the creation of Web pages by content providers. This choice was widely viewed as contrarian at the time. Other major players, including mobile phone manufacturers such as Nokia and network operators such as Vodafone, were championing the rival Wireless Application Protocol (WAP) as the standard for creating Web pages for handheld wireless devices. The DoCoMo team opted for c-HTML because the language permitted content providers to adapt their existing Web sites for i-mode access at very low cost.

DoCoMo supported other standard Internet formats. These included the HyperText Transfer Protocol (HTTP) for transmitting data between the phones and servers and the standard protocol (SSL) for transmitting the secure data needed for financial transactions over the Internet. It also decided to support the Music Instruments Digital Interface (MIDI), a sound format widely used in karaoke-on-demand services. MIDI became the standard format for downloading i-mode ringtones.[40]

Rely on others for content. DoCoMo decided from the start to go two-sided. It relied on the market for the provision of diverse content to end users rather than supplying everything itself. This ran counter to con-

39. www.nttdocomo.co.jp/english/corporate/investor_relations/referenc/annual/pdf_02_e/2002.pdf;   http://www.nttdocomo.com/companyinfo/subscriber.html; http://www.nttdocomo.com/companyinfo/subscriber.html.

40. The MIDI standard was adopted by the electronic music industry for controlling all devices (including synthesizers and sound cards) that emit music.

ventional industry wisdom at the time, not to mention the advice DoCoMo received from McKinsey—that wireless platforms needed to *own* the content they supported and to block entry by competing third-party content providers if they were to maximize network revenues. DoCoMo rejected the closed garden for the open one.

In Mr. Natsuno's view, it was essential to assist third-party content providers in joining i-mode—for example, by lowering their fixed costs. The combined innovative power and resources of outside providers, he reasoned, far exceeded that of any single platform vendor. A large variety of creative offerings attracts more users to the service, and a large potential market stimulates yet more creative effort on the part of independent providers.

Develop a billing system. I-mode's unique billing system was its third strategic pillar. DoCoMo set up the network to charge users according to the amount of data, measured in packets, they downloaded rather than the amount of time they spent online.[41] In addition, they made this billing system available to content providers so that these providers could charge small monthly fees for their services; i-mode charges 9 percent of the gross billings as its fee for providing this to the content providers.[42] Users therefore got the convenience of a single monthly bill, while content providers got reliable billing service for a fraction of the cost of doing it themselves.

It is interesting to contrast i-mode's strategy with that employed by Vodafone during its failed attempt to introduce wireless 3G services in Europe. In 2000, this British network operator partnered with the French media conglomerate Vivendi to launch the Vizzavi service for mobile phones.[43] Like all European operators at the time, Vizzavi relied on WAP as the protocol for displaying content. Therefore, content providers with

41. "Traditionally, Telco's billing models have been designed to handle voice traffic . . . and, as in the traditional voice world, charges were usually based on prices per minute. With content services and new GPRS technologies, where data connection will be 'always on,' this model is no longer valid." Alain Lefebvre, "Not all kilobytes are equal," *Telecommunications International*, March 1, 2002.

42. This offer is restricted to official content providers.

43. Ian Lynch, "Vodaphone Clinches Vizzavi Purchase," *vnunet.com*, August 30, 2002.

traditional Web sites had to rewrite their pages from scratch in order to make them accessible through Vizzavi-enabled mobile phones. Furthermore, Vizzavi was not an "always on" mobile Internet service like i-mode, so users had to establish a dial-up connection to an access number in order to browse wireless content, tying up the phone the way fixed-line telephone modems displace voice communications. Time spent online was billed exactly like a voice call at the same per-minute rate, an inefficient and very expensive arrangement for both the operator and the user. Vizzavi attracted very little interest from third-party content providers, but both Vodafone and Vivendi were confident that the content they were able to supply themselves through Vivendi's ownership of Universal (Music and Studios) would be sufficient to attract a critical mass of subscribers, whereupon third-party developers would find the service more interesting.

Despite Vodafone's and Vivendi's investment of €1.6 billion[44] in Vizzavi, the portal's revenue and subscriber growth were both disappointing. After one year of operation Vizzavi had 2 million subscribers, compared to i-mode's 5.6 million subscribers, and after about two years Vizzavi had 4.2 million subscribers, compared to the Japanese service's 21.7 million. By May 2002, the portal was spending €1.02 million per day without any profit in sight, and its stock market valuation, which had been €20 to €50 billion at the height of the Internet bubble, had dropped to almost nothing by the time Vodafone bought out Vivendi's 50 percent stake in Vizzavi in August 2002.[45]

Evangelization

Given the explosive success of i-mode with subscribers, DoCoMo found itself overwhelmed with propositions from many diverse content and

44. Dan Roberts, "Survey—Creative Business Vizzavi," *Financial Times*, June 12, 2001.

45. "Vivendi Universal Announces 24% Revenue Growth to 7.3 Billion Euros and 90% Ebitda Growth to 1.5 Billion Euros in Third Quarter for Media & Communications Businesses," Vivendi Universal press release, October 30, 2001; Dan Roberts, "Survey—Creative Business Vizzavi," *Financial Times*, June 12, 2001; "Vivendi considers sale of stake in new media portal Vizzavi," *The Canadian Press*, August 20, 2002, Ian Lynch, "Vodaphone Clinches Vizzavi Purchase," *vnunet.com*, August 30, 2002.

application providers. In October 2000, a little more than a year and a half after the service's introduction, there were already 1,200 official sites from 665 companies and approximately 28,000 nonofficial ones.[46] These sites already covered the four major content categories initially identified by DoCoMo: information (news updates, weather, sports results), e-commerce (mobile banking, securities trading, ticket purchases), databases (telephone directories, restaurant guides, maps, dictionaries), and entertainment (games, fortune telling, clubs, ringtone and character download). Content providers were attracted by the subscribers, the ease of porting content to the i-mode platform as a result of its standard formats, and the fact that they got to keep 91 percent of their revenues.

Having made wise strategic decisions in designing i-mode, DoCoMo didn't need to stoke the fires continually under the content providers who were the application developers for this platform. Since its launch, DoCoMo has never had to seek new content. Its major challenge has instead been how to select among the many applicants that want to become "official" i-mode sites. I-mode is an open platform, and therefore content providers don't need permission to make themselves available. However, i-mode helps ensure the quality of its content through a certification program that labels some sites "official." The company organizes regular meetings bringing together the content editors from each of its regional subsidiaries to discuss their views on what content should or should not be included as official, in marathon sessions that sometimes last for two days. In May 2004 the 4,100 official providers accounted for 40 percent of i-mode network traffic, while the 70,000 unofficial content providers accounted for the remainder.[47]

DoCoMo does not organize conferences for its application developer and content provider community. Nor does its Web site have space and resources specifically dedicated to its developer-content providers like the other software platforms we have encountered.[48] It doesn't need to provide any special tools since its platform is intentionally composed of

46. Natsuno, *i-mode Strategy*, pp. 9–10.

47. Natsuno, *i-mode Strategy*, pp. 64–65; http://ojr.org/japan/wireless/1084495929.php.

48. Compare http://www.nttdocomo.co.jp/english/index.shtml; www.symbian.com; www.palmsource.com; www.microsoft.com; and www.apple.com.

already successful and widely used technologies, such as c-HTML and Java, that already have strong developer communities. Its technology partners provide and advertise their own tools.

Pricing

To access i-mode, users must purchase i-mode–enabled handsets from DoCoMo, which acquires them from a variety of manufacturers, including Fujitsu, NEC, Panasonic, and Sharp. From the beginning DoCoMo has employed a loss-leader strategy, selling handsets for roughly $80 to $170 less than it pays the manufacturers.

DoCoMo began by charging end users roughly $2.50 per month and 2.5 cents per 128-byte packet. The maximum-length email (500 alphanumeric characters, or 250 kanji characters)[49] costs a user less than 80 cents to send. These prices were in force as of late 2005 for users of older 2G handsets. However, those who used 3G phones paid $1.25 per month and less than 2 cents per packet. DoCoMo also offers volume discounts.

DoCoMo has always allowed content providers to keep the lion's share of their revenues in order to encourage them to provide diverse and innovative content. The only charge to content providers is the 9 percent fee levied on official sites that choose to piggyback on i-mode's billing system. In 2004, for example, DoCoMo derived $10 billion in revenues from traffic charges to users and only $90 million from fees charged to content providers.

The I-Mode Platform

Consider a day in the life of Yoshiko, an avid i-mode user in the summer of 2005. During her one-hour commute to the trendy Ebisu area in central Tokyo, where a branch of her company is located, she uses her pink NEC N700i phone to send ten emails to her friends, her boyfriend, and her mother in Kobe. She also buys advance movie tickets for that evening's *Lost in Translation* showing at a nearby Toho Cinema (Japan's biggest chain of movie theaters). When she gets to the theatre she will get her tickets by simply waving her mobile phone—equipped with a FeliCa chip for contactless payment—in front of a reader placed at the entrance.

49. Youngme Moon, "NTT DoCoMo: Marketing i-mode," *Harvard Business Online*, July 17, 2002, p. 4.

At lunchtime she goes to an Italian café for lunch. She has to pay cash for the only time that day because they don't take FeliCa yet. While eating with a colleague, she books a flight to Seoul on All Nippon Airways (ANA) for the next weekend to visit a high school friend. She gets an e-ticket and notices that she can even do e-pre-check-in, so that at Narita airport she will get her boarding pass by simply waving her phone in front of a reader close to ANA's counter. As the meal ends, she takes a picture with her camera phone of herself and her colleague and emails it to her mother.

That evening, on the way to the movie theater by subway, she leafs through a fashion magazine and uses her phone to scan the QR code next to an ad for Shiseido makeup. This opens an on-screen window giving more details about when the makeup line will become available, as well as prices and recommended accessories. Distracted, she can't find the movie theater. With her almighty *keitai* (mobile phone), she goes to Japan Teletext Co.'s Web site, pulls up an interactive map of the movie theater and, after 2 minutes of deft navigation, finds her way there. She meets her boyfriend, who is passing the time furiously playing an online i-mode game provided by locally famous publisher Enix.

After the movie, she starts talking with her boyfriend about how they both like Green Day's "Holiday" and they decide to have it as a ringtone. Her phone is more advanced than his, so she uses i-mode and the Chaku-Uta music service to search and download the song in two minutes. She also gets her favorite animated cat character from Chaku-motion, which will move in sync with the song when her phone rings. Then she beams the song to her boyfriend's phone through infrared. Meanwhile, her boyfriend was checking baseball results on i-mode because they missed an important Yomiuri Giants' game to see the movie, which they didn't much like.

This is reality in Japan, especially for the young. It is made possible by the invisible engine of the software platform. It is already revolutionizing industries in Japan beyond mobile phones. DoCoMo is becoming a leading payment system and disrupting the existing industry. The success of i-mode in Japan is the result of a technology that was just right for the economic and social circumstances of that country. While some of the story told above may remain uniquely Japanese, some of it will no doubt become reality in many parts of the world.

Which Is the Platform for Mobile Phones?

After encountering so many "platforms" in the mobile phone industry, one wonders, who exactly controls (and in what sense) the mobile phone platform? Indeed, one interesting feature of this industry that has become particularly salient with the rise of smart phones is the struggle between handset manufacturers, mobile operators, software platform providers, and standard setters (such as Qualcomm) to dominate the entire ecosystem. There is of course competition within each of these layers—Nokia versus Motorola, Vodafone versus Verizon, Microsoft versus Symbian—but, more interesting, there is also intense competition between layers. Mobile phone operators would 'like handset manufacturers to yield to their demands and design the phones in accordance with the operators' specifications. Handset makers, on the other hand, wish to maintain the strength of their brand name and are not very keen on customizing their devices for each individual operator, both because it is costly and because it would give operators too much control. Finally, given the importance computer-like features have gained in consumers' minds, software platform vendors see a good reason for both mobile operators and handset makers to bend to *their* will. Things are in fact even more complicated, as some actors in this ecosystem participate in several layers. Take Nokia, the primary sponsor and leader of the Symbian consortium. Through its strong brand name it hopes to maintain the high ground it has traditionally had over U.S. and European mobile phone operators. At the same time, its Symbian efforts have been in no small part motivated by the desire to pre-empt Microsoft (or any other software platform producer, for that matter) from taking control of the mobile phone industry. To counter this, as we have seen above, Microsoft has temporarily allied itself with the other layer, mobile operators, by using Asian device manufacturers and branding Windows-powered phones with the operators' logos.

That Nokia and Microsoft, two companies with very different products and business models, can be considered to be competing against each other illustrates the complex platform relationships in the mobile phone industry. After all, no one would argue that Dell is competing with Microsoft for control of the PC industry.

That dominance of the software platform is a critical asset in the competition for dominance of the industry seems to be clear to everyone. The handset makers were quick to realize this, which led to the creation of Symbian. More recently the major mobile operators have taken a strikingly similar step by establishing a London-based organization, the Open Mobile Terminal Platform (OMTP), to promote standards that will give mobile phone owners a more universal user experience while still allowing mobile operators to customize their offerings. The OMTP alliance is a clear indication that mobile operators want more control of the handsets

(continued)

used on their networks. Through this alliance, operators will be able to define standards regarding handsets and operating systems that major mobile phone vendors such as Nokia, Samsung, and Motorola will be expected to follow.[50] And Qualcomm, the company behind CDMA 3G mobile telephone standards, is also staking a serious claim with its Brew software platform, which has risen to prominence recently through the success of another Japanese operator, KDDI, and its au mobile Internet service, a serious rival to NTT DoCoMo's i-mode.

It is not yet clear what exactly "control" or "dominance" of the mobile phone industry means. "Ownership" of the customer seems to be an important element and one helping to tilt the balance of power in favor of mobile operators. But those same customers are rather sensitive to handset brands and design—witness the success of the latest Razr phone by Motorola—so that one popular model can make its producer a dominant player. Last but not least, consumers today care more and more about the variety and quality of features and content available on their phones, which depend crucially on the underlying software platforms. This gives software platform providers considerable say and influence over the evolution of the industry, which explains why participants from all layers are keen on being involved in a software platform.

Thus, if one defines dominance or control as the ability to drive innovation and ultimately extract the lion's share of profits, the dominant position in the mobile phone industry is still up for grabs. In particular, it is telling that mobile phone industries in different countries have different power structures. Japan's NTT DoCoMo, for instance, is the envy of mobile operators worldwide for its ability to dictate technical specifications to handset makers (including Panasonic, Sony, Sharp, Fujitsu, and NEC) and even downplay their brand names. The situation is very different in Europe and in the United States, where mobile operators have little leverage with giant handset makers such as Nokia and Motorola, and therefore little ability to drive innovation throughout the industry.

It is not at all clear, as we write these lines, that the traditional operating system platform as we know it from PCs and PDAs is necessarily the relevant software platform in the smart phone space. As David Nagel, once head of Palm, pointed out to us, it might turn out to be a different type of platform, say a network standard or a mobile Internet platform such as i-mode, which commoditizes all the layers underneath.

---

50. "Mobile operators unite to influence handset evolution," *EE Times UK*, June 23, 2004.

INSIGHTS

• Because mobile telephone operators have generally controlled what phones subscribers use, what software platforms run those phones, and what applications can be downloaded onto them, the mobile phone business has been an unusually complex environment for software platforms. This control is being challenged by both handset makers and software platform providers.

• The Symbian OS, Microsoft's Windows-powered OSs, and Palm OS are the leading operating systems and software platforms for mobile phones. Symbian, with by far the largest market share, is a joint venture formed by leading mobile operators in an effort to standardize on non-Microsoft operating systems.

• Some mobile operators/manufacturers control middleware platforms that sit on top of the mobile phone operating system; handset maker Nokia and mobile operator DoCoMo are the leading examples.

• Although industry fragmentation and efforts by mobile operators to control the customer experience have slowed the growth of application developers, there are now multibillion dollar markets for ringtones and games.

• Japan's DoCoMo, a mobile operator, has built a highly successful software-platform–based ecosystem that provides third-party content and applications to phone users. DoCoMo uses its significant share of mobile phone sales to persuade handset manufacturers to, for example, equip phones with contactless FeliCa chips that make it possible to pay with one's phone.

• Several key DoCoMo decisions defied conventional wisdom. It chose standard formats and protocols with which Internet providers and developers were familiar, relied on the market to develop content rather than producing it themselves, and made money by charging users for data downloaded rather than air time consumed.

8

Dangerous Intersections

When you're playing Bobby Fischer—and you want to win—don't play chess. Make sure whatever game you're playing—be it network delivery of media vs. stand-alone PC, whatever you're in—that you're not playing a game someone else has mastered when you have an option to play another game.
—*Rob Glaser, Founder of RealNetworks, May 2001*[1]

INSIDE THIS CHAPTER

· The elements of digital media platform technology

· The major players and their diverse business models

· Competition among intersecting digital media platforms

White headphones dangle from the ears of many employees at the Microsoft campus in Redmond, Washington. These almost always connect to iPods. Apple had sold 15 million of these digital music devices by mid-2005. Since it came on the market in 2001, the iPod has dominated the market for digital media devices with hard disks.[2]

Microsoft must find this grating. iPod users live in an almost entirely Apple world when it comes to music. Apple makes the devices with its proprietary digital software system built in. While iPods can be used with Windows-based personal computers, iPod owners can download music from their computer into their iPods and manage their iPod music only

1. Amy Johns, "If I Knew Then What I Know Now: Rob Glaser vs. Goliath," *Business 2.0*, May 30, 2001.

2. Apple 10-Q, 2nd Quarter of the financial year 2005, p. 15.
"Apple's iPod Available in Stores Tomorrow," Apple press release, November 9, 2001 (http://www.apple.com/pr/library/2001/nov/09ipod.html).

Chapter 8: Digital Media Timeline

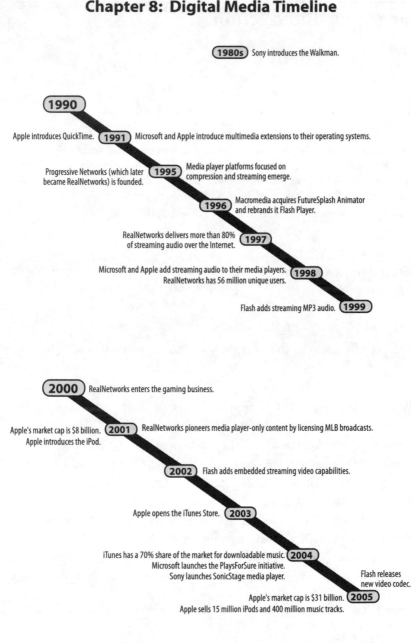

1980s Sony introduces the Walkman.

1990

Apple introduces QuickTime. **1991** Microsoft and Apple introduce multimedia extensions to their operating systems.

Progressive Networks (which later became RealNetworks) is founded. **1995** Media player platforms focused on compression and streaming emerge.

1996 Macromedia acquires FutureSplash Animator and rebrands it Flash Player.

RealNetworks delivers more than 80% of streaming audio over the Internet. **1997**

Microsoft and Apple add streaming audio to their media players. RealNetworks has 56 million unique users. **1998**

Flash adds streaming MP3 audio. **1999**

2000 RealNetworks enters the gaming business.

Apple's market cap is $8 billion. Apple introduces the iPod. **2001** RealNetworks pioneers media player-only content by licensing MLB broadcasts.

2002 Flash adds embedded streaming video capabilities.

Apple opens the iTunes Store. **2003**

iTunes has a 70% share of the market for downloadable music. Microsoft launches the PlaysForSure initiative. Sony launches SonicStage media player. **2004**

Flash releases new video codec.

Apple's market cap is $31 billion. **2005**
Apple sells 15 million iPods and 400 million music tracks.

with Apple's iTunes application. And they can generally download music, that is paid for, from the Internet only through Apple's iTunes store.[3] (We mention some exceptions later.)

With its digital music device, Apple has again followed a single-sided, vertically integrated strategy rather than a multisided platform strategy. So far it has worked. Apple's profits have soared. The financial markets appear to believe that iPods have turned Apple around. Apple's market capitalization has increased from $8 billion in 2001, when the iPod was introduced, to $31 billion in 2005. (Compare this 280 percent increase to the Nasdaq, which rose only 7 percent during the same period.[4])

Bill Gates, though, holds the same view on the iPod as he did on the Mac. In May 2005 he conjectured:

I don't think the success of the iPod can continue in the long term, however good Apple may be. . . . I think you can draw parallels here with the computer here [sic], too, Apple was once extremely strong with its Macintosh and graphic user interface, like with the iPod today, and then lost its position.[5]

Of course, back in 1985, when Gates sent his famous letter to Jobs about licensing the Mac OS, his interests were aligned with Apple's. A bigger market for Macs would have made a bigger market for Microsoft's applications. Twenty years later Apple is one of many competitors populating handheld devices with software platforms that do not come from Microsoft. The digital media system that Apple uses for its iPod empire is one that competes with Microsoft in many dimensions. Indeed, the iPod is but one facet of competition among media platforms for encoding, streaming, playing, managing, and limiting the piracy of digital music.

3. RealNetworks has recently reverse-engineered Apple's proprietary scheme, so that currently iPod users can use the RealPlayer to purchase and transfer songs to their iPods; however, Apple has warned that future software and hardware improvements mean that this scheme may not work in the future (Brian Dipert, "Song Wars: Striking Back Against the iPod Empire," *EDN*, June 9, 2005).

4. Market Capitalization on June 22, 2005, was $31 billion, according to Yahoo! Finance. Market Capitalization Apple 10-K, 2001. The Nasdaq closed in December 2001 at 1950.4 and in June 2005 at 2091.07.

5. "Report: Gates Says iPod Success Won't Last," *ABCNews.com*, May 12, 2005.

This chapter is about that competition—one that is quite different from what we have seen for other computer platforms. Elsewhere the competing firms had similar business models and were making money on the same side of the platform. They were all playing more or less the same game. While Microsoft and Apple followed different integration strategies, for example, both earned the bulk of their revenues from computer users. With digital music systems each major player has a quite different business model and source of revenue than the other. Apple is making its money increasingly from selling hardware, while Microsoft's profits come from increased sales of operating systems, and selling content is a growing source of RealNetworks' revenues.

How these intersecting platforms (see Chapter 3) compete with each other is one of the issues we address. The lessons from the digital media player wars are relevant well beyond this narrow category. Software platforms increasingly collide with each other in a process that is sometimes called, wishfully, convergence. They are also colliding with other multisided platforms, as the faltering advertising-supported media industry can attest in the face of the onslaught from Google, Yahoo!, and other Web-based software platforms.

Digital media platforms provide a contrast in many other ways to the software platforms we have discussed thus far. They also, however, have numerous similarities. Multisided pricing strategies have been key to igniting these platforms. Finding marquee customers on one side has been key, too. And, as with all code-based products, they compete by adding features—and thus grow larger—over time. (Most of the platforms we discuss work with digital video data as well as digital audio data. We focus on the audio part of these platforms and especially its relationship to the online distribution of music. Much of what we say, though, has parallels for video and the online distribution of movies.)

Digital Music Technology

The software technology for creating, delivering, and playing back digital music files has several components that help shape competition among the digital music platforms. These are different from the technologies we have discussed thus far.

To begin with, the music has to be in digital form. Much recorded music is already digital. But the raw digital files are too big for distributing music over the Internet or downloading music into smaller devices as digital music files. For those who want to store their music on their computer hard drives, Beethoven's nine symphonies would take up 3,500 megabytes of hard disk space if they were downloaded directly from the CDs.

The invention of software-based algorithms for compressing these large digital audio files on one computer and decompressing the resulting smaller files on another computer has been critical for the use of digital music on computer networks and smaller devices. This software is called a "codec," short for *c*ompression/*dec*ompression. The codec used by iTunes, for example, reduces the size of the original file by up to 90 percent, making all nine of Beethoven's symphonies fit into a more manageable 350 megabytes.

Most codecs make the original file smaller by eliminating portions of the sound that humans cannot hear, such as very high-pitched tones, or by eliminating portions of the file that will not reduce the quality too much. The codec also pulls other tricks to make the file smaller. (Media players have separate codecs for audio and video; some have a codec only for audio.) When the user wants to listen to music, the software decompresses the file to reproduce the song as close to the original as the technology permits. (Users can often choose the degree of compression. Greater compression results in smaller files but poorer sound quality.)

After it has been compressed through one of these algorithms, audio data are put into a "container"—a data file—that can be used for transport and storage. The container file is often referred to as the format. A song stored in an MPEG container file, for example, is in the MPEG format. Most container files can contain multiple audio and video tracks encoded with different codecs. The container also has a label that describes various characteristics of the media data, including the type of compression. In the case of audio and video files this label has information that helps synchronize the audio and video tracks when they are played back. (There isn't necessarily a one-to-one correspondence between a codec and a file format; indeed, codecs are often independent of the format. However, some pairs of the file formats and codecs have been developed jointly and are used together for legal or technical reasons. The Windows Media codecs that are usually stored in a Windows Media file format are one example.)

The container may also have information related to digital rights management (DRM). A music file downloaded from iTunes, for example, is subject to a license agreement that Apple has with the owners of the music. The agreement says that users can play a song on no more than five authorized computers but can download it to an unlimited number of iPods. After a track is encoded to reduce its size, DRM technology will also encrypt it so that it can be decrypted and played only with the proper set of keys or passwords and thus so that only authorized users can play it.

You must have a media player on your computer to be able to play audio files that you have received from a content provider over the Internet. As a practical matter, that means that you have to have installed a media player that can read the file sent by the content provider and decompress it. Your media player must be compatible with the format and codec used by the content provider. Moreover, it must also understand the DRM technology if one is used. The firms that make digital media platforms have, however, chosen different formats and codecs.

So how do all these components fit together?

For you to buy Charlie Parker's rendition of "Salt Peanuts" for your iPod, "Salt Peanuts" takes the following journey. For iTunes to carry "Salt Peanuts," Apple has to have a deal with the Savoy Jazz music label, which owns the right to this track. Most likely Apple has worked out a deal with Savoy Jazz for many of its songs. Apple provides the publisher the iTunes Producer tool (including the "signed iTunes labels") to encode their music using the AAC codec. After Savoy Jazz has encoded the master tracks of the songs that it has agreed to distribute through iTunes, it provides iTunes with these encoded tracks for distribution. (It is possible that Apple rather than Savoy does the encoding.) Apple uses its media system software to put it on its servers in an MPEG format file, the container used by iTunes Music Store.

You now have to have iTunes software installed on your computer to buy "Salt Peanuts" from Apple and download it onto your machine. (You couldn't have used another media player to download the iTunes song. Even though it would probably understand both the MPEG format and the AAC codec, Apple uses proprietary DRM technology that prevents other players from playing that track.) After you pay the 99 cents for the track, Apple's web server will deliver the song to you over the Internet, along with the keys needed to unlock the DRM protection. The iTunes software arranges to store it on your hard drive.

You can use the iTunes software to play "Salt Peanuts" on your computer as often as you want. Each time you listen, iTunes retrieves information from the file, decrypts and decompresses the audio data, and plays the song. If you want to download it onto your iPod, you just direct iTunes to do that after connecting your iPod. But your iPod has its own software platform that coordinates with iTunes. As on your computer, if you want to hear a song, the iTunes software on the iPod retrieves the file, decrypts, decompresses, and plays. You can also download the song to other computers and devices, but the DRM will stop this if you try to do this for more than five computers.

Of course, much digital audio is not destined for an iPod, nor is it necessarily even distributed over computers. Much content still comes on CDs or DVDs. People "rip" music from these onto their computers. Their media players will most likely give them choices on the extent to which they want to compress the music. People can generally download the music from their computers onto their digital devices. So you could buy a Charlie Parker album with "Salt Peanuts" and download it onto your iPod that way—or onto your MP3 player or other digital music devices.

People also get audio and video content "streamed" to them over the Internet. They get to see or hear the content just as they would watch a movie on television or listen to a radio broadcast. It is possible to listen to hundreds of radio stations over the Internet. Many content providers such as cnn.com offer audio clips and in some cases video clips on their sites. And this technology is being used on cable and other systems for "video on demand," which plays movies over communication networks.

As with listening to the radio or watching television, you often can't save streaming files without special tools.

Nevertheless "streaming technology" has been one of the other key innovations driving the growth of digital media systems. The audio and video signal is sent to the device and it plays an infinitesimal time after the signal leaves the transmittal device. The streaming server does this by sending small portions of the file, called packets. These are stored in a buffer on the computing device and played back. The streaming server continues to replenish the buffer. As a result, when all this works properly, the user perceives the file as playing in real time.

If there is too much traffic on the Internet, there may be a delay in replenishing the file, and the user will see that a movie has frozen or a song has been interrupted. Moreover, the quality of the playback is highly dependent on the speed of the user's Internet connection; slower speeds require the use of greater compression and thus entail greater loss of quality.[6] Indeed, streaming has become viable only because improvements in codecs have made it possible to reduce file size without sacrificing too much quality, and the spread of broadband has increased the size of the data pipe going into many homes and offices.

Many software components have helped create the now vibrant market for distributing audio and video content over the Internet. Media players are key ones and the component that most people use.

Evolution of Digital Media Systems

Software to create and manage digital audio files dates back to at least the early 1980s. Before the early 1990s, however, PCs did not have enough computing power to use media to any substantial degree.

In 1991, Microsoft and Apple both introduced "multimedia extensions" to their software platforms. These additional services, made available through APIs, provided support for media-related tasks, such as playing audio. For the most part, these early multimedia features were

6. With downloaded content, large, high-quality files can be transmitted via slower connections, albeit with correspondingly longer download times.

used by software applications for sound effects or by CD drives for playing music CDs. IBM, the other major contender in PC operating systems at the time, also introduced multimedia features into its operating system (OS/2) in the early 1990s.[7]

Apple and Microsoft evangelized the use of media-related APIs use by developers. Microsoft released the Microsoft's Multimedia Developers Kit and Apple its QuickTime Software Developer Kit. Both companies released significantly improved tools for developers and content providers starting in 1995.[8] At this point, media players were two-sided platforms, appealing to users and developers.

Interestingly, unlike many other platform services, Apple and Microsoft each ported their media-related services to each other's platforms by providing separate applications that ran on each other's platform. We return to this later in the chapter.

The Internet made another platform side possible. From the news to the blues, many Web-based businesses started providing audio and video content that consumers could download onto their PCs. The *New York Times* began to provide online content through its @Times services via AOL. The House of Blues posted interviews with artists online, as well as broadcasts of concerts.[9] Apple, Microsoft, and other media player vendors encouraged these content providers to make their content

7. "Microsoft Ships Windows with Multimedia Extensions 1.0," *Business Wire*, August 21, 1991; Erica Schroeder, "Apple's Multimedia Effort Gains Support; QuickTime Backers Meet at MacWorld," *PC Week*, January 20, 1992. IBM bundled Multimedia Extensions to Program Manager (MMPM/2) with OS/2 2.1 in June 1993 (Gabrielle Gagnon, "OS/2. IBM's OS/2 2.1 Operating System," *PC Magazine*, May 31, 1994).

8. John Sayers and Rockley Miller, eds., "A Look Back: The Year in Review," *Multimedia & Videodisc Monitor*, January 1, 1992; "Apple Ships Quicktime for Windows to Provide Cross-Platform Multimedia Standard," *PR Newswire*, November 10, 1992; "Apple Rolls Out QuickTime 2.1 for Macintosh," *Multimedia & Videodisc Monitor*, October 1, 1995; Andrew Singleton, "Wired on the Web: It's Not Just for Breakfast Anymore," *BYTE*, January 1, 1996.

9. Mark Berniker, "'Times' and NY 1 Team for CD-ROM (*Telemedia Week*) (includes related article on combining TV with multimedia)," *Broadcasting & Cable*, January 9, 1995; Marilyn Gillen, "House of Blues Stands at the Interactive Crossroads: (Company Forms the House of Blue Media)," *Billboard*, January 14, 1995.

available for their media platforms. Each vendor provided software that read the digital content, encoded it using their codec, and put it into a file format that their media players could read. Many content providers made content available for the major media player platforms. Media players were three-sided platforms.

Beginning in 1995, with the growing popularity of the Internet, media player platforms started emerging that focused more on compression and streaming so that users could receive music and video files over the slow telephone lines that were the predominant method of connection to the Internet in the late 1990s. Shortly thereafter, software for compression and streaming video over the Internet also started appearing. (Streaming audio technology is a prerequisite for streaming video content, which generally has a sound track.) Apple, Microsoft, Motorola, Oracle, Precept Software, Progressive Networks (RealNetworks), VDONet, Vosaic LLC, Vextreme, and Xing Technology Corporation were some of the pioneers in the creation of streaming audio and video media software. Many of these firms, largely unremembered a decade later, were acquired by other players or folded.

Among the startups, Progressive Networks, which became RealNetworks, was the main success story. Its RealAudio media player, introduced in April 1995, enabled content providers to stream audio content over the Internet and enabled computer users to play this content over the slow dial-up connections that were mainly used at that time. By 1997, RealNetworks was delivering more than 80 percent of streaming audio over the Internet.[10]

As is typical in these platform industries, firms engaged in leapfrog competition to offer better compression, streaming, and other features than their rivals. Consider the innovation that has taken place in digital media platforms since 1995. RealNetworks was the first to add streaming video to its player in early 1997. Apple followed, adding streaming audio to its media player in March 1998, and Microsoft did the same in

10. Archived news on RealAudio.com (http://web.archive.org/web/19961220180029/www.realaudio.com/prognet/prognews.html [downloaded June 18, 2005]); Thomas W. Haines, "RealNetworks Hopes to Make Real Profits When Net Matures," *The Seattle Times*, October 1, 1997.

Table 8.1
Media Player Features Over Time

Date	Product	Features Added
Aug. 1991	Multimedia Extensions for Windows	Media Player can start, stop and pause the playback of sound or animation files. Music Box can play and catalog audio CDs.
Dec. 1991	QuickTime 1.0	Multimedia extension added to Mac OS System 7. Users could combine animation, sound, and video, and incorporate the results into Macintosh applications.
July 1995	RealAudio 1.0	RealAudio 1.0 released. It can stream audio from the Internet (in the RealAudio format and codec).
Dec. 1996	Flash 1	Macromedia acquires FutureSplash Animator and rebrands it the Flash Player.
Jan. 1997	RealVideo 1.0	RealVideo released and bundled with RealAudio in RealPlayer. Plays and streams video.
May 1997	Flash 2	Adds sound capabilities, including support for synchronizing. WAV and AIFF (Audio Interchange File Format) sounds to animations.
Mar. 1998	QuickTime 3	Introduces real-time streaming of digital content over the Internet.
July 1998	Windows Media Player	Streams audio and video.
May 1999	RealJukebox	RealJukebox introduced. Users can play, record, organize, and search for music from single interface, rip CDs, find and download music from the Internet, sync with portable device.
May 1999	Flash 4	Adds streaming MP3 audio.
June 1999	QuickTime 4	Allows streaming of both live and stored video and audio over the Internet. Uses nonproprietary industry standard RTP and RTSP protocols.
Aug. 1999	Window Media DRM	Windows Media integrates DRM.
July 2000	Windows Media Player 7	Integrated a digital audio and video player, "jukebox" features, and Internet radio tuner. Capable of CD burning and copying.

Table 8.1
(continued)

Date	Product	Features Added
Jan. 2001	iTunes 1.0	iTunes, jukebox software-introduced. Users can listen to audio CDs, MP3, or Internet radio, rip CDs and store them on hard drive in MP3 format, maintain music library, burn CDs, and download songs to certain MP3 players.
Apr. 2001	QuickTime 5	Full support for MPEG-1 standard and Flash 4.
Dec. 2001	RealOne Player	Combines functions of RealPlayer and RealJukebox with a media browser. Includes support for audio and video streaming, burning CDs.
Nov. 2001	iTunes 2.0	Adds MP3 CD burning, an equalizer, and cross fading.
Mar. 2002	Flash 6	Macromedia allows developers to embed video streams for playback in the Flash Player.
May 2002	QuickTime 6	Support for MPEG-4, AAC, DVC Pro (PAL), and more.
July 2002	iTunes 3.0	Adds Smart Playlist feature—allows user to automatically create mixes from songs in music library based on chosen criteria.
Aug. 2002	RealOne Player 2.0	Supports all major file formats. Adds DVD playback support.
Sept. 2002	Windows Media Player 9	Built in support for Fast Streaming technology.
Apr. 2003	iTunes 4/ Quicktime 6.2	Integration of iTunes Music Store; music sharing between Macs. Adds DRM.
June 2003	QuickTime 6.3	Support for 3GPP enables users to share video, audio, and text on wireless devices.
Oct. 2003	iTunes 4.1	First version of iTunes for Windows.
Apr. 2004	RealPlayer 10	Supports all major media formats and codecs (RealAudio, RealVideo, AAC, MP3, MPEG-4, Windows Media, QuickTime) and the ability to play music from all major online music stores. Integrated music download store. Ability to fast forward and rewind within streams without delay, and to pause live streams. DRM included.

Table 8.1
(continued)

Date	Product	Features Added
Sept. 2004	Windows Media Player 10	Built-in Digital Media Mall gives users choice of online stores. Supports Janus DRM, which allows time-sensitive DRM (secure clock technology).
June 2005	QuickTime 7	Preview release. Supports playing and streaming high-definition video.
June 2005	iTunes 4.8	Streams QuickTime Video.
Aug. 2005	Flash 8	Integrates new video codec for improved performance.

July 1998.[11] Other companies entered with media players. Adobe's Flash became a leading media player for the distribution of video content almost overnight in 2005. Table 8.1 shows the major media player platforms that were introduced between 1995 and 2005, their capabilities, and their major components. (In addition to these media systems, a number of open-source and small commercial systems have also been introduced.)

These media player vendors were not all in the same business. They were pursuing different strategies for making money, as we see next. But they did have one important thing in common: they gave away the media players to users.

Competition Between Intersecting Platforms

Hardly anyone pays directly for using a media player. All of the major media player developers have Web sites where you can download the latest versions of their basic media players for free. So if you want to get the most recent version of RealNetworks' media player, as of June 2006 you could go to real.com and click on the free download link

11. "Progressive Networks Ships RealAudio System," RealNetworks press release, July 25, 1995; "QuickTime 3 and QuickTime 3 Pro Available Now," Apple press release, March 30, 1998; "Key Corporations, Internet Sites and Industry Vendors Announce Deployment, Support," Microsoft press release, July 7, 1998.

to get a copy of RealPlayer 10.5. Real made its stand-alone media player available for free from the start. When asked, "What's the best move you've made?" Rob Glaser, its chief executive and founder, responded, "Probably making the RealPlayer free."[12] Many PCs for home use come with several media players at no extra charge. These include the media players that are included in the Mac OS and Windows as well as several other media players, such as MusicMatch or RealPlayer. Media players are also included in other products such as music devices or services such as AOL.

Some media player vendors sell premium versions of their players. Apple, for example, charges $29.99 for a beefed-up version of Quick-Time, and RealNetworks charges $19.99 for a premium version of the RealPlayer, RealPlayer Plus. (The premium RealPlayer Plus is also available bundled with the Real SuperPass service for a fee of $12.99 a month.) But nothing suggests that any company sees media players as a significant source of revenue. The financial statements for companies such as Apple and RealNetworks do not break out media player sales, nor do they suggest that these sales provided a material source of earnings. Instead, vendors of media player software hope that through free distribution they will achieve profits from increased sales of complementary goods and services. The mix of such goods and services varies across vendors and, for some vendors, has varied across time as well.

Where Does the Money Come From?

So how do media player vendors make their money? What motivates them to make the significant investment in developing complex media platforms and giving the media players away for free? We consider the answers to these questions next. Table 8.2 summarizes the results for easy reference. Like other software platforms, media players subsidize one customer group to get other customer groups on board. Unlike other software platforms, different media software platforms secure profits from different customer groups. We illustrate this with a detailed discussion of Apple and RealNetworks.

12. Johns, "If I Knew Then What I Know Now."

Table 8.2
Sources of Revenue from Media Players

	Media Player Software (Free Version)	Media Server Software	Content Providers	Application Developers	Hardware Sales	Content Sales	Computer Operating Systems	Major Source of Profits
Apple	—	0	0	+	+	+	+	Hardware sales, and operating systems
RealNetworks	—	+	+	+	0	+	0	Content sales
Microsoft	—	0	+	+	0	+	+	Operating systems
Adobe	—	+	+	+	0	0	0	Media server sales

Apple   Apple first demonstrated the QuickTime product at an Apple developer conference in May 1991.

Apple released QuickTime as a separate add-on in December 1991 and included it as part of the Mac OS System 7 the next year. It also ported QuickTime to Windows and started shipping that version in 1994. As a result, most copies of QuickTime—and the related iTunes software introduced in 2001—run on Wintel computers and not on Macs.[13]

Apple also made the software necessary for distributing QuickTime files available for free. It eventually made the source code for its streaming server software available so that others were free to create versions for non-Macintosh servers. Like other software platforms, with the exception of video games, Apple has made the API-based services in QuickTime available to developers for free, has provided free software to developers to help them write programs using QuickTime, and has spent effort evangelizing its media platform among the developer community.[14]

This poses a mystery: How does Apple make money from its considerable investment in improving and porting QuickTime?

The inclusion of QuickTime with the Mac OS does not require much explanation. As with any feature added to an operating system, it makes the operating system more valuable to some end users and therefore tends to increase sales and possibly the price that the vendor can charge. While it is impossible to know the extent to which QuickTime increased sales of Macs, we note that a 1 percent increase in sales would generate revenues of about $50 million per year.[15] It is not a bad strategy, and it is in any case one followed by many software platforms. We return to this in Chapter 11.

Apple had to make a trade-off in considering whether to port QuickTime to Windows. On the one hand, making its media technology

13. Schroeder, "Apple's Multimedia Effort Gains Support"; Carolyn Said, "QuickTime 2.0 Now Plays on Windows," *MacWEEK*, November 28, 1994; "Apple Unveils New iMacs with CD-RW Drives and iTunes Software," Apple press release, February 22, 2001.

14. http://developer.apple.com/darwin/projects/streaming/. Apple does charge for the SDK for QuickTime.

15. According to the Apple 10-K filing for 2004, Macintosh net sales were $4,923,000,000 (p. 28).

available for free to developers and users of competing software platforms strengthens those platforms and therefore harms Apple. On the other hand, making its media player technology available for these rival software platforms encourages content providers to make content available for that technology. That in turn makes the Mac OS with Quick-Time more appealing to end users. Apple presumably decided that having a popular media player for its software platform was more important than losing some sales to competing software platforms. Microsoft made the same decision.

Apple's investment in QuickTime, however, began paying significant dividends by the turn of the century when it introduced the iPod/iTunes music system. Apple introduced the now-iconic iPod in October 2001. These devices could download music (at first only using the Mac OS, and later using Windows) using iTunes. iTunes is based on the Quick-Time media player and allows consumers to do many of the things they can do with other media players.[16]

Apple opened its iTunes Store in April 2003. It charged consumers 99 cents per downloaded song. Apple, however, doesn't try to earn significant profits from the iTunes Store. Instead, the iTunes store and media player platform are designed to increase sales of iPods and to some extent Macs. As we discuss later, Apple has tried to design the iTunes/iPod system so that it doesn't work with competing media players or devices. That helps ensure that Apple doesn't lose revenues to others. Thus Apple has adopted a "give away the blades and sell the razor" strategy. That pricing strategy is unique among the industries we have considered.

Apple had sold 50 million iPods by March 2006, and 1 billion music tracks by February 2006. The iPod/iTunes music system helped Apple earn record profits in 2005 and accounted for 32 percent of Apple's net sales in 2005. One brokerage firm has estimated that sales of the high-margin iPod portable players will top 24 million units in 2006.[17]

16. "Apple Unveils New iPods," Apple press release, July 17, 2000; "Apple Launches iTunes for Windows," Apple press release, October 16, 2003.

17. "iTunes Music Store Downloads Top One Billion Songs," Apple press release, February 23, 2006; Apple 10-K for financial year 2005 and quarterly statements 2006; Howard Wolinsky, "What's next for iPod? Popular gizmo may get makeover," *The Chicago Sun Times*, February 19, 2006.

RealNetworks   Rob Glaser, the force behind RealNetworks from its beginning, worked on Microsoft's media platform in the early 1990s. He left and formed Progressive Networks in early 1994. This startup launched its RealAudio Player in April 1995. In early 1996, the *Seattle Post-Intelligencer* reported that more than 3 million people had installed the RealAudio Player.[18] That was about three times more installations than Xing, its nearest competitor, had achieved.

Progressive Networks adopted two classic multisided strategies to establish its position.

First, it made its player available for free. As it noted in its first 10-K filing two years after it launched RealAudio, "From its inception the Company has strategically chosen to offer its RealPlayer software to individual users free of charge to promote the widespread adoption of its client software and speed acceptance of internet multimedia."[19] With the development of browsers and the expansion of the Internet, it was able to distribute its free player easily through Web sites where people could download it.

Second, it developed the second side of its platform, the content providers. According to the *Seattle Post-Intelligencer*, "Progressive has teamed with a host of companies and organizations to serve up a cornucopia of internet audio, from the State of the Union address to the music of Madonna and Meatloaf to a historical tour of the Oscar Mayer Wienermobile."[20] Progressive Networks gave content providers the encoder software they needed to make their content available for RealAudio.

During its early years, Progressive's main source of revenue was from the sale of RealAudio servers—the software that content providers needed to stream audio to users. And even here it appears that Progressive gave away a basic version of the server software, charging only for more advanced versions that streamed content to a large number of users.

18. http://web.archive.org/web/19961220183228/www.realaudio.com/prognet/pr/prodannounce.html; Warren Wilson, "Now Hear This: Seattle Company Leads the Way with 'Streaming Audio' for Internet Sound," *Seattle Post-Intelligencer*, February 19, 1996.

19. RealNetworks 10-K filing for 1998, p. 4.

20. Wilson, "Now Hear This."

Glaser's company changed its name to RealNetworks and went public in November 1997. Its first 10-K filing with the Securities and Exchange Commission provides more insights into the strategy followed by this innovative firm. By this time RealNetworks had expanded from streaming audio into streaming video. At that time its businesses consisted of the RealSystem for streaming audio and video, "a web-site designed to promote the proliferation of streaming media products," and a network of Web sites that were supported by advertising revenues. About 78 percent of its revenues came from software licenses. Although these aren't broken out, they appear to come mainly from licensing server software. (RealNetworks also introduced a premium version of its player in late 1996, from which it received licensing revenues.)

It made RealPlayer widely available to consumers. According to its filing with the SEC,

This strategy has been pursued through various means, such as offering the Company's RealPlayer and Basic Server free of charge over the internet, bundling the Company's products with those of other major vendors and using multiple distribution channels, including both direct sales and indirect original equipment manufacturer ("OEM") and retail relationships.[21]

In the two years since it introduced RealAudio it had made considerable progress. RealNetworks reported in its SEC filing that more than 40 million copies of RealPlayer had been downloaded, more than 260,000 Web pages had content encoded in RealPlayer, and more than 1,200 software developers had joined its development program.[22]

RealNetworks envisioned pursuing three related businesses as of 1997:

1. Licensing server software. Content providers need this software to make audio and video available to RealPlayer users.

2. Expanding its Internet commerce business for content providers and developers. At the time this included RealNetworks products, streaming media tools and utilities for developers, and training.

3. Aggregating content for streaming media. It appears that RealNetworks hoped for advertising revenue from building a network of Web sites that had streaming content.

21. RealNetworks 10-K filing for 1998, p. 5.
22. Ibid., pp. 2–20.

In light of RealNetworks' subsequent evolution, it is interesting that the company at this point in time did not seem to envision that it would make money by providing its own content.

RealNetworks quickly built a five-sided platform consisting of users, content providers, developers, server manufacturers, and other partners. In 1998 it had 56 million unique users of its players. That year CNN, ESPN, ABC, Bloomberg, SportLine USA, and Broadcast.com started offering content in Real. The RealGuide provided users with access to more than 1,700 live radio and television stations. The company added 850 registered developers in 1998, giving it more than 2,000 in its program.[23] And finally, RealNetworks had persuaded America Online, Netscape, and a number of PC manufacturers to bundle its RealPlayer with their products.

But profits were elusive. They were not going to come from free media players for consumers. And unlike Apple and Microsoft, RealNetworks had no prospect of earning money from operating system sales. Nothing prevented the company from pursuing the hardware-centric strategy that later proved successful for Apple. But RealNetworks had always specialized in software. It didn't have hardware in its genes.

Over time, RealNetworks shifted its pursuit of profits from selling server software toward selling content that relies on its digital media platform. As of the summer of 2005, RealNetworks had three major content offerings.

First, its Real Music Store had more than a million songs. Consumers could download these to more than a hundred different digital music devices. Its Rhapsody service provided a variety of subscription services; the basic version allowed users to play songs on their computers but not take permanent possession of the music. This subscription service also worked with portable devices through its Rhapsody To Go program. In December 2005, Real's Music Store had about a 1 percent share of the online digital music market, compared to iTunes' share of 82 percent.[24] In addition, Rhapsody provides access to more than fifty radio stations, including many without advertisements.

23. Ibid., p. 4; RealNetworks 10-K filing for 1999, p. 4.
24. NPD Musicwatch Digital, February 2006.

Second, RealNetworks offered audio and video content through its SuperPass program. Video content included films from iFilm, broadcasts from CNN, ABC, and BBC, and sports radio. Audio content includes access to the radio stations mentioned above. Users also got some free music downloads as part of the package. In May 2005, RealNetworks had 1.85 million paying subscribers, one million of those being to its music subscription services.[25]

Finally, RealNetworks got into gaming in 2000. According to Glaser,

The game strategy is to be publisher, developer and distributor to focus on platforms used by regular consumers, not just hard-core game lovers. You don't need to purchase a special console and we believe that the accessibility of the games is a key to broad demographic penetration. With[in] the foreseeable future, the most important . . . platform for us is the PC. The second most important one, which will grow . . . is the mobile phone.[26]

As part of these efforts RealNetworks has purchased several game-related companies, including GameHouse and Mr.Goodliving.[27] Real-Networks has two major game offerings: RealArcade, which allows people to play games online, and RealArcade GamePass, which allows people to download games.

As a result of these content-related strategies, RealNetworks has obtained a greater portion of its revenue from consumer subscriptions and less from licensing software for corporate customers. In 2004, RealNetworks earned as much as 70 percent of its revenue from content sales, though it had earned no such revenue before 2000.[28] Within consumer products, about half of revenues were from sales of video (including the Real SuperPass subscription service), 30 percent were from music sales, and the remaining 20 percent were from game sales.

25. RNWK Q1 2005 RealNetworks Earnings Conference Call, May 4, 2005.

26. Ibid.

27. "RealNetworks Revenue Grows 29% in First Quarter of 2004," RealNetworks press release, April 28, 2004; "RealNetworks Enters Mobile Games Market: Acquires European-Based Mr. Goodliving Ltd.," RealNetworks press release, May 11, 2005.

28. RealNetworks 10-K filings for 1998, 1999, and 2005 (p. 22); Erich Leuning, "RealNetworks Turns on Subscription Service," Associated Press Newswires, August 15, 2000.

There's an important strategic complexity here: RealNetworks competes increasingly with other content providers, who themselves have different strategies for making money from various sides of their platforms. Many of these content providers—Yahoo! for example—earn revenues mainly from advertising rather than selling content.

Platform Integration and Interoperability

The companies that have built media software platforms differ in two other related ways that affect how they compete with each other. One involves the extent to which they operate particular sides of the platforms themselves—that is, the extent to which they integrate into one of the business sides as opposed to encouraging other firms to provide those services. The other concerns the extent to which they interoperate with other platforms.

At one extreme is Apple. Its iPod/iTunes platform is integrated into the hardware and content-provider sides of the media platform, and it doesn't interoperate with any other platform. At the other extreme is Microsoft, whose media platform is integrated into neither hardware nor content and which interoperates with all other media platforms that allow it to do so. In the middle are vendors like RealNetworks, which limit interoperability—but not completely—and integrate—but only partially—into the content provider side.

Figure 8.1 summarizes where the various media platforms fall in terms of integration and interoperability. For each it shows whether the platform is integrated fully or partly into a hardware device or the provision of content and the degree of interoperability with other platforms. Apple and Sony operate vertical silos that do not interoperate, at least intentionally, with anyone else. Microsoft and many of the media players that rely on its APIs are unintegrated and highly interoperable. RealNetworks' RealPlayer lies in between.

Why do these companies choose such different business models for the same line of products? As we have noted, each company has different strengths, and their goals vary.

Apple has kept the iTunes/iPod platform tightly integrated. It has leveraged its strength of having software and hardware engineers work closely together to create products that are elegant and easy to use for

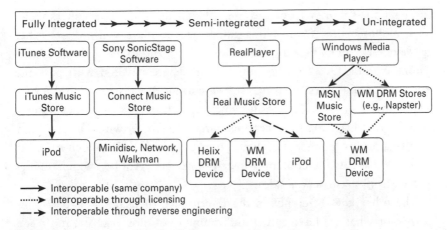

Figure 8.1
Models of varying integration and interoperability in media players.

consumers. For now, at least, this has given Apple a significant competitive advantage over rivals.

RealNetworks has built a more open media player platform than Apple. It is trying to increase the reach of its media player and content provision to the widest scope of devices and industries. It has deepened its relationships with cable operators and mobile phone producers.[29] And, as we noted before, it has developed Rhapsody To Go for increasingly popular mobile devices.

Microsoft also operates an open media player platform. The Windows Media Player platform enriches the overall Windows software platform. The more open and interoperable the Windows Media Player platform is, the more attractive the Windows platform becomes.

Microsoft thereby earns revenues from increased Windows sales.

Product Differentiation and Multihoming

Digital media platforms differ from other software platforms we have discussed in two significant ways. First, in all of the industries we have discussed, competing firms served roughly the same platform sides and earned their profits from similar sides. Makers of PC operating systems

29. "Wall Street Web Stocks: Napster and RealNetworks CEOs Sound Off on Yahoo—Update 2," *AFX International Focus*, June 17, 2005.

all make their money from end users, video game console makers make their money mainly from selling games or securing royalties from other game makers, PDA makers make money from end users, and smart telephone manufacturers make money from device makers, who pass the costs on to end users. In contrast, the current models for digital media platforms range from Microsoft, which earns its return on media systems mainly from licensing its operating system; to Apple, which increasingly earns its profits from selling digital music devices; Real, which earns its profits mostly from content subscriptions; and Adobe, which makes profits from Flash server sales.

The other key difference is the importance of usaging several platforms, or what we have called multihoming. In most sectors, most end users use a single software platform; that is the case with PCs, PDAs, and smart mobile phones. People may have more than one video game console, but they seldom buy two of the most recent generation. Multihoming is more prevalent on the other sides of these industries. Application developers often write for multiple platforms and sometimes port applications (especially games) from one platform to another. Some of the large hardware manufacturers also engage in some multihoming. For example, IBM and Hewlett Packard sell computers with different software platforms. Most makers of PDAs and mobile telephones, however, use just one software platform.

In contrast, multihoming is prevalent on almost all sides of media platforms. Many people use several media players. Some might watch a movie using QuickTime, listen to streaming music using RealPlayer, and manage their music collection using iTunes and listen to it on their iPods. About 40 percent of consumers who used media players use two or more every month.[30] Most content providers make their audio and video material available in several formats. More than 85 percent of the most popular Web sites had content in at least two of the following formats: Windows, Real, QuickTime, or MPEG formats. On average they had files in 3.1 different formats as of late 2005.[31] (Stores operated as part

30. Nielsen NetRatings, Custom Rollup Reports, January 2005 to December 2005.

31. Media Metrix, Top 1000 Website Survey, Dcember 2005.

of one of the vertical silos such as iTunes and Google's videostore are the key exceptions.) Many PC manufacturers install multiple media players for their users, though digital music devices and mobile phones typically have just one. A 2006 study found that large manufacturers install an average of 5.6 media players on consumer and small-business computers sold in the United States.[32] (Multiple media players are not common, however, on mobile phones and other small computing devices.)

Multihoming appears to be prevalent for media platforms for several interrelated reasons. For one, media player platforms provide many distinct services valued differently by heterogeneous consumers. These platforms provide both audio and video, downloading and streaming, and interoperability with non-PC devices. It doesn't cost consumers much to use several platforms—it is easy to get several media players for a PC and to switch between them, depending on the task. Their choices are based on what they want to do, whether the task is streaming a movie clip or downloading a song from iTunes or Napster. One reason is that the decision by consumers to use a particular media player depends on decisions by content providers to make material available for particular media players. Consumers might prefer to use Windows Media Player with their iPods, but Apple's iTunes store prevents that. In other cases content providers make decisions to use a particular media format because it is better in some relevant respect; that is why many streaming video providers rely on Flash.

Another reason, though, is that media player platforms have differentiated themselves to appeal to different consumers. They have developed different looks and features that appeal in varying degrees to different users for different uses. For the past several years, for example, *PC Magazine* has recommended MusicMatch for organizing and playing downloaded music but not for playing video or streaming content (for which MusicMatch offers minimal capabilities). iTunes, on the other hand, has distinguished itself by being very good at managing music libraries and working with the popular iPod. The newest release of

32. LECG, "Survey and Analysis of Media Players Installed on New PCs Sold in Europe and the United States," March 2006.

Windows Media Player is recommended for organizing mixed media libraries, such as those that include music as well as photos. RealPlayer is currently the only player that allows users to integrate music tracks with different DRM protection schemes, so a person can put songs bought from iTunes and those purchased from Real's Music Store in the same playlist.[33] Flash is the most compact player, which makes it very quick to download. That is a plus for content providers who want to standardize on a particular media player of their choice. They automatically download it to the PC of the consumer who tries to view their content.

Making content available exclusively for a single media player is another important differentiation strategy. RealPlayer pioneered this approach in 2001. It struck an exclusive deal with Major League Baseball to host audio broadcasts of games and video highlights that would only be available to people who had a subscription with Real and used its RealPlayer. Other exclusives followed. As of June 2005, the newest album of the popular rock band the White Stripes was only available before its official release on Real's media platform. Also, all free online content from the hit television show "American Idol" will be offered only in Real's formats.[34] Apple adopted a similar tactic with iTunes. Although people can obtain many of the songs on iTunes from other online music stores, the iPod is designed so they should only be able to use it with songs they have purchased and downloaded from the iTunes store. (As of this writing, RealNetworks has been able to reverse Apple's iPod technology to sidestep these restrictions, but this compatibility is likely to be eliminated by Apple in the next software or hardware update of iTunes or the iPod.)

33. Matthew P. Graven, "MusicMatch Jukebox 8.1," *PC Magazine Review*, November 11, 2003; Matthew P. Graven, "MusicMatch Jukebox 7.5," *PC Magazine Review*, February 1, 2003; "Microsoft Windows Media Player 10," *PC Magazine Product Guide*; http://www.pcmag.com/article2/0.1759.1641331.00. asp "RealPlayer 10.5," PC *Magazine Product Guide*, http://www.pcmag.com/article2/0.1759.1654038.00.asp.

34. Derek Caney, "Major League Baseball Inks 3-Year Pact with Real Networks," *Reuters News*, March 27, 2001; Brian Garrity, "Billboard.biz: Real Grabs White Stripes Exclusive," *VNU Entertainment Newswire*, June 6, 2005; Carl Bialik, "RealNetworks to Stop Providing Services to Baseball Site," *Dow Jones Business News*, February 5, 2004.

Digital Rights Management

Media software platforms are central to the growing market for the distribution of audio and video content over the Internet to PCs, digital music devices, and mobile phones. DRM technologies are a critical component of these platforms. Without these technologies the owners of content—the artists, music publishing companies, and movie studios—would never have assented to the distribution of their otherwise easily pirated content online.

DRM is perhaps best thought of as a software platform in itself, although in practice, the DRM software platform is an integral part of the overall media software platform. The DRM platform provides a mechanism for granting people permission to use certain content, preventing those without permission from using that content, and managing payment terms for using one or more copies of that content. DRM platforms used for content distributed online typically have five components:

1. Software that locks up the content so that it can only be accessed with the proper key
2. A "rights expression language" that describes how the content can be used
3. Software that manages and distributes the keys to unlock the content
4. A method for collecting payment for the usage rights
5. Software on the consumer's device that monitors usage and locks or unlocks content, depending on the rights the consumer has to a copy of the content and payment for that copy

Like the media platform overall, the DRM technology is distributed across several different parts of the platform.

Most DRM technologies work in a very similar way. Audio or video tracks are first encoded using a codec. The resulting encoded track is encrypted and stored in a container. When a user purchases the track online, the track is downloaded onto the user's computer. The unique decryption key along with relevant rights information (number of authorized computers, expiration date, number of allowed playbacks, and so on) is stored in a key depository on the customer's computer and also on the music store servers. Alternatively, when one transfers the track onto a portable media player, the key is also transferred into that player's key depository. When the user wishes to play the track, the proposed usage is checked against the associated right: Is this computer authorized? Has the allowed number of playbacks been exceeded? Finally, if authorized, a key is retrieved from the depository and the track is decrypted (DRM), decoded (codec), and then played (media player).

Like many of the software platforms we have discussed, DRM makers have to get several groups on board their platform to make it a success. The content owners are a particularly critical platform side for DRM, though. They have to be convinced that the DRM solution strikes the right balance between persuading consumers to buy the content and preventing consumers (and others) from pirating songs, movies, and other valuable intellectual property. Finding the right balance is more important than it seems. Before iTunes there were many unsuccessful attempts at selling digital music and video protected by DRM. Interestingly, iTunes wasn't successful because its DRM technology, FairPlay, was better or more secure but because it was more user-friendly. Apple pioneered the concept of "good enough" protection: good enough to keep innately honest customers pretty honest while making DRM as invisible to them as possible. Apple recognized that dedicated hackers will eventually break through any protection and, accepting that inevitability, decided to make the experience pleasant for everybody else.

Content owners like EMI and content service providers like Yahoo! find content protection solutions useful because these solutions allow them to charge for content while discouraging nonpayers from gaining access to the content. Many content owners and content service providers have, of course, used content protection solutions of varying degrees of sophistication for a long time. Those solutions range from producing printed material in forms that discourage photocopying to encrypting broadcasts for satellite television. Stricter solutions generally impose greater cost and inconvenience on content users. Consequently, content owners and providers have always faced trade-offs deciding whether and to what extent to rely on content protection solutions.[35]

35. For example, "the tone of the discussion by music industry interests is one of enabling flexible business models and avoiding consumer backlash, as much as it is about controlling piracy. In this respect, the music industry may be

As RedMonk analyst Stephen O'Grady notes, "It comes down to the rights of consumers vs. the rights of business. What people want is fair use of content purchased at a reasonable price."[36] The adoption of DRM solutions for digital music devices illustrates the importance of these trade-offs. Apple FairPlay is not regarded as the "best" DRM solution in terms of eliminating piracy or managing content licensing.[37] But it is regarded as good enough, relative to the constellation of economic factors, that content owners must consider.[38] Just as important, FairPlay is the DRM feature associated with the iPod player, which is by far the most popular digital music device on the market today. (DRM solutions are features of media software platforms and are one of many ways in which these platforms differentiate themselves. Each of these DRM features, however, is substitutable from the standpoint of content owners, store owners, and music consumers.[39])

As with other multisided platforms it is difficult to get one side on board without simultaneously attracting the other sides. People who

---

learning a positive lesson from its early experiments with DRM." Bill Rosenblatt, "Microsoft and Music Industry Discuss Future of CD Copy Protection," *DRM Watch*, September 23, 2004.

36. Byron Acohido, "IBM raises stakes in digital media circle," *USA Today*, April 19, 2004 (http://www.usatoday.com/tech/news/techinnovations/2004-04-19-ibm-digital-rights_x.htm, downloaded August 26, 2005).

37. Apple's iTunes and its FairPlay solution have been undermined a number of times: "programmers have worked to strip out the anti-copying features, called FairPlay, included with every song purchased from the iTunes store. Several programmers have created software that does appear to remove the FairPlay protections altogether, allowing the purchased songs to be distributed without restriction." Ina Fried, "Apple Disables iTunes Song-Swapping Tool," *CNET News.com*, April 29, 2004; http://asia.cnet.com/news/personaltech/0,39037091,39177444,00.htm (downloaded August 26, 2005).

38. "Apple's Own FairPlay Copy Protection Tools Have Also Won the Big Record Labels' Approval and Form the Heart of the Company's iTunes Music Store." John Borland, "MP3 getting antipiracy makeover," *CNET News.com*, March 2, 2004.

39. Analysts see these as providing similar benefits to consumers and content owners: Sony, Microsoft, and Apple, along with several others, all have music stores which sell content and have their own content protection solutions. "Sony to take on iTunes in Europe," *Reuters Newswire*, September 30, 2004.

license content over the Internet or wireless networks need to have the DRM software installed on their computing devices. Generally that means having a media player that uses the same DRM technology as has been used by the content owner. Likewise, the content providers need to be on board. Some of them act as intermediaries between the DRM solution providers and the content owners, while others, such as Apple, are both the DRM solution provider and the content provider, and still others, like Sony, are the content owner, content provider, and DRM solution provider (although Sony makes its content available to other providers and subject to other DRMs).

The Future

Between 2000 and 2004, the number of hours that American households spent surfing the Web increased from 1.1 to 2.7 billion. About 75 percent of American households used the Internet on a regular basis by February 2006. An increasing amount of commerce is being done on the Web. In the United States, the total dollar amount of sales through Web-based transactions (excluding travel) increased from $34 billion in 2001 to $86 billion in 2005.[40] From 2000 to 2005 the percentage of American households with broadband connections increased from 5 percent to 60 percent.[41] These changes are all interrelated: the more users there are, the more content that is created for them; the more content there is, the more use there will be; and greater use drives an increased demand for high-speed connections. All of these trends are happening in many countries outside of the United States— usually less rapidly, as in Germany, but sometimes far more rapidly, as in Korea.

Media platforms are useful without access to the Web—people play CDs and DVDs and download them to other devices, for example. But media platforms have become far more popular for users, content

40. "Two-Thirds of US Web Users Now On Broadband," *eMarketer*, March 2006. http://www.emarketer.com/Articles/Print.aspx?1003875.

41. Jeffrey Grau, "Retail E-Commerce: Future Trends," *eMarketer*, February 2006. Ben Macklin, "The Broadband Report," *eMarketer*, April 2001; Ben Macklin, "North America Broadband," *eMarketer*, March 2005.

providers, application developers, and hardware makers because of the growth of Web-based delivery mechanisms for digital content. In 2005, American consumers downloaded more than 353 million songs legally. (Estimates suggest that they also downloaded more than 430 million songs illegally that same year.[42])

Digital media systems will play an important role in the emerging markets for digital content. Predictions are always hazardous, but it seems clear that the rapid growth we have seen in recent years will continue, especially as digital content becomes downloadable and playable on more devices.

Consider the possibility that smart mobile telephones will be used for this purpose. Mobile telephones are ubiquitous: more people globally have them than PCs. It is anticipated that by 2008, almost 15 percent of the mobile phones shipped will be "smart" and therefore capable of downloading and playing digital content. That is 130 million devices.[43]

Alternatively, iPod and similar devices may continue their rapid growth and become the device of choice for consumers. One analyst predicts that more than 180 million portable media devices will be sold in 2009.[44]

Beyond this, as DRM technology has advanced, more content owners have seen digital distribution as highly desirable. The music companies that once sued to shut down Napster embraced, after initial skepticism, the idea of paid downloadable music. The movie studios are following, and several "movie stores" have emerged on the World Wide Web.

A further development concerns home entertainment. As more content is distributed over the Internet, it is inevitable that consumers will have a computer, with a software platform, wherever they watch television. The only question is what form that computing platform will take. We return to this subject in Chapter 12.

42. Jeffrey Grau, "Retail E-Commerce: Future Trends," *eMarketer*, February 2006. Ben Macklin, "The Broadband Report," *eMarketer*, April 2001, p. 45.

43. http://www.ifpi.org/site-content/press/20050119b.html. Yankee Group, "Pumping Up the Volume for Online Music Services," January 23, 2004.

44. Alex Slawsby, Allen M. Leibovitch, Randy Giusto, Kevin Burden, David Linsalata, and Ramon T. Llamas, "Worldwide Mobile Phone 2005–2009 Forecast and Analysis" (IDC report no. 33290), April 2005, tables 5 and 6.

INSIGHTS

• All digital media software players are available at no additional cost as part of a software platform or as a free application and all add features over time to attract additional users, developers, and hardware makers.

• Some providers of digital media platforms have integrated them into their overall software platform and derive revenue from overall software platform sales (Windows); others have provided separate platforms and tried to earn money from the provision of content (RealNetworks); and still others have tried to earn revenue from an integrated hardware/software/content platform (Apple).

• Apple has pursued a single-sided strategy in which it has integrated into all possible sides of the digital media software platform business. It has adopted a unique "sell the razor/give away the blades" strategy: it earns profits from the sale of its hardware (iPod) and loses money or breaks even on its software platform and content provision (iTunes).

• Multiple software platforms with conflicting strategies have survived in part as a result of differentiating themselves to appeal to varying segments of consumers, content providers/owners, and application developers.

• As with other software platforms pricing low to one side, evangelization of the platform, and feature accretion through bundling have been important competitive strategies.

9

With a Little Help . . .

Do not hold the delusion that your advancement is accomplished by crushing others.

—*Marcus Tullius Cicero*[1]

> *INSIDE THIS CHAPTER*
>
> · The design of software platform ecosystems
> · Advantages and disadvantages of one-sided versus multisided strategies
> · Why software platform integration varies across industries and over time

This chapter and the next two focus on three key strategic decisions faced by software platform vendors. The first, considered in this chapter, is the scope and integration of the business. Should it produce complements that work with the software platform or leave that to others? Should it operate a multisided platform, and if so, what sides should that platform have? The second decision, examined in Chapter 10, involves how to price to get all the sides on board and to interact with each other. Should it levy a fixed charge for accessing the platform or a variable charge for using it—or both? How much of its profit should it seek from each side? The third decision, considered in Chapter 11, involves what features and functionality to include in the software platform itself. Should it offer several alternative platforms or just one?

In the preceding five chapters, we saw that some software platform vendors define the scope of their activities quite narrowly. In recent years

1. http://www.orangejobs.com/nz/graduates/articles/interviews.htm.

PalmSource, for instance, has focused on developing and licensing the Palm OS operating system. Others define the scope of their activities more broadly and have offered most or all components of the complete system. That is the case with the iPod/iTunes platform. We have seen differences in integration within industries, Apple versus Microsoft being perhaps the most familiar contrast. Over time, Palm's metamorphosis from a complete systems provider to a supplier of only operating systems (PalmSource) has been perhaps the most striking. Many platform vendors have been partially integrated into applications, producing some themselves and, in a variety of ways discussed in this chapter, encouraging third parties to produce others. Overall, the industries we have studied have tended to exhibit less integration over time, though the process has hardly been steady or uniform. This chapter attempts to make sense of all this.

Ecosystem Participants and Structures

The first strategic issue a software platform vendor must consider is the structure of the ecosystem that surrounds it. What groups participate in this ecosystem or could? How might they best contribute to helping get the platform off the ground and contribute to long-term profitability?

End users, the final customers for the systems built around the software platforms, are common to all platforms. They typically are interested in working systems, not unconnected components, but whether they obtain those systems from one firm or from several varies from industry to industry and from time to time. Sometimes the software platform vendor deals directly with end users (an example is Sony's PlayStation), but it is at least as common to reach end users only through a third party (Microsoft's Windows Mobile). In some cases end users can be profitably divided into subgroups for pricing purposes, as we discuss in the next chapter.

End users apart, every other participating group is a potential *complementor*, a provider of products or services that are complements to the software platform and that therefore enhance the value of the platform when their quality increases or their price falls.[2] Hotel rooms in Las Vegas and flights to Las Vegas are complements; hotel rooms in Las Vegas and hotel rooms in Honolulu are substitutes. If software platform vendors decide not to produce a particular complementary product themselves, they need to encourage complementors to affiliate with their platform and to invest in making their complementary products better and cheaper.

Producers of basic *hardware*—the systems, containing one or more CPUs, on which the software platform can run—are important complementors in all the industries we have examined so far (they won't be for two industries we look at in Chapter 12). Within platform industries, there is variation in the extent to which the same firms make the hardware and software platforms; the key exception is video game providers, in which all successful firms have made integrated hardware and software platforms. RealNetworks has never been in the hardware business. Apple has never left it.

When an ecosystem includes independent hardware producers, they need to be courted by the software platform provider. Microsoft needs to convince computer makers to build computers that run on Windows. PalmSource must convince companies to design and produce PDAs based on the Palm OS. This courtship takes the form of a rather intricate dance in periods of rapid innovation and changing technical standards, since quick changes in hardware and software need to be coordinated among independent firms if systems are to function well and the ecosystem as a whole is to prosper. At the same time, independent hardware vendors frequently also serve as distributors of the software platform to users. PalmSource does not license the Palm OS directly to end users. Instead, the Palm OS is licensed to device makers, and the latter install them on their products before selling systems to end users.

An interesting exception is the mobile phone industry, in which *mobile network operators* are mainly responsible for the distribution of mobile phones (the basic hardware) and their software platforms to end users. Symbian deals with phone manufacturers, and they in turn deal with the network operators. Microsoft, on the other hand, has not had much luck

2. Karl Case and Ray Fair, "Principles of Economics," 3rd ed. (Upper Saddle River, N.J.: Prentice Hall, 1994), pp. 82–83.

persuading major manufacturers to use its mobile phone operating system; it has therefore concentrated on selling phones made by second-tier manufacturers directly to mobile network operators. In the case of i-mode, the software platform sponsor, NTT DoCoMo, is also the network operator and thus the distributor of mobile phones equipped with i-mode to end users.

The production of *peripheral equipment* is a significant business in many of the industries we have examined. This is just as true for Apple iPods in 2005 as it was for Windows PCs in 1995. The boundary between hardware and peripheral equipment is to some extent dependent on both the state of technology and hardware makers' design decisions, of course. Microsoft's early operating system for the IBM computer didn't have a graphical user interface (GUI) and didn't need a mouse. That changed with the development of Windows. However, it turns out that computer makers have relied on third parties to make mice rather than doing it themselves. Interestingly, many are made by Microsoft, which integrated into mouse production in 1983 mainly to be sure that the sort of mouse specified by its nascent Windows system would be available in the marketplace. Microsoft developed and patented a mouse that could connect to a PC through an existing serial port rather than to a special card installed within the computer. This innovation reduced the cost of the mouse and thus of mouse-using computers running Windows. Apple as a vertically integrated hardware and software platform maker has always produced its own mice.

Applications are the third major category of complements. Applications are products that are typically licensed directly to end users. Ranging from word-processing programs to "shoot-'em-up" games to ringtones, they are key actual or potential participants in software platform ecosystems. Many software platforms begin by providing their own applications. That was the case with the Apple Newton and Palm Zoomer and many of the video game consoles. Others begin with a small stock of third-party applications. The original IBM PC began with Microsoft's languages along with a few applications such as VisiCalc that were ported by their developers from CP/M. Almost all software platforms end up relying mainly on third-party developers as they mature.

Finally, *content* is an important complement for many media-oriented software platforms. There is very little evidence that software platforms produce their own content. They typically encourage third parties to make it available. That is the case with media players: Apple, Microsoft, Real, and others facilitate content providers and content owners to make everything from songs to news to videos available for their media platforms. In some case media-oriented platforms license content, sometimes exclusively, and then provide it to end users. That's the case with Apple's iPod/iTunes platform and RealNetwork's Rhapsody music service. Some software platforms, such as iMode, work as actively with content providers as others work with application developers, to sustain a rich ecosystem of complementary content provision.

When one describes the extent to which a software platform is integrated into its ecosystem, it is important to recognize that partial integration is common and varies importantly in extent. Microsoft writes some applications to run on Windows and some games for the Xbox, for instance, but third-party vendors are important in both cases, and their importance has varied over time. For a time Apple did license the Macintosh operating system for use on third-party hardware, but these licensees were never very important in aggregate, while Symbian licensees produce all of the smart phones that run the Symbian platform. Some changes in integration, particularly partial integration, reflect accidents of history and the marketplace. If third parties had offered a quality two-button mouse in 1983, it seems unlikely that Microsoft would have gotten into the mouse business. Similarly, Microsoft's Word and Excel products were successful on the Macintosh platform when Microsoft was still working with IBM to develop OS/2, and this earlier experience clearly contributed to the success of these products in the Wintel segment. It is hard to imagine that this was the outcome of a conscious long-term plan, as evidenced by Bill Gates's plea to Apple's Scully to make the Mac OS platform ubiquitous (see Chapter 4).

The closeness of the contractual and informal relationships between participants in different parts of a business ecosystem varies from arm's-length, anonymous spot market transactions, as in the textbook wheat market, to long-term, joint-venture–like arrangements that are hard to distinguish from integration by ownership. In the case of the software platforms we have examined, even the weakest relationships are far deeper than the arm's-length relationships one sees in many one-sided industries. Software platforms can't have direct relationships with the thousands of small developers, hardware makers, and peripheral device makers. Yet they document and make APIs available to developers, provide interface information to hardware and peripheral makers, and make sure their platforms have the relevant drivers for the peripherals. And they develop relationships through large developer conferences and small focus groups that bring some of these smaller players together. At the other extreme, software platforms often have deep relationships with several larger partners. These relationships involve regular exchange of information and joint work on defining new standards and specifications. They may also involve joint investments in product development or marketing. Representatives from Microsoft's Xbox and Sony's PlayStation divisions, for instance, both spend a great deal of time with Electronic Arts. At the furthest extreme, Symbian spends a great deal of time with its major backers, especially Nokia.

Key Determinants of Integration

Transactions Costs

The economic literature on determinants of the scope of firms' activities effectively began with Ronald Coase's classic 1937 paper titled "The Nature of the Firm."[3] Coase argued that competition generally forces firms to operate at least cost. For instance, an auto producer will make its own steel if and only if it is cheaper to make steel than to buy it. This of course has a touch of tautology to it. The novel and powerful aspect of Coase's analysis was his focus not on the production cost of making steel but on comparing the *transactions costs* of alternative methods—firm and market—of organizing the relationship between steel and auto production, of achieving coordination and motivation. Further work by

3. Ronald Coase, "The Nature of the Firm," *Economica* 4 (1937): 386–405. A very nice summary of the main themes in this literature, with references, is provided by John Roberts, *The Modern Firm* (Oxford: Oxford University Press, 2004), chap. 3.

economists following Coase has enhanced our understanding of the determinants of these important costs.[4]

For some kinds of goods and services, the market is generally superior, and integration is correspondingly uncommon. To focus on a polar case, banks use lots of pencils, but not even the biggest banks make their own. On the one hand, entry into pencil production seems relatively easy, so banks can count on competition to hold pencil prices close to costs. Moreover, it is relatively easy to specify pencil quality, to compare pencils from different vendors, and to switch from one pencil supplier to another, so arm's-length spot market competition can be relied on to produce both good quality and low prices. On the other hand, there is no reason to believe that banks are particularly good at producing pencils, and devoting top management time to pencil production takes it away from competing in banking.

The economics literature argues that changing any of the conditions enumerated in the preceding paragraph tends to tilt the organizational decisions toward integration. If the relevant market is not competitive or if the buyer has special advantages in production, for instance, integration becomes more attractive. Partial integration is sometimes used as a device to deal with upstream market power, because it both adds competition and makes an implicit threat of further integration. And when technical change is rapid, or standards are in flux, or interface specifications are evolving, the software platform provider may be able to optimize system performance only by also producing other system components.

A factor that is particularly relevant in this context is the difficulty of writing a contract that deals acceptably with all contingencies. Suppose, for instance, that Sony believes that a *great* submarine game would be a powerful complement to PlayStation 2 and thus sell millions of copies, but that no such game exists yet, so it decides to contract with a third party to develop one. Sony can write a contract for the development of a submarine game with a long string of specified technical properties. It would be reasonably straightforward to verify whether such a contract

4. The work of Oliver Williamson has been particularly important. See Oliver E. Williamson, *The Economic Institutions of Capitalism* (New York: Free Press, 1985).

had been breached. It would also be straightforward to write a contract that required a *great* game by specifying that it had to achieve a particular sales target. But it would be hard to determine if the failure to achieve greatness was the fault of the developer or because of a poor console platform. Moreover, if the project were technically adventurous, it might fail either because the developer didn't do a good job or because the project was infeasible. It would be difficult for a court or anyone else to decide objectively which was the case and therefore enforce the contract. Integration is one way to deal with these sorts of problems. Management decides whether or not the game its own staff produces is great or the reasons why the project failed, little or no time is spent writing a formal contract, and litigation is essentially ruled out.

Contracting problems can be an important impediment to innovation in systems businesses.[5] If, for example, the interface between hardware and operating system is well defined and unchanging, independent hardware and operating system vendors can take it as a specification and innovate more or less independently.[6] But if innovation is architectural and involves changes in that interface and thus in key technical specifications, coordination is essential and contracting generally does not work well, as both the Pentagon and many buyers of custom homes have learned to their sorrow.

The Multisided Solution

Instead of making a complement internally (integration) or buying it from a third party (contracting), platform vendors often induce a third party to supply it directly to end users and, possibly, to pay for the privilege. Suppose Sony persuades one or more independent developers that a great submarine game for PlayStation 2 would sell millions of copies, and it provides development tools that make it easy to develop games. If the royalty Sony charges on PlayStation 2 games is reasonable,

5. Kevin Boudreau, "How Does 'Openness' Affect Innovation? Evidence from Mobile Computing" (MIT Sloan School of Management working paper) (Cambridge, Mass.: MIT, 2005).

6. This is, of course, the modular approach to design discussed in Chapter 2. See Carliss Baldwin and Kim Clark, *Design Rules I: The Power of Modularity* (Cambridge, Mass.: MIT Press, 2000).

developers will have strong incentives to invest in the hope of developing a great submarine game: a great game will make a lot of money (probably a large multiple of what Sony could pay in-house developers), while a lousy game will return little or nothing (certainly less than Sony would likely pay its in-house developers if their game bombed). Because of these strong incentives, which are aligned with Sony's interests, no game-specific contract is necessary. Similarly, Microsoft doesn't have to try to use a contract to persuade Dell to produce high-quality, inexpensive computers, since Dell already has very strong incentives to do just that.

This multisided approach has its own problems, though.[7] First, if there are only a few possible suppliers of a key complement, there is a pricing problem.[8] Suppose firm *A* sells software platform *a*, firm *B* is the only producer of compatible hardware product *b*, consumers are interested only in systems that combine the two products, and *A* has adopted a multisided approach in which both it and *B* set prices independently. Because products *a* and *b* are complements, if either *A* or *B* raises its price, sales of both products will fall. But when *B* considers raising its price, it will take into account only the resulting fall in its sales, not the reduction in *A*'s sales. The reverse holds for *A*. The result will be a total system price (for *a* plus *b*) that is *above* the profit-maximizing level. Thus *A* has to share system profits with *B*, and those system profits are lower as a result of independent pricing than they would be through coordination.

What is the cure? From *A*'s point of view, one cure is to have many competing producers of good *b*. Competition will then hold the price of *b* close to cost (including a reasonable return on capital) regardless of *A*'s pricing, so that *A* both effectively determines the system price (via the price of *a*) and captures all the economic profit. Generally, it is more

7. Annabelle Gawer and Michael Cusumano (Platform Leadership: How Intel, Microsoft, and Cisco Price Industry Innovation [Boston: Harvard Business School Press, 2003]) provide interesting discussions of several of the points made in this paragraph and the next in the context of the computer industry.

8. Testimony of Kevin Murphy in *United States v. Microsoft*, No. 98-1233.— Augustine Cournot, *Researches into the Mathematical Principles of the Theory of Wealth*, trans. Nathaniel Bacon (New York: Macmillan, 1927) (original in French, 1838).

attractive to rely on others to supply a complement (instead of buying it or making it), all else equal, if there are many producers of that complement who compete intensely. Hence the common strategic advice, "Commoditize the complements."

On the other hand, potential complementors will invest only if they expect their investments to earn a reasonable return in the marketplace. That often depends critically on how they expect the platform vendor to behave. This raises some interesting dilemmas. For instance, while partial integration into production of complements can provide a hedge against failure of the market to produce what is needed, it can also, by threatening more intense competition, inhibit desirable third-party investment. (Similarly, Chapter 11 notes that software platforms commonly innovate by adding features and functionality that had previously been supplied by third-party applications. While this process makes platforms more valuable to both end users and application developers, it in effect intensifies the competition expected by the latter.) Expectations are not nearly so important for internal development or development by contract.

Finally, while the provider of a complete system can determine the direction of technical change internally and informally, this process becomes much more complex when system components are supplied by different parties. Sometimes a single entity, often the software platform provider, emerges as the driving force and system regulator. This seems clearly the case in video games, for instance, where console vendors both drive innovation and serve as gatekeepers for game developers to promote both quality and variety. DoCoMo plays a similar gatekeeper role in the i-mode ecosystem. But, as the world of PC games illustrates, the existence of a gatekeeper is not inevitable. The costs of setting up and operating an effective gate vary from case to case, as do the net benefits of managing entry (and thus to some extent limiting creativity).

Moreover, when several ecosystem participants have critical knowledge, leadership in the innovation process is often shared. And the identity of the leaders is not necessarily predetermined. In personal computers, for instance, IBM initially played the lead role in driving innovation but soon lost it to a combination of Microsoft and Intel. Microsoft needs to work with Intel, hardware makers, and application developers to ensure that the systems in which all have a financial stake take full advantage of advances in a wide range of technologies.

Among the platform vendors we have discussed, DoCoMo has arguably the most complex task of coordinating innovation around its mobile Internet i-mode platform. Whenever it adds a new feature or service (e-payment, for example), it has to work with handset makers to include the corresponding chip or software in their phones. Then it has to explain to content and service providers how to build services based on the new feature. And of course it needs to do some plumbing itself on its network, adding software on its application servers or even upgrading the physical network gear. Nokia, to take another smart phone example, seems the main driver in the Symbian ecosystem. Fear of being thereby disadvantaged at the hands of a leading competitor may have led to Motorola's partial defection from that community.

This last example illustrates a final issue that arises with some regularity in the multisided businesses we've discussed. Before Motorola's defection, Nokia and Motorola collaborated in managing Symbian while competing to sell handsets. Similarly, between 1998 and 2003, Palm both collaborated with Handspring, to make sure the Palm OS and Handspring's hardware worked well together, and competed with it in the sales of integrated hardware-software systems. These are necessarily complex relationships, and keeping both collaborative and competitive dimensions healthy is not simple. It is often hard for individuals to both collaborate with each other and compete effectively against each other, so that these functions are often handled at the working level by different units within the organization. Top management, of course, cannot divide itself in this fashion.

Nokia faces these issues when licensing its Series 60 middleware platform to makers of Symbian-based handsets that compete against Nokia's own phones. As mentioned in Chapter 7, to alleviate licensee concerns, the company decided to raise a high internal Chinese wall between the Mobile software division, which is in charge of developing and licensing Series 60, and the hardware division. This sort of arrangement is not without its costs, of course, since there are efficiency gains from allowing hardware and software developers to communicate.

Merchants or Two-Sided Platforms

Software platforms have a choice between two models when it comes to the provision of applications, games, or content. The first is a multisided model: platforms provide support for interactions among the various customer groups supported. Each customer group needs access to the multisided platform to reach the other groups. The platform doesn't substitute itself for any customer group in these interactions. For example, it doesn't buy applications or games and resell them to end users. This multisided model is used for at least two customer groups by most software platforms we have encountered with the exception of the iPod/iTunes digital media platform.

To take one example, i-mode is a three-sided platform. It sells *access* to both users and content providers. It never takes ownership of content. Each content provider receives revenues directly from i-mode users, depending on how popular or appealing her content is. Each i-mode content provider therefore cares a great deal about how many people buy i-mode phones, because this determines the size of their target markets. And this implies that, in turn, each content provider cares about how many other content providers support i-mode and how good their content is as well, because the overall availability of content drives users to i-mode. Also, although DoCoMo does buy i-mode phones from contract manufacturers and resells them to end users, a significant fraction of i-mode phones are sold by manufacturers through other retail channels. This means that handset manufacturers need to be induced to produce and sell i-mode phones,[9] and each of them necessarily cares about the overall popularity of the i-mode system.

The second business model is a *merchant* or single-sided model. The platform buys the complementary products or services and resells them to users. It substitutes for the user when dealing with the maker of complementary products—that is, it buys and takes ownership of these products—or it makes these complementary products itself. Indirect network

9. As we have seen in Chapter 7, the inducement to produce is a particularly complex one, as DoCoMo works very closely with its associated phone manufacturers to help them include the specifications needed to take advantage of the features offered by the i-mode service.

effects are no less important for the merchant model than they are for the two-sided model. They are just managed directly by the platform owner rather than through the multisided strategies we discussed in Chapter 3.

iPod/iTunes is the only example of a pure merchant model we have seen among software platform–based businesses. Apple buys or makes all the pieces necessary for making the iPod (with the exception of a variety of peripheral equipment), and it in effect buys the music from publishers and owners on behalf of iTunes users. It has acted on behalf of consumers in negotiating directly with the music publishers and owners. At the end of 2005, the publishers were trying to persuade the digital music industry to adopt variable pricing that would charge more for hit songs than for older ones; Apple is vigorously defending its 99 cent price for all model—and is therefore reserving royalty fees that depend on popularity—on the grounds that this is the best model for the ecosystem.

Many software platforms, however, have adopted partial merchant models in the sense that they either integrate into a side or buy the complementary product or services on behalf of consumers. That is Apple's approach on the hardware side for its computers. It makes its own computers and either makes or buys some of the peripheral equipment that come with its computers. And it was Palm's approach as well initially; it made or bought all the relevant pieces for the Pilot.

What Exactly Does It Mean to Be Two-Sided?

According to the general definition we provided in Chapter 3, a platform is running a two(multi)-sided business model whenever it connects two (or more) groups of agents, each of which benefits from the participation of the other(s), *and* the platform provides the support for direct interaction between the two (or more) sides, without taking the place of any of these sides. Sony PlayStation is clearly multisided: the more independent game developers it signs up, the more consumers will buy it, and vice versa. And game developers sell their games directly to PlayStation users. The same holds for i-mode, Windows, and Palm.

As pointed out above, however, Apple's iPod platform functions as a one-sided business, although there are positive indirect network effects from its adoption by music publishers and users. To throw some light on

(continued)

what may sometimes appear as an obscure distinction, consider a retailer like Wal-Mart.

In the first scenario, Wal-Mart functions like your average village merchant who wakes up early in the morning to go acquire (many different types of) produce from suppliers, and then resells it to consumers at its local store. In this case the transactions Wal-Mart conducts with members of the two groups, suppliers and consumers, are largely independent of each other. First, Wal-Mart takes the place of buyers when dealing with suppliers, and then it substitutes itself for sellers when dealing with consumers. Suppliers could not care less about how many people visit Wal-Mart's stores, they are only interested in the price Wal-Mart bids for their products and the quantity it buys. Similarly, consumers care only about the prices at which Wal-Mart sells and the quality of the product it supplies, not the prices at which it buys.

Imagine now that Wal-Mart becomes more sophisticated and offers each supplier a contract specifying the price per unit of its product, a quantity it commits itself to buy, and also a price at which the supplier has to repurchase any unsold units. This type of contract is likely to improve efficiency by allowing Wal-Mart to order larger quantities upfront rather than restricting itself to a minimum in order to avoid accumulating unsold inventories. Short-run risk is now shared between Wal-Mart and its suppliers. At the same time, however, this contract also introduces indirect network effects. In deciding whether or not to accept such contracts, suppliers now have to take into account the visitor traffic Wal-Mart's stores generate, because it determines sales and ultimately their profits: more consumer traffic means fewer unsold items and therefore higher profits. And since consumers are clearly more likely to visit Wal-Mart if it offers a greater variety of products, each individual supplier ultimately cares about how many other suppliers (particularly of complements and substitutes) contract with Wal-Mart.

This example illustrates simply how even in the context of a one-sided merchant, two-sided indirect network effects may appear just by the nature of the contracts it writes with its suppliers. Nonetheless, the merchant's business is still not two-sided in any meaningful sense. Furthermore, this example is not directly relevant to software platforms, since "buying back unsold units" does not make any sense for digital applications, games, or content. Inventory is not an issue in the digital economy.[10]

There is, however, a way in which Wal-Mart's business can become clearly two-sided, which is also directly relevant to software platforms.

10. For a more detailed discussion of the scope of the platform, see Kevin Boudreau, "The Boundaries of the Platform: Vertical Integration and Economic Incentives in Mobile Computing" (working paper, MIT Sloan School of Management, Boston, 2005).

(continued)

> Imagine that instead of buying all products and reselling them, thus effectively taking ownership, Wal-Mart rents shelf space to some suppliers, say to Kellogg for its cereals, to Coke for its cans, and to Sony for its electronic devices. The suppliers are responsible for supplying, displaying, pricing, and advertising their merchandise within the space allocated by Wal-Mart, and they receive the revenue from sales to consumers. Again, putting aside suppliers' costs of visiting multiple stores, this contract is likely to result in cost savings because it provides suppliers with both flexibility and incentives to use price, advertising, and display to maximize profits, and thus allows Wal-Mart to charge high rents. (On the other hand, some efficiency might be lost because suppliers have no incentive to take into account the effects of their in-store actions on other suppliers.) In this case, Kellogg, Coke, and Sony are more than a little interested in the traffic Wal-Mart generates, since this determines how many consumers are likely to stop by their stands and eventually buy their products. It makes sense to think of them as "on board" the Wal-Mart platform. Renting shelf space to third-party vendors in the material world is akin to being a portal in the digital world. Conversely, i-mode can be described as offering "virtual shelf space" to its content providers, which the latter can manage as they choose. As Wal-Mart surely would in this example, DoCoMo in fact reserves the right to pick and choose which firms are awarded the most prominent spaces (that is, are designated official providers), as well as how the entire space is managed.
>
> Naturally, one can come up with many other contractual specifications that transform pure merchants partially or fully into two-sided platforms. These specifications may enhance efficiency by better aligning interests and incentives between the platform or merchant and its suppliers or complementors.

Patterns of Integration Over Time

At the most general level, the computer-based industries studied in this book have tended to become less integrated over time. The computer industry, for instance, started off with mainframe suppliers such as IBM providing fully integrated, stand-alone systems, including hardware, software platform, some applications, and peripheral equipment. An independent software industry emerged later, along with suppliers of peripheral equipment. Then, as computers became smaller and the workstation and PC revolutions unfolded, third-party suppliers of applications and peripheral equipment became more important. Some software platform vendors, such as Apple and Sun, continued to provide both hardware and software platforms, while Microsoft produces operating systems and some applications but no computer hardware platforms and no major peripheral equipment.

A similar evolution (although on a much shorter time scale) has taken place in the PDA and smart phone industries: these devices have evolved from single-purpose electronics products supplied by individual manufacturers into small computers based on software platforms that support a variety of application vendors and hardware suppliers. Similarly, the video game industry has evolved from single-game systems such as Home Pong through multiple-game systems provided by the same manufacturer (Fairchild's Channel F, Atari's VCS 2600) and ultimately to video game consoles (PlayStation, Xbox) that integrate hardware and software and are supported by hundreds of third-party game developers and publishers, as well as middleware providers.

The most plausible industry-wide explanation for this trend is the development of competitive markets for system components, which depends on the emergence of both accepted standards that are relatively stable and platforms that are perceived as viable. The analysis of changes in integration over time goes back at least to Adam Smith, who asserted in *The Wealth of Nations* that "the division of labor is limited by the extent of the market." In a famous 1951 paper, Nobel Laureate George Stigler argued that this proposition implies that "vertical disintegration is the typical development in growing industries, vertical integration in declining industries."[11]

Stigler noted that at the inception of new industries, vertical integration is necessary because the technologies involved are unfamiliar. It is therefore hard for firms to persuade outsiders to participate in a business with uncertain prospects and with which they have had little or no experience. If and when the industry grows and becomes viable, many of the tasks involved in the production processes are sufficiently well defined and are performed on a sufficient scale to make it possible for an integrated early entrant to turn them over to specialized firms, either as suppliers or as complementors. It is also profitable to do so *provided*

11. George Stigler, "The division of labor is limited by the extent of the market," *Journal of Political Economy* 59 (June 1951): 185–193.

the market of specialists is sufficiently competitive, as we discussed above, and that generally depends on the industry being large enough to support multiple specialist firms. Disintegration frees previously integrated firms to concentrate on those parts of the final product on which they have a comparative advantage. They may become specialists, or system vendors that buy components from specialists and assemble them.

Naturally, the industries Stigler had in mind were traditional one-sided ones, such as cotton textile machinery: the system vendors just bought parts and sold final integrated products. However, his insights apply to the modern digital industries we discussed here, and with particular force in some respects. It is not just that software platform vendors *can* rely on specialist firms to provide complements as an alternative to buying them. Rather, it seems that they *must* rely on third parties: increasing technological complexity and consumer demand for more diverse and better products make it impossible for the same firm to innovate effectively throughout the entire system; enlisting the cooperative participation of outsiders via well-defined interfaces becomes a must. In the words of Takeshi Natsuno, i-mode's chief strategist, "given the complexity of today's IT businesses, one technology or one firm alone cannot lead a new service."[12]

As the applications software industry matured and became more competitive, platform software vendors could turn from writing applications for their platforms to managing relations with third-party suppliers. The development of the IBM PC and its clones allowed Microsoft to offer a successful software platform without getting into the hardware business. Disintegration of the video game business both required and enabled the emergence of a vibrant industry of independent game developers. When Palm had managed to establish itself as a viable platform, it could enable the creation of the "Palm economy" of third-party complementors.

The video game industry took at least an additional step further on the disintegration path than the other industries did. A second wave of disintegration followed the emergence of the third-party game providers. As consoles became more complex, resulting in a longer and more

---

12. Takeshi Natsuno, *i-mode Strategy* (New York: John Wiley & Sons, 2002), pp. 31–48. Interview with the author.

complex development process, the game development side of the market separated into game development studios and game publishers. As described in Chapter 5, the former do the actual coding, whereas the latter specialize in managing relationships with console vendors, providing initial financing for developers and marketing for their games, and managing financial risks by spreading investments over a broad range of games. We have also seen the gradual build-up of a third wave of disintegration with the appearance of pure middleware firms that specialize in providing development tools to game developers for specific console platforms. Their market opportunity was created mainly by the increasing complexity of 3D graphics programming and especially the rise of online games, which require sophisticated networking solutions. And, of course, consoles such as PlayStation and Xbox welcomed the appearance of these firms, as they lowered the entry costs and expertise required of game developers.

Digital media platforms represent an interesting partial exception to this general tendency. In adopting its integrated iPod/iTunes platform, Apple apparently believed, for example, that the relationships among the various sides—such as inducing music companies to license their songs for online distribution—were too delicate to leave to others. It also may have believed that Apple's organizational advantage comes from producing cool integrated solutions. Moreover, it may be naive to think that Apple, whose genes come from Steve Jobs, could run a software-centric ecosystem as it is to think that Microsoft, whose genes come from Bill Gates, could make fashion accessories.

To explore these trends in more detail, it is useful to consider integration between platform software and applications separately from integration with hardware and peripheral equipment.

Applications Software

Our overviews of the evolution of computer-based industries suggest that the main reason why software platform vendors integrate into applications is to overcome the difficulty of attracting multiple complementors to new platforms with uncertain market prospects—the so-called chicken-and-egg problem, with technical uncertainty and complexity on top. If a PC operating system, for instance, lacks enough attractive applications, users will not adopt it, and therefore independent developers will not have any reason to write applications for it. Similarly, nobody wants to buy a video game console for which there are no good games, and nobody wants to write video games for a console that nobody will buy. There may be other ways to make developers more optimistic, of course, and evangelization certainly has a role.

In fact, DoCoMo relied on a "pure evangelization" strategy before the launch of its i-mode platform and has followed the same pattern when introducing major new features. It initially solved the chicken-and-egg problem by enlisting sixty-seven providers of attractive and diverse content; it was perhaps able to do this because its large share of the gadget-loving Japanese mobile phone business made i-mode seem highly likely to succeed. DoCoMo has always made it a point neither to buy content nor to provide any by itself, in order to preserve the incentives of third-party content providers. The company thinks that if it entered the content business, third parties would be reluctant to participate for fear that any innovative service they might come up with would eventually be imitated and competed away by DoCoMo. Likewise, if it bought content, providers would have an incentive to write content likely to appeal to DoCoMo, not to i-mode users, and would stop development once they sold it.[13]

On the other hand, integration—and the actual production of applications—provides more credibility to a software platform with uncertain prospects than evangelization by itself. In combination with evangelization, integration amounts to putting the platform vendor's money where its mouth is. Thus, most of the platforms we have encountered in this book initially opted for an approach involving writing some attractive applications or good games internally, so that end users had a reason to buy the platform and independent software vendors had a concrete reason to bet on its viability. Naturally, if and when its viability is established, it often makes sense to focus development efforts on the platform itself and tools for developers, and to work to bring independent developers on board as participants in the platform's ecosystem. Even in mature systems, though, doing some applications in house may provide

13. Natsuno, *i-mode Strategy*, pp. 62–63. Interview with the author.

valuable information on the quality of its development tools (eating one's own dog food, so to speak) and be a useful device for showcasing new platform features.

Palm provides the best example of gradual disintegration as a strategy. As we saw in Chapter 6, Palm thought that, in the wake of the failure of previous PDAs, including its own Zoomer, application developers would be quite reluctant to develop applications in time for the launch of PalmPilot. Therefore Palm decided to write the core applications itself and bundle them with the device. When it had established a significant base of users it could turn its attention to getting independent software application developers on board and creating the Palm economy. Palm's emphasis on getting others to write applications is particularly noteworthy because Palm began as an application developer for small computing devices. Even when it developed the PalmPilot it contracted most of the work for pieces other than the applications out to others.

Another example is provided by the video game industry. When Sony entered with its highly successful PlayStation in 1994, the dominant players, Nintendo and Sega, each had more than half the games for their respective consoles developed in-house. In large part this stemmed from the fact that both companies had been major players in the arcade industry before entering the home video game console market and therefore had a lot of in-house game development talent and stocks of proven games. Before launching the PlayStation and the Xbox, Sony and Microsoft acquired several prominent game publishers in order to ensure the presence of a few good games at launch: Psygnosis (Lemmings) for Sony, Rare (Battletoads, Golden Eye 007) and Bungie (Halo) for Microsoft. But only one of the twenty-six games was developed in house when PlayStation 2 was released in 2000,[14] and both Sony and Microsoft relied primarily on effectively courting the independent game developers that had emerged since the industry's creation. After the launch of major consoles, the fraction of games by console vendors has generally remained small: the proportion of games

14. David Canter and Jeb Haught, "Fans of Sony Will Find PlayStation 2 Satisfies," *The San Diego Union-Tribune*, November 14, 2000.

available in North America and developed in house is about 10 percent for GameCube, 8 percent for PlayStation, and 8 percent for Xbox.[15]

In the PC world, Apple's early computers mainly ran Apple-developed applications, but there soon emerged a set of independent vendors—of which Microsoft was an important member—creating applications for the Apple II and then the Macintosh. By the late 1980s Apple had less than a 10 percent share of the market for Macintosh applications. Today Apple makes less than 1 percent of the applications available for Mac OS.[16]

Microsoft's role over time as a supplier of applications for PCs running its operating systems was more complex, both because of its history and because a vigorous applications software industry was already in place when the IBM PC was launched. As we noted in Chapter 4, Microsoft began as a developer of programming languages and tools for 8-bit computers and the CP/M operating system. While it was selling the DOS operating system for IBM PCs and their clones, it was also selling applications with GUIs for Apple computers. In 1988, seven years after the IBM PC was launched, independent software vendors provided the leading word processor (WordPerfect), spreadsheet (Lotus 1-2-3), and database (Ashton-Tate dBase) for the DOS software platform.[17] Microsoft accounted for only 18 percent of the sales of spreadsheets and 8.5 percent of the sales of word processors for DOS-based PCs. It played a larger role in applications for the Apple platform, accounting for 75 percent of Macintosh spreadsheet sales and 60 percent of the Macintosh

15. http://www.us.playstation.com/games.aspx (note that SCEA is a division of Sony); http://www.xbox.com/en-us/games/default; http://www.nintendo.com/games.

16. Of the 18,247 software products available for Mac OS X, Apple Computer created only 43 (http://guide.apple.com/action.lasso; advanced search of software performed December 29, 2005).

17. "Strategies for Microcomputers and Office Systems: PC Spreadsheet Software: Market Review and Forecast, 1988" (IDC report no. 4389), November 1999; "Word Processing Software, 1989" (IDC report no. 5019), December 1990; "PC Database Management Systems Software" (IDC report no. 4258), September 1989; "PC File Management Software: Market Review and Forecast, 1988" (IDC report no. 4413), November 1989.

word-processing sales.[18] With the rise of Windows 3.0 and its GUI and the appearance of processors capable of running graphics-intensive programs at acceptable speeds, Microsoft's experience in the Macintosh world became relevant to computers running its own operating systems. Its word processor (Word) and spreadsheet (Excel) quickly became category leaders, and the Office package built around them rapidly attained a similar status. By the late 1990s, Microsoft accounted for about 20 percent of the revenue earned by makers of Windows applications.[19]

Although integration into applications/games/content can help a software platform vendor deal with the chicken-and-egg problem of end-user and complementor skepticism at launch, it is neither necessary nor sufficient for the solution of this problem. In addition to i-mode, examples of apparently successful platforms that did not initially integrate into applications include Linux and Symbian. Likewise, the digital media platforms offered by Apple, Microsoft, and RealNetworks didn't integrate into the provision of content (although there was plenty of content available) or into applications that used the APIs provided in those platforms.

Most of these platforms had other sorts of integration that served to reduce initial doubts as to their viability. For example, in mobile phones Symbian had the backing of the major hardware manufacturers, and Windows CE was sponsored by a company that had already built up a reputation for persistence in the face of market apathy. Others had different strategies that didn't require the development of an ecosystem. Linux has developed mainly as an operating system used for specialized applications, such as doing the special effects for the film *Titanic*, operating the Google search engine, or running task-specific servers. Its similarity to UNIX and its open nature also made it relatively easy to port existing applications. RealNetworks started as an application itself that ran on top of Windows. For a while it was the only streaming audio game in town and could leverage that to attract content.

18. Ken Siegmann, "Microsoft's Dominance Continues: Resellers, Competitors Cite Concerns with Developer's Huge Share of Mac Market," *Macintosh News*, December 11, 1989.

19. "Worldwide Software Market Forecast Summary, 2000–2004," (IDC report no. 22766), August 2000. Calculation excluded "system software."

The history of media devices suggests that integration into content, for example, can even be harmful if incentives within the integrated enterprise are not in line. In this business, Sony trails Apple's iPod by three years and tens of millions of consumers. Before iPod's launch, Sony had the successful Walkman mobile media device and possessed an unmatched amount of content (Columbia, CBS Records, and MGM), whereas Apple was prominent in neither players nor content. But Sony's media player and music download service, designed to compete with iTunes, were significantly slowed by internal conflicts between its hardware and media divisions, the latter claiming that digital music players would increase the threat of piracy and therefore would significantly hurt its revenues. Meanwhile, Apple demonstrated that a well-designed software platform such as QuickTime/iTunes can be made attractive both to consumers, by allowing them to purchase music through the iTunes Web site, encrypt it in AAC or MP3 format, and transfer it to their iPod, and to music publishers, by managing digital rights effectively and thus providing a healthy source of revenues.

Interestingly, we are aware of no examples of software platforms that initially integrated into the applications/games/content that subsequently exited that business entirely. On the other hand, almost all such platforms have adopted a two-sided strategy and made significant investments in attracting third-party suppliers. Partial integration is the norm. The only exceptions are those successful software platform vendors that launched without integration; they have remained out of the applications business.

Hardware and Peripherals

The tendency of computer-based industries to disintegrate over time is even clearer—with interesting exceptions—when we consider integration with the supply of basic hardware and peripherals. In the early mainframe days, these were tightly linked to operating system software. Not only were there no specialist vendors to attract in these early days and no standardized hardware-software interfaces to provide to them, but different vendors made different technical choices, and there was necessarily great uncertainty regarding the viability of individual platforms. For instance, until 1998, when Apple introduced the iMac with USB ports, Apple used nonstandard interfaces to connect peripherals such as printers, keyboards, and mice, and it bundled a computer mouse and display with those systems.[20] It continues to bundle hardware with its Mac OS.[21] Because Microsoft entered the platform business later and in partnership with IBM, whose viability was not in much doubt at that date, it has never been in the hardware business and is only a marginal supplier of peripherals.

Accidents of history and birth shape what firms are good at, their core competencies, and this has a long-lived effect on overall strategy and integration decisions. One can't presume that Apple could have created the rich ecosystem that Microsoft did, or that Microsoft could have created the style and veritable cultural icons that have helped Apple survive where so many others failed.

As we discussed in Chapter 4, Apple's strategy enables it to coordinate hardware and operating system changes internally, without intercorporate negotiation, and, because the Mac OS runs only on Apple hardware, to test all hardware/OS packages thoroughly before they are offered to end users. Microsoft's strategy requires it to invest heavily in working with hardware vendors and makes it impossible to test its software platforms with all hardware configurations end users will encounter. On the other hand, its hardware complementors have very strong incentives to produce quality machines at low cost, as both Dell shareholders and those who lost their investments in firms that used to compete with Dell can attest. One can imagine Apple's strategy winning in a world in which technological change drove frequent, radical changes in hardware and software architectures, so that the ability to manage those changes internally and produce more reliable systems was an

20. "Hands On–Mac–Universal Solution," *Personal Computer World*, February 1, 1999; "Mac Ports, Past and Present," http://charm.cs.uiuc.edu/users/olawlor/ret/mac_ports.

21. As we noted in Chapter 4, Apple briefly (from 1994 to 1996) pursued a policy of partial integration in hardware. But this pursuit was both brief and timid: Apple's licensees never accounted for more than 21 percent of the sales of computers running Apple operating systems. "Macintosh Clone," http://www.answers.com/topic/macintosh-clones; John Poultney, "Dataquest Posts 1997 Mac Tally," February 23, 1998.

enormous advantage, but that is not the world in which the computer industry has operated in the last few decades.

The Microsoft strategy of having the hardware complement its operating system produced by a competitive, technologically dynamic industry has served to make its operating systems more valuable and to speed their market penetration. Microsoft is not above using integration on occasion to stimulate important markets for complements, as its entry into mouse production, discussed earlier, illustrates.

Palm, discussed in Chapter 6, provides another interesting example of disintegration over time. It began as a developer of PDA applications that teamed up with others to create a PDA. It learned the downsides of lack of integration from that failed experience: it was hard to design a product by committee. So when it made another try at this business, it adopted a fully integrated strategy, not in the sense that it made everything but in the sense that it controlled all aspects of the software and hardware design process and treated other firms as subcontractors rather than partners. Following its success, it intentionally let this tight integration unravel. It started licensing its operating system to other hardware manufacturers—makers of PDAs, mobile phones, code bar readers, and other devices—in 2000 in order to increase its attractiveness to application developers. Eventually, Palm went all the way by disintegrating in 2003 into PalmSource, the software platform vendor, and PalmOne, the hardware manufacturer.

It did so mainly to liberate itself from the delicate conflicts of interest it was facing by licensing its operating system to PDA manufacturers that competed against Palm's own devices, the same problem Nokia is addressing by building a Chinese wall around its Mobile Software division. Disintegration allowed PalmSource to focus clearly on building a software platform that would appeal to a variety of device manufacturers.

Palm was responding to the competitive pressure of Microsoft's Windows CE, the software platform that is currently the biggest challenge for Palm OS in the PDA business and that relies entirely on third-party hardware producers. The now independent PalmSource would be in a better position to compete for the attention of those same hardware producers. In the words of David Nagel, PalmSource's CEO "As an independent company, PalmSource can accelerate the acceptance of Palm OS."[22] In doing so, Palm explicitly stated that it did not want "to go the way of Apple and become a niche player."

Microsoft is pursuing the same strategy in smart phones, treating the hardware (handsets) as a commodity. The major producers of handsets have responded with Symbian, which can be viewed as an attempt to turn the operating system into a commodity. (This interpretation is reinforced by Symbian's design: hardware-specific middleware must be developed in order to make Symbian fully functional [with an end-user interface] with each manufacturer's handsets.) Although Symbian looks from some angles to be a nonintegrated software platform, its close links with Nokia have naturally made other handset producers nervous. Continuing this theme, i-mode can be viewed as an attempt, using Java middleware and other additions to its platform (e-payment in particular), to commoditize both handsets and operating systems to some extent; if end users and content providers can interact through i-mode interfaces regardless of their underlying hardware and software, then operating systems become less important. Thus, for instance, i-mode users can download Java applications through the i-appli service regardless of the particular handset model they have and the operating system it uses. And, as in other sectors, Linux is both a nonintegrated software platform and a nonstandard sort of competitor.

In addition to Apple in PCs, there are two other clear exceptions to the general pattern of disintegration of software platforms from hardware over time. The first of these is Apple's iPod media device, which integrates a hardware platform, software platform, and, through Apple's iTunes service, content. As noted earlier, it is hard to know whether this is no more than Apple's staying true to a corporate strategy that favors integration across the board or whether it reflects some nonobvious technical advantage to coupling hardware and software tightly—or even whether this tight integration is a permanent state of affairs.

The second clear exception is the video game industry. All successful providers of video game systems integrate hardware and platform

22. Palm, "PalmSource Spin-Off and Handspring Acquisition Approved by Stockholders," Palm press release, October 28, 2003.

software. We believe the explanation for this departure from the norm stems from special features of video game consoles. These are computers designed for only one type of application, interactive games in which graphics are typically very important. To provide the best possible gaming experience, sophisticated graphic designs must be rendered with high speed and great accuracy. Poor performance is visible, literally, to customers. To be competitive, system vendors have designed all platform components, hardware and software, to squeeze the best possible gaming performance out of the underlying microprocessor, and market leaders clearly have no interest in developing industry standard designs or interfaces. For example, the Emotion Engine processor at the core of PlayStation 2 and the entire architecture surrounding it were new, "the result of brilliant, out-of-the-box thinking."[23] It was built for one purpose: to generate amazing 3D graphics and digital sound. It was not as fast as Intel's Pentium II CPU for some operations, but, not surprisingly, its graphics processor had 1,000 times more bandwidth than PC graphics processors at the time of its introduction. Just as devotees of PC games have typically demanded the hottest PCs, so it seems that on average, video game systems need to be closer to the technological cutting edge (or, as is sometimes said, the bleeding edge) than PCs. This is just the sort of environment in which the flexibility in innovation provided by integrating hardware and platform software is most likely to pay off.

Still, it would be a great surprise if the enormous success of Microsoft's "commodity hardware" strategy in the PC business had not attracted imitators in the video game industry. This is at least one way to look at the short-lived 3DO Multiplayer discussed in Chapter 5. Trip Hawkins, its creator, had focused on specifying the best possible gaming technology and intended to license hardware production to multiple manufacturers—Panasonic, Sanyo, Creative Labs, and AT&T. As we noted, the other novelty in Hawkins's strategy was Multiplayer's pricing: the console was very expensive for end users ($699), while developers were charged remarkably low royalty rates ($3). It is hard to know which novelty was the main cause of failure, and, as we discussed in Chapter

23. Steven L. Kent, *The Ultimate History of Video Games* (Roseville, Calif.: Prima Publishing, 2001), p. 560.

5, the pricing strategy was clearly unsound. On the other hand, Michael Katz, former CEO of Sega of America, suggests that licensing hardware production was also unworkable in video games:

I'd like to think that we would have had the smarts at Sega to market the 3DO in the conventional, successful way and not create this, if you'll forgive the expression, ridiculous new model that Trip came up with of how to market and sell 3DO. I mean, not manufacturing the hardware himself and licensing the technology to other people—it's ridiculous. Why would more than one company want to compete against someone else with exactly the same product? Why would a retailer want to buy the same product from more than one company? Everyone in the industry thought that was ludicrous.[24]

At first blush, Mr. Katz seems to be saying that the exact strategy that made Bill Gates the richest man in the world was "ludicrous." But the sectors are different. Third-party hardware production may work in the PC world because machines that are differentiated in buyers' eyes can still run Windows successfully. We talk of Wintel PCs as commodities, but this is only approximately true: the major manufacturers produce many models and configurations and advertise their superior features and functionalities loudly. This is perhaps even clearer in PDAs and smart phones, where different devices running the same applications on the same software program can be highly differentiated via differences in hardware design. The ability to differentiate and innovate in these sectors holds out the prospect of high profits. In the video game arena, however, it may be necessary for all vendors to produce "exactly the same product" in order to generate a satisfactory gaming experience. And, as Mr. Katz indicates, manufacturers would much rather differentiate their products, if only slightly, than produce a pure commodity.

Still, Microsoft itself, although it seems to have been fully aware of the failure of 3DO's Multiplayer eight years before, decided to try the same model again when it launched the Xbox in 2001. After all, if someone could successfully bring the PC platform model into the video game industry, who else better than Microsoft? But, as we saw in Chapter 5, Microsoft was quickly rebuffed by the third-party PC manufacturers it tried to enlist—quite probably a blessing in disguise. In a rephrasing

24. Kent, *The Ultimate History of Video Games*, p. 486.

of Mr. Katz's words, Michael Dell told Microsoft upon refusing the Xbox deal offered to him:

When Sony cuts the prices on their PlayStations, their stock price goes up. Every time I cut prices, my stock price goes down. If you don't understand why that happens, you don't understand the console business. I understand why this is strategic to Microsoft. I don't understand why this is strategic to Dell.[25]

Competing Ecosystem Structures

In most of the preceding chapters, we have encountered examples of competing software platform vendors with very different scope and integration strategies and thus, typically, very different business models. Apple versus Microsoft in PCs is the most familiar example, and Microsoft versus Symbian versus i-mode is perhaps the most complex. Rivalry of this sort raises economic issues that do not arise in the traditional world of bricks, mortar, and widgets. How does competition *across* the various layers of the mobile phone industry (mobile network, handset hardware, handset operating system) differ from competition *within* the same layer?

The managerial and strategic issues this sort of competition poses are interesting and difficult. As PCs and video games compete to become dominant as home entertainment centers, should video game manufacturers encourage or discourage conversion of video game consoles into PCs? As PDAs and smart phones both seek to become the single indispensable device in every purse and pocket, what sorts of complementors should they seek to attract, or should they focus on integrated strategies? Should Apple's competitors emulate its one-sided model, or should they be confident that multisided strategies will ultimately win out in media devices, as they have elsewhere?

INSIGHTS

• Software platform vendors are participants in complex ecosystems that include end users as well as producers of complements (such as

25. Dean Takahashi, "Opening the Xbox," *Prima Lifestyles*, 2003, p. 168.

hardware devices, software applications, and content), and, in mobile phones, mobile operators.

• Platform vendors are more likely to find a multisided strategy most effective when technical interactions with complementary products are stable and well defined, and the markets for those complementary product markets are competitive. These conditions tend to be more prevalent in more mature markets.

• At the start, software platform vendors often also produce applications and hardware because third parties can't be attracted until a base of end users has been built. Over time, software platform vendors generally become less integrated, though partial integration into applications is very common.

• In a multisided strategy, the software platform mainly facilitates interactions between the sides of the platform (particularly applications vendors and end users). In a single-sided (or merchant) strategy, the platform either produces the complementary products itself or buys them and resells them to end users.

• Most software platform vendors adopt a multisided approach with respect to at least two sides, although they may take a merchant approach with other sides. The major exception is the iPod/iTunes platform, which operates as a merchant with regard to all sides: hardware, software, and content provided to its customers.

10

Some Lunches Are Free

"Oh, 'tanstaafl.' Means 'There ain't no such thing as a free lunch.' And isn't," I added, pointing to a FREE LUNCH sign across room, "or these drinks would cost half as much. Was reminding her that anything free costs twice as much in the long run or turns out worthless."
—*Robert Heinlein*[1]

INSIDE THIS CHAPTER

- The basics of software platform pricing
- When to use fixed versus access fees
- Where software platforms have sought profit

When you go to a video game arcade, you have to pay every time you start a game. At home, once you have bought a game for your video game console, you can play it as often as you like. And if you play online, you can also play as often as you like, but only if you pay a monthly fee. When you play music on your computer, you can either use the media player that came with it or download others for free and use them instead. RealNetworks sells its digital content by subscription; Apple charges 99 cents per song. Computer manufacturers can pay Microsoft for the right to install Windows (with larger manufacturers receiving a volume discount) or they can install Linux for free. Software developers can either pay Sony a royalty for each copy of a PlayStation game they sell or they can get Apple's help to write games for the Macintosh and pay Apple no royalties at all. Mobile phone users in the United States

1. Robert A. Heinlein, *The Moon Is a Harsh Mistress* (New York: Tom Doherty Associates, 1997).

are generally charged according to the number of minutes they are connected to the network, with various volume discounts available, while i-mode users in Japan pay according to the amount of data they send or receive, regardless of how long they are connected.

This chapter tries to explain why different industries have chosen different pricing methods to get both sides on board and maximize profits from the participants in their ecosystems. In so doing it provides insights into the pricing policies that new businesses based on software platforms should consider. We begin by explaining the basic economics of pricing in multisided platform businesses. We then consider three important dimensions of pricing for software platforms. First, what is priced? Some businesses based on software platforms charge for access to their platform, some charge for use of the platform, and a few charge for both. Second, how do prices vary across the customers on a given side of a platform (game developers, for example)? One price does not fit all in either theory or practice. Third, who gets the (nearly) free lunch? Contrary to Milton Friedman's observation that there's no such thing as a free lunch, in the industries we have examined, the customers on one side get services for free, or at least for a price that at best covers out-of-pocket cost.

Pricing in Multisided Businesses

In single-sided businesses, pricing analysis mainly focuses on the level of price, both at introduction for new products and at maturity, and on price discrimination—differences in price paid by different customers. The profit-maximizing price for a single product depends on the cost of supplying an additional unit—the incremental or marginal cost—and on the responsiveness of demand to price. Demand will be more responsive to the price of a particular product—economists would say the price elasticity of demand will be higher—the easier it is for buyers to reduce purchases of the product in question when its price rises, either by switching to competitive products or by doing without, and the less likely competitors are to match price increases or ignore price cuts. The higher a product's price elasticity of demand, the lower is the optimal markup of that product's price over marginal cost.

Pricing is more complex for new products and for firms that produce multiple products. Firms sometimes engage in "penetration pricing": they charge low introductory prices to get the attention of buyers and penetrate a new market, then raise these prices over time as the market matures. Under other conditions firms practice "cream skimming," charging high prices to early, eager buyers and then lowering prices over time to capture a larger market. Similarly, firms that produce several products must adjust prices to take into account that some may be substitutes for each other (pricing high reduces cannibalization of sales from substitutes) and some may be complements for each other (pricing low boosts the sales of complementary products).

Even in these and other more complex cases, pricing in single-sided markets always begins with product-specific marginal cost. This tight connection between the incremental cost of a product and its price weakens considerably in multisided businesses in ways that have important implications for pricing strategy.

The fact that there is a tight connection between prices and costs in single-sided businesses doesn't mean that all customers get charged the same price. In fact, many firms charge higher markups over cost to some customers (or groups of customers) than others, depending on their intensity of demand. Economists gave this practice the name "price discrimination" before "discrimination" acquired such negative connotations.[2] Not only is price discrimination common in market economies, but often it enhances economic welfare by, for example, better enabling firms to recover the costs of research and development and thus increasing incentives to perform R&D.

Price discrimination turns out to be important in multisided businesses as well, as we discuss later in this chapter. As background for these discussions, it is helpful to summarize the three major types of price discrimination that economists have identified.

Firms would like to be able to charge every individual buyer the absolute most they would be willing to pay. That is what a very good used car salesperson tries to do: he tries to figure out the most each buyer

2. Mankiw, "Principles of Economics," p. 334; Carlton and Perloff, "Modern Industrial Organization," pp. 297–299.

would pay and then quotes just a little bit less. (Economists would say he is practicing first-degree price discrimination.) In practice, sellers rarely have enough information to pull this off, so they try a couple of cruder methods.

One common method involves various bulk or volume discount schemes that give customers a lower average cost per unit the more units they buy. (Economists call this second-degree price discrimination, or nonlinear pricing.) The simplest bulk discount is called a "two-part tariff," because customers have to pay both a fixed charge to buy anything (an access charge) and a per-unit charge for each unit purchased (a usage charge). The average cost per unit falls as more units are purchased.[3] In principle, firms can generally increase profits by using both access and usage charges, though collecting both charges sometimes entails higher transactions costs that swamp any potential profit gain. If there are costs associated both with providing access and with providing usage, it seems more common for firms to make the bulk of their profits from usage, which measures strength of demand, rather than from access. That is, to use the most familiar example, giving away the razor (or selling it at cost) and making money on the blades seems to be more common than selling the blades at cost and making profits on the razor.

Another method of price discrimination reflects the fact that it is often much easier for firms to guess how much, on average, a particular group would be willing to pay than to guess how much a particular individual might pay. An airline may not know how much a particular individual will pay for a seat, but it does know that people who travel at the last minute are typically business travelers who are willing to pay much more than people who book weeks in advance. The airline can therefore charge the group of last-minute travelers more than advance-booking passengers. Of course, to engage in this group method of pricing, the seller must find groups of buyers who have different sensitivity to the product's price, who can be identified and therefore charged separate prices, and

3. The classic exposition is Walter Oi's "A Disneyland Dilemma: Two-Part Tariffs for a Mickey Mouse Monopoly," *Quarterly Journal of Economics* 85 (1971): 77–96. For a more technical treatment, see Richard Schmalensee, "Monopolistic Two-Part Pricing Arrangements," *Bell Journal of Economics* 11 (Autumn 1981): 445–466.

who can't defeat the scheme by having the low-price group sell to the high-price group. Although there are challenges here, many businesses in practice figure out ways to engage in this sort of discrimination. (This is known as third-degree price discrimination.)

Pricing for Balance . . .?

We have emphasized that in theory and in practice, multisided firms have to balance the demand on the two sides by pricing, and that they often do this by pricing low to one side and high to another. Any student of basic economics, though, should question this statement for any platform in which the two sides interact directly with each other. After all, under textbook competition it doesn't matter whether the government imposes a product-specific tax (2 cents per bushel of wheat, for instance) on buyers or on sellers, since sellers will pass the full amount of the tax through to the buyers. Now consider payment cards. Card systems typically charge cardholders a zero price for using their cards and charge merchants about 2 percent of the transaction amount when cardholders use their cards to pay. This effort to tilt pricing in favor of cardholders would be defeated if merchants imposed a surcharge of 2 percent on all transactions using a card. Then the cardholder would end up paying, and the merchant wouldn't.

Could a similar result be true for video game consoles? Does it matter whether the console maker collects royalties from game developers or from game users? If game developers pass the royalty cost on to the users, the users end up paying in the end anyway.

In practice, it generally does matter which side pays, because two key assumptions made in the textbook discussion don't apply. First, there are often significant transactions costs that prevent the customers on the two sides of most markets from just "sorting it out" themselves. Take the payment card example. Although most card systems prohibit merchant surcharging because it degrades the value of their product to cardholders, several countries have barred card systems from imposing such a no-surcharge rule. In those countries, however, most merchants don't surcharge. One reason is that it is costly to impose small charges on customers. Those merchants that do surcharge often charge more than they are charged by the card system—an indication that they are using the fact that a customer wants to use her card as a basis for groupwise price discrimination.

The effects of transactions costs are visible in many two-sided markets. We discuss their likely role in video games below.

Second, competition in most real markets is less intense than in textbook markets. Competition among suppliers on at least one side of two-sided businesses is often imperfect, either because there are only a few major sellers or because products are differentiated. In this case, per-unit charges on that side generally are not passed on dollar for dollar. The exercise of market power (which leads to output restrictions) on that side may complicate the problem of balancing the two sides, and the presence of excess profits (deriving either from market power or from a few highly successful differentiated products) makes it more attractive to charge that side.[4]

When balance matters in a mature two-sided business, the pricing problem is much more complex than in a single-sided business. Marginal cost and price responsiveness on both sides matter for both prices, and so does the pattern of indirect network effects. In general, if side A cares more about side B than B cares about A, then, all else equal, A will contribute more total revenue. Thus, newspapers make their money from selling advertising, not from selling papers.

The textbook pricing formula for a single-sided market gives the optimal markup over marginal cost as 1 over a measure of price responsiveness (the price elasticity of demand), so low price responsiveness implies high markups. The corresponding formula for a two-sided business involves marginal costs on both sides, price responsiveness on both sides, and measures of the strength of indirect network effects in both directions. In particular, balance may require charging a price below marginal cost to a group with low price responsiveness, something a single-sided business would never do, if it is critical to attract members of that group in order to get members of the other group on board.

4. For a general discussion of the issues discussed in this paragraph and the remainder of this section, see Jean-Charles Rochet and Jean Tirole, "Two-Sided Markets: A Progress Report," mimeo, IDEI and GREMAQ, Toulouse, France. On the effects of imperfect competition, see Andrei Hagiu, "Pricing and Commitment by Two-Sided Platforms," *Rand Journal of Economics*, 37 (2006): forthcoming.

As we mentioned in Chapter 3, most two-sided businesses earn all or almost all of their profits from only one of the customer groups they serve. The standard economic theory of pricing in these businesses indicates that such pricing structures may be optimal, but it does not imply that they should be the norm. One explanation for the observed pattern is that sensitivity to price typically differs substantially between the two sides, so that it is optimal to price low to the price-sensitive side in order to attract the price-insensitive side, which can then serve as the main source of profit.[5] Another explanation is that the standard theory neglects the transactions costs of collecting revenue from two sides rather than one. If, for instance, standard theory says that an 80/20 revenue split between two sides is optimal, but the costs of monitoring usage and excluding nonpayers required to collect the 20 would be significant in practice, the true optimum, taking those costs into account, may be 100/0.

Entry and Platform Competition

Two other strands of the economic literature would seem to be relevant to software platforms. The first deals with entry strategies. Recent work has argued that it may be necessary for new two-sided businesses to use a "divide and conquer" pricing strategy to deal with the chicken-and-egg problem, or the reluctance of either side to come on board without the other. The idea is initially to subsidize one side (or, more generally, to do whatever it takes) in order to get it on board even though the other side is not yet on board, and to use the presence of the subsidized side to attract the other side.[6] This differs from the single-sided penetration pricing strategy discussed above because the key here is to generate indirect network effects, to use the subsidized side as a magnet to attract the other side. After entry has been successfully effected and both sides are on board, of course, the rationale for the initial subsidy vanishes, and

5. The technical argument that "corner solutions" of the 100/0 sort are the rule under the most plausible assumptions is given by Wilko Bolt and Alexander F. Tieman, "Skewed Pricing in Two-Sided Markets: An IO Approach" (working paper 13, De Nederlandsche Bank, Amsterdam, October 2004).

6. Bernard Caillaud and Bruno Jullien, "Chicken and Egg: Competition Among Intermediation Service Providers," *Rand Journal of Economics* 34, no. 2 (Summer 2003): 521–552.

one would expect to see a corresponding shift in pricing policy. One of the regularities we discuss below, however, is that pricing structures—the relative amounts paid by the various sides—appear fairly robust over time; there are not many examples of pricing low to one side at first and then raising prices significantly later.

A slightly different entry problem arises when members of one side must be attracted before members of the other side.[7] In order to attract buyers for a new video game console, for instance, an array of attractive games must be available at the console's launch, but this won't happen unless developers have been persuaded earlier to invest in developing those games. Developers, of course, won't make those investments unless they expect the console to be popular. This requires at least that they expect the console to be sold for a low price. In order to create such expectations, console makers often commit publicly to low prices months before their products are launched, in announcements directed at both game developers and end users. Steve Race, then president of Sony Computer Entertainment, describes such an announcement he made at a large trade show six months before the launch of Sony's Playstation[8]:

Olaf [Olafsson, President of Sony Electronic Publishing] was about two-thirds of the way through his speech when he said, 'I would like to call up Steve Race to tell you a little bit more about the Sony Playstation.' So I walked up. I had a whole bunch of sheets of paper in my hands, and I walked up, put them down on the podium, and I just said '$299,' and I walked off to this thunderous applause.

The other relevant strand of the economic literature considers competition among multisided platform businesses. At one level, the standard pricing formula mentioned above deals with this: as in single-sided markets, the presence and behavior of competitors are important determinants of price responsiveness of demand. A new element here is the distinction between "single-homing" and "multihoming." When faced with two or more competing platforms, a business or household is said to single-home if (because of switching costs or for other reasons) it can deal with at most one of them; it is said to multihome if it is able to deal

7. Andrei Hagiu, "Pricing and Commitment by Two-Sided Platforms," *Rand Journal of Economics* 37 (2006): forthcoming.

8. Steven L. Kent, *The Ultimate History of Video Games*, 2001 p. 516.

with two or more of them. In the PC world, most households single-home, while many software developers multihome.

This is a fairly general pattern: most members of one side single-home and most members of the other multihome. While it seems plausible that this difference should affect pricing, it is less clear which side should benefit in general. The standard theory says that pricing on one side will tend to be lower, all else equal, when the number of single-homing members increases on that side and higher when the number of multi-homing members increases.[9] The argument is that if members on one side become more inclined to single-homing—which happens, for example, if their switching costs become higher—then competition will be more intense on that side, since it becomes competition for all of a member's business, not just for some of it. On the other hand, casual observation of the video game industry suggests that as multihoming has become more common among video game developers over time, their royalty rates have come down substantially. This is consistent with the opposed argument that the easier it is for an important player on one side to multihome, the lower its switching costs and thus the greater its ability to shift its business between competing platforms. This in turn enhances its bargaining power vis-à-vis platforms and thus its ability to command lower prices. Perhaps in part for this reason, as we discuss below for most software platforms, end users, who generally single-home, contribute much more to the net revenue of the platform business than application or content developers, who commonly multihome.

What Is Priced?

Most of the preceding section implicitly assumed a platform business that charged only usage fees. In fact, an important choice in the industries studied here is between access fees and usage fees, which can be exemplified as the difference between buying a video game for home use, and thereby getting the right to play it as often as you like, versus being

9. Jean-Charles Rochet and Jean Tirole, "Platform Competition in Two-Sided Markets," *Journal of the European Economic Association* 1, no. 4 (2003): 990–1029.

charged each time you play a game in an arcade. Even though, as we discussed above, it is theoretically preferable to employ both kinds of fees, we know of only one case in which this is done—most plausibly because of transactions costs. That case is massive, multiplayer online role-playing games (MMPRPGs to gamers), where players do face a two-part pricing regime—and more.

Price Discrimination in MMPRPGs

Online gaming has spawned several new and original pricing business models, which have first appeared on the PC platform and are now increasingly emulated by console manufacturers and console game publishers.[10]

Most of these novel pricing models have been created by the developers of online massive multi-player role-playing games (MMPRPG), which are hosted on the publishers' servers and played online simultaneously by thousands of users who enter and exit the game 24 hours a day, 7 days a week.[11] The basic pricing is a simple two-part tariff: users pay a fixed fee to buy the game CD, usually around $50, after which they are charged monthly subscription rates. (For example, the current monthly fee for Sony Online Entertainment's Everquest is $12.99, and the one for Electronic Arts' The Sims Online is $10.) However, the very successful MMPRPGs realized that they could profitably sell expansion packets and game enhancements.[12] Everquest, for example, started offering a premium server, Everquest Legends: for an extra $30 per month, players gain access to additional content, guidelines, and events. Other MMPRPGs have pushed price discrimination even further by selling additional game characters and objects. Players of Electronic Arts' Ultima Online can get advanced characters (alchemists and magicians) for $30. It was not long before a secondary market appeared on eBay, where players trade characters among themselves.[13]

Noticing these developments, console makers realized the revenue-generating potential they offered and sought to capture it. Xbox 360, with

10. This has a lot to do of course with the fact that PC online gaming has largely predated console online gaming, which has only become a key aspect of platform competition with the last two console generations.

11. IGDA Online Games white paper (2003).

12. A hit like Everquest reached 500,000 users, whereas more recently, Korea's NCSoft shattered all records when it announced that its Lineage MMPRPG had an astounding 4 million paying customers.

13. "Patti Waldmeir: Cyber World Is Heading for Regulation," *Financial Times*, March 30, 2005.

(continued)

> its centralized and proprietary online service, is in a particularly good position to create an online marketplace where players can trade game artifacts (levels, characters, weapons, and so on). PlayStation will find it more difficult to do this, since its online service is decentralized.
>
> These practices open up the very interesting possibility of "piecemealing" games, transforming them from unitary packaged goods into completely modular, mix-and-match collections of products. It is easy to imagine publishers selling bare-bones versions of their games on CDs and then price discriminating among users by offering additional levels, characters, features, weapons, and so on for sale individually. This would present console manufacturers with the opportunity of charging users each time they downloaded a game piece through their online services. This would be broadly akin to the per-data packet charges levied by mobile network operators such as Japan's NTT DoCoMo on users downloading content on their mobile phones through the wireless network.

For video game consoles that connect to the Internet, one could imagine emulating MMPRPG pricing and charging both an access fee (the purchase price of the console) and a variable (per-month or per-game) fee for games played at home on the console. In theory, using both forms of pricing would generally increase profits somewhat. In reality, collecting a usage fee for console-based games would certainly increase the seller's costs, and that cost increase would almost certainly swamp any theoretical increase in profit. Moreover, charging a usage fee to consumers who have always been able to play "their" games as much as they want would almost certainly provoke a serious consumer backlash. As this example illustrates, the pricing instruments that each software platform can use on each side of its market depend to a large extent on the transaction costs involved, on the institutions of that particular market, and on the available technology.

Exclusion and Piracy

For a software platform to be able to charge a positive access or variable price to a certain side of its market, it first needs the means to exclude members of that side who don't pay. On the end-user side, this is a relatively small problem when the software platform is integrated into the hardware. Even if the software platform can be easily copied, it is useless without the basic hardware, and there are many ways (including using nonstandard components and nonpublic designs) to make cloning the hardware difficult. It is thus not surprising that we are unaware of any allegations of substantial piracy of Apple computer systems.[14]

On the other hand, it does not seem easy to exclude makers of peripheral devices. In any case, we are unaware of any serious attempt to do so in the industries studied here.

When the software platform is not bundled with the basic computer hardware, software piracy can become a major problem, particularly if (as is the case for PCs designed to run Windows) there are numerous third-party hardware producers using standardized components and working with well-documented hardware-software interfaces so that the necessary hardware is easy to buy or build. In this case, the software vendor almost certainly needs to devote resources to fighting piracy. It might license its systems only to hardware vendors who agree (on pain of heavy penalties) not to ship hardware without operating systems, for instance, and devote resources to enforcing that contract provision. It might also hire agents to attempt to buy pirated copies of its system and hand the sellers over to the authorities.

Because these and other sorts of antipiracy measures are costly, whereas copying software is essentially free, some amount of piracy of popular platforms is almost certain to occur. Since the higher the price of the platform, the more tempting it is to copy it illegally, a strategy of selling software separate from hardware fits best with a strategy of selling the software for a relatively low price.

One other aspect of licensing platform software to hardware makers deserves mention. Microsoft has long offered discounts on operating system licenses to computer makers to design and build machines that meet certain standards. These offers are a part of the Market Development Program, and their conditions typically include selling more than

14. Although Apple's June 2005 announcement that they would be switching to Intel architecture started rumors that such piracy might be a concern in the future.

a certain percentage of computers with certain minimum technical specifications (memory, CPU speed, and so on). The rationale is to provide incentives for improving the quality of the computers that reach end users, which in turn stimulates demand for Windows. This is also one method for coordinating innovation across corporate boundaries and, from Microsoft's point of view, of reducing the number of end users who are unhappy that advertised features of Windows don't work on their new computers.

Developers of applications, games, or media content cannot be automatically excluded from using operating systems. It is hard to keep APIs secret (they need to be documented for internal developers, for instance) or to prevent developer tools and programming languages from being copied, especially if they are being sold for a high price. All video game consoles obtain exclusion by using a security chip to prevent games produced by unauthorized developers from running, and one cannot use a mobile phone purchased from one carrier on another's network without the other carrier's SIM card. We are unaware of any other exclusion device that has been used successfully in the industries studied here at any significant scale.

In the smart phone industry, third-party vendors could initially supply applications freely, as in the PC industry. However, realizing that the quality of applications available had a significant impact on the overall user experience, network operators and handset manufacturers began to create *signing programs* for third-party software. These programs resemble the distinction DoCoMo makes between official and unofficial content: nobody is completely excluded, but not every application can obtain official approval. Users know that signed applications satisfy certain quality standards. In 2003, Symbian introduced what has become the most significant signing program, Symbian Signed, endorsed by Symbian's hardware licensees as well as network operators. In addition to granting signed applications a public seal of approval, handset manufacturers such as Nokia and Sony Ericsson, as well as operators such as Orange and T-Mobile, open their distribution channels only to applications that are Symbian-signed. (Developers pay modest fees to Symbian in this process: $350 for registration and from €185 to €560 for testing.[15]) We understand that it is technically possible on at least some phones for network operators to go a step farther and block end users from installing nonapproved applications on their handsets, and that some are at least considering this step.

Intensity of Use

If it is possible to exclude potential participants, the next choice is whether to do so and to charge something for access or usage. If a positive price is to be charged, access fees, which do not vary with intensity of usage, are typically (but not always) easier to charge than usage fees in the markets we've discussed here. This is because it is easy to monitor purchase, but purchase in these settings typically enables usage at widely different levels of intensity. (Arcade video games provide a counter example: it is much more natural to charge each time a game is played than to sell the rights to unlimited play.) Once I've bought a video game for my Xbox, I can play it every waking hour or toss it in the closet and forget it. The developer would like to charge more in the former case than in the latter, though he would generally like to charge something (an access fee) in the latter case as well. But, as we discussed above, it is simply not easy to monitor and charge for postpurchase usage in this case.

Things are changing with the advent of online gaming. Console online games have followed PC online games by adopting a subscription model; users pay a monthly subscription fee to play.[16] This isn't pure usage pricing, though; that would involve charging for time spent online or at least for each login. This sort of pricing would seem to be feasible; perhaps it is not done for the same reason that most U.S. consumers pay a flat monthly fee for unlimited local (land-line) telephone calls: consumers value having a predictable monthly bill and don't like having to

---

15. https://www.symbiansigned.com/app/page/faq, https://www.symbiansigned.com/app/page/testhouses. Registration is done by VeriSign, Inc., and testing by either CapGemini, Mphasis, or NSTL; all are Symbian partners.

16. As we have seen, however, on Xbox Live, users pay a monthly fee to Microsoft and have access to all Xbox-supported online games, whereas the PlayStation online service leaves it to each individual game developer to charge subscription fees to users.

think about the cost consequences of their actions on a minute-by-minute basis.

The access/usage issue arises in slightly different form with applications developers. A software platform vendor could, in principle, charge each third-party application or game developer only a fixed fee for access to its system. One can argue that Apple, Microsoft, Symbian, and Palm-Source do this, but their fees for developer tools and related information at best just cover the costs involved. In fact, one can think of this policy as offering negative prices to credible developers, with more attention devoted (and thus, in effect, a larger subsidy given) to developers that produce the most popular applications—thus, roughly, a negative usage charge on that side of the market.

Any attempt to make significant profit from access charges to developers would run into the exclusion problem discussed above. Moreover, such a policy would clearly be inefficient. Game developers, for instance, differ enormously in scale, and a fee that Electronic Arts would notice would likely exclude most of the firms in the industry. The pricing scheme actually adopted by video game platforms, a royalty for each game sold, is in effect a usage fee for game developers: it charges them more if they derive more value from access to the platform. But, as we discussed above, it leads to access pricing, not usage pricing, of individual games to end users.

Some platforms do have the potential to monitor intensity of usage, at least approximately. If the number of songs downloaded from iTunes were a good measure of iPod usage, Apple could use song pricing on iTunes to levy a usage charge on iPod owners. However, as we discussed in Chapter 8, Apple has decided not to do this and to sell songs on iTunes on roughly a break-even basis. This may be simply a continuation of Apple's long-standing strategy of seeking profit in hardware rather than software, or it may reflect worries that piracy would make higher prices for music unsustainable. RealNetworks' Rhapsody service, in contrast, charges users monthly fees for unlimited streaming access to a million songs, but it does not allow downloading, so that when they stop paying they no longer have access to any songs they have heard before.

In Chapter 7 we noted that one of the main features of i-mode is its sophisticated billing system, which allows NTT DoCoMo to charge users based on the amount of data they receive and send to and from their i-mode phones. This is arguably a reasonable proxy for consumer usage of (and thus value derived from) the platform. While clearly imperfect, it seems superior to the much less accurate alternative that was used by WAP-based services such as Vizzavi that charged based on time spent on the network. Today, virtually all wireless service providers around the world charge usage fees based on the amount of data transferred or levy a flat fee for unlimited data transfers.

Particularly with ubiquitous access to the Internet, it is possible in principle to monitor intensity of end-user usage for essentially any software platform. One could, for example, imagine that every time a PDA using the Palm OS is linked to a computer connected to the Internet, it would report CPU usage to PalmSource, which would automatically generate a monthly charge to the owner's credit or debit card, just as some Internet service providers do now.[17] But this sort of monitoring is not free, and in most cases suppliers seem to have found it more efficient on balance to let the cheapest method of transacting (per session at video game arcades and per game for home systems) determine whether access or usage is priced, and not to incur the extra cost of instituting a two-part tariff or other more sophisticated pricing system.

Price Discrimination

Like many, if not most, businesses, software platform vendors have employed a variety of forms of price discrimination, some traditional and some not, in order to enhance their profits. For instance, license fees for the Palm OS are negotiated separately for each licensee, while Symbian uses the same price schedule for all its licensees (who are also its owners). From 2002 to 2004 Symbian earned an average of almost half its revenue from providing consulting services to its licensees, helping them to adapt the Symbian operating system to their hardware, but consulting fees have become less important over time, and in 2004 they constituted only one-fourth of total revenue. We do not know how the use of these services varies across licensees or how, if at all, they are marked up. Like

---

17. After a certain amount of CPU usage, the system could be set up to deny the end user access to applications until it had been linked to the Internet.

Microsoft, both Palm and Symbian offer bulk discounts, so that larger licensees pay lower per-unit license fees.

In video games, it has been argued that console pricing reflects cream skimming, which is a form of intertemporal price discrimination: prices typically decline over the life spans of particular consoles so that on average, the most eager buyers pay higher prices. On the other hand, it is likely that costs decline over time as well, as learning occurs and component prices fall, so the extent of discrimination is not clear. It is our understanding that Sony and Microsoft charge lower per-unit royalties for games that sell many copies.[18] This interesting form of nonlinear pricing strengthens game developers' incentives to focus on a few good games rather than many mediocre games.

Without a detailed knowledge of costs, it is difficult to know whether some pricing strategies have an element of discrimination. I-mode users pay on the basis of the volume of data transferred and iTunes users pay for each song downloaded, while subscribers to RealNetworks' Super Pass service pay monthly fees independent of usage. The first two seem better designed to measure individual differences in demand, while the subscription scheme, which resembles the way local phone service has traditionally been priced in the United States, is no doubt a response to consumers' preference for flat, known fees.

Two relatively unusual pricing practices encountered in these industries reflect the multisided nature of most platform businesses. First, as we noted in Chapter 5, video game console vendors generally offer lower royalties and joint marketing arrangements to developers that develop exclusively for that console.[19] Note that there is no forcing: developers are free to choose whether or not they wish to develop exclusively for a

18. Email correspondence with Nanako Kato and Gerald Cavanagh of SCEI, May–August, 2005, and Dean Takahashi, *Opening the Xbox* (Roseville, Calif.: Prima, 2002). SCEI.

19. Authors' interviews at SCEI. In the economic literature on multisided markets, developers who focus on a single platform are said to single-home, while others are described as multihoming. For a discussion of the strategic implications of these behaviors, see Rochet and Tirole "Platform Competition in Two-Sided Markets"; Jean-Charles Rochet and Jean Tirole, "Tying in Two-Sided Markets and the Impact of the Honor All Cards Rule" (mimeo, IDEI University of Toulouse, 2003); Jean Charles Rochet and Jean Tirole, "Two-Sided Markets: An Overview" (mimeo, IDEI University of Toulouse, 2004).

particular platform. (This differs from the exclusive contracts used by Nintendo in the late 1980s and early 1990s, which left independent developers with no choice but to support NES exclusively if they wanted to be granted any access at all.) The motivation for offering better prices to exclusive developers is simply that exclusivity offers the console maker a competitive advantage over rival platforms in competition for the end users that constitute the other side of the market. This is especially true for killer games, whose sole presence on a console is sometimes sufficient to entice many users to purchase that console. Another software platform offering better deals in exchange for exclusivity is RealNetworks, which paid Major League Baseball $20 million in exchange for making game coverage available exclusively through RealPlayer.[20]

In the video game industry, game developers also seek exclusivity. As we noted in Chapter 5, movie and sports tie-ins are important sources of value to game publishers. Accordingly, significant licensing fees are paid to Hollywood studios and professional sports leagues in exchange for the rights to feature their images, characters, and players in games. And publishers pay significantly higher amounts for exclusive rights: Electronic Arts' exclusive NFL license was rumored to be close to $200 million for five years, whereas their NBA license cost well below that amount, as it was shared with rival game publishers (the NBA sold nonexclusive rights to five game makers for a total of $400 million).[21]

The second unusual pricing practice is discrimination among complementors based on "quality." Microsoft has given more favorable license terms to computer makers that offer machines meeting certain design standards. These arrangements do not reflect Microsoft's costs or differences among computer manufacturers; rather, they reflect the greater value of "quality" computers as complements to Microsoft's operating systems. In addition, as we noted above, NTT DoCoMo offers better deals in the form of additional services to "official" i-mode content providers (those endorsed by DoCoMo) than to others, and the Symbian

20. "RealNetworks pays $20M for baseball audio rights," *UPSIDE Today*, March 27, 2001.

21. "NBA Grants Videogame Rights to 5 Publishers for $400 Million," *The Wall Street Journal*, March 22, 2005.

Signed program is administered by some network operators and handset providers in a similar fashion. Finally, video game consoles simply exclude poor-quality games completely by denying them the necessary security chips. Multisided platforms have strong interests in raising the quality of the products supplied by complementors to end users.

Price Structures of Multisided Platforms

A fundamental decision facing all multisided platform businesses is choice of a price structure: How much should the platform vendor charge each side relative to the others? Since transactions involving some sides may have significant associated variable costs (the production and distribution costs of video game consoles, for instance), the most illuminating way to analyze observed price structures is to look at the contributions of each side to gross margin or variable profits: revenue minus side-specific variable cost. Should a two-sided platform derive most of its gross margin from one side of the market, and if so, which side, or should it choose a more balanced structure, with both sides making significant contributions to gross margin?

Like all multisided platforms, the pricing structures of the software platforms we have encountered in this book reflect the need to get all unintegrated sides on board: end users, application/game/content developers, and manufacturers of hardware and peripheral equipment. The structures we have examined have three remarkable features. First, all of them are extremely skewed: almost all earn a disproportionate share of their variable profits on only one side of the market, either end users or developers. Second, for all but video games, the platform earns the bulk of its net revenues from end users. The third remarkable feature, which we consider in the next section, is that these structures have been stable over time.

Main Characteristics

As we have seen in Chapter 4, PC operating system vendors such as Microsoft and Apple make virtually all of their profits on the end-user side of the market. Since applications developers tend to multihome and end users tend not to, this is somewhat at odds with the theoretical prediction, noted above, that *all else equal*, pricing tends to favor the side of the market that does not multihome. Of course, all else is never equal.

Apple makes profits from end users directly by selling Apple computers based on the Mac OS. Microsoft, on the other hand, charges most end users indirectly, through the licensing fees it levies on OEMs, which the latter pass through in the final prices of their computers. (Some Windows users do buy upgrades themselves.) As one would expect in this highly competitive industry, these fees appear to be passed through roughly dollar-for-dollar.[22] Apple's variable costs on the user side are the marginal costs of producing each Macintosh computer and installing its software on it, whereas Microsoft has essentially zero marginal costs. (Microsoft distributes master CDs; the computer manufacturers do the copying.)

On the developer side, Apple, Microsoft, and most other operating system vendors devote significant resources to supporting application developers through development tools, conferences, and direct assistance. The prices charged for these services are set to at most cover costs. In fact, some development tools are available for download for free from the software platforms' Web sites.[23] Somewhat less attention is paid to makers of peripheral equipment, in part because they need less information to produce compatible devices. But neither Apple nor Microsoft seeks profits from the provision of this information.

The pricing strategies of PalmSource and Symbian are very similar to Microsoft's strategy in PCs, which in turn is very similar to Microsoft's strategy in PDAs and smart phones. PalmSource and Symbian, like Microsoft, make most of their profits in the form of licensing fees charged to manufacturers of devices running their operating systems, and both offer a great deal of support to third-party developers in exchange for fees that are generally set just to cover costs.

NTT DoCoMo's i-mode mobile Internet platform also earns a disproportionate share of its profits from end users, in this case through

22. Interview with Microsoft.

23. Many of Apple and Microsoft's SDKs are available free of charge on their developer Web sites, and there are some other tools that are sold, but we believe that these are sold at close to cost. See http://developer.apple.com/; http://msdn.microsoft.com/.

network usage charges. We have seen that DoCoMo also earns some revenues from "official" content providers who choose to use DoCoMo's billing system, but this accounted for only around 1 percent of total revenue from users in 2004. Furthermore, although these revenues are designed to cover the costs of providing the billing service to official content providers, it is unlikely that they cover the overhead costs DoCoMo incurs in connection with the teams that monitor and select official content.

Net profits from i-mode's hardware side are negative, as DoCoMo buys the handsets from manufacturers and resells them at a significantly lower price to consumers in order to encourage adoption of the i-mode platform and thus to generate more revenues from network usage charges.[24] This practice, known in the mobile phone industry as "handset subsidies," is yet another version of the cheap razor/expensive blades or two-part-tariff policy we've discussed before. Selling a handset both produces profits directly and generates future profits by increasing network traffic. The presence of this second effect makes the optimal handset price lower than it would otherwise be. If this effect is strong enough, it can drive the optimal price below marginal cost, as it apparently does for DoCoMo and other network operators.

As we discussed in Chapter 8, the leading digital media platforms employ markedly different business models. But in all these models, end users are the primary source of variable profit: in Microsoft's case through licensing of Windows, in RealNetworks' case through licensing access to content, and in Apple's case through sales of iPods. None of these vendors extracts profit from content owners, and indeed, Apple and RealNetworks pay for content.

Video game console manufacturers are the single, striking exception to the general "end users pay" pattern in these industries. These firms derive most of their variable profits from games, both by charging royalties to independent or third-party game developers and through sales of games produced in-house (so-called first-party games). Ever since Atari introduced the VCS 2600 and the cheap razor/expensive blades business model in 1977, game consoles have been most often priced at

24. Interview with Takeshi Natsuno of DoCoMo, March 2005.

or below marginal cost.[25] However, due to falling costs of components and learning effects, there commonly exist periods of time over a console's life cycle when price exceeds marginal cost.

For example, a Sony executive in 2004 stated that there is a "positive gross margin" on PlayStation 2 sales,[26] a statement that our interviews at Sony Computer Entertainment Inc. (SCEI) have confirmed. It is most likely that Sony originally sold the PlayStation consoles below marginal cost, but over time it has been able to make manufacturing more efficient and derive positive gross margins. Nonetheless, even now the largest share of SCEI's PlayStation variable profits come from royalties levied on third-party publishers of video game software and sales of first-party games—between 60 and 70 percent, according to our interviews. In addition, game developers must also pay a fixed fee for the necessary game development tools, but this fee is very small relative to royalty revenues. The published price for a three-year Tools and Middleware license for the PlayStation 2 was approximately $12,000.[27] That is equivalent to typical $8 royalties levied on only 1,500 copies of a PlayStation game, when hits like Tomb Raider sell millions of copies.

The Xbox console also has had negative gross margins. The average selling price of an Xbox console has been $160 since 2002, yet the average cost of producing it for the same period has been $304. Microsoft's newest console, the Xbox 360, is also being sold at a loss. The company released the Xbox 360 in November 2005, but does not expect any profits until 2007. By contrast, from its 2001 launch and through December 2003, the company received $961 million in revenues from software sales—direct sales of its own games plus $7 per-unit royalties levied on third-party games—and $313 million from sales of

25. Leonard Herman, *Phoenix: The Fall and Rise of Videogames* (Union, N.J. Rolenta Press, 1997); Southwest Securities "Interactive Entertainment Software: Industry Report," Fall 2000; Peter Coughlan, "Competitive Dynamics in Home Video Games," *Harvard Business Online*, June 13, 2001.

26. "kelly s i." *Mirror*, March 4, 2000; quotation from Takao Yuhara, Sony Corporation Senior Vice President and Group CFO, Sony Corporation earnings conference call, January 28, 2004.

27. Tools & Middleware License for PlayStation(R)2, Sony Corporation, September 8, 1999.

peripherals such as game controllers, memory cards and other plug-ins, and remote controls. First-party games accounted for roughly 70 percent of total game software revenues.[28]

Some Explanations

What determines these pricing structures? In particular, how can one make sense of the fact that video game consoles have chosen to earn the bulk of their profits on the game developer side of their market, whereas all other software platforms studied here make most of their profits from end users? It is clear that transactions costs can't be the driving force, since extra costs for a security system must be incurred to exclude games from unlicensed developers.

We offered one explanation in Chapter 5, based on the assumption that the number of games purchased by an individual console owner is correlated with the value he or she places on the video game system. Under this assumption the optimal pricing policy is that first introduced with the Atari VCS 2600: price the console low to generate penetration and build demand for games, and make most profit on the games. Once this pricing model has become established, it is difficult for any firm to depart from it by charging a high price for the console and a low price for games, as 3DO learned to its sorrow, since it is hard for a high-priced console to get penetration unless it somehow manages to launch with an unusually large number of great games, and without penetration it won't get great games in the first place.

We have encountered a variety of related alternative explanations that deserve discussion. Many of our interviewees stress that one important reason why PC operating system vendors do not generate variable profits from their application developers is that PC platforms are open. In principle, anyone can develop applications for Windows or Mac OS without explicit consent from Microsoft or Apple. (You don't even need development tools, which are relatively expensive in any case.) In other words, the openness of these software platforms means that their sponsors have

28. Arik Hesseldahl, "Microsoft's Red-Ink Game," *Business Week Online*, November 22, 2005; Andrew Hendley, Adam Holt, Phil Michelson, and Derek Wong, J.P. Morgan North American Equity Research, "Microsoft Corporation: Patience Is a Virtue," January 6, 2004, table 12.

forfeited the ability to exclude developers and therefore the ability to charge them for access and usage of the platform. The same is true for Palm and Symbian and for Microsoft's PDA and smart phone operating systems. In contrast, video game consoles have always been closed platforms and have maintained the ability to exclude through the use of a security system that locks out unauthorized developers. These security systems are necessary to be able to charge royalties to third-party game developers.

Of course, simply having the ability to charge game developers does not explain why they should in fact be charged. Moreover, video game platforms are closed because their owners spent money to close them, and this begs the question of why other platforms have remained open. It is not that hard to imagine Microsoft, Apple or Palm devising software security systems to lock out unauthorized application developers. (Note, in particular, that video game developers pay royalties only for video games that run on consoles; royalties are not charged for games that run on PCs and other open platforms.) If these companies have chosen not to do this, the reason is unlikely to be technological; it is most probably because the costs exceed the benefits. In particular, if it were optimal for operating system vendors to charge independent software developers substantial royalties, similar to those charged by video game consoles, the potential revenues created would likely justify the fixed cost of developing a security system. If, on the other hand, it is not optimal to charge much anyway, then leaving their platforms open is the most cost-effective solution.

When discussing why the price of consoles is set low, manufacturers often argue that their prime customers are particularly price-sensitive and reluctant to pay too much for a platform mainly designed for playing games. They also stress the importance of obtaining a large installed base of users right away in order to reward game developers and give them incentives to keep writing games for that particular console.[29] On the other hand, the price of consoles is generally highest at launch. Manufacturing cost is also highest at launch, of course, and consoles are typically priced at or below marginal cost at launch.[30] As we have suggested

29. Interview with Nanako Kato and Gerald Cavanagh of SCEI, April 2005.
30. Coughlan, "Competitive Dynamics in Home Video Games."

above, subsequent price cuts reflect both cost reductions and, plausibly, intertemporal price discrimination: eager early adopters pay higher prices and, plausibly, contribute more to variable profits than less interested, late adopters.

The recent economic literature on two-sided markets implies that optimal price structures are determined by side-specific marginal costs, price elasticities of demand on both sides of the market, and the relative intensities of externalities between the two sides.[31] One general result that has emerged is that the side that "cares" more about the other side should pay more, all else equal. It's rather difficult to compare indirect network effects or side-specific price responsiveness in software platform industries, however, and examining side-specific costs doesn't discriminate between, say, Apple's computers and Sony's video game consoles.

The only economic modeling framework that has been specifically designed for studying two-sided software platforms is that of Hagiu.[32] He shows that the greater is user demand for variety of applications/games/content, the greater is the optimal share of platform profits contributed by developers (as opposed to end users). When demand for variety is higher, products (applications, games or content) are less substitutable, so there is less competition among developers. This allows developers to charge higher prices to end users and some of them to earn high profits, making it harder for the software platform to earn profits directly from end users and easier to extract them from developers via royalties.

Although user demand for product variety is difficult to quantify precisely, it is quite clear that video game users care about product variety

31. Rochet and Tirole, "Platform Competition in Two-Sided Markets," "Tying in Two-Sided Markets and the Impact of the Honor All Cards Rule," and "Two-Sided Markets: An Overview"; M. Armstrong and J. Wright, "Two-Sided Markets, Competitive Bottlenecks and Exclusive Contracts" (mimeo, University College, London, and National University of Singapore, 2004); Wilko Bolt and Alexander F. Tieman, "Skewed Pricing in Two-Sided Markets: An IO Approach" (DNB working paper no. 13, October 2004); Wilko Bolt and Alexander F. Tieman, "A Note on Social Welfare and Cost Recovery in Two-Sided Markets" (DNB working paper no. 24, December 2004).

32. Andrei Hagiu, "Two-Sided Platforms: Pricing and Social Efficiency" (http://www.princeton.edu/~ahagiu/job%20market%20paper%204%202.pdf).

more than users of computers, PDAs, or smart phone applications. One reason is durability: consumers quickly grow tired of one video game and frequently demand new ones, while we have been using the same basic word-processing program since around 1995. Video game console users buy an average of 3.5 games per year.[33] On the other hand, when it comes to computers, PDAs, smart phones and even mobile Internet services such as i-mode consumers use a remarkably low number of different products, and they stick to the same ones for long periods of time. Put otherwise, video games are more substitutable (interchangeable) from the point of view of consumers than applications for computers, PDAs, or mobile phones. Hence, one would expect to see video game platforms make a larger share of profits on developers relative to the other software platforms. And this is precisely what we observe.

Evolution of Pricing Strategies

It is natural to ask how software platforms' pricing strategies evolve over time. Based on our case studies, the surprising answer is, to a first approximation, they don't. Both what is priced and the basic pricing structures tend to remain constant over time. The only major shift in pricing strategy that we have observed occurred in 1977, when Atari began selling its new VCS game console below manufacturing cost, planning to make its money selling games. This razor/blades strategy has persisted in video games ever since. This continuity in pricing strategies is somewhat surprising, since the environments that software platforms face when they are established in the market differ dramatically from the ones they faced at their inception.

In principle, at least, all two-sided platforms face a rather difficult chicken-and-egg problem at launch. Application/game/content developers, along with third-party hardware and peripheral equipment manufacturers, are naturally reluctant to invest in supporting a new software

---

33. Schelley Olhava, "Worldwide Videogame Hardware and Software 2004–2008 Forecast and Analysis: Predicting the Future," (IDC report no. 31260), May 2004. Installed base for consoles is 123,368 and software shipments were 434,715.

platform unless they expect it to have a substantial installed base of end-users, and end users are generally reluctant to adopt a platform unless they expect it to be supported by an attractive array of applications, hardware, and peripherals. Economic theorists have argued that platform vendors' initial pricing structures should be designed to overcome this startup problem. The divide-and-conquer strategy calls for subsidizing the participation of one side of the market through fees low enough (possibly negative) to attract it, regardless of the participation of the other side (divide), and then charge positive prices to the latter, who knows that the first side will participate no matter what (conquer).

Once both sides are on board and the platform is clearly viable, of course, there is no need to subsidize the participation of either side in this fashion. Thus, a platform following a divide-and-conquer strategy would be predicted to subsidize participation of at least one side but to do so only temporarily; price should rise substantially to the initially subsidized side. But we have seen no such behavior by any of the platform software businesses we have studied.

On the other hand, we *have* seen changes in platform businesses' scope and integration that may play a similar role. In the extreme case, Palm removed all doubts about the availability of hardware, applications, and peripherals by being completely integrated into all these market sides at the launch of the PalmPilot. Over time, as it became established and these sectors matured, it was able to withdraw and focus on the software platform. Similarly, in video games both Sony and Microsoft acquired several high-profile game developers before releasing their consoles so that both end users and other game developers could reliably expect their consoles to have a number of high-quality games. It may be that because integration decisions are less easily changed than price policies, they serve as more credible devices to affect expectations when products are launched. Price policies, in contrast, seem to be selected with the long run in mind, though it is a bit surprising that so many firms apparently managed to get those policies right from the beginning. In any case, the fact is that price policies have been more stable than integration and scope strategies in the computer-based industries studied in this book.

INSIGHTS

• In principle, the pricing problem for software platforms (and other two-sided businesses) is complex, since it must consider the interdependencies of costs and demands (particularly indirect network effects) linking all sides.

• There is much variety in what software platform vendors charge for, and this is expanding as technology progresses. A general rule of thumb is that even though it is more profitable *in theory* for software platforms to charge both access and usage fees, they generally charge only one or the other.

• Like most businesses, software platform vendors use a variety of forms of price discrimination in order to ignite the market for their products and services. This helps firms target the most profitable customers and enables the most efficient and profitable bundling of services.

• Software platform vendors generally earn the bulk of their profits from only one side of the market, typically end users. The exception is video game console producers, who subsidize end users and incur extra costs to enable them to charge royalties to game developers. A plausible explanation is that the number of games purchased correlates with end users' demand for video game systems, so that making money on games enables console vendors to earn more from those who have the highest demand.

• Pricing strategies of software platforms have been remarkably stable. There are no examples of a software platform–based business pricing low to one side at first and then raising prices after getting that side on board. The pricing structure that ignites the business is generally the pricing structure that persists over time.

11

When Bigger Is Better

"I want a pair of jeans—32–28," I said. "Do you want them slim fit, easy fit, relaxed fit, baggy, or extra baggy?" she replied. "Do you want them stonewashed, acid washed, or distressed? Do you want them button-fly or zipper-fly? Do you want them faded or regular?" "I just want regular jeans. You know, the kind that used to be the only kind."
—*Barry Schwartz, "The Paradox of Choice"*[1]

INSIDE THIS CHAPTER

· How and why software platforms have expanded over time
· The software platform value proposition
· The economics of bundling features into software platforms

As we first noted in Chapter 2, when measured by lines of code, software platforms have grown steadily and substantially over time.

This pattern holds across software platforms for the same computing device. Linux, the Mac OS, and Windows have all grown rapidly. And it is true across different computer-based systems. Software platforms have gotten larger for handheld devices, mobile telephones, and video game consoles as well as for personal computers.

Table 11.1 shows the growth in the number of lines of code of various software platforms over time. Although numbers are not available for every year, the data show a consistent pattern. The average annual growth rate is about 50 percent. That means that the number of lines of code doubles about every two years.

1. http://www.aarp.org/bulletin/yourlife/many_choices.html.

Table 11.1
Size of Operating System by Year

OS	1992	1993	1994	1995	1996	1997	1998	1999	2000	2001	2002	2003	2004	2005	Compound Annual Growth Rate (%)
Measured in millions lines of code															
Red Hat Linux						9		16	27		42	50			33
Windows			3		15		18			35	40				30
Windows CE									0.4			2	2.5		58
Linux Kernel			0.1	0.2	0.5			1.1		2.2		3.8			50
Measured in megabytes															
Macintosh						70	200	250		1,500				4,000	66

Source: Red Hat Linux source code (http://research.microsoft.com/projects/SWSecInstitute/DIMACS-report.pdf); Linux Kernel source code; Apple system requirements.

This might not seem surprising, since hardware is becoming more powerful at a rapid rate, and hardware and software platforms are tightly coupled. The processing power and memory of computing devices have risen because the costs of producing microprocessors and memory have declined rapidly as a result of technological change and scale economies. But those forces cannot explain the growth of software platforms. Innovations such as object-oriented programming and the open-source model have made it more efficient to write platform code, but not dramatically so. There is certainly no Moore's Law operating in the labor-intensive process of computer programming. And while there are scale economies from using the same software platform across an increasing number of devices, there are, as Chapter 2 noted, *diseconomies* from expanding the size of the software platform itself.

Besides, there is something fundamentally different between what's happened with hardware and with software. Hardware has generally gotten smaller and more powerful. In contrast, software platforms have gotten bigger.

Increases in computer speed and storage capacity have indirect effects that help explain some of the growth in software platforms. More code is needed to control more complex and capable hardware. With more memory available, software platform architects and programmers have less incentive to economize on code. Neither effect is large enough, however, to explain the historical growth of software platforms.

The main driver is clear: software platforms have added code primarily to provide *more features* to end users and application developers. They have done this in tandem with the hardware platform that has provided *more features* with which the software platform can work. This chapter documents this expansion over time of the scope of software platforms and describes the economic and technological forces behind it.

Feature Accretion

Three patterns emerge from our study of software platforms across different computing devices:

• Every release of each software platform contains significant new features, and some features are even introduced between releases.

• Over time, software platforms incorporate many features that had been provided by third parties on a stand-alone basis.

• Software platforms generally include the code for all available features; they are seldom offered with a list of optional features from which customers can pick and choose.

More Features

Over time, software platform producers add features that appeal to end users, to application developers, and sometimes to both. They have to do this in part to get end users to buy another version of the software platform, since software platforms, like diamonds, don't wear out. They also have to do this to get software developers to write or modify their applications and thereby increase the value of the software platform. Applications don't wear out either, and new services made available through Application Programming Interfaces (APIs) will enable and entice developers to write new ones or upgrade existing ones.

The Palm OS is a good example. As we discussed in Chapter 6, when the original version was introduced in 1996, it included a feature called Graffiti that recognized a special kind of script. This enabled users to convey written information to the device by stroking a "pen" (a stick) over the screen. It also included a calculator, notebook, address book, calendar, and a utility to synchronize files and contacts in the PDA with desktop computers. The fourth version, released in 2001, added support for Bluetooth wireless technology and bundled America Online and utilities for reading and editing Microsoft Office documents. At the same time, it added many software services for developers, including some for telephony-based applications.[2] By 2004, the Palm OS, now in its sixth version, included APIs that enabled developers to take advantage of modern wireless networks, as well as headset and hands-free support for users, who were increasingly using their PDAs as telephones. It also includes a Web browser and supports advanced Web technologies, multimedia, and sophisticated security.

2. Cameron Crouch, "Palms Gain Expansion Options, Keep Popular, Sleek Design," *PC World*, May 2001; "Palm Revamps Operating System, Adds APIs," *Network World*, July 2, 2001.

Apple's Mac OS has also added features that have made it more valuable to end users and developers. The very first Mac OS in 1984 included a graphical user interface (GUI), calculator, notebook, a simple puzzle game, and a clipboard tool called Scrapbook to move text between applications. By 1988 it also included a color user interface that could be displayed on multiple monitors. Three years later it bundled AppleTalk and AppleShare, which enabled users to share files and printers across a network. In 1994, now on to Mac OS 7.5, Apple included Stickies—a desktop application that provided an electronic version of Post-It Notes. Version 9.0, released in 1999, had an updated version of Sherlock, Apple's search engine, which searched the user's hard drive and the Internet. Video chatting was included in 2003.[3] The most recent version, released in early 2005, includes Dashboard, a visually appealing utility that lets the user run many useful mini-applications called widgets. Among the widgets included are a stock ticker, a weather forecast, a flight tracker, a dictionary, and a translation tool. Over this period Apple also added more APIs that developers could use. These included a sophisticated set of media APIs associated with the QuickTime media platform (discussed in Chapter 8) that have been used by a large number of media applications available on the Mac, including Adobe's Premiere, a popular video editor.[4] Other APIs let developers take advantage of new technologies like Bluetooth and the visual technology behind the Mac OS's good looks.

All software platforms have added features over time that helped users and developers avail themselves of the new opportunities made available by the rapid development of the World-Wide Web. Table 11.2 shows when each of the major platforms on which we have focused added Internet communication protocols, a Web browser, an email client, and a

3. http://www.macos.utah.edu/Documentation/MacOSXClasses/macosxone/macintosh.html.

4. http://www.mackido.com/History/EarlyMacOS.html; http://www.macos.utah.edu/Documentation/MacOSXClasses/macosxone/macintosh.html; Gene Wilburn, "Some Bugs to Iron Out in Mac OS," *The Toronto Star*, January 5, 1995; Steve Wood, "Mac OS O9. I Think I Like It!" *A View from the Classroom*, November 8, 1999 (http://lowendmac.com/macinschool/991108.html); http://adobe.es/aboutadobe/pressroom/presskits/pdfs/premiere50/PREaag.pdf.

Table 11.2
Feature Accrual Across Platforms

	Platform						
Feature	Windows	Mac OS	Palm OS	Windows CE	Symbian	Xbox	Play-Station
Networking	1995	1994	1997	1996	2000	2001	2000
Web browser	1995	1998	2003	1996	1999	NA	NA
Email	1993	2001	1997	1996	1999	NA	NA
Media player	1991	1993	2002	2000	2000	2001	2000

media player.[5] In some cases these additions came in the form of code that was integrated into the operating systems. Microsoft, for example, wove various browser-related features (such as an HTML-rendering engine) into Windows 98. In other cases this came through bundling an application with the software platform. For example, Palm OS 3.0 included a stand-alone Expense application that eased the task of tracking business trip expenses.

5. Bernard J. Reddy, David S. Evans, and Albert L. Nichols, "Why Does Microsoft Charge So Little for Windows?" (National Economic Research Associates paper), October 9, 1998; "Windows For Workgroups 3.11 Launched" (Network Week APT Data Services no. 94), October 15, 1993; "Microsoft Ships Windows with Multimedia Extensions 1.0," *Business Wire*, August 21, 1991; http://kb.iu.edu/data/abmc.html; "What Changed in Mac OS X Version 10.1?" Mac OS History, http://www.macos.utah.edu/Documentation/MacOSXClasses/macosxone/macintosh.html; David Flynn, "New Pilots Fly Higher," *Sydney Morning Herald*, June 3, 1997; "Where is Palm OS 6?" (http://www.palminfocenter.com/view_story.asp?ID=6393); Ian Cuthbertson, "Multimedia on the Move: Sony Clie NX70VG," *The Australian*, February 11, 2003; Marty Jerome, "Put Windows in Your Pocket," *PC/Computing*, January 1, 1997; Jack Schoefield, "Third Strike for Windows CE in Palm Territory," *The Guardian*, April 19, 2000; "Symbian OS Version 6.x Detailed Operating System Overview" (http://www.symbian.com/technology/symbos-v6x-det.html); "Symbian Releases Latest EPOC Technology for Future Smartphones and Communicators," Symbian press release, June 15, 1999 (http://www.symbian.com/press-office/1999/pr990615.html); http://reviews.cnet.com/Microsoft_Xbox/4505-6464_7-7853769-3.html?tag=top; "Playstation2 Launch Drawing A Crowd," *Sun-Sentinel-Ft. Lauderdale*, March 19, 2000; "kelly s. i.," *Mirror*, March 4, 2000.

Features Already Provided by Others

Many features were available, in some form, to users or developers as third-party "add-ons" before they were incorporated into software platforms. This is most obvious in the case of PCs. Internet browsers, file encryption and compression, firewalls, and many other applications were available to end users before they were incorporated into either Mac OS or Microsoft Windows. Similarly, third-party media players preceded integrated ones on both Palm and Symbian operating systems. Third-party console accessories enabled network connectivity and online game downloads as early as 1983, nearly two decades before such functionality was integrated into the major consoles.

Some new features were provided first to developers rather than to end users, sometimes by third-party vendors offering libraries and tools that enable developers to take advantage of new technologies or innovations. In 2000, for instance, Extended Systems released a set of tools that enabled manufacturers to add Bluetooth support into their Palm OS–based devices, a year before Palm added this capability into the Palm OS. Similarly, SoftConnex provided USB connectivity APIs a couple of years before they were incorporated into the Symbian OS.[6]

Several dynamics are at work here. Platform releases need to occur at discrete intervals, and they can only include features that have been fully tested by the release data. For this reason, some features are not released promptly. Other vendors sometimes fill in the resulting gaps by offering add-ons that improve the platform in some dimension. Independent software developers also come up with ideas that the platform developers hadn't even thought about. Many of these attract very few interested users, but others become quite popular. If the original developer doesn't have intellectual property rights on her idea, the software platform vendor can incorporate these innovative features into its own product.

In the late 1980s, for instance, Apple and Microsoft decided to develop their own scaleable font technology instead of using Adobe's PostScript.

6. "Extended Systems Ships Bluetooth Software Development Kit for Handheld Devices," *M2 Presswire*, April 4, 2000; "USB On-The-Go Frees Digital Devices for Direct Connectivity Without A PC," *Business Wire*, November 18, 2002; "SoftConnex Joins Symbian Platinum Partner Program and Announces USBLink Host Software Solution," *Business Wire*, February 18, 2003.

Each was concerned about Adobe's per-font royalties and chose to bypass Adobe and develop their own technology. They collaborated on TrueType, which was included with both firms' respective operating systems in the early 1990s. Other times, though, the software platform has had to license technologies developed by others or acquire these firms in order to build in the feature promptly. That was the case with Internet Explorer, Microsoft's Web browser, which was originally built with technology that Microsoft licensed from Spyglass in 1995.

Of course, this means that making third-party add-ons for software platforms can be bit like making souvenirs for the latest Olympics. The market opportunities may be fleeting and might disappear as soon as the platform vendor catches up. The add-on developer can survive only by providing more value than the platform vendor. Many software products have disappeared after a short life when the platform vendor caught up.

One such example is the Watson browser add-on for Mac OS X. Watson, released in 2001 by Karelia Software, enabled users to access the Web in a novel and efficient way. Apple named it 2002's "Most Innovative Mac OS X Product." However, a year later, Apple's new Sherlock 3 search tool essentially supplanted it, and Watson was discontinued in 2004. Similarly, when ARM released MPEG-4 codecs for the Symbian platform in late 2000, the Symbian OS did not include that functionality. Newer versions of the OS, however, have come with support for MPEG media included, and ARM does not offer the codecs any more.

However, inclusion of a feature in the platform does not mean certain death for related third-party offerings. Third-party utilities have been able to distinguish themselves in various ways from the corresponding platform functionality. One such example is the Norton Utilities suite of disk and system repair and diagnosis utilities. Since its introduction in 1982, the Norton suite has had to adapt continuously as the functionality it offered has been added to both major desktop operating systems. Over time, disk compression, disk repair, defragmentation, disk optimizing, encryption, and other tools have all been added to both Mac and Windows platforms. Nevertheless, Symantec still offers Norton Utilities as a part of its SystemWorks bundle.

Versions and Options

Unlike automobiles and Chinese restaurants, software platforms tend not to offer different models or options. Consider the original Mac OS, introduced in 1984. It contained many fairly obscure features, but users and developers had to take all of them—or none. The same is true for the 2005 version. You can buy only one version of Mac OS X Tiger, and you cannot get it without Safari, the Apple browser, or Spotlight, Apple's search engine. Similarly, your Palm or Symbian-based smart phone will include a Web browser, a calendar, and an address book. You must take the option to play CDs on your Xbox or PlayStation 2 or to browse the Web via your i-mode phone even if you don't ever want to exercise it.

There are two exceptions to this pattern.[7] Software platforms for servers—the computers that serve as nodes and perform specialized tasks on networks (including "serving" content requested over the network)—often come in several versions for different uses. These versions are offered mainly to enable pricing to be tailored to differences in user requirements. More advanced versions are almost always supersets of the basic versions and usually come with better software support. The other exception concerns software platforms that are embedded in devices, such as cash-dispensing machines. Here, memory, performance, and power consumption concerns drive the market to small systems with targeted functionality. Often different versions target different sets of devices, or the manufacturer can pick and choose from the different components that make up the platform. Manufacturers can use utilities such as the Windows Embedded Studio to select components and build a system.

7. A third exception exists by order of the European Commission: since January, Microsoft has made two versions of Windows XP available to computer manufacturers. One makes Windows Media Player available to end users and makes the corresponding APIs available to developers; the other does not. Since they cost the same, no major computer manufacturer has licensed the second version. "Microsoft to Release Windows XP Home Edition N and Windows XP Professional Edition N in Europe," Microsoft press release, June 8, 2005 (http://www.microsoft.com/presspass/press/2005/jun05/06-08XPNEuropePR. mspx).

The Economics of Bundling

Software platforms differ from most other products in the number of features that are included in the product and in the growth of that number over time. But the difference is a matter of degree. Most products are bundles of components that could be provided separately and sometimes are. You cannot buy this chapter alone; you must buy the whole book. Men's laced shoes always come with laces, although it is possible to buy laces separately. Airlines cannot purchase the Airbus A380 without also buying the software system for flying it. And numerous products besides software platforms include features that others used to provide as add-ons.

"I haven't the slightest idea who he is. He came bundled with the software."

Many years ago automobiles were designed so that customers could purchase an air conditioning unit and have it installed after they bought the car. Today, almost all automobiles sold in the United States come with a factory-installed air conditioner. In the 1980s, PC users had to purchase an additional chip, a math coprocessor, if they wanted to do significant numerical calculations. By the 1990s these numerical capabilities had been integrated into all microprocessors used in PCs.

In all these cases, firms made two related decisions. One concerned product design and scope. What should be included, and how should the parts interrelate? The other decision concerned the firm's product line. Should the firm offer only one product, or should it offer several with different combinations of features? Economists have examined these questions, as we describe in this section, and the answers help explain the scope and bundling patterns we observe for software platforms, as we show in the next section.

Product Design and Product Lines

Almost all products consist of components. Take something simple such as salt. Few consumers purchase pure salt. If you buy Morton's iodized salt in the United States you get salt, iodine, and a box. More complex products are combinations of even more components. The typical personal computer has hundreds of separate parts. A credit card provides two major distinct features: the ability to pay for things and the ability to finance those things.

These products could be designed differently—and historically were. Long ago salt did not contain iodine and did not come in easy-to-use containers. If you wanted a CD-ROM drive for your computer in the late 1980s you had to buy it separately and attach it with a cable. Charge and debit cards allow people to pay but not to finance.

To illustrate the decisions that firms make about how to design their products and what products to offer to consumers, consider a simple case in which there are two components, *A* and *B*, each valuable to consumers in its own right. The possible products are listed in Table 11.3. Three cases are particularly important:

• *Components selling* occurs when the firm offers *A* and *B* separately (cars and bicycle racks).
• *Pure bundling* occurs when the firm only offers *A* and *B* together as a single bundled product, *AB* (men's laced shoes).
• *Mixed bundling* occurs when the firm offers the bundle *AB* and either or both of its components, *A* and *B* (such as the Sunday *New York Times* and the *New York Times Book Review*).

With two components, there are three possible "products" and seven possible product lines, as shown in Table 11.3. The number of products and product lines increases dramatically as the number of components

Table 11.3
Products That Can Be Sold Based on Two Components

	A	B	AB
Components selling	×	×	
Components selling	×		
Components selling		×	
Pure bundling			×
Mixed bundling	×		×
Mixed bundling		×	×
Mixed bundling	×	×	×

increases. Thus, with three components there are seven possible products and 127 possible product lines, while with five components there are thirty-one possible products and over 2 trillion possible product lines.[8]

Firms make different decisions on product designs and product lines within the same industries. Some may offer only components, while others may offer only bundles, and still others may engage in mixed bundling. Consider the most popular midsize automobiles sold in the United States, the Ford Taurus, Honda Accord, and Toyota Camry. The Accord comes in six models that have between zero and two options. The Camry has three models with between nine and twelve options. And the 2004 Taurus had four models with between three and thirteen options. Across car segments there is even greater variation. For example, Porsche is famous for having an enormous number of options that allow purchasers to customize their cars. All of these automobile makers

8. Mathematically, the simplest way to formulate the general problem is to ask ourselves how many different subsets of K objects you can conceive. Line up the objects in whatever order you like: for each of them, there is a simple binary decision, to include it in the current subset or not, and one needs to make this decision for all objects. Note that modifying the decision for one object results in a different subset; therefore there is a total of 2 to the power K (2^K) different subsets. This includes, of course, the empty set, which is obtained by opting for noninclusion for each individual object; therefore the total number of distinct nonempty product lines based on K products is $2^K - 1$.

include tires on their cars. They all purchase tires from third parties, and none of these automakers sells tires separately.[9]

Minimizing Producer and Consumer Costs

Bundling decisions affect costs for both producers and consumers. In both cases it is useful to divide these into costs that vary with each unit (marginal costs) and costs that are lumpy over a range of units (fixed costs). There may be diseconomies of scope from producing multiple separate products that raise both sorts of cost.

For example, studies of automobile manufacturing have found that making many options available increases what are called "complexity costs," which do not vary much with sales. Similarly, maintaining and managing different SKUs (Stock-Keeping Units) costs money, regardless of sales volume. Separate products require separate packaging and shelf space, each of which raises costs. To offer multiple versions of its Linux distribution, Red Hat Linux would have to create distinct packages and probably obtain additional shelf space at software retailers to display all versions. Marginal costs may also rise with product variety. It is cheaper to produce and distribute one pill that contains both cold and headache medicine than two separate products. Likewise, it is less expensive for operating system vendors to distribute a single CD with both an oper ating system and Internet communication functionality (for example, support for TCP/IP protocols) than to distribute these separately.

It is also possible, of course, that combining features may increase fixed or marginal costs directly by making products more complex and harder to make. And complexity may have costly indirect effects as well, such as raising the likelihood of products breaking down, raising support costs for customers, and increasing the costs of repair. As software platforms have gotten larger, it has become harder to manage their production, the likelihood of bugs has gone up, since more modules interact with each other in ways that are difficult to anticipate entirely, and security problems have escalated. Likewise, combining drugs together

9. David S. Evans and Michael Salinger. "Why Do Firms Bundle and Tie? Evidence from Competitive Markets and Implications for Tying Law," *Yale Journal on Regulation* 22 (Winter 2005): 37–89.

increases the risks of unintended and unanticipated side effects. The marriage of computers and automobiles provides other examples of the potential disadvantages of bundling. Owners of Dodge 2001 minivans have, according to the *New York Times*, "posted anguished cries . . . about electronic gremlins that stop windows from rolling all the way up, that unexpectedly dim the interior lights, that drain batteries or that make engines sputter."[10]

Unless they dislike the components that are bundled, consumers are likely to realize savings from bundling. If you like to read about sports and arts every day, it is cheaper to get a newspaper with both than to have to buy two papers, even if you have to throw away the style section. And if you have both a cold and a headache, it is more convenient to get a single package of pills. Letting the producer make choices for you can save you time as well. When we go to the hospital for surgery, most of us would prefer to leave most of the choices of most of the components to the experts rather than make them ourselves. Downloadable music lets us pick individual songs for our collections. But many might prefer the bundles the artists and publishers put together and distribute as albums. Choice is costly because it takes time and effort to make informed decisions, ones that others may be able to do more efficiently, and bundling reduces consumers' transaction and search costs.

But bundling may also impose costs on consumers. Consumers may prefer to mix and match components—a common strategy in building home entertainment systems and increasingly popular for music collections. Although automobile manufacturers have reduced variety over time, many car buyers like having some choice, and some no doubt resent option packages that require them to take a moon roof to get a more powerful engine.[11]

These sorts of costs help explain how businesses choose the finite set of products they actually do offer from among the essentially infinite number they could offer. Firms must weigh the demand for a particular product offering against the costs of making it available as a stand-alone

10. "What's Bugging the High-Tech Car?" *The New York Times*, February 6, 2005, p. 14.

11. Example of an options package for Ford Taurus from Evans and Salinger, "Why Do Firms Bundle and Tie?"

product or as part of another product. Many products are not offered at all because there is not enough demand to cover the costs of producing and distributing them. Some men would no doubt prefer to get their shoes without shoelaces because they have a favorite shoelace brand or color they like to use. But there are probably so few shoelace aficionados that it would not pay to offer this option. Other products are offered only separately because few people want them as a system. Although this is changing, many families buy their own ingredients for dinner rather than prepackaged meals. And in other cases there is enough demand for the components and the bundle for producers to offer both—to engage in mixed bundling.

In some cases, it isn't profitable for producers to offer bundles versus the individual components. Consider a simple example. One hundred consumers would pay up to $10 for A; fifty different consumers would pay up to $6 for B, and a third group of ten would pay up to $20 each for AB. It costs $1 to produce each unit of A and B and $2 to produce each unit of AB. It costs $200 to make each of these three products available at all; these might be the fixed costs of creating and stocking any one of these products. In this case the average per-unit cost, if all demand is met, of A is $3 (= $1 + $200/100), of B is $5 (= $1 + $200/50), and of AB is $22 (= $2 + $200/10).

Both A and B could be provided separately for a profit, since the consumer willingness to pay for each unit is greater than the average cost of producing it ($10 vs. $3 for A and $6 vs. $5 for B). However, the bundle cannot be provided profitably because the unit costs exceed what people will pay; it costs $22 to make AB on average, but consumers will only pay $20. The problem here is lack of demand. Not enough people want the bundle to make it profitable to provide, given the significant fixed cost involved.

On the other hand, firms sometimes offer *pure bundles* because, even though some consumers do not value portions of the bundle, it is cheaper to sell the components together. To see the intuition, consider the extreme case in which each of several types of consumers wants one component but none of the others. If the fixed cost of providing each of the components is high enough, it may nonetheless pay to combine them all together. It may be cheaper to give consumers a component they do not want than to provide the component they do want separately. The manufacturer then saves money, and the consumer often gets a lower price than she would otherwise.

A simple example illustrates this. There are two consumers. Person 1 is willing to pay $5 for *A* and nothing for *B*; person 2 is willing to pay $5 for *B* but nothing for *A*. It costs the manufacturer $2 per unit to make the components *A* and *B*. The per-product fixed cost of offering a product at all is $1. The manufacturer could sell a unit of *A* and a unit of *B* separately for $5 each, collect $10 in revenue, incur $4 in manufacturing cost and $2 in product-offering cost, and make a profit of $4. Or it could sell a bundle *AB* to both consumers for $5 each, collect $10 in revenue, incur $4 in manufacturing cost and $1 in product-offering cost, and make a profit of $5.

Bundling is the best strategy in this example: it saves $1 of fixed cost. In this example the manufacturer pockets the difference, but some of the cost savings would get passed on to the consumer in a competitive market. Moreover, if the fixed cost of offering a product were $5, it would not be profitable to offer *A* or *B* separately (the additional $4 in fixed cost would wipe out the profit of $4), but it would be profitable to offer *AB* (the manufacturer would earn $1 of profit).

Although these examples are contrived, they illustrate why firms offer only a fraction of the products—defined by combinations of components—that they could. The examples above involve just two components, for which there are three possible products. As we noted above, with three components there would be seven possible products (*ABC, AB, AC, BC, A, B, C*); with ten there would be 1,023. Even minimal fixed costs of offering individual products would encourage producers to reduce the number of products in their product lines to those for which there is significant demand. If you think about the products you buy, while you may have a great deal of choice, you have infinitely less than you could if firms offered all possible combinations of components that some customers might like.

Exploiting Demand

Firms bundle components because it enables them to sell more and usually make more profits. That can be true for demand-related reasons, as well as to save costs.

One obvious reason to add features to a product is to increase the demand for it. Perhaps surprisingly, this does not necessarily lead to a higher price. Speaking a bit loosely, it all depends on what sort of new buyers are attracted by the new features. Features that attract price-sensitive buyers—perhaps because they are particularly eager to save the cost of buying a separate product with those features—will tend to reduce the profit-maximizing price. Conversely, features that attract price-insensitive buyers will tend to raise the seller's profit-maximizing price. In the case of software, it is common for firms to add features without increasing the price. Since it introduced QuickTime in 1991, Apple has added many new features such as streaming audio and video, and support for new formats, yet Apple continues to offer the QuickTime player free of charge. Similarly, RealNetworks has added DVD playback and CD ripping to its player, which it still offers for free.

It is common to bundle together products that are complements, such as automobiles and tires, but firms may find that it pays to bundle products that aren't complements. We already saw an example of this above. Bundling persuaded two consumers to buy a product even though each wanted only a single component. This saved the manufacturer costs.

The idea that bundling of noncomplements can be used to enhance profits goes back to a classic paper by Nobel Prize winning economist George Stigler. Stigler tried to explain why movie distributors at one time required theaters to take bundles of pictures.[12] Suppose for movie *A*, theater 1 is willing to pay $8,000 and theater 2 $7,000; for movie *B*, theater 1 is willing to pay $2,500 and theater 2 $3,000. If the distributor rents the films separately, it would charge $7,000 for *A* and $2,500 for *B* to attract both theaters and collect $9,500 from each, for a total of $19,000. But consider how much the exhibitors would pay for a bundle of both movies: theater 1 would pay $10,500 and theater 2 would pay $10,000. Thus, if the distributor charged $10,000 for the bundle, it would collect $20,000 and make more money.

More generally, businesses can exploit the law of large numbers when they are producing products that have many components. Consumers place different valuations on the various features available to them. You

---

12. George J. Stigler, "*United States v. Loew's Inc.*: A Note on Block Booking," *Supreme Court Review* 152 (1963): 152–157.

value the arts section of the newspaper highly, while your spouse does not care much for it; your spouse values the sports section highly, while you do not care much for that section. The valuations for any component can be quite dispersed across consumers with different tastes. If you combine all these components into a single product, the variations tend to cancel each other out, and, relative to the corresponding average value, there will be less dispersion in the value consumers place on the product than on the individual components. This makes it easier for the firm to sell to a large fraction of the market at a price that captures a large share of the product's economic value.[13]

This of course means that many people are getting components that they do not value. But if it does not cost much to provide these components, if it costs little or nothing for consumers to ignore or dispose of these components, and if it is expensive to offer multiple product versions, bundling components together into a single product typically expands demand efficiently. These assumptions are especially likely to hold for software and other information goods for which the marginal cost of providing the product (and any component of it) is approximately zero, and the cost of developing and distributing the product is high.

Newspapers are a good example. They provide many features—from crossword puzzles to astrology tables, stock market quotes, and dance reviews—that only a portion of their readers care about. But, relative to the cost of producing and distributing a newspaper, these features are not that expensive to add. By including them the newspaper brings in more readers at its typical price, sells more copies, and therefore covers more of the fixed costs of producing the paper. Consumers who don't want to read these features can easily ignore them. Such bundling can benefit consumers by providing products that either would not be produced or would be more expensive absent bundling.

As is often the case, firms make money bundling this way because they are providing a service to consumers. Consumers get to pick and choose what they want. They can ignore choices they don't care about at little

13. For formal analyses, see Richard Schmalensee, "Gaussian Demand and Commodity Bundling," *Journal of Business* 57, no. 2 (January 1984): S211–S230; Yannis Bakos and Erik Brynjolfsson, "Bundling Information Goods: Pricing, Profits, and Efficiency" Management Science 45 (December 1999): 1613–1630.

cost. Few people care that their eyes may wander over horoscopes in the daily newspaper or that the paper weighs a bit more from the extra newsprint or that a software program takes up a smidgeon more memory because of code for a feature they'll never use.

Aggregating Demand

Suppose that the first tenth of the population of 100 persons would be willing to pay $10 for component 1, the second tenth would pay $10 for component 2, and so forth up to component 10. Each would be willing to pay only $2 for each of the other nine components. Costs are zero. If the firm sells each component separately, it could charge $2 for each, sell all ten to all customers, and thereby make $2,000. Or it could charge $10 for each but sell each to only ten customers, and thereby make $1,000. However, every consumer would pay $28 ($10 + 9 × $2) for the bundle of all ten components. By bundling, the firm could get all 100 consumers to buy the bundle and make $2,800. Bundling this way can make consumers better off because they can get choices they wouldn't otherwise get. Moreover, producers of information goods can use this approach to cover the fixed costs of developing and offering products.

Bundling can be used in a different way to facilitate price discrimination, which we discussed in the preceding chapter.[14] That is, if different groups of consumers place different values on groups of components, bundles can be designed so that those with stronger demand pay more. The idea is possible to design bundles of components that cause consumers to sort themselves by the bundles they choose into groups with different willingness to pay. (Marketers call this "segmentation.") In the case of autos, some will want the car with the sports package, while others will want only the basic package. The seller can then charge a premium to groups that have a particularly high demand for a particular package and offer an especially aggressive price to consumers that are very sensitive to price but are also willing to take the no-frills deal. For this to work, there must be a predictable correlation

14. For a different potential use of bundling for price discrimination, see Richard Schmalensee, "Commodity Bundling by Single-Product Monopolies," *Journal of Law and Economics* 25, no. 1 (April 1982): 67–71.

between combinations of components and demand (for example, price-sensitive consumers generally have a low demand for frills). A number of studies have found, for example, that automobile companies have much higher markups on luxury models than on base models.[15]

Multisided Platforms

Bundling decisions by multisided platforms are particularly complex because they have to take into account all customer groups.

All of the considerations discussed so far still apply to multisided platforms. The principles just have to be adjusted to take into account the fact that there are several distinct groups of customers linked by indirect network effects. Newspapers—advertiser-supported media platforms—include style sections that appeal to younger women, who are valuable to advertisers. Video game console manufacturers may bundle joysticks not only because players want them, but because developers can produce cooler games if they know that all players will have joysticks.

Multisided considerations affect bundling decisions in three other ways.

Bundling customers. In some cases one can think of a platform provider as bundling customers together on one side to offer them to customers on the other side. Take shopping malls. Mall developers rent space to stores. But they are selective as to which stores they allow in the mall. They try to offer a diverse group of shops that match their intended customers. That means choosing particular quality levels of stores and limiting duplication. Most mall developers would reject a second bookstore even if it offered to pay the same rent as the first bookstore. That is in part because having greater diversity attracts more shoppers and therefore makes the mall more valuable to merchants, which in turn will pay more for more foot traffic. The same considerations apply to the content that mobile telephone operators offer to their subscribers and the types of articles that magazines offer their readers.

15. Steven Berry, James Levinsohn, and Ariel Pakes, "Automobile Prices in Market Equilibrium," *Econometrica* 63 (July 1995): 841–890.

Bundling negatives. Multisided platforms may also bundle components in ways that harm side 1 directly but create value to side 2 and, by attracting more customers on side 2, benefit side 1 indirectly. A shopping mall again provides a good illustration. You may have noticed that some malls, especially vertical ones, are not designed to minimize the amount of time it takes the customer to walk between stores. Instead, they are sometimes designed to increase the distance customers need to walk and therefore the number of stores they pass en route. That increases the foot traffic that passes by each store.[16] Payment cards are another example. Merchants that agree to accept cards from a system generally have to agree to take cards from all customers who present cards from that system and refrain from charging card customers more than customers who pay in other ways. Both rules impose costs on merchants and reinforce the bundling of all customer cards. But each rule benefits cardholders directly and merchants indirectly. (These rules have been challenged under the competition laws in various countries. In the United States, merchants can now take credit cards without taking debit cards, while in the United Kingdom, merchants can surcharge card transactions.)

Bundling for externalities. Multisided platforms pay particular attention to harvesting externalities among customer groups. Some features may be bundled because doing so promotes interactions between the two sides. Singles-oriented clubs often bundle drinks with admission; an example is the two-drink minimum. One explanation for this is that it promotes social interaction. Similarly, i-mode has signed a deal with Macromedia that enables it to include (bundle) the Flash Player plug-in in the platform it offers content providers, in order to encourage them to build Web sites with enhanced visual effects that are presumably more appealing to users. And, as we have noted before and will discuss in more detail below, including APIs in software platforms helps developers provide services to end users.

16. Beyard, Michael D, *Shopping Center Development Handbook*, 3rd ed. (Washington, D.C.: Urban Land Institute, 1999).

What Is Bundled, What Is Not; Why and Why Not?

As we have noted, the steady growth in the size of software platforms (as measured by lines of code) has been driven by the steady addition of features—most of which could have been provided by separate applications, and many of which once were—for developers and users. And customers don't get to pick and chose their features. Models are few and options are rare.

But it isn't as if software platforms have an irrational appetite, like PacMan, for absorbing everything in sight. The Sony Playstation doesn't have a word processor, although some of its customers might like to have one included. And Microsoft has kept Windows and Office for Windows separate, even though all Office customers need Windows too.

Then again, platforms' appetites do seem pretty voracious. As we mentioned earlier, i-mode phones can substitute for payment cards at stores in Japan. You just wave the phone over a sensor and press your thumb for further verification. The software for PDAs now helps people to make telephone calls, as well as to send emails and manage their calendars. Video game consoles and PCs are both racing to become media hubs that will help people manage and play music, videos, and television programs.

One reason software platforms have added more features is quite simple: they can.

Technology

Changes in the hardware for computing devices have made it possible to include more features in the software platform. The mobile phone operating systems of today, for example, simply could not fit in the memory that was available on mobile phones ten years ago. But advances in the underlying hardware have also created more opportunities for software platform vendors to devise features that can attract one or more groups of customers.

The cost of storage has declined for all computing devices. Figures 11.1 and 11.2 show the trends in the cost of random access memory (RAM) and hard disk storage for PCs. Between 1984 and 2005, the price per megabyte of RAM declined from $1,000 to less than 25 cents. Over the same period, the price per megabyte of hard disk storage declined from

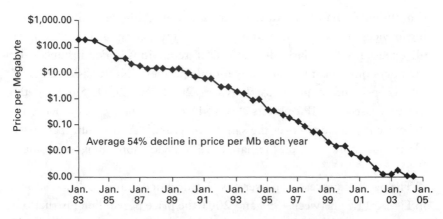

Figure 11.1
The price of hard disk storage in personal computers, 1983–2005, log scale. (Source: Data from 1983 to 2001 are from Steven J. Davis, Jack MacCrisken, and Kevin M. Murphy, "Economic Perspectives on Software Design: PC Operating Systems and Platforms," in *Microsoft, Antitrust and the New Economy: Selected Essays*, ed. David S. Evans [Boston: Kluwer, 2002]. Data from 2002 and beyond are from archived prices taken from compusa.com.)

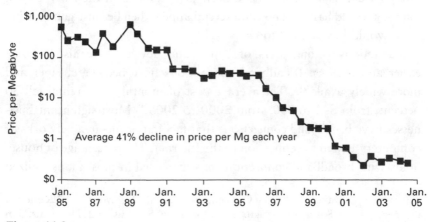

Figure 11.2
The price of random access memory (RAM) in personal computers, 1984–2005, log scale. (Source: Data from 1983 to 2001 are from Steven J. Davis, Jack MacCrisken, and Kevin M. Murphy, "Economic Perspectives on Software Design: PC Operating Systems and Platforms," in *Microsoft, Antitrust and the New Economy: Selected Essays*, ed. David S. Evans [Boston: Kluwer, 2002]. Data from 2002 and beyond are from archived prices taken from compusa.com.)

slightly more than $100 to less than a penny. Although other comput-
ing devices use different memory and storage components, they have
all experienced similarly dramatic cost reductions.[17] For instance, the
memory component used in many mobile phones, "NOR flash memory,"
fell 42 percent in price just between 2003 and 2004. Similarly the
memory used in MP3 players, "NAND flash memory," experienced a
20 percent price drop over the same two years.[18] As a result, it is possible to put more code on the hardware and do more things with more
RAM.

The price of processing power has also declined dramatically, as shown
in Figure 11.3. Between 1993 and 2001 the price per million instructions
per second (MIPS) declined from slightly more than $12 to less than 10
cents for Intel microprocessors. Today this cost has fallen to about a
nickel for Intel's Pentium 4 chips. Similar changes occurred for other
microprocessors. These changes have allowed software platform developers to provide complex new features that perform quickly enough to
be of value to developers and customers. Many of the visual effects for
today's video games could have been programmed in the early 1990s,
but they would have had no commercial appeal then because games using
them would have played too slowly.

Interactions among users of computing devices have also become
easier and cheaper. Broadband connections have become cheaper and
more widely available. The average cost of monthly DSL rental fell 30
percent, from $42 to $30, from 2000 to 2005.[19] Most significant businesses have broadband connections that facilitate wide-area networks of
computers as well as connection to the Internet. The percentage of households with broadband connections has increased in most industrialized

17. Steven J. Davis, Jack MacCrisken, and Kevin M. Murphy, "Economic
Perspectives on Software Design: PC Operating Systems and Platforms," in
Microsoft, Antitrust, and the New Economy, ed. David S. Evans (Boston: Kluwer,
2002), fig. 1.

18. Takuya Inoue, Mario Morales, and Soo-Kyoum Kim, "Worldwide Flash
Memory Forecast 2005–2008" (IDC report no. 32854), February, 2005.

19. Point Topic, "Long Term Trends in Broadband Pricing: 2000–2005,"
May 18, 2005 (http://www.point-topic.com/content/operatorSource/dslreports/
Longtermtrendsinbroadbandprices2000-2005.htm).

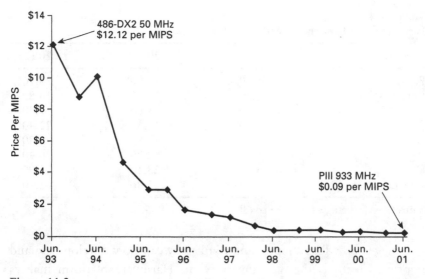

Figure 11.3
The price of processing power in personal computers, 1993–2001, Intel Processor MIPS. (Source: Steven J. Davis, Jack MacCrisken, and Kevin M. Murphy. "Economic Perspectives on Software Design: PC Operating Systems and Platforms," in *Microsoft, Antitrust and the New Economy: Selected Essays*, ed. David S. Evans [Boston: Kluwer, 2002].)

countries, as shown in Table 11.4, with almost one-third of U.S. households connected through cable or DSL in 2004.

In addition to these general trends, most computing devices have experienced decreases in the prices of other important components. The cost to computer assemblers of a CD-ROM drive declined from about $500 in 1991 to about $30 in 2005. The cost to mobile telephone manufacturers of a SIM card declined 25 to 30 percent from 2002 to 2003.[20]

The hardware and software platforms have a symbiotic relationship. These incredible advances in the hardware platform make it possible for the software platform to do far more than it could previously. Software platform makers see more capacious hard drives, faster microprocessors,

20. A SIM card is a component of most mobile phones that carries identifying information about the mobile customer as well as some address book information. "High-end cards and growing applications enable smart card manufacturers to leave behind a troubled 2002," *M2 Presswire*, August 6, 2003.

Table 11.4
Percentages of Households with Broadband Services

Country	2002	2003	2004
France	5.40%	11.00%	23.10%
Germany	7.20	10.20	14.80
Italy	4.10	8.60	17.00
Spain	5.90	13.60	22.40
UK	5.10	12.80	22.30
Western Europe[21]	8.20	12.70	20.40
US	15.70	23.10	29.90
Canada	28.10	35.80	42.70

Source: eMarketer, "Europe Broadband," April 2005.

and bigger broadband pipes, and think they can now develop new and improved features that consumers want. Hardware platform makers understand this. They recognize that it makes sense to invest in these hardware improvements in part because they can depend on software platforms, and the applications they support, to make use of the increased capability those improvements will produce. These positive feedbacks reinforce each other and lead to the addition of features—and tremendous innovation—through the various ecosystems based on computer hardware and software platforms.

Feature Accretion

One of Microsoft's lawyers once remarked, famously and flippantly, that he thought that Microsoft should be allowed to bundle a ham sandwich with Windows if it wanted to.[22] Why doesn't it—with mustard and pickles on the side, for that matter? Or, more seriously, why has it included Windows Media Player but not Office? On the other hand, why do some mobile phones, supported by their software platforms, come with cameras, email, instant messaging, and games, not to mention the ability to make a dinner reservation?

21. Austria, Belgium, Denmark, Finland, France, Germany, Italy, Netherlands, Portugal, Spain, Sweden, and the United Kingdom.
22. Todd Bishop, "Microsoft Loses Crucial EU Ruling; It Must Split Off Media Player While Appealing," *Seattle Post-Intelligencer*, December 23, 2004.

Most developers and users rely on only a portion of the features included in the software platform they are using. For example, any given software program typically would call on a small percentage of all the APIs provided by Windows. But different developers use different ones: game developers make much more use of the platform's graphics capabilities than developers of personal finance programs, for instance. Most consumers use only a few of the features included in Windows. Have you ever used the on-screen keyboard? Or explored the fonts installed on your system using Character Map? We haven't, and we suspect few others have either.

Similarly, few individuals read newspapers from cover to cover. Most pick and choose articles that interest them. The most popular section of U.K. newspapers, sports, is read by fewer than half of newspaper readers, while most sections are read by fewer than a third.[23] Some of us never read the sports section, while others never read the marriage announcements or obituaries. Similarly, a typical basic cable television package comes with seventy channels,[24] but we suspect most people watch a handful or two and ignore all the rest. There probably isn't much overlap between the regular viewers of Comedy Central, Home and Garden TV, the Discovery Channel, and ESPN2. This isn't surprising. As we noted above, bundling different things together is a particularly good business strategy for information goods, for which the marginal cost of adding and distributing another feature is typically very small.

There is a simple explanation for the steady feature accretion we see in software platforms. Technological advances in hardware have given software platforms more to work with and have all but eliminated hardware-related constraints on their size, at least for the time being. Software platforms add features in the hope that more users will find the platform worth its price because they can find the particular features they want and that more developers will write to the platform because they

23. PR Week Media Snap—"National Newspaper Readership Patterns," *PR Week*, May 10, 1990.

24. Comcast standard cable package comes with seventy channels in the Boston area, RCN "Full Basic" comes with seventy-five channels (http://www.comcast.com/Support/ChannelGuide.ashx); http://www.rcn.com/cabletv/lineupDetails.php?lineupID=13.

can find some subset of APIs that helps them write profitable programs. Because platforms are multisided businesses, these additional users and developers increase demand indirectly as well as directly. A platform is more attractive to end users if it has more applications, and it is more attractive to developers if it has more users.

But if more is always better, why no ham sandwich? The answer lies in comparing the additional consumers brought in by adding new features with the cost of adding them. Take Office. There were 63 million Microsoft-licensed copies of Office in use in 2004.[25] The average price of an Office upgrade was upward of $250, and a new license for Office for businesses was upward of $350. And there were about 515 million Microsoft-licensed copies of Windows in use in 2004. Users interested in upgrading their version of Windows can purchase the latest edition from retailers—an upgrade of XP is $90 on average, or a new license is upward of $150.[26] Many business customers do not need Office on their computers because they use specialized software. Insurance company employees, for example, typically spend their days using customized software for dealing with claims and other insurance-specific matters. And many households do not need the firepower in Office either. By keeping Office separate, Microsoft can charge companies that do not need word processing and the other Office features a lower price and companies that do need those features a higher price. In this case the fixed cost of offering separate products is probably fairly small relative to the additional profits that can result from selling Office and Windows separately. But what if most customers who bought Windows also wanted Office? Then it might well make sense, in terms of both Microsoft's profits and total cost to society, to bundle Windows with Office.

This example highlights the fact that the features that get bundled into software tend to be of two extreme sorts. It makes business sense to bundle features that are used by relatively few users, as long as those

25. http://www.microsoft.com/msft/speech/FY05/Raikes_CapposelaFAM2005.mspx.

26. Survey of Office products on Amazon.com; AI Gillen and Dan Kusnetzky, "Worldwide Client and Server Operating Environments 2004–2008 Forecast: Microsoft Consolidates Its Grip" (IDC report no. 32452), December 2004, tables 1 and 2; survey of Windows products on Amazon.com.

users value the features in question highly enough, because it will generally cost little to add these features relative to the additional sales brought in. (Of course, at the far extreme we have features that are simply not worth developing in the first place because so few end users care about them that there is no way to cover their development cost. We are ignoring those features here—as software platform vendors try hard to do in practice.) And it makes sense to bundle features that are used by most users. If most users want a calendar with their PDA, there is nothing to be gained by incurring the extra cost of selling it as a stand-alone product.

Between these two extremes, it could make business sense to offer the components separately or to offer multiple versions, some of which don't have certain features. Looking across software platforms, however, it appears that this sort of mixed bundling is seldom used. Software platforms either include a feature in the platform or they don't. Unlike cars or cereals, there are almost never multiple versions of the platform to choose from. (Of course, as with everything, this can change with developments in technology [innovations in making modular software, for example], consumer demand [segments develop that want a specific feature set], and competition policy [some competition policy authorities have argued that Microsoft should offer multiple versions of Windows].)

The multisided nature of software platforms helps explain this. Users want to know that the applications they license will run on their version of the software platform, while developers want to know that their applications will work for customers who have the software platform to which they are writing. This assurance is particularly important, since developers and end users are making decisions at different points in time. If there are multiple versions of a software platform on the market, the developer may not be able to conduct the advertising necessary to tell you which is the right version. Thus, standardizing software platforms tends to help both end users and applications developers.

Most commercial vendors of Unix have made their versions proprietary, and more than twenty versions are currently available. Applications written for one version might not run on another. Given its roots in Unix, Linux has been particularly careful to prevent similar fragmentation or "versioning" of its software platform. The GPL prevents Linux vendors from appropriating the source code to build a proprietary version of Linux (or for any similar purpose).

Innovation Through Bundling

One only has to take a look at ads for Apple's Mac OS X Tiger to see that a major source of innovation in software platforms comes from bundling new features. Although Apple has made lots of improvements to the core of this operating system over the years, consider what it is highlighting for consumers in Figure 11.4: a search program (Spotlight), a Web browser (Safari), video and audio conferencing (iChat), a media player (QuickTime), and an email program (Mail). All in all Apple says there are more than 200 new features in Tiger.

Some of these features were included in previous versions of the operating system but have undergone considerable improvement. Others are new, such as Spotlight. And while products similar to each of these features are available from independent application developers (Firefox for browsing and RealPlayer for media, to take two examples), Apple users benefit from having these features available to them as part of a single integrated platform. Consumers, for example, don't have to find and install their own browser, media player, and email client. They can just trust Apple to provide a good package. And a number of reviewers have commented that these additional features make Tiger an innovative and desirable software platform. They claim that "even casual Mac users will immediately see the difference,"[27] because "Tiger is the best version of Mac OS X yet. . . . The performance improvements are immediately noticeable. Every major bundled application has been improved. There's an unprecedented number of substantial, totally new features and technologies: Spotlight, Core Image and Video, Quartz 2D Extreme, Dashboard, and Automator, just to name a few."[28] Of course, if an Apple-supplied feature is a dog, end users always have the option of ignoring it and using something else.

27. "Apple Mac OS 10.4 Tiger," *Cnet Review*, April 29, 2005 (http://reviews. cnet.com/Apple_Mac_OS_10_4_Tiger/4505-3673_7-31256837-2.html?tag= top).

28. http://arstechnica.com/reviews/os/macosx-10.4.ars.

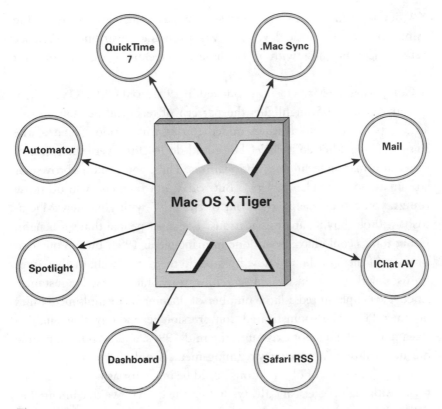

Figure 11.4
Diagram based on a screen shot of Apple's online promotion of Mac OS X Tiger.
(Source: http://www.apple.com/macosx/.)

Mac OS X Tiger doesn't just provide innovative new features to end users. Apple marketing highlights the new features it has provided to developers. For example, Apple's QuickTime 7 technology "features an ultra-efficient new video codec . . . that delivers stunning video quality,"[29] while Core Image "unlocks the performance of today's powerful graphics hardware for ultra-fast, pixel-accurate image processing."[30] Reviews geared toward developers have also noted the value of these additions. Reviewers have described Mac OS X Tiger as "a milestone in Mac OS

29. http://www.apple.com/macosx/features/quicktime/.
30. http://www.digitalhub.com/macosx/overview/advancedtechnology.html.

X's development process."[31] This system has some developers saying things like "being a Mac developer was a fun and rewarding experience before Tiger, but now with all of these new technologies, our jobs got even easier."[32]

Comparing the Mac OS 7, introduced in 1991, to the Mac OS X Tiger, introduced in 2005, highlights the pattern of technical advance. Table 11.5 lists some of the features added during this period. Some of the things you couldn't do in 1991 but could do in 2005 were the result of other information technology innovations. Thus, you couldn't browse or stream audio and video in 1991. But today, not only can you do those things, you can do them "right out of the box" with your new Macintosh, without buying any applications. For most people that's a benefit. Other things could have been done in principle in 1991, but no one had thought of them or didn't know how to do them very well, or there was no use for them. Sophisticated searching was unnecessary, for instance, since few people stored a large number of documents or multimedia files on their PCs. The sophisticated compression technology that enabled streaming media did not exist until the mid-1990s, and even then, people did not realize how popular streaming media would become.

These same sorts of observations could be made for any software platform. Although bigger isn't always better, the growth we documented at the beginning of the chapter has enabled users and developers—and, we should note, makers of hardware and peripheral equipment—to do more with their software platforms.

Convergence

There seems to most of us to be a qualitative difference between Palm OS including a browser and DoCoMo turning its phone into a payment device. The former seems like a natural expansion within a relatively well-defined category, while the latter seems like one category setting out unexpectedly to conquer another. But there is really nothing unexpected about it. Increasingly, computer platforms—sometimes led by the software platform, at other times working hand-in-hand with the software platform—have invaded nearby, and not so nearby, categories.

31. http://arstechnica.com/reviews/os/macosx-10.4.ars.
32. http://maczealots.com/reviews/tiger/developers/.

Table 11.5
Some of the New Features Added to Mac OS Since System 7

Multimedia functionality (QuickTime and iTunes)
DVD support and recording
Email and Internet functionality
Disk and Internet searching
Java support
Handwriting recognition
Stickies—Post-It-like application
Bluetooth
Power management
Better disk management
Encryption
Support for multiple users
Password management, voice passwords
Modern multiprocessing

Mobile telephones, for example, are starting to compete with digital music devices to download, store, and play music. And increasingly these devices are able to play television—for now, specially designed short soap operas—to help entertain subway and train commuters, among others. We've gotten used to seeing them used for email and instant messaging.

Game consoles are competing with other home entertainment technologies. They include DVD drives and therefore compete with manufacturers of DVD players; they have the ability to store, manage, and play music, and thus compete with a variety of music-related devices; and they can download, store, and edit television, and are therefore competitive with products like TiVo.

The fact that computer platforms can combine all these features does not necessarily mean that consumers will embrace them. Many fortunes have been lost by those who believed the 1990s' hype about digital convergence—witness the AOL Time Warner merger. Companies like Microsoft have been working on ways to get PCs into the living room for more than a decade. Thus far consumers seem to like their PCs and their home entertainment systems to be separate boxes in different rooms. Yet convergence may occur slowly and by stealth.

The home entertainment system of the future, like the automobile of the present, may not look or feel like a PC. But at its heart it is likely to have a microprocessor and a software platform. It may look like an obvious product, but in fact it will probably be the result of the accretion of features in various software and hardware platforms over time. Bundling drives innovation and creates industries.

INSIGHTS

• The ability to select bundles of features to sell helps firms segment their customers, control costs, and enhance profits. Bundled products offer consumers convenience, lower costs, and products tailored to their needs and wants.

• Bundling decisions by multisided platforms, such as software platforms, are more complex since they must take into account the effect on all customer groups. Multisided businesses must consider both the additional customers they get on one side as a result of including a new feature and the additional customers they will get on the other side from having those additional customers. They may also include features that harm one side directly but benefit the platform overall by getting more customers on board on another side.

• Bundling makes sense for businesses whenever the cost of adding additional features is lower than the additional sales generated thereby—even if most purchasers do not value or use all the features in a product bundle.

• Software platforms double in size roughly every two years mainly as a result of adding new features; all software platforms have attracted new users and innovated in this way. This behavior is a response to demand that has been made possible by the plummeting costs and rapidly increasing capabilities of computer hardware.

• Software platforms tend not to offer models or options. They come bundled with features that users and developers have to take in total, even if those features are not widely used.

12

Swept Away

Look to the future, because that is where you'll spend the rest of your life.
—*George Burns*[1]

INSIDE THIS CHAPTER

· Why software platforms create, destroy, and transform industries
· The enormous potential of Web-based software platforms
· How auction-based and search-based platforms are transforming the retail sector

Introduction

Software platforms march relentlessly across the economic landscape, forming new industries, transforming others, and sometimes shattering old ones in their wake.

Video game platforms have gradually pushed board games to one side. In 2004, people spent twelve times as much on video games as they did on board games; twenty years earlier they had spent more than seven times as much on board games as on video.[2] The PC software platform made the typewriter a museum piece within a generation. In 1985 the

---

1. http://en.wikiquote.org/wiki/George_Burns.
2. http://money.cnn.com/2005/04/29/news/midcaps/bored_games/; "The Profit In Games People Play," *New York Times*, December 31, 1986; "Video Game Wars Heating Up: Firms Hawk New Generation of Machines," *Los Angeles Daily News*, August 24, 1993; Schelley Olhava, "Worldwide Videogame Hardware and Software 2004–2008 Forecast and Analysis: Predicting the Future" (IDC report no. 31260), May 2004.

typewriter industry had U.S. sales of $1.1 billion; about two decades later it was less than a tenth as large.[3] The destruction isn't confined to old industries. Fax machines started a global revolution in real-time communication in the 1980s. Slowly, email and other document delivery platforms are making the fax machine passé. Nor are software platforms protected from their brethren, as the Palm OS learned from the platforms that have powered smart mobile phones. And, like amoebae, software platforms envelope their own. Regularly, they add features such as Internet communication capabilities that had been provided by stand-alone applications.

The malleability of code makes software platforms particularly adept at moving into old industries and starting new ones. Sometimes this is as simple as adding a block of code to an existing software platform—more or less like adding another section to a newspaper. For example, the Safari browser that Apple added to the Mac OS took up just over 6 megabytes of this 500+ megabyte software platform. Other times it requires more substantial work. Yet both Symbian for mobile phones and MS-DOS for PCs were completed in less than a year by building on code that was created for other purposes, much as a writer might build a novel from a short story.

Creative destruction has been a hallmark of economic progress for millennia, but it has proceeded at a glacial pace for most of history. The Industrial Revolution sped this process up. Even so, it took decades for change to filter through the economy following innovations such as the spinning jenny, steam engine, and electric generator. The information technology revolution has quickened the pace of industrial change greatly. The plummeting costs of computer processing and storage make it possible to create products and industries that were not only infeasible but also unimaginable a few years earlier. Software platforms further accelerate the process of creative destruction, mainly because code is digital and malleable. Think how easy it is to add a new feature to a software platform and distribute that change electronically over the Internet to potentially billions of computing devices around the world.

3. "What's New in Typewriters," *New York Times*, March 9, 1986. "Clack of Typewriter Still Stirring Minds," *USA Today*, June 20, 2003.

As we look ahead, there are signs that the pace at which software platforms transform the economy will accelerate even further in the coming decades. People have speculated about some of these transformations for years.

The control of the living room is perhaps the best example. As of 2006 there is little doubt that software platforms in some form will dominate home entertainment. Many of these platforms have crept into the television ecosystem without much notice.

People usually think of TiVo as a digital video recorder (DVR) maker: it makes a box that records television shows and skips over commercials. In fact, the hardware in that box is built around a hard disk drive and didn't require much inventive effort. The software platform is the secret behind the TiVo service and the strategy that this company has adopted for home entertainment.

To make inroads, TiVo followed strategies with which we are now familiar. It priced the box low to penetrate the market and earned revenues from subscription fees. At first this was a familiar one-sided "give away razor and sell the blades" strategy. However, this pricing approach was designed to create a critical mass of TiVo users. Once developed, those users could be used to attract two other sides.

One is familiar: developers. TiVo is evangelizing its software platform by providing tools and offering prizes for the best applications in several categories, including games, music, and photos.

The other side is perhaps surprising: advertisers. As a verb, "to TiVo" has entered American slang as the process of skipping over commercials—not a development likely to thrill the companies that spend billions every year on television advertising. As a software platform, however, TiVo provides tools that allow television advertisers to provide creative services to users. Viewers can select advertisements they are interested in and can download infomercials and other more detailed product information that they can't get in a 30-second spot. Whether TiVo will succeed with this strategy is not obvious as of this writing. (It is facing stiff competition from low-priced DVRs offered by cable companies.) But using the invisible engine in its DVR, TiVo is trying, at least, to transform the television advertising model, and with it how we consume home entertainment.

Automobiles provide another instructive example. Although we doubt software platforms will transform the auto industry, they will surely take on a more significant role in automobiles. Microprocessors now control more than thirty mechanical systems in automobiles, from power windows to antiskid systems, as well as features that provide entertainment and information such as radio and navigation.[4] Many different operating systems, some of which are dedicated to particular microprocessor-based features, run these computing devices.

The dashboard now comes with separate technologies that are ripe for integration through a software platform. The navigation system, for example, is currently a self-contained computer application. Many developers have created map-based applications on the Web. Drivers will soon relish the ability to download these applications onto their automobiles. At the same time, automobile makers are increasingly incorporating new entertainment technologies into cars, including the ability to use iPods, MP3 players, and satellite radio. These create a demand for a more flexible software platform that can facilitate in-car entertainment. In addition, consumers are interested in more wireless speech-enabled applications in their cars, which is a natural for a software platform.

Not surprisingly, several vendors have been working on developing in-car software platforms. Enea, a Swedish company, for example, offers three operating systems for automobiles. These operating systems share a common set of APIs and environment for writing applications. As of late 2004, automobile companies wrote customized applications to run on in-car software platforms in their vehicles. Over time we would expect more third-party developers to produce applications for these platforms. Moreover, cars are increasingly becoming connected computing devices. One source estimates that sales of global positioning systems (GPSs) have increased 33-fold between 1998 and 2004, and about 60 percent of consumers plan to purchase a GPS system with their next vehicle.[5] More-

4. http://www.epn-online.com/page/18332/embedded-software-platform-for-automobiles-the-replacement-of-mechanical—.html.

5. "Microsoft bolsters auto application software," *Network World*, July 18, 2005. "Enea Introduces Embedded Software Platform for Automobiles," *Business Wire*, December 2, 2004. "Cost of Getting Lost Is Higher Than Ever," *PR Newswire*, May 19, 2005; "You are here," *The Virginian-Pilot & The Ledger-Star*, December 20, 2004.

over, the increased use of wireless technology with cars through mobile phones could enable Internet access and the integration of in-car software platforms and Web services into the dashboard.

Enterprise software is another example of an industry that software platforms will change. Oracle, Microsoft, SAP, and other software developers have written large, complex applications that large enterprises use to handle tasks such as human resources, accounting, and supply chain management. Globally, enterprises spent more than $21 billion on such software in 2004.[6]

Enterprise software is evolving into middleware platforms that themselves support a developer community. Rather than adding their own features to their applications, the large enterprise software makers are making the system services provided by various modules in their products available to third-party developers. That includes publishing APIs and providing software developer kits to help other companies develop applications. SAP, for example, announced in early 2005 that it was making its Netweaver development platform publicly available. That platform includes more than 1,200 services that are available through APIs that developers can use. Later in the year Oracle introduced its competing Java-based Fusion middleware. Both companies are making developer tools available for free to actively encourage developers to "get on board" the platform. SAP includes the core components of Netweaver for free with its mySAP ERP and mySAP Business Suite while Oracle offers Fusion's Java IDE, called JDeveloper, for free.[7]

Over the next decade invisible engines will transform economic life well beyond our living rooms, cars, and offices. They will change how we buy and pay for things. And they will cut a wide swath of destruction across many industries that have heretofore helped buyers and sellers find and do business with each other.

The market capitalization of the newspaper industry provides a leading indicator of what's to come. From December 2004 to December

6. Paul Hamerman and R "Ray" Wang, Forrester Research, "ERP Applications —The Technology and Industry Battle Heats Up," June 9, 2005.

7. http://www.zdnet.co.uk/print/?TYPE=story&AT=39192233-39020466t-20000007c; "Oracle JDeveloper 10g," http://www.oracle.com/tools/jdev_home. html; Ellen O'Brien, "NetWeaver for Free? Not Quite," *SearchSAP.com*, September 30, 2004.

2005, each of the ten largest newspaper companies in the United States lost market value; their market capitalization fell 23 percent over this period, while the S&P 500 rose by 4 percent. New York Times Company's market value declined by $2 billion (35 percent), and Gannett, the largest, lost $6 billion (29 percent).[8] A major factor behind this is Internet-based advertising. And behind Internet-based advertising search engine–based software platforms that are using multisided strategies to drive the growth of vast ecosystems. The source of this cataclysmic change is the subject of this concluding chapter.

Web-Based Software Platforms

Many of the software platforms we have discussed are married to a hardware platform. That's the case with PC and video game console platforms. Being a couple enables the software and hardware to play as much as possible to each other's strengths. Specialists talk about "optimizing" the software for the hardware. Other software platforms can't indulge in monogamy. They have to work well with several hardware platforms because the industry is fragmented along hardware lines. That's the case with mobile phones. It became the case for PDAs as software platform makers such as Palm realized that mobile phones provided both opportunities and challenges. A few others are "distributed platforms." Digital media platforms and i-mode have pieces that reside on the devices that people use (often called the client) and other pieces that reside on computers that sit in the backroom (often called the server).

It has always been possible to design a software platform that resides entirely on servers. Indeed, one of the businesses we discuss in the box below, payment systems such as Visa, are server-side platforms. The software platform resides on servers on a network and does virtually all the work necessary to execute transactions. The clients—payment cards with magnetic stripes and terminals at the point of sale—do little (like the computer screens called "dumb terminals," that long ago connected people to mainframes).

8. Pulled from Bloomberg on December 28, 2005 (http://finance.yahoo.com/q?s=%5EGSPC).

Two related developments have made server-based software platforms increasingly attractive. For one, the World Wide Web has grown dramatically. The number of computers sold for use as Web server activities grew 60 percent from 2000 to 2005.[9] For another, communications capacity has grown: more households and businesses globally have broadband connections, and those connections have increasing rates of throughput. As we've noted, this piping has extended to mobile telephones and other handheld devices. Not surprisingly, businesses have developed software platforms that live on the Web.

As consumers, we tend not to think about the code that lies at the heart of many Web-based enterprises. Yet, putting aside whether this code comprises a software platform, it is a major source of value for companies like Amazon. Instead of building factories, they construct software programs that process information on mainframes or, more commonly, massive arrays of server computers. They innovate through adding features in their software, such as Amazon's feature, "Customers who bought this book also bought. . . ."

Most Web-based enterprises do not, in fact, operate what we've called software platforms. They run computer applications that, while innovative and admirable, do not have the defining feature of a platform: the provision of software services to third parties. But others have followed multisided strategies by making software-based services available through APIs and encouraging the growth of developers and other third-party complementors.

This chapter focuses on two software platforms that facilitate transactions on the Web: eBay and Google. Before we discuss them in detail, we need to take a quick, relatively painless detour into economic history.

Driving Down Transactions Costs

Economic textbooks often describe an idyllic world in which everybody has perfect information for free. Pricing is transparent. Quality is known. Search is costless. With intense competition in such a world, resources

9. IDC Server Workload Data, 2005.

flow effortlessly to their highest-valued uses. Adam Smith's "invisible hand" of self-interested behavior inevitably leads to the greatest good.

Like the frictionless plane of introductory physics class, this economic nirvana is unreachable. Yet over centuries, societies have gotten closer to it through the development of institutions that facilitate trade among people and businesses. We have grown so accustomed to some of these institutions that we forget how innovative they were in their times, and the enormous values they created for humankind.

In the Western world, some of the most important innovations of this sort date to very ancient times. The Lydians introduced the first money—standard gold and silver coins that were an easy way to exchange and store value—in the seventh century B.C. The Babylonians held the first auction for which there is a record, in around the fifth century B.C.[10] The village market that brought buyers and sellers together in a central location had been around for millennia before the Roman Forum opened its doors to traders.

Further innovations that facilitated buying and selling arose as Europe came out of the dark ages. The development of checks in twelfth-century Florence was the major monetary one. Stock exchanges—bourses—began several centuries later. The predecessors of today's modern exchanges were firmly in place by the first part of the nineteenth century. The invention of printing with moveable type in 1450 vastly increased the rate at which information could be disseminated throughout the world. London newspapers printed advertisements regularly by the seventeenth century.[11]

During the early nineteenth century, at least in the United States, retailers started allowing customers to buy on credit. People could charge their purchases and pay at the end of the month. Many larger retailers offered installment plans that allowed people to buy durables, such as sewing machines, over time. In 1950, Diners Club—the first payment card that could be used by individuals at many merchants—gave birth to the modern global industry of debit, credit, and charge.[12]

10. "Auctions . . . A History" (http://www.jjmanning.com/selling.htm).

11. *Encyclopedic Dictionary of Semiotics, Media, and Communication*, edited by Marcel Danesi, 2000.

12. David Evans and Richard Schmalensee, *Paying with Plastic*, 2nd ed. (Cambridge, Mass.: MIT Press, 2005).

Over the course of economic history there have also been many innovations in transportation. These have ranged from the early traders, who traversed the known world, to the development of shipping and rail, and eventually automobile and air transportation. The world became a more connected place. We had a global economy that allowed financial and physical resources to move relatively freely well before the birth of the commercial Internet in 1995.

All these innovations have lowered transactions costs and thereby made exchange cheaper and broader. The Lydian invention of coins, for example, made trade cheaper and more secure. It also permitted trade that might not have taken place because buyers or sellers were more likely to have a common medium of exchange and unit of account.

Consider a simple modern-day example. I have a car I am willing to sell so long as I get more than $10,000. You are willing to pay up to $12,000 for my car. Suppose it costs $500 between the two of us to find each other and consummate the deal. Then we can share in $1,500 of value that is created by moving the car from me (the lower-valued user) to you (the higher-valued user). How much we each capture depends on our bargaining power and the sales price we negotiate. But in the end there's $1,500 of hard value to be had net of transactions costs.

Institutions can help consumers and businesses obtain value through exchange in two major ways. They can make it cheaper. If you and I could find each other and consummate our deal for $100 less, we'd have $100 more value to share. They can also make trade that was impossible possible. Suppose you and I couldn't find each other and do a deal without a particular institution—an auction, an advertisement, or a payment card. Then we might not be able to obtain the $1,500 of value at all, or we might end up with less desirable trading partners and obtain less than $1,500.

Summed across all people and businesses and all possible transactions, innovations that can reduce transactions costs or make more trades possible have immense value. A little arithmetic reinforces the insight. An innovation that could reduce the cost of retail transactions in the United States by 0.1 percent of the value of those transactions would result in savings of almost $4 billion annually.[13] That's one of the reasons

13. http://www.census.gov/svsd/advretl/view/adv44x72.txt.

payment systems compete to shave off seconds on transactions at the point of sale.

Payment Cards

The payment card remains both an important vehicle for reducing transactions costs and an intriguing computing device. Even in its magnetic stripe form it provides a primitive interface with a vast global computer network that allows people to obtain cash and conduct other transactions around the world. It is also the most popular computer-related device in the world. There were more than 2.2 billion payment cards in circulation in 2004 compared with 1.5 billion mobile phone subscribers.[14]

The technological basis for making the payment card the most widely available computing device in the world has already been laid. Smart cards, which contain a computer chip with considerable storage capacity, have held the promise of replacing the magnetic stripe technology since they were invented in the early 1970s. Yet virtually all cards in the United States remain based on magnetic stripes. Smart cards are more popular in Europe—they were introduced in France in the early 1990s, and MasterCard and Visa have recently provided strong incentives for all banks in Europe to deploy the next generation of these cards.[15]

Although their considerable hardware intelligence remains largely untapped, it is not for lack of an operating system. The major card networks have sponsored software platforms for smart cards that could promote the development of applications for these cards. MasterCard adopted the MULTOS operating system in 1997, while Visa uses Sun's Java Card, also developed in 1997, and American Express uses both.[16] These software platforms provide software services through APIs and make it possible to create applications that will run on the smart cards' microprocessors. So far, however, relatively few such applications have been created.

Smart cards have not succeeded in generating the sort of indirect network effects between the hardware and software that has helped other platforms overcome their chicken-and-egg startup problems and grow quickly. They have faced several problems.

14. Alex Slawsby, and Allen M. Liebovitch, "Worldwide Mobile Phone 2004–2008 Forecast Update" (IDC report no. 31080), July 2004. Source: *The Nilson Report*, no. 829, March 2005.

15. http://www.cartes-bancaires.com/EN/groupement/historique.html.

16. http://www.javarss.com/java-timeline-10years.html; Kim Min-hee, "MasterCard Takes on Visa in Smart Card," *The Korea Herald*, November 15, 2004; Donald Davis, "Brand Awareness: The Four Big Payment Brands Are Counting on Contactless Chips to Inject Some Excitement into Their Smart Card Programs," *Card Technology*, March 1, 2005.

(continued)

While reductions in microprocessor costs have lowered the cost of smart cards over time, these cards are still significantly more expensive than magnetic stripe cards. Without a killer application that some group—merchants, cardholders, issuers, or other players in the system—values highly, there is little demand for smart cards in the United States. (In Europe they serve to provide enhanced security that is provided in other ways in the United States.[17]) On the other side of the market, without a base of smart cards there is little incentive to develop applications for them, and no killer application for smart cards has emerged to spark their widespread adoption. One possible killer application that we will return to below is "contactless"—these are chip-based cards that use radio waves to connect to a reader at a short distance.

The payment card industry has faced a problem similar to one experienced by mobile telephone producers but even more severe. Banks issue credit and debit cards. Although card associations such as MasterCard and Visa can encourage the development of applications that run on all cards, each bank has a strong incentive to differentiate the cards it issues from those issued by other banks. The cards, after all, are part of the service that banks are providing their depository customers, in the case of debit cards, or often part of a lending relationship, in the case of credit cards. Banks are interested in applications that help them sell these broader relationships in competition with other banks. Unfortunately, that reduces their incentives to promote the development of applications. The card issuers have a further incentive for maintaining a walled garden around their devices: security. Either the card issuer or the cardholder faces significant liability if the card is breached. Two developments could provide the indirect network effects necessary for supporting a software platform-based ecosystem for payment cards. The first involves the marriage of two popular computer devices—the payment card and the mobile phone.

In Japan, NTT DoCoMo has incorporated the ability to pay for goods and services in some of the mobile phones it provides subscribers. It relies on Sony's FeliCa contactless chip. Consumers scan items at merchants that have contactless readers that can communicate with the phones. Based on an early 2005 report, there were a million phones with this payment ability and 13,000 merchants with readers.[18] In Japan, most of these bricks-and-mortar transactions are going through the DoCoMo billing system in addition to the Internet billing system we discussed in Chapter 7. Of course, Japan is one of a kind in so many ways, as we have noted—DoCoMo's success as a payment system partly results from the fact that payment cards were much less popular than cash; DoCoMo got people paying by phone

17. Evans and Schmalensee, *Paying with Plastic.*

18. Matt Richtel, "Momentum Is Gaining for Cellphones as Credit Cards," *New York Times*, January 10, 2005.

(continued)

> before it got them to pay by card in effect. And DoCoMo is the largest mobile phone operator in Japan.
>
> The other development is contactless payment as a possible killer application that could appeal to cardholders and merchants. Chip-enabled cards have not become popular because no one had figured out a way to generate significant value for customers that would warrant the initial cost. With few chip-enabled cards around, combined with the walled garden issue raised above, there wasn't much incentive to write applications. Several U.S. payment card issuers have been introducing contactless cards to their cardholders and trying to persuade merchants to install the necessary terminals. It is too early to tell, but the growth of contactless may seed the market with enough chip-based cards to increase the growth of applications.

Multisided platforms were behind most of the institutions that have formed to facilitate transactions. Consider three examples.

• The first recorded auction, at least according to Herodotus, involved the marriage market. Women were auctioned for the highest price, which could be positive or negative. Men paid for some women, while other women had to offer a dowry to attract a mate. What this lacked in romance it made up for in efficiency. It provided good information and transparent pricing. Other exchange platforms followed relying on many variants of the original highest-bid auction.

• The first money had to get buyers and sellers on board in the same way that American Express needs to get merchants and cardholders on board today. Traders could still have bartered their oxen and kettles or continued to use the irregular metal slugs that were then used as stores of value. The Lydian coins became popular because, like modern-day payment cards, buyers and sellers agreed on this means of exchange and store of value.

• The early advertising-supported media had to get advertisers and eyeballs on the same platform. Magazines were, for many years, resistant to advertisers and, in an effort to protect readers, only permitted them on the back. But publishers quickly learned that advertising boosted sales and covered the high first-copy costs. By the end of the nineteenth century, many magazines were in the business of delivering readers to advertisers.[19]

19. James Twitchell, "Media and the Message," *Advertising Age*, March 29, 1999.

The prevalence of multisided platforms in facilitating transactions historically is not surprising. By definition, these platforms solve transaction problems, broadly construed, between different groups of customers that would like to interact with one another. A multisided platform is often the solution to market frictions.

The Internet provides a technology that can help these multisided platforms operate more efficiently. But that flat description, though true, is an immense understatement. The development of Web-enabled software platforms is leading to the creation of new institutions that can dramatically reduce transactions costs and drastically expand the scope of trade among buyers and sellers around the world. It is this revolution to which we now turn.

eBay

For the fun of it, Pierre Omidyar decided to write the code for an auction program over Labor Day weekend in 1995.[20] He started Friday afternoon. By Monday, September 4, he had a program that would allow users connected through the Internet to list, view, and bid on items. He posted AuctionWeb, as he called it, as one of several home pages on his URL—ebay.com—and announced it on several Internet newsgroups to help attract interest. Slowly, it did.

Omidyar had created several categories of things to list. They included computers, antiques, comic books, and a few others. People started placing items. In the first few weeks these included an autographed poster of Michael Jackson, a Toyota Tercel, and a Mattel Nintendo Powerglove. The buyers and sellers were on their own. The successful bidder paid the seller directly and the seller made arrangements to deliver the merchandise to the successful bidder.

Omidyar didn't charge users for AuctionWeb and hadn't originally intended to turn it into a business. However, as the traffic increased, his Internet service provider complained about the amount of capacity ebay.com was taking and decided to increase his monthly fees. To defray these costs, Omidyar decided to charge sellers 5 percent of the sales price

20. Adam Cohen, *The Perfect Store: Inside eBay* (Boston: Little, Brown, 2002).

for items that sold for less than $25 and 2.5 percent for items that sold for more. Buyers didn't pay anything to look, bid, or buy, and sellers only paid when they made a sale.

The growing community of buyers and sellers was self-policing at first. Omidyar encouraged them to behave ethically and to trust one another. Most did. But, as Webmaster, Omidyar was the natural person to appeal to when they didn't. To help govern the community, Omidyar developed the Feedback Forum. He noted,

Most people are honest. Some people are dishonest. Or deceptive. This is true here, in the newsgroups, in the classifieds, and right next door. It's a fact of life. But here, those people can't hide. We'll drive them away.[21]

He encouraged people to rate those with whom they transacted on a scale of −1, 0, and +1 and to provide any comments they wished. He barred people who had accumulated several negative ratings from the site.

eBay evolved from these beginnings.[22] The story is told well elsewhere, so we will fast forward to 2005. The code for eBay has grown from the few lines Omidyar wrote over a long weekend to about one million lines of C++ in 1999, and now to more than 6 million lines, mainly written in Java EE. It has gone from running along with many other things on Omidyar's home computer to running on an array of over 9,000 servers in multiple locations. As of the third quarter of 2005, it had 168 million registered users around the world exchanging goods in about 50,000 categories. In 2005 it earned $4.5 billion of revenue on sales of more than $25 billion. Its market capitalization was $62 billion as of January 4, 2006.[23]

The invisible engine that powers this transaction platform has grown enormously from the code that Omidyar wrote and patched together

21. The first part of this section is based in large part on Cohen, *The Perfect Store: Inside eBay*, p. 27.

22. The following is based on interviews with Michael Dearing and Chris Donlay of eBay, December 2005.

23. http://www.auctionbytes.com/cab/abn/y04/m06/i26/s01; Jeffrey Schwartz, "Dot Coms Need You," *VARBusiness*, July 22, 2002; "'Bot' Networks on the Rise, According to Symantec Report," *Bangkok Post*, October 19, 2005; www.sec.gov; http://finance.yahoo.com/q?s=ebay.

from whatever freeware he could find to do the job that Labor Day weekend in 1995. As with all the software platforms we have seen, this growth resulted in large part because eBay kept adding features that were valuable to its community. Of course, if computer code was all there was to eBay, it wouldn't be a software platform in the sense that we've used that term in this book.

In fact, eBay decided to make services provided by its code available to others through APIs. These APIs have resulted in eBay creating an ecosystem of developers that create applications for sellers. Moreover, eBay has provided various tools to sellers themselves that better enable them to benefit from the power of its software engine. Before we explore this aspect of the eBay software platform, we first summarize how this huge online marketplace promotes transactions between buyers and sellers.

eBay helps buyers and sellers come together in two main ways. A number of sellers offer merchandise at a fixed price—"Buy It Now." They are like traditional shopping mall retailers. This model accounted for about 30 percent of eBay sales during the third quarter of 2005.[24] Many other sellers use eBay's auction engine. Auctions have been eBay's long-term focus and what we concentrate on here.

Most auctions start with a minimum price and a fixed length of time over which the seller will accept bids. They usually follow a "second-price"—the highest bidder wins but pays the price offered by the second-highest bidder. This type of auction provides a lot of information to buyers and sellers, and it is transparent. In practice, if not in theory, it tends to avoid the winner's curse, which arises when the high bid is based on overestimation of an item's value, since the winner pays only the second-highest bid. Sellers can also opt to have a reserve price at which they can decline to sell the item. This price is higher than the minimum price; the fact that there is a reserve is disclosed to bidders, but the amount isn't.

eBay could make money in various ways. It could charge buyers to get into its marketplace or for bidding in auctions. It could charge sellers for accessing its platform, using the resources available for establishing

24. "EBay Faces Threat from Google on Fixed-Price Business," Dow Jones News Service, October 25, 2005.

stores, for listing items, or for selling things. Although it has progressed beyond the simple commission fees for sellers that Omidyar established when he was pressed for cash, eBay has maintained a relatively simple pricing structure, one designed to encourage certain behavior as well as to raise revenue.

Buyers don't pay anything directly. They can browse, bid, and buy for free. Sellers pay an insertion fee for each item. These fees are similar to the access or fixed fees that we discussed in Chapter 10; they are independent of whether the item sells or how much it sells for. Sellers also pay a commission on items that are sold. This commission is similar to the variable fees we discussed in Chapter 10. The commission is based on a sliding scale: 5.25 percent for the first $25, 2.75 for the next $975, and 1.5 percent for anything at or beyond $1,000. Finally, sellers can pay to have a reserve price, which varies from $1 for less than $50, $2 for $50 to $199.99, and 1 percent for more than $200.

Omidyar's Feedback Forum has evolved into a critical aspect of eBay. Buyers and sellers are encouraged to provide these ratings. The ratings are aggregated and reported for each registered user as a buyer or seller. Our own experience with eBay is that people are fanatical about these ratings. People don't want negative ratings because it affects their ability to do business with a broad community. Sellers in particular value high ratings because it provides buyers assurance for merchandise that they can't see (except in pictures) from a seller who exists mainly as an email address. These buyer and seller ratings are a valuable asset for eBay and for its community.

Like many exchange platforms, eBay has to satisfy both buyers and sellers. It maximizes revenues more by encouraging sales rather than trying to get the highest price for every sale. The second-price bidding scheme encourages buyers who are fearful of the winner's curse—the tendency for winners of high bid auctions to have overpaid. Sellers are encouraged to adopt low minimum bids and reserves. The rating system provides information on the reliability of buyers and sellers.

As a result, eBay—and rivals around that world that have followed similar approaches—has reduced transactions costs and expanded the scope of trade. We're sure economists will examine the social value that eBay and its imitators have created. It is likely to be enormous, for the reasons we mentioned earlier. eBay has reduced transactions cost for many buyers and sellers. While these savings are likely small relative to transaction values, when accumulated across buyers and sellers and compounded over time they are likely huge. But, more important, some of the transactions that take place on eBay probably wouldn't have taken place at all. The entire value from trade net of transactions costs would have been left unrealized.

If that were all, eBay would be a revolutionary transaction platform but not one that fits into this book. In fact, eBay is fundamentally different from the London Stock Exchange, Sotheby's, and manheimauctions.com because it allows two groups of businesses to use services provided by the software platform: sellers and developers. And, as a result, it lies at the center of an expanding ecosystem of businesses that benefit from eBay and in turn make eBay a more valuable platform for the eBay communities.

eBay provides sellers with a variety of tools that help them run their businesses through eBay's platform. Much of this involves free tips and advice. Sellers can also attend local "eBay universities" and seminars that provide further instruction. eBay has developed a variety of software programs that help these sellers. Turbolister, for example, is a free application that helps sellers list multiple items on eBay, design the listings, and manage the schedules. Other programs are available for small monthly charges after a 30-day trial period. Selling Manager, for example, helps larger sellers manage their entire eBay program, including downloading sales data from eBay.

Moreover, sellers can also obtain software tools from third-party developers that have built programs that rely on the software services eBay makes available through its APIs. Like the other software platforms we have seen, it didn't take long in its evolution for eBay to realize the importance of a vibrant developer community for helping its buyers and sellers. The eBay Developers Program was started in November 2000. It provides developers with

· Software services available through APIs
· Software development kits that facilitate writing applications
· A "developer zone" that provides, for example, access to tools, sample code, and technical support

• A "developer sandbox" that provides a place where developers can test their applications
• Member forums for online discussions with other developers

Web Services comprise an important set of APIs. They enable developers to create Web-based applications that can conduct business on eBay. These applications, which can be written in any programming language that is capable of making Internet data requests, enable users to do all the things they could do from the eBay desktop, including conducting auctions and managing their stores. There were roughly 2.5 billion calls to the Web Services APIs monthly in 2005, and almost half of the traffic on eBay came through these Web-based applications.

As of the end of 2005, about 21,000 developers have registered for the developer program. Thus far they have developed more than 1,600 applications that buyers and sellers can use with eBay. These include tools for managing auctions, productivity tools, and wireless applications.

Terapeak.com, for example, provides users with access to data on the hundreds of millions of eBay listings, along with analytical tools for examining buying habits and trends for specific categories. It is targeted to sellers who want to better understand the marketplace in which they are competing. Vendio's Ticket Manager is an example of software that is designed to help sellers in a particular category. According to its marketing material, it will "increase your listing capacity, manage your live listings to boost sell through, and fulfill orders with powerful post sale management." Auction Wireless Alerts, by Prisma Corporation, is designed for bidders: it will alert you on your mobile phone when an auction is about to end.

As with many other platforms we have seen, eBay has an annual contest for the "best application" for eBay. The grand prize winner of the "eBay Developer Challenge 2006" was UnWired Buyer, which calls a buyer on her mobile and lets her bid by phone. The first place winner was Auction Contact, which helps online publishers place ads for items on eBay. It also holds an annual developer conference.

Initially, eBay charged developers fees for accessing their APIs. These were intended in part to encourage developers to design efficient software that minimized the load on the software platform. In November

2005, eBay decided to eliminate all developer charges. It is providing free use of the APIs (so long as developers use the most recent version of the platform), membership, and certification, as well as live technical support. eBay also provides a place where developers can promote their applications to the eBay community.

The eBay community is transforming the traditional retail industry. It has made the process of buying and selling more efficient and is providing serious competition for everything from shopping malls to used car dealers. Time will tell the extent to which this software platform destroys traditional businesses. But perhaps the most remarkable aspect of eBay is that it has swept into the economy many transactions that wouldn't have occurred without it.

Google

Google is a software platform, with a search engine at its core, that controls a massive array of Web servers. It derives revenue and profit from facilitating transactions between buyers and sellers. It doesn't, as of the end of 2005, facilitate these transactions directly in the way eBay does. Rather, it does so indirectly through advertisements that point users to particular businesses that can meet a need those users seem likely to have. Virtually all of its revenues and profits come from charging businesses for some form of advertising.

It didn't start that way. We briefly summarize Google's evolution from search engine par excellence to advertising-supported search engine–based transaction platform before examining the business model pursued by this software platform.[25]

As the number of sites and amount of content on the Web expanded rapidly in the mid-1990s, it became apparent that people needed tools for finding things. Programmers began writing search engines. These software applications automatically searched (or "crawled") the web to recover its content, indexed this content in some way that facilitated people finding things, and provided a user interface, including a search

25. Much of the following discussion is based on John Battelle, *The Search: How Google and Its Rivals Rewrote the Rules of Business and Transformed Our Culture* (Huntington, N.Y.: Portfolio Press, 2005).

method for recovering information from the index. AltaVista, created by Digital Equipment Corporation in its death throes, was launched in December 1995.[26] One of the most successful of the early search engines, it handled more than 4 billion search queries during its first year. It became a popular portal and made money by selling display advertising. More sophisticated search engines followed AltaVista. They tried to deliver better search results to users by, for example, conducting statistical analyses of word relationships between Web pages.

Google began as an academic research project conducted, famously, by Stanford engineering graduate students Larry Page and Sergey Brin. Page started working on a doctoral dissertation concerning the mathematical characteristics of the Web. The Web can be thought of as a map of interrelated links. Page's idea was to study who links to whom—a simply stated but computationally difficult problem. Brin joined him. They brought to bear a set of tools that were developed initially by Professor Eugene Garfield. Garfield was a pioneer in the field of information science who did groundbreaking work on the analysis of scientific citations.

To see the idea behind this, consider the sorts of ranking that academics obsess over. Who, for example, is the best evolutionary biologist in the world? One can't really answer that question objectively, so let's pose a different one: Whose scientific papers on evolutionary biology are cited most often? One can answer that question objectively by looking at the citations in academic papers to other academic papers. Papers that are cited more often are presumably more influential and therefore more important. One can refine the analysis—and this is where Garfield's breakthroughs came in—by weighting the citations by the importance of the paper making the citation. So citations by papers that hardly anyone cites (and therefore are presumably not very good) count for less than citations by papers that many people cite (and are therefore presumably very good). This analysis can be extended to the ranking of academic departments, journals, and countries by aggregating across the papers relevant for each.

Applying this concept to the Web, one can ask simply how many Web sites are linking to each Web site. That leads to a simple ranking of Web

26. http://www.clubi.ie/webserch/engines/altavist/history.htm.

sites. One can also ask how many "important" Web sites are linking to each Web site. A simple measure of importance, following scientific citation analysis, is how often a Web site that, itself, has many links is linking to a particular Web site. Web sites that are linked often by other Web sites that are linked often are in some sense better, or at least more interesting.

The Stanford team developed a program that crawled the web and documented the links between sites. Using this program, dubbed BackRub, to collect data on the entire Web on an ongoing basis required an immense amount of computer resources. They then developed an algorithm, PageRank, that ranged pages based roughly on the number of other highly cited pages that cited them. These rankings were married to the standard index that emerges from crawling the Web based on words. The index identifies the Web sites that seem to be relevant to a particular word search. The ranking then identifies the importance of these Web sites.

Computer search is about helping people find the best answers to their questions. Page and Brin made a huge leap forward in doing that. They made their search engine available through Stanford. It was a quick success.

They then started their own search—for a financial return on their innovation. For the first 18 months they tried to sell the technology to some other established search-based Internet businesses. The founder of Infoseek, one of the leading portals of its time, says, "I told them to go pound sand." As more or less did everyone else. The problem, according to John Battele's book on Google's early years, *The Search*, was that the Web portals viewed search as a commodity technology and one that only had to be "good enough."

Page and Brin needed money, though. Between the exponential growth of the Web, which had increased the computing demands for constructing their searches, and the exponential growth of people using their search engines, which had increased the computing demands for handling the searches, they needed more hardware and space than Stanford was able to offer for free. They raised start-up funds and incorporated as Google, Inc., on September 7, 1998.

Google initially earned revenue by licensing its search engine to other companies such as Netscape and Yahoo. They eventually turned to advertising. This was the way that other Web portals with search features supported themselves. Several questions were already apparent. First, should the pricing scheme entail charging for the number of eyeballs that see an ad or the number of people who click on an ad? Second, should the advertising be separate from the search, such as display ads on a portal that happens to have a search engine, or be integrated into the search, so that advertising that is relevant to the search appears? Third, should the search engine alter the search results—in particular, the order in which results are presented—based on payments made by companies?

The answers to these questions may be apparent in hindsight now, but they were not clear around the turn of the twenty-first century to Google's founders or to many others in search of Internet business models. Battelle's book provides an interesting discussion of how the advertising-supported search industry and Google decided to resolve these issues. We fast-forward to Google's answers.

It is useful to begin by recalling what a Google search result page looks like. Consider a search for "BMW series 6." The top of the page (on December 21, 2005) had two sponsored links by automobile Web portals—edmunds.com, which has reviews as well as links to dealers, and southbankleasing.com, which leases cars. Below this, on the left-hand side of the page, are the ranked search results. Not surprisingly, www.bmwusa.com is the first. On the right-hand side of the page are more sponsored links—on the first page of the search results all of these are places where you could find out about leasing or buying a BMW.

Google settled on charging for the number of clicks. The supported links only pay Google if people click on them. While this is a natural approach for Web-based advertising, the fact that it is used instead of the traditional pay-per-eyeball approach distinguishes Google, and similar firms, from the traditional advertising-supported media industry.

Google also decided to have only search-related advertising, and even then only text-based advertising. There's no reason the BMW page couldn't have an ad that isn't directly related to the search—a Pepsi ad, for example—or a display ad for a local BMW car dealer. But it doesn't. (This reflects a typical two-sided trade-off. In this case, Google decided that it was better to give up certain advertising revenue than to degrade the quality of the product to the users. By making the search more appealing that increased the number of users and therefore the amount of advertising revenue from those users.)

Finally, Google decided not to take payment for altering the search results. There are many ways to climb the Google charts. Some of these are encouraged, such as selecting keywords that help the search engine make the proper linkages. Others are discouraged, and Google, often to the ire of entities that care about where they are displayed, makes changes in algorithms to defeat gaming of the rankings.

Google operates a bidding process for appearing as a sponsored link. Entities bid on a price per click. However, Google cares about the number of times an advertisement is clicked, as well as on the amount it gets per click. As a result, the actual ranking of the sponsored links on the search pages depends on the price-per-click bid as well as the number of times that the link has been clicked on. Thus, if two entities had bid the same per click, the links with the greater number of clicks will be first; if two links have the same number of clicks, the link with the higher bid will be first. As of 2005, 99 percent of Google's $6 billion revenue came from pay-per-click advertisements—its AdWord program for its own site and its AdSense program for external sites.[27]

Google, as just described, is an advertising-supported search engine that competes mainly with other advertising-supported media. Like other advertising-supported media, it is a multisided platform that supports advertisers and eyeballs. Unlike most traditional advertising-supported media (although like the Yellow Pages), it uses valuable search results to attract eyeballs rather than using content such as *Lost* for ABC or Paul Krugman's column for the *New York Times*. If that were all, as we said for eBay, Google would be a fascinating business, but not one for this book.

The invisible engine behind Google is a software platform that provides services through APIs to software developers. As of the end of 2005, Google offered four major sets of APIs. All of these promote the development of applications that either drive traffic to Google, and

27. http://www.sec.gov/Archives/edgar/data/1288776/000119312506056598/
d10k.htm.

therefore enable it to obtain advertising revenue, or enable Google to export advertising to other Web sites or devices.

Web APIs give developers access to the Google search engine so that their programs can pull information from the Web. That could include, for example, sending out periodic search requests to update information on a subject. At the end of 2005, this program was still experimental, and developers who wanted to create commercial services needed to get permission.

AdWords APIs permit developers to write programs that interact with Google's AdWords server. They are particularly helpful to advertisers who want to write internal applications for managing their "sponsored links" on Google's search and developers who want to write applications that they can sell to advertisers—both of which will make advertising with Google more attractive.

Desktop APIs concern a search engine program that Google has made available for local use. The Google Desktop applies Google's search technology to the storage contained on computers used by individuals or enterprises. Google makes APIs available that permit developers to write applications that use this search capability on these computers that are under the control of the individual or enterprise (as opposed to computers that are on the Web).

Map APIs allow developers to write programs that use Google's mapping service. Google has constructed a database of maps and satellite images of the world. It made APIs available to developers for creating applications in June 2005.[28] As of the end of 2005, these APIs were available only for applications that were free to the public. Businesses can use this to develop applications to help people find locations so long as they don't charge for it.

Accessing Google's Web and AdWords APIs imposes costs on Google because they result in additional traffic on its servers. That is quite unlike the APIs in software platforms that reside on local computing devices. It doesn't cost Apple anything when a person runs an application on the computer that relies on a software service that Apple has made available through an API in the Mac OS. Not surprisingly, Google limits the use

28. "Google, Yahoo Offer Maps APIs," *CMP TechWeb*, June 29, 2005.

of APIs that result in traffic on its system. In the case of Web APIs, Google limits users to 1,000 queries a day and, since this is still experimental, doesn't provide any method, aside from negotiating with Google, for obtaining more. In the case of AdWords, Google provides advertisers with a quota of "units" with their advertising account. Different operations based on the AdWords APIs consume various numbers of these units. The quota is tied to the amount of advertising spending. In January 2006, Google began providing a mechanism for commercial developers to obtain larger quotas. As of the end of 2005, Google was not charging for accessing its Map APIs, although it was reserving the right to place advertising on Web pages that relied on these APIs.

Seven years after its formation, Google is at an early stage in creating the kind of developer community that has surrounded other computer-centric software platforms, and is also behind eBay in this regard. Nevertheless, the direction is clear. Google Maps, for example, created an enormous flurry of developer activity quickly. Developers have created applications, some of which can be run from mobile phones, for finding cafés or wireless hotspots and showing criminal activity such as burglaries in small neighborhoods. At the end of 2005, there were at least 500 applications written on these APIs.[29] Google's APIs are poised to support a significant ecosystem of application developers. Google stands to benefit from these APIs by charging for access to its search engine and databases, driving traffic to its site from which it derives advertising revenue, and exporting its paid advertising services to linked sites.

Google is not alone in taking these approaches, although it is the largest Internet advertising-based business, with 2005 revenues of $6 billion, and the one with the highest market capitalization, $125 billion as of the end of 2005.[30] Yahoo has taken somewhat different approaches to developing an advertising-supported platform. Microsoft introduced Windows Live in late 2005 as a Web-centric platform that would compete in many dimensions with Google. In all these cases, the platforms are vehicles for lowering search and transactions costs for

29. There were about 500 Google Maps applications listed on the "Google Maps Mania" blog on December 23, 2005.

30. http://finance.yahoo.com/q?s=goog; http://www.sec.gov/Archives/edgar/data/1288776/000119312505065298/d10k.htm.

consumers and businesses. The ultimate driver of revenue and success is facilitating transactions. Not surprisingly, Google and Microsoft are both developing payment systems that, much like PayPal on eBay, can help their users consummate transactions.

These software platforms are sweeping away traditional industries.We noted earlier, to take one example, newspapers' collapsing stock market valuations. There are several Internet-related reasons behind this, but a major one is that Google and similar platforms can eliminate two major inefficiencies in traditional advertising. Think about all of the advertising dollars that beer manufacturers such as Miller in the United States spend. A large proportion of Americans don't drink beer. Miller ads have no chance of resulting in additional sales from them. It is inefficient both for these "eyeballs" and for Miller for them to spend time glancing at or hearing a Miller ad. Moreover, in the end, Miller has a very limited ability to figure out the extent to which its advertising expenditures result in increased sales. There isn't any convenient way to link exposure to an advertisement to a subsequent sale. (This can only be done, imperfectly, through expensive consumer surveys.) Google and its competitors, however, can tailor the insertion of advertisements to signals from users that they are possibly interested in a topic—buying a BMW for example, or being interested in French restaurants in Tokyo, or where to get the cheapest Miller Lite in Boston.

These software platforms also have the promise of altering significantly how people buy things and how stores sell things and how payments are made. First, along with the auction-based platforms, advertising-supported platforms are likely to move more transactions from physical to virtual stores. Second, the search engine platforms are likely to change the way people buy things at physical stores. For example, wireless devices could be used to find merchandise, compare prices, and guide the user to a store. These devices could also quickly capture feedback on the retail experience, which could be fed back to the software platform. That would extend the important online feedback system to off-line. In both these cases, although eBay and Google have made relatively limited advances thus far, we would expect, based on the other software platforms that we have studied, that developers will create a vast number of applications for auction-centric and search-centric software platforms. It would be hard to overstate the likely importance of these applications for stimulating innovation in the ecosystems supported by software platforms such as eBay and Google.

Back around the turn of the century there was a great deal of talk about the third industrial revolution, the new economy, and how the Internet would transform the economy as we knew it. Then the dot-com bubble was pricked. Trillions of dollars of value disappeared from stock market valuations in a few short months.[31] Those who hyped the new economy were seen as foolish if not in a few cases criminal. With the benefit of hindsight, though, it looks like the bust was at least as much an overreaction as the bubble. We think three things are clear.

We are about 25 years into a third industrial revolution that is built on microprocessors and, what is often overlooked, the software platforms that use the underlying computer technology to provide powerful services to a wide variety of applications. The first industrial revolution lasted from 1760 to 1830. It was based on innovations such as the steam engine and iron production. The second industrial revolution went from 1850 to 1930. Important developments included the invention of the electric generator and the rise of the chemical industry. Although a longer perspective may change our views on this, it appears that the third industrial revolution started around 1980 with the incorporation of the microprocessor into PCs and video games and the subsequent development of software platforms to create vast ecosystems of businesses around these hardware-software platforms. The second leg of this information technology revolution is the invention of the Internet, which had its commercial birth in 1995.

Just as electric generators drove the development of diverse industries in the second industrial revolution, software platforms have been the invisible engines behind the third industrial revolution. That is not to understate the importance of hardware innovations, which have been essential to what this third revolution has accomplished. Nor is it to minimize the importance of the innovations that led to the Internet: these will ultimately go down in history, we suspect, as some of the most

31. http://catablast.blogspot.com/2005/07/kozmocom-relic-of-dotbomb-bust.html.

important organizational innovations economic history has seen. It is to say, though, that software platforms have played a critical role in sustaining businesses based on microprocessor technologies and are likely to do so for those based on the Internet as well. At a purely technological level, these software platforms permit the software industry to obtain vast scale economies by providing application developers, hardware makers, and content providers with services they all need; the software platforms thereby enable the ecosystem to avoid significant duplication of effort. At a business level, these software platforms permit the formation of ecosystems that create value through the symbiotic relationships between diverse communities.

Software platforms naturally lead to multisided businesses. Almost all of them discussed here have done so. By their nature, multisided platforms reduce the cost of doing business for buyers and sellers. From Apple's OS at the early end of the historical spectrum we have considered to eBay at the late end, these businesses have followed similar multisided strategies to get multiple distinct groups on board and generate value for separate communities of users. Their success, generally, has resulted not from following the dot-com hype of building share quickly and at whatever cost, but from nurturing mutually interdependent communities. In the main, that has meant providing software services for free or at subsidized prices to numerous third parties. That results in the software platform being enveloped in a rich ecosystem of complementors who together provide great value for themselves and for consumers.

History teaches us that it takes decades for technological changes to work their way through the economy, destroying, creating, and transforming industries. The third industrial revolution got off to a quick start. We suspect that it will continue through at least the first few decades of the twenty-first century and that our invisible engines will ultimately touch most aspects of our business and personal lives.

INSIGHTS

• Software platforms have powered new industries such as personal computers and mobile phones, destroyed traditional industries such as typewriters, and disrupted industries from music to payment cards.

- Software platforms are powerful engines of change because of the malleability of code, which makes it easy for them to march across industry boundaries, and because their multisided nature enables them to create vigorous ecosystems of complementors.

- Web-centric platforms that facilitate transactions and lower transactions costs are poised to disrupt the retail sector and advertising-supported media. The 24 percent drop in the market capitalization of the major newspaper publishers between 2004 and 2005 is just one signal of the upcoming transformation.

- The leading Web-centric platforms based on auctions (eBay) and search (Google) have developed multisided strategies based on providing services through APIs to developers and other third parties and encouraging the creation of vibrant ecosystems around their platforms.

- Software platforms are critical players in the third industrial revolution that started around 1980. The first leg of this revolution focused on software platforms that run on dedicated computing devices. The second leg, which began around 2000, is focused on software platforms that run on Web servers and that help businesses and consumers buy goods and services.

Selected Bibliography

Books

Allan, Roy A. *A History of the Personal Computer: The People and the Technology.* London, Ontario: Allan Publishing, 2001.

Andrews, Paul, and Stephen Manes. *Gates.* New York: Touchstone, 1994.

Babbage, Charles. *Passages from the Life of a Philosopher.* In *The Works of Charles Babbage*, ed. Martin Campbell-Kelly. London, U.K.: Pickerings, 1989.

Baldwin, Carliss Y., and Kim B. Clark. *Design Rules.* Cambridge, Mass.: MIT Press, 2000.

Battelle, John. *The Search: How Google and Its Rivals Rewrote the Rules of Business and Transformed Our Culture.* Huntington, N.Y.: Portfolio Press, 2005.

Beyard, Michael D. *Shopping Center Development Handbook*, 3rd ed. Washington, D.C.: Urban Land Institute, 1999.

Brooks, Frederick P. *The Mythical Man-Month: Essays in Software Engineering.* New York: Addison-Wesley, 1975.

Butter, Andrea, and David Pogue. *Piloting Palm.* New York: John Wiley & Sons, 2002.

Campbell-Kelly, Martin. *From Airline Reservations to Sonic the Hedgehog: A History of the Software Industry.* Cambridge, Mass.: MIT Press, 2003.

Carlton, Dennis, and Michael Perloff. *Modern Industrial Organization.* Boston: Addison-Wesley, 2005.

Carlton, Jim. *Apple: The Inside Story of Intrigue, Egomania, and Business Blunders.* New York: HarperCollins, 1997.

Carroll, Paul. *Big Blues: The Unmaking of IBM.* New York: Crown Publishers, 1993.

Case, Karl, and Ray Fair. *Principles of Economics.* Upper Saddle River, N.J.: Prentice Hall, 1994.

Cohen, Adam. *The Perfect Store: Inside eBay*. New York: Little, Brown, 2002.

Cournot, Augustine. *Researches into the Mathematical Principles of the Theory of Wealth*, trans. Nathaniel Bacon. New York: Macmillan, 1927 (original in French, 1838).

Cusumano, Michael, and Annabelle Gawer. *Platform Leadership: How Intel, Microsoft and Cisco Drive Industry Innovation*. Boston: Harvard Business School Press, 2003.

Cusumano, Michael A., and Richard W. Selby. *Microsoft Secrets*. London, U.K.: HarperCollins, 1995.

Demaria, Rusel, and Johnny L. Wilson. *High Score! The Illustrated History of Electronic Games*. Berkeley, Calif.: McGraw-Hill/Osborne, 2002.

Duncan, Ray. *The MS-DOS Encyclopedia*. Redmond, Wash.: Microsoft Press, 1988.

Estabrooks, Maurice F. *Electronic Technology, Corporate Strategy, and World Transformation*. Westport, Conn.: Greenwood Publishing, 1995.

Evans, David, and Richard Schmalensee. *Paying with Plastic*, 2nd ed. Cambridge, Mass.: MIT Press, 2005.

Freiberger, Paul, and Michael Swaine. *Fire in the Valley*. New York: McGraw-Hill, 2000.

Friedman, Jon, and John Meehan. *House of Cards: Inside the Troubled Empire of American Express*. New York: Kensington Publishing, 1992.

Harper, Stephen C. *The McGraw-Hill Guide to Starting Your Own Business*. New York: McGraw-Hill, 2003.

Hennessy, John L., and David A. Patterson. *Computer Architecture: A Quantitative Approach*. New York: Elsevier Science & Technology Books, 2002.

Herman, Leonard. *Phoenix: The Fall and Rise of Videogames*. Union City, N.J.: Rolenta Press, 1997.

Ichbiah, Daniel, and Susan L. Knepper. *The Making of Microsoft: How Bill Gates and His Team Created the World's Most Successful Software Company*. Rocklin, Calif.: Prima Publishing, 1991.

Kent, Steven L. *The Ultimate History of Video Games*. Roseville, Calif.: Prima Publishing, 2001.

Kingaard, Jan. *Start Your Own Successful Retail Business*. Santa Monica, Calif.: Entrepreneur Press, 2002.

Linzmeyer, Owen W. *Apple Confidential*. San Francisco: No Starch Press, 1999.

Mankiw, Gregory. *Principles of Economics*. New York: SouthWestern/Thomson, 2003.

McConnel, Ben, and Jackie Huba. *Creating Customer Evangelists*. Chicago: Dearborn Trade Publishing, 2003.

Moon, Youngme. *NTT DoCoMo: Marketing i-Mode.* Cambridge, Mass.: Harvard Business School, 2002.

Mykland, Robert. *Palm OS Programming from the Ground Up.* Berkeley, Calif.: Osborne/McGraw-Hill, 2000.

Nagle, Thomas T., and Reed K. Holden. *The Strategy and Tactics of Pricing*, 3rd ed. Englewood Cliffs, N.J.: Prentice-Hall, 2002.

Natsuno, Takeshi. *i-Mode Strategy.* West Sussex, U.K.: John Wiley & Sons, 2002.

Rhodes, Neil, and Julie McKeehan. *Palm Programming: The Developers Guide.* Sebastopol, Calif.: O'Reilly & Associates, 1999.

Roberts, John. *The Modern Firm*, Oxford, U.K.: Oxford University Press, 2004.

Scotchmer, Suzanne. *Innovation and Incentives.* Cambridge, Mass.: MIT Press, 2004.

Shapiro, Carl, and Hal Varian. *Information Rules.* Cambridge, Mass.: Harvard Business School Press, 1998.

Sheff, David. *Game Over: Press Start to Continue.* Wilton, Conn.: GamePress, 1999.

Stallings, William. *Operating Systems: Internals and Design Principles*, 4th ed. Upper Saddle River, N.J.: Prentice Hall, 2001.

Stross, Randall E. *The Microsoft Way.* Reading, Mass.: Addison-Wesley, 1996.

Takahashi, Dean. *Opening the Xbox.* Roseville, Calif.: Prima Publishing, 2002.

Williamson, Oliver E. *The Economic Institutions of Capitalism.* New York: Free Press, 1985.

Articles

Armstrong, M., and J. Wright. "Two-Sided Markets, Competitive Bottlenecks and Exclusive Contracts" (mimeo). University College, London, and National University of Singapore, 2004.

Arthur, Brian. "Increasing Returns and The New World of Business." *Harvard Business Review* 74 (July–August 1996): 100–109.

Bakos, Yannis, and Eric Brynjolfsson. "Bundling and Competition on the Internet." *Marketing Science* 1 (Winter 2000): 63–82.

Bakos, Yannis, and Erik Brynjolfsson. "Bundling Information Goods: Pricing, Profits, and Efficiency." *Management Science* 45 (December 1999): 1613–1630.

Baxter, William. "Bank Interchange of Transactional Paper: Legal and Economic Perspectives." *The Journal of Law and Economics* 26 (October 1983): 541–588.

Brandenburger, Adam. "Power Play (C): 3DO in 32-bit Video Games" (case study). *Harvard Business Online*, April 10, 1995.

Berry, Steven, James Levinsohn, and Ariel Pakes. "Automobile Prices in Market Equilibrium." *Econometrica* 63 (July 1995): 841–890.

Bolt, Wilko, and Alexander F. Tieman. Skewed Pricing in Two-Sided Markets: An IO Approach. Working Paper 13, De Nederlandsche Bank, Amsterdam, October 2004.

Bolt, Wilko, and Alexander F. Tieman. A Note on Social Welfare and Cost Recovery in Two-Sided Markets. DNB Working Paper 24, December 2004.

Boudreau, Kevin. How Does "Openness" Affect Innovation? Evidence from Mobile Computing. MIT Sloan School of Management working paper, Cambridge, Mass., 2005.

Boudreau, Kevin. The Boundaries of the Platform: Vertical Integration and Economic Incentives in Mobile Computing, MIT Sloan School of Management working paper, Cambridge, Mass., 2005.

Caillaud, Bernard, and Bruno Jullien. "Chicken and Egg: Competition among Intermediation Service Providers." *Rand Journal of Economics* 34, no. 2 (Summer 2003): 521–552.

Church, Jeffrey, and Neil Gandal. "Network Effects, Software Provision and Standardization." *The Journal of Industrial Economics* 60 no. 1 (March 1992): 85–104.

Coase, Ronald. "The Nature of the Firm." *Economica* 4 (1937): 386–405.

Coughlan, Peter J. "Competitive Dynamic in Home Video Games (B): Nintendo Power" (case study). *Harvard Business Online*, June 13, 2001.

Coughlan, Peter J. "Competitive Dynamics in Home Video Games (K): Playstation vs. Nintendo 64" (case study). *Harvard Business Online*, June 13, 2001.

Davis, Steven J., Jack MacCrisken, and Kevin M. Murphy. "Economic Perspectives on Software Design: PC Operating Systems and Platforms." In *Microsoft, Antitrust and the New Economy: Selected Essays*, ed. David S. Evans. Boston: Kluwer, 2002, p. 361.

Evans, David. "The Antitrust Economics of Multi-Sided Platform Markets." *Yale Journal on Regulation* 20 (Summer 2003): 325–381.

Evans, David. "Is Free Software the Wave of the Future?" *Milken Institute Review* (4th Quarter 2001): 33–41.

Evans, David, Albert L. Nichols, and Bernard J. Reddy. "Why Does Microsoft Charge So Little For Windows?" In *Microsoft, Antitrust and the New Economy: Selected Essays*, ed. David S. Evans. Boston: Kluwer, 2002, p. 93.

Evans, David, and Michael Salinger. "Why Do Firms Bundle and Tie? Evidence from Competitive Markets and Implications for Tying Law." *Yale Journal on Regulation* 22 (Winter 2005): 37–89.

Evans, David, and Richard Schmalensee. "The Industrial Organization of Markets with Two-Sided Platforms." Working paper, August 2005. Available: http://ssrn.com/abstract=786627.

George, Lisa, and Joel Waldfogel. "Who Benefits Whom in Daily Newspaper Markets?" NBER Working Paper no. 7944, October 2000.

Hagiu, Andrei. *Platforms, Pricing, Commitment and Variety in Two–Sided Markets*. Doctoral dissertation, Princeton University, 2004.

Hagiu, Andrei. "Pricing and Commitment by Two-Sided Platforms." *Rand Journal of Economics* 37 (2006): forthcoming.

Hagiu, Andrei. "Two-Sided Platforms: Pricing and Social Efficiency." Harvard Business School and Research Institute of Economy Trade and Industry working paper, Cambridge, Mass., 2005.

Katz, Michael, and Carl Shapiro, "Systems Competition and Network Effects." *Journal of Economic Perspectives* 8 (Spring 1994): 93–115.

Kurtzman, Joel. "An Interview with W. Brian Arthur." *Strategy+Business* 11 (1998): 95–103.

Lerner, Joshua, Parag Pathak, and Jean Tirole. "The Determinants of Open Source Contributions." *American Economic Review Papers and Proceedings* 96 (May 2006).

Lerner, Joshua, and Jean Tirole. "The Open Source Movement: Key Research Questions." *European Economic Review* 45 (2001): 819–826.

Lerner, Joshua, and Jean Tirole, "The Scope of Open Source Licensing." *Journal of Law, Economics and Organization* 21, no. 1 (April 2005): 20–56.

Lerner, Joshua, and Jean Tirole, "Some Simple Economics of Open Source." *Journal of Industrial Economics* 50 (June 2002): 197–234.

Liebowitz, Stan, and Stephen Margolis. "Network Externality: An Uncommon Tragedy." *Journal of Economic Perspectives* 8 (Spring 1994): 133–150.

Moon, Youngme. "NTT DoCoMo: Marketing i-mode" (case study). *Harvard Business Online*, July 17, 2002.

Oi, Walter. "A Disneyland Dilemma: Two-Part Tariffs for a Mickey Mouse Monopoly." *Quarterly Journal of Economics* 85 (1971): 77–96.

Rochet, Jean-Charles, and Jean Tirole. "Platform Competition in Two-Sided Markets." *Journal of the European Economic Association* 1 (June 2003): 990–1029.

Rochet, Jean-Charles, and Jean Tirole. "Two-Sided Markets: A Progress Report" (mimeo). IDEI and GREMAQ, Toulouse, France.

Rochet, Jean-Charles, and Jean Tirole, "Tying in Two-Sided Markets and the Impact of the Honor All Cards Rule" (mimeo). IDEI, University of Toulouse, 2003.

Schmalensee, Richard. "Commodity Bundling by Single-Product Monopolies." *Journal of Law and Economics* 25, no. 1 (April 1982): 67–71.

Schmalensee, Richard. "Gaussian Demand and Commodity Bundling." *Journal of Business* 57, no. 2 (January 1984): S211–S230.

Schmalensee, Richard. "Monopolistic Two-Part Pricing Arrangements." *Bell Journal of Economics* 11 (Autumn 1981): 445–466.

Stigler, George. "The Division of Labor Is Limited by the Extent of the Market." *Journal of Political Economy* 59 (June 1951): 185–193.

Stigler, George. "*United States v. Loew's Inc.*: A Note on Block Booking." *Supreme Court Review* 152 (1963): 152–157.

Thomke, Stegan, and Andrew Robertson. "Project Dreamcast: Serious Play at Sega Enterprises Ltd." (case study). *Harvard Business Online*, September 9, 1999.

Market Research

Burden, Kevin, Jennifer Gallo, Alex Slawsby, and Weili Su, "Sync or Swim: Worldwide Smart Handheld Devices Forecast and Analysis, 2002–2006." IDC report no. 26865. http://www.idc.com, April 2002.

Burden, Kevin, Randy Giusto, Allen M. Liebovitch, David Linsalata, Ramon T. Llamas, and Aley Slawsby, "Worldwide Mobile Phone 2005–2009 Forecast and Analysis." IDC report no. 33290. http://www.idc.com, April 2005.

Burden, Kevin, Randy Giusto, Allen M. Liebovitch, David Linsalata, and Ramon T. Llamas, "Worldwide Mobile Phone 2005–2009 Forecast Update and 1H05 Vendor Analysis." IDC report no. 34408. November 2005.

Burden, Kevin, Randy Giusto, Dave Linsalata, Ross Sealfon, and Alex Slawsby, "Worldwide Smart Handheld Devices Forecast and Analysis, 2003–2007." IDC report no. 29586. http://www.idc.com, June 2003.

Burden, Kevin, Randy Giusto, David Linsalata, and Ramon T. Llamas, "Worldwide Smart Handheld Device 2005–2009 Forecast and Analysis: Passing the Torch." IDC report no. 33415. http://www.idc.com, May 2005.

Burden, Kevin, Randy Giusto, David Linsalata, and Alex Slawsby, "Worldwide Smart Handheld Device 2004–2008 Forecast Update: First Quarter Triggers Downward Revision." IDC report no. 31554. http://www.idc.com, August 2004.

Burden, Kevin and Alex Slawsby, "Hand Check: The Smart Handheld Devices Market Forecast and Analysis, 2000–2005." IDC report no. 24859. http://www.idc.com, July 2001.

Byron, Dennis, Richard Heiman, Gary Ingram, R. Paul Mason, and Melita Marks, "Worldwide Software Market Forecast Summary, IDC report no. 22766. http://www.idc.com, 2000–2004." August 2000.

Gikas, Anthony N., and Stephanie S. Wissink, "The Video Game Industry," Piper Jaffray. April 2005.

Gillen, Al, and Dan Kusnetzky, "Worldwide Client and Server Operating Environments 2004–2008 Forecast: Microsoft Consolidates Its Grip." IDC report no. 32452. http://www.idc.com, December 2004.

Gillen, Al, and Dan Kusnetzky, "Worldwide Linux Operating Environments 2004–2008 Forecast and Analysis: Enterprise Products Pave the Way to the Future." IDC report no. 32416. http://www.idc.com, December 2004.

Gillen, Al, Milla Kantcheva, and Dan Kusnetzky, "Worldwide Linux Operating Environments 2005–2009 Forecast and Analysis: Product Transitions Continue." IDC report no. 34390. http://www.idc.com, December 2005.

Golvin, Charles S., "Sizing the US Mobile Messaging Market." *Forrester Research*. July 30, 2004.

Grau, Jeffrey, "E-Commerce in the US: Retail Trends." *eMarketer*. May 2005.

Grau, Jeffrey, "Retail E-Commerce: Future Trends." *eMarketer*. February 2006.

Hammerman, Paul, and R. "Ray" Wang, "ERP Applications—The Technology and Industry Battle Heats Up." *Forrester Research*. June 9, 2005.

Heiman, Richard V., Sally Hudson, Henry D. Morris, Albert Pang, and Anthony C. Picardi, "Worldwide Software Forecast Summary, 2003–2007." IDC report no. 30099. http://www.idc.com, September 2003.

Heiman, Richard V., and Anthony C. Picardi, "Worldwide Software 2004–2008 Forecast Summary." IDC report no. 31785. http://www.idc.com, August 2004.

Hendley, Andrew, Adam Halt, Phil Mickelson, and Derek Wong, "Microsoft Corporation: Patience Is a Virtue," J.P. Morgan North American Equity Research. January 6, 2004.

House, Jill, "Market Mayhem: The Smart Handheld Devices Market Forecast and Analysis, 1999–2004." IDC report no. 22430. http://www.idc.com, June 2000.

House, Jill, and Diana Hwang, "Pocketful of Palms: The Smart Handheld Devices Market Forecast Update and Outlook, 1999–2003." IDC report no. 21177. http://www.idc.com, December 1999.

Hwang, Diana, "Technology Road Map of Smart Handheld Devices." IDC report no. 16225. http://www.idc.com, June 1998.

IDC Server Workload Data. http://www.idc.com, 2005.

Inoue, Takuya, Soo-Kyoum Kim, and Mario Morales, "Worldwide Flash Memory Forecast 2005–2008." IDC report no. 32854. http://www.idc.com, February 2005.

Kevorkian, Susan, "Worldwide Compressed Audio Player 2004–2008 Forecast: MP3 Reaches Far and Wide." IDC report no. 31811. http://www.idc.com, August 2004.

Kevorkian, Susan, "Worldwide and U.S. Compressed Audio Player 2005–2009 Forecast and Analysis: MP3 All Over the Place." IDC report no. 33932. http://www.idc.com, September 2005.

Kevorkian, Susan, and Josh S. Martin, "U.S. Paid Music Service Provider 2004–2008 Forecast and Analysis: Sounding Better and Better." IDC report no. 31426. http://www.idc.com, June 2004.

Levitt, Mark, and Bruce Stephen, "Worldwide PC Market Review and Forecast 1990–1995." IDC report no. 6077. http://www.idc.com, December 1991.

Liebovitch, Allen M. and Alex Slawsby, "Worldwide Mobile Phone 2004–2008 Forecast Update." IDC report no. 31080. http://www.idc.com, July 2004.

Linsalata, David, Schelley Olhova, and Lewis Ward, "U.S. Wireless Gaming 2004–2008 Forecast and Analysis: Gaming . . . Together." IDC report no. 32644. http://www.idc.com, December 2004.

Macklin, Ben, "Europe Broadband." *eMarketer.* April 2005.

Macklin, Ben, "North America Broadband." *eMarketer.* March 2005.

Macklin, Ben, "The Broadband Report." *eMarketer.* April 2001.

Media Metrix. Top 1000 Website Survey, Fall 2004.

Nielsen NetRatings data.

The Nilson Report no. 829, March 2005.

Olhava, Schelley, "Tales of the Gamer: IDC's 2004 Videogamer Survey." IDC report no. 31768. http://www.idc.com, September 2004.

Olhava, Schelley, "Worldwide Videogame Hardware and Software 2004–2008 Forecast and Analysis: Predicting the Future." IDC report no. 31260. http://www.idc.com, May 2004.

Olhava, Schelley, "Worldwide Videogame Forecast and Analysis, 2001–2006." IDC report no. 26906. http://www.idc.com, April 2002.

O'Rourke, Brian, "Video Game Consoles: Sony, Nintendo and Sega Brace for Microsoft Challenge," In-Stat. December 2000.

"PC Database Management Systems Software." IDC report no. 4258. http://www.idc.com, September 1989.

"PC File Management Software: Market Review and Forecast, 1988." IDC report no. 4413. http://www.idc.com, November 1989.

"Personal Computer Industry Service Worldwide Shipments and Forecast." *Dataquest.* 1988.

"Personal Computers U.S. Vendor Segmentation: 1998." *Dataquest.* April 19, 1999.

"Pumping Up the Volume for Online Music Services," *Yankee Group.* January 23, 2004.

Ramsey, Geott, "The eCommerce: B2C Report." *eMarketer.* March 2001.

Rau, Shane, "Worldwide PC Processor 2004 Vendor Shares." IDC report no. 33398. http://www.idc.com, May 2005.

"Strategies for Microcomputers and Office Systems: PC Spreadsheet Software: Market Review and Forecast, 1988." IDC report no. 4389. http://www.idc.com, November 1989.

Ward, Lewis, "U. S. Wireless Ring Tone 2004–2008 Forecast and Analysis." IDC report no. 34713. http://www.idc.com, August 2004.

"Word Processing Software, 1989." IDC report no. 5019. http://www.idc.com, December 1990.

Index